CONSTRUCTING AUTOCRACY

CONSTRUCTING AUTOCRACY

ARISTOCRATS AND EMPERORS
IN JULIO-CLAUDIAN ROME

MATTHEW B. ROLLER

PRINCETON UNIVERSITY PRESS
PRINCETON AND OXFORD

Copyright © 2001 by Princeton University Press
Published by Princeton University Press, 41 William Street,
Princeton, New Jersey 08540
In the United Kingdom: Princeton University Press, 3 Market Place,
Woodstock, Oxfordshire OX20 1SY
All Rights Reserved

Library of Congress Cataloging-in-Publication Data

Roller, Matthew B., 1966–
Constructing autocracy : aristocrats and emperors in Julio-Claudian Rome /
Matthew B. Roller.
p.   cm.
Includes bibliographical references and index.
ISBN 0-691-05021-X (alk. paper)
1. Rome—History—The five Julii, 30 B.C.–68 A.D.   2. Aristocracy (Political science)—
Rome.   3. Emperors—Rome.   4. Class consciousness—Rome.   I. Title.

DG281 .R65 2001
937'.07—dc21   00-056511

This book has been composed in Sabon.

The paper used in this publication meets the minimum requirements of
ANSI/NISO Z39.48-1992 (R1997) (*Permanence of Paper*)

www.pup.princeton.edu

Printed in the United States of America

10 9 8 7 6 5 4 3 2 1

*For my sisters Emily and Elinor,
and for Rhonda*

CONTENTS

ACKNOWLEDGMENTS   ix

ABBREVIATIONS   xi

INTRODUCTION   3

PART ONE: ETHICS AND IMPERIAL IDEOLOGY   15

CHAPTER ONE
The Ethics of Civil War: Competing Communities in Lucan   17

1. Overview   17
2. Traditional Roman Ethical Discourse   20
3. The "Assimilating" Viewpoint   29
4. The "Alienating" Viewpoint   36
5. Ethics and Armies in Conflict   43
6. The Narrator   47
7. Lucan and Early Imperial Aristocratic Ideology   54

CHAPTER TWO
Ethics for the Principate: Seneca, Stoicism, and Traditional Roman Morality   64

1. Overview   64
2. Stoicism's Two Regimes of Value   66
3. Where Does Moral Value Reside? Stoic and Traditional Ethics   70
4. Who Judges and How? Dilemmas of Internal and External Evaluation   77
5. The Problem of Exempla   88
6. Ethics in Julio-Claudian Society: Military Glory and Senecan virtus   97
7. Ethics in Julio-Claudian Society: Flattery and Stoicism   108
8. Conclusion   124

PART TWO: FIGURING THE EMPEROR   127

CHAPTER THREE
The Emperor's Authority: Dining, Exchange, and Social Hierarchy   129

1. Overview   129
2. Giving a Dinner: The Convivium as Object of Exchange   135

3. *Speech and Power: Amicable and Hostile Reciprocity in the Convivium* 146
4. *Dining with Rulers: The Construction of Imperial Authority* 154
5. *Imperial Authority and Gift Giving* 173
6. *The Emperor as Gift-Debtor* 193
7. *Conclusion* 210

CHAPTER FOUR
Modeling the Emperor: The Master-Slave Relationship and Its Alternatives 213

1. *Overview* 213
2. *Freedom and Slavery: A Social Metaphor in Political Discourse* 214
3. *Father or Master? Two Models for the Emperor in Julio-Claudian Literature* 233
4. *Competing Paradigms for the Early Principate* 247
5. *Social Inversion and Status Anxiety* 264
6. *Status Anxiety and Stoic Remedies* 272
7. *Conclusion* 286

BIBLIOGRAPHY 289

INDEX 301

ACKNOWLEDGMENTS

IT IS A *locus communis* of the acknowledgment genre to affirm that one in fact cannot acknowledge, much less reciprocate, all the debts one has incurred in producing a book. A *locus communis*, to be sure, but also a true statement. I will therefore do what the conscientious Roman aristocrat of the early imperial period is advised to do in this situation: since I cannot offer concrete recompense to my benefactors in equal or greater share to the services they have rendered me, and thereby fully acquit myself of my obligations to them, I must settle for singing their praises to the widest possible audience.[1]

Some of the arguments developed in this book first saw the light in a 1994 dissertation at the University of California at Berkeley. That project was guided by Daniel Melia, Charles Murgia, and in particular by Tom Habinek, the director; portions of it also benefited from probing readings by W. S. Anderson, Martin Bloomer, and Tony Long. Two years of uninterrupted writing were generously funded by a Mellon Fellowship in the Humanities and a Mellon Dissertation Fellowship. A dissertation is not a book, however, and the conversion of the former into the latter required that everything be rethought and rewritten, with much material cut out and a much larger amount of new work added in; in this process an entirely new set of debts was incurred. David Konstan and Elaine Fantham read the entire work in its dissertation form; they gently but firmly indicated how much needed to be done, and at the same time offered many pointers for approaching the daunting task ahead. Among those students, colleagues, and friends who subsequently discussed aspects of the work with me or read portions of the manuscript are John Baldwin, Shadi Bartsch, Richard Bett, Tony Corbeill, Cynthia Damon, Craig Dethloff, Allen Grossman, Susan Hahn, Brian Krostenko, Ann Kuttner, Deborah Lyons, Miriam Pelikan Pittenger, Robert Rodgers, Michael Schaffer, Giulia Sissa, Gabrielle Spiegel, Elizabeth Sutherland, Brian Warren, and Raymond Westbrook; I richly commend all of them for their intellectual generosity, critical acumen, and patience. Special thanks go to Andrew Riggsby for his careful readings and for untold hours of discussions on every conceivable issue over the years; to Bob Kaster for his formidable critiques at several stages; and to Kirstie McClure and other colleagues who partici-

---

[1] According to the younger Seneca, I can be grateful simply by having warm feelings toward the following persons and groups, even if I do and say nothing whatsoever, either here or in any other context (see chapter 2 below). But to adopt this view would make for a jejune acknowledgment indeed.

pate in the Program in Political and Moral Thought at Johns Hopkins University—they have provided a genial yet exigent interdisciplinary audience for my ideas, and supplied invaluable reality checks ("You classicists have a very odd idea of what normativity is"). The referees for Princeton University Press, Bob Kaster and Brad Inwood, provided page upon page of criticisms and suggestions, by which the final version was greatly improved. None of the above, of course, is to be held accountable for the views expressed in this book, or for the errors and infelicities that remain. All translations are my own unless otherwise noted; yet I must inevitably echo from time to time the translations of earlier scholars, from whose labor and learning I have profited. Notable among these are the translations of Seneca by Basore (1928) and Gummere (1920), and Braund's (1992) lucid version of Lucan.

The bulk of chapter 1 appeared in an earlier version as an article entitled "Ethical Contradiction and the Fractured Community in Lucan's *Bellum Civile*," *Classical Antiquity* 15 (1996) 319–347. The substance of that article is reprinted here by kind permission of the University of California Press and the editors of *Classical Antiquity*. I am also grateful to the Department of Classics at Johns Hopkins, which granted me a one-course teaching reduction in the Fall term of 1997, at a crucial moment in the development and coalescence of this project. The editorial and production staff at Princeton University Press has been professional and efficient throughout, shepherding the manuscript through its various reviews and revisions and into production without a hitch; I thank classics editor Chuck Myers in particular for saving me, at a very late stage, from utterly despairing of a title.

Finally, I acknowledge a few debts that go broader and deeper than the current book. My teachers at Stanford in the mid-1980s were responsible for bringing me into the field in the first place. Mark Munn and Marsh McCall have the most to answer for, persuading me to begin Greek and then reeling me in like a fish when I still believed I ought to be a physicist; Susan Stephens, Sue Treggiari, Mike Jameson, Tony Raubitschek, and Gregson Davis were also complicit in their distinctive ways. My parents went along with this undergraduate volte-face of mine, against their better judgment; their love and support has always made everything seem both possible and worthwhile. Last, there are three women to whom I owe debts both ancient and immediate. To them alone concrete reciprocity is forthcoming here: for it is to them that I dedicate this book.

Baltimore, Maryland
April 2000

ABBREVIATIONS

Standard abbreviations, sometimes slightly expanded or compressed, are used for authors and works cited in the notes, or parenthetically in the main text. For these, see the *Oxford Latin Dictionary* (= *OLD*) pp. ix–xxiii, or the *Oxford Classical Dictionary,* 3rd ed., eds. S. Hornblower and A. Spawforth, Oxford 1996, xxix–liv. I use the following abbreviations for scholarly journals or reference collections:

AJP	*American Journal of Philology*
BMC	*Coins of the Roman Empire in the British Museum* (ed. H. Mattingly et al., London 1923–)
CIL	*Corpus Inscriptionum Latinarum*
CQ	*Classical Quarterly*
HSCP	*Harvard Studies in Classical Philology*
ILS	*Inscriptiones Latinae Selectae* (ed. H. Dessau, Berlin 1892–1916)
JRS	*Journal of Roman Studies*
LS	(= Long, A. A., and David Sedley, 1987)
OLD	*Oxford Latin Dictionary* (ed. P. G. W. Glare, Oxford 1968–82)
PIR	*Prosopographia Imperii Romani* (First edition: eds. E. Klebs, H. Dessau, P. de Rohden, Berlin 1897–98. Second edition: eds. E. Groag, A. Stein, L. Petersen, Berlin 1933–)
RE	*Paulys Realencyclopädie der classischen Altertumswissenschaft* (eds. A. Pauly, G. Wissowa, and W. Kroll, Stuttgart 1894–)
RIC	*Roman Imperial Coinage* (First edition: ed. H. Mattingly et al., London 1923–94. Second edition, vol. 1 only: eds. C. H. V. Sutherland and R. A. G. Carson, London 1984)
SVF	*Stoicorum Veterum Fragmenta* (ed. H. von Arnim, Leipzig 1903–24)
TAPA	*Transactions of the American Philological Association*
TLL	*Thesaurus Linguae Latinae* (Leipzig 1900–)

Certain citations of Dio Cassius appear in a form of the following sort: Dio 63(62L).17.2. The first number represents the book number as given in Boissevain's standard edition of Dio. The number in parentheses labeled "L," if it is present, indicates the book number given in the more widely available Loeb edition, which sometimes differs from Boissevain.

CONSTRUCTING AUTOCRACY

INTRODUCTION

THE YOUNGER SENECA, in his treatise "On Anger," provides the following account of the goings-on at a Persian royal dinner party:

King Cambyses was excessively fond of wine. One of his dearest friends, Praexaspes, advised him to drink more sparingly, declaring that drunkenness was disgraceful in a king, whom everyone's eyes and ears followed. To this the king responded, "That you may know how much I am in control of myself, I will prove that both my eyes and my hands are serviceable after drinking wine." He then drank even more freely than before, from even bigger cups, and now heavy and sodden he bid that his detractor's son go out beyond the threshold, and that he stand with his left hand raised over his head. Then he bent his bow and struck the boy through the very heart, which he had said was his target. Cutting open the boy's chest, he pointed out the arrow tip sticking in the heart itself, and looking back to the father he asked whether he had a sufficiently steady hand. Whereupon the father declared that even Apollo could not have shot more accurately.

Cambysen regem nimis deditum vino Praexaspes unus ex carissimis monebat ut parcius biberet, turpem esse dicens ebrietatem in rege, quem omnium oculi auresque sequerentur. ad haec ille "ut scias," inquit, "quemadmodum numquam excidam mihi, adprobabo iam et oculos post vinum in officio esse et manus." bibit deinde liberalius quam alias capacioribus scyphis et iam gravis ac vinolentus obiurgatoris sui filium procedere ultra limen iubet adlevataque super caput sinistra manu stare. tunc intendit arcum et ipsum cor adulescentis (id enim petere se dixerat) figit rescissoque pectore haerens in ipso corde spiculum ostendit ac respiciens patrem interrogavit satisne certam haberet manum. at ille negavit Apollinem potuisse certius mittere. (*Ira* 3.14.1–2)

This hair-raising sequence of events cries out for explanation on several points: What possessed Praexaspes to reproach Cambyses for heavy drinking in the first place? What is the meaning of the king's savage display of what he calls, paradoxically, his "self-control"? And why, in the end, did Praexaspes praise the king's aim? Seneca, never one to stint on interpretation, offers answers to all of these questions in the sentences immediately following this anecdote. First, he condemns Praexaspes for complimenting the king on his accurate shooting: he calls this courtier a "slave in spirit rather than in legal status" (*animo magis quam condicione mancipium*, §15.3), since he took the murder of his own son as "an opportunity for flattery" (*occasionem blanditiarum*). Next Seneca directs his invective against the king: he denounces Cambyses for his bloodthirstiness, and for "breaking up dinner parties with punishments and corpses" (*convivia suppliciis funeribusque solventem*); and he declares that the king is himself a worthy target of arrows, to be shot at him by his own friends (§15.4). Finally, regarding Praexaspes' initial comments to the king, Seneca suggests that it was not wise to chastise the king for drinking too much wine, when the real problem was that he might drink blood instead of wine, and since his hands were better filled with wine cups than with weapons. Yet Seneca concedes that Praexaspes was trying to do his king a service: he concludes that this courtier "was added to the number of those who showed, by the great disasters they suffered, how great was the cost, for the friends of kings, of giving good advice" (*accessit itaque ad numerum eorum qui magnis cladibus ostenderunt quanti constarent regum amicis bona consilia*, §15.6).

This anecdote, of course, is not so much about a specific Persian aristocrat's relationship with his king as about the relationship between aristocrats and kings more generally and, by implication, about how Roman aristocrats relate to their own ruler, the emperor. For, while the date of composition of this text cannot be fixed with great precision, it was probably written late in the reign of the emperor Claudius (Griffin 1976: 396)—about a century after Julius Caesar defeated all his rivals in battle, definitively swept away the old republican sociopolitical order, and established himself as the undisputed master of the Roman world; also some eighty years after Augustus put in place the institutional arrangements of the new sociopolitical order that modern scholars call the "principate," and thereby made himself the first of what we conventionally call the "emperors."[1] By the time Seneca (himself a high-ranking aristocrat) wrote this treatise, then, Roman aristocrats were familiar with the necessity of coping in a world that had an emperor in it; yet, as I will argue in this book, alternative visions of how the emperor did or might or should impact the actions and values of aristocrats continued to be fiercely contested. That Seneca borrowed this anecdote (suitably modified) from Herodotus (3.34–35), and that the figures involved are Persians rather than Romans, in no way detracts from its contemporary relevance: for Seneca has retold the tale, in Latin, within a treatise ("On Anger") that overtly urges particular patterns of behavior and mental discipline upon an audience of contemporary Roman aristocrats, Seneca's own social peers (indeed, the treatise is explicitly addressed to Seneca's own brother Novatus). Moreover, Herodotus provides none of the lengthy ethical commentary that Seneca appends to the anecdote:

[1] The Romans themselves, however, called their ruler by a variety of names under different circumstances; some of these alternatives, and their implications, are discussed in chapter 4 below.

this is Seneca's own contribution for the edification of his audience; it is this commentary in particular that stitches the story into contemporary Roman aristocratic modes of thinking and connects it to elite anxieties.

I have begun with this passage because the situation it describes, and Seneca's commentary on the actions and motives of the participants, encapsulates a variety of conceptual and constructive engagements with the imperial regime on the part of aristocrats—ways in which aristocrats think about their situation in a society dominated by an autocrat, and through which they position themselves relative to him so as to avoid harm, preserve their traditional prestige, and gain various social advantages. First, there is the dinner-party setting, where aristocrat and ruler interact face-to-face over food and wine: we will see later (chapter 3) that the dinner party, with its wealth of social nuances and implications, was a particularly fruitful locus for working out and comprehending the character of the ruler-aristocrat relationship. Second, there is the matter of reciprocity: the aristocrat, according to Seneca, gave his ruler good advice, yet was rewarded by having his son gruesomely executed before his very eyes; the aristocrat in turn responded with praise for the king, which appears to be completely inappropriate to these circumstances; and Seneca himself bestows blame liberally on both parties. As we will see (again chapter 3), exchanging goods and services with the emperor was another common way in which Roman aristocrats articulated and manipulated this relationship. Third, the aristocrat's initially rather frank criticism of his ruler, followed later by a compliment that Seneca condemns as "flattery," raises the question of "speaking to power": what kinds of things an aristocrat can or should say to his ruler under various circumstances, and what the consequences of such speech are for both parties (chapters 2 and 3). Fourth, Seneca speaks briefly of the aristocrat paradoxically as a "slave," though he alerts us that this usage is figurative by noting that it is a slavery of mind or soul (*animus*) rather than of legal status (*condicio*). This is an insult to the aristocrat, implying that it would better befit his high status to have acted or spoken otherwise than he did; but to speak or act otherwise would necessarily be to challenge the ruler, to call his legitimacy into question: for this aristocrat is a "slave" only if the king stands as "master," and to be free is to be rid of the master (chapter 4). In a subsequent anecdote similar to this one (*Ira* 3.15), Seneca carries this "slavery" metaphor much further, suggesting that an oppressed aristocrat can always "free" himself from an oppressive ruler by committing suicide. This kind of "freedom" has a whiff of the philosophical about it (again chapter 4), and we will see in general that philosophical ethics can provide aristocrats with ways of thinking about their relations with emperors that differ from established, longstanding patterns of aristocratic ethical thinking (chapter 2). Indeed, some aristocratic authors articulate their relations with the emperor and his regime precisely by placing alternative value systems, linked to alternative sets of interests, in competition with one another (chapters 1 and 2). This one anecdote, then, adumbrates a range of issues that will be addressed in this study, all related to the question of how Roman aristocrats living in the early principate conceptualized, shaped, and sought to manage the autocracy in which they lived. There will consequently be no surprise that I discuss this anecdote several further times, from different points of view, in the chapters that follow.

Let us step back and take a broader view. The advent of the emperor in Roman society, and of the imperial regime we call the principate, marked a massive and unprecedented relocation of power and authority in the Roman world: as I will soon discuss further, it came to be concentrated in the hands of a single person (along with a small group of select associates), while the authority of other persons and institutions, in which social and political power had been vested through the five centuries of the republican regime, was correspondingly diminished. My aim in this book is to examine the terms, or the conceptual frameworks, in which and by which Roman aristocrats who lived under the Julio-Claudians—the first dynasty of emperors[2]—comprehended and molded the emergent sociopolitical order that was the principate, with its distinctive relocations of power and authority. I contend that, in this period, the emperor was being invented on the fly, through various feats of imagination, as a social figure who related in particular ways to other members of society, and particularly to elites. This invention of the socially contextualized and integrated ruler was a dialogical process: different visions of the ways in which the emperor and his power intervened, or could potentially intervene, in aristocratic values and social practice were proposed and placed in competition with one another. Ultimately, these contestations and negotiations were moves in power struggles between different segments of the aristocracy, in which the competing groups sought to articulate the character of the principate in ways most advantageous to themselves, and to persuade others of the correctness and legitimacy of these articulations.

It is primarily in literary texts that I seek evidence for this dialogical, contested thinking-out and shaping of the principate, for it is here that the material for this investigation is richest. The group whose involvement in this process is most in question is the aristocracy, for aristocrats

[2] I date the beginning of the new regime to the victory of Octavian (later Augustus) over Antony at Actium in 31 B.C. (other scholars may prefer 27 or 23 B.C.); the Julio-Claudian dynasty ended with the death of Nero, Augustus's last surviving male descendent, in A.D. 68.

were the primary producers and consumers of literary texts—activities that presupposed significant leisure time and education, hence a degree of wealth.[3] At Rome, the aristocracy consisted minimally of equestrians and senators, and the authors of the texts examined in this study were all members of one of these orders.[4] I do not take the view that these authors were nothing more than mouthpieces for a collective aristocratic class consciousness; on the contrary, their representations of the new order, and of the relationship between emperor and elites, were substantially their own uniquely individual constructions, as will be obvious from the discussions below. However, they wrote for an audience of other aristocrats, and they presumably hoped that their representations would be found compelling and persuasive by that audience. Thus it seems reasonable to examine these texts for representations of the principate that engaged the interests of the elites—the group that included both author and audience, and that was most immediately affected by the emergence of the principate.

Modes of representing are linked to social and economic structures. It is appropriate, then, to sketch briefly certain broad changes in these structures that occurred in the transition from republic to principate, to provide a general background against which the arguments developed in this book will play out. This information is well known, has received much detailed discussion, and is (I take it) broadly uncontroversial. In the longstanding sociopolitical order of the Roman republic, the aristocracy dominated society in a number of ways. Its dominance was economic, since aristocrats monopolized society's material resources, primarily through their ownership of or control over land. It was political, in that aristocrats competed for and occupied all the positions of power in the government, through an oligarchic system of collegial magistracies of annual tenure. It was social, to the extent that they subordi-

---

[3] See Kautsky 1982: 24, 79, who defines an aristocracy, broadly, as a "ruling elite" composed of those who competed for magistracies and other positions in the government, and who did not labor themselves but derived their livelihood from the labor of peasants. Kautsky's work is a cross-cultural study of aristocracies and their political and economic role in primarily agrarian, noncommercialized, premodern societies, societies that he calls "traditional aristocratic empires" (pp. 3–27). For him an aristocrat is defined primarily by his role in such a society, and not strictly by the source of his income: his definition does not require an "aristocrat" to be a member of the landed nobility that lives directly off the peasantry, but admits also those (exceptional) persons in agrarian economies who derive some or much of their income indirectly from the peasantry by taking it from other aristocrats, or, even more exceptionally, have significant income through trade (pp. 79–83). Throughout my book I use "aristocracy" and "elites" interchangeably.

[4] As Hopkins 1983: 44–45, 110–11 argues, equestrians and senators constituted a single elite which, although it contained many different subgroups with competing political interests, was largely unified by birth, acculturation, socialization, and economic interests.

nated to themselves, more or less directly, many other inhabitants of the state though patronal activities, slaveholding, and sometimes brute force. With the advent of the principate, however, significant shifts in the distribution of power and authority began to occur in each of these categories. In no case did any nonaristocratic social group acquire significant power: the modes of production did not change hands, nor did the class structure of society change, so there was no revolution in a Marxist sense.[5] Rather, power and authority began to be redistributed within the aristocracy. Its collective, oligarchic dominance in the areas described above faded, and power became increasingly concentrated in the hands of one aristocrat in particular — the emperor — and a group of other persons distinguished and empowered primarily by their proximity to him: family members, certain equestrians and senators who were particularly close friends or associates, and certain freedmen within the imperial household.[6] Economically, the emperor was by far the wealthiest individual in society, owning or controlling more land, slaves, and other forms of capital than anyone else. Politically and socially, emperors from Augustus onward maintained dominance in large part by exploiting their superior capitalization to co-opt other individuals and groups. For through distributions of foodstuffs and other goods, money, offices, and other sorts of honors to persons of every social rank and position, they kept others in their debt; in particular, they took care to appoint handpicked men to the most important positions in the government and in the military, rather than entrusting the allocation of these positions to the vagaries of the electoral process and other longstanding modes of aristocratic competition. (Note, however, that the traditional magisterial principles of annual tenure and collegiality did not apply to the emperor qua emperor, for the tenure of this role involved no preset time limitation or, usually, any recognized equal in power.) Since he dominated established modes of aristocratic competition, the aristocracy at large was forced to seek new arenas of compe-

---

[5] Whether, or to what degree, the term "revolution" usefully describes the changes that took place in the Roman world between 60 B.C. and A.D. 14 (Syme's periodization in his provocatively titled 1939 study, *The Roman Revolution* [p. vii]), between 80 and 49 B.C. (approximately the years covered by Gruen 1974; see esp. pp. 1–5), or in any other interval one may choose, has long been debated. However, a consensus seems to have emerged that even though the modes of production and the class structure of society did not change, nevertheless significant changes did occur in many aspects of Roman culture. This topic is now revisited in a collection of essays entitled *The Roman Cultural Revolution* (Habinek-Schiesaro 1997); for a brief history of the characterization of these changes as "revolutionary," see pp. xv–xvi, along with Wallace-Hadrill's essay, esp. pp. 3–7.

[6] Wallace-Hadrill 1996: 285, 299 discusses power derived from proximity to the emperor, especially power of this sort exercised by women and freedmen. He speaks of the emperor's normal entourage as a "court," resurrecting an earlier idea of Friedlaender.

tition, new ways of competing both among themselves and with the emperor. My project is not to examine these shifts in the locations of power and authority per se, though aspects of some of these shifts will receive detailed discussion. Rather, these shifts both stimulated and were in turn affected by the ideological activity, the conceptualizing and constructing, that is my primary object of study.

My thinking about the linkages between sociopolitical change and conceptual change in ancient Rome has been helpfully informed by the work of scholars who have investigated this interrelationship in other societies. One scholar whose work in this area has been seminal is Clifford Geertz. In his 1964 essay "Ideology as a Cultural System," he argues that sharp changes in an established political and social order may lead to "a loss of orientation," "social dislocation and psychological tension," and "conceptual confusion" among those whose ordered social universe has been swept away. Such confusion, he contends, leads to intensive ideological activity: a "search for a new symbolic framework in terms of which to formulate, think about, and react to political problems" (Geertz 1973 [1964]: 219–21). While his insight that social and conceptual change are linked is vitally important, Geertz seems to present this link as unidirectional: social change precedes, stimulates, and drives conceptual change; the latter is a reaction to the former. More recently, this approach has been nuanced by a group of political theorists who embrace the idea that our conceptual categories do not simply mirror a preexisting social reality, but at least partly constitute that reality. One of these theorists, Quentin Skinner, cites as an example Elizabethan entrepreneurs who, in an attempt to give moral legitimacy to their commercial activities, borrowed from the language of the church and referred to themselves as "religious"—a term with positive connotations that implied pious, selfless, conscientious behavior. Yet, Skinner argues, this self-construction imposed effective limits on the kinds of commercial activities in which these men could participate. For in calling themselves "religious," they subjected themselves to a larger set of expectations for what constitutes "religiosity," expectations that accompanied this term in its original ecclesiastical domain of reference. These entrepreneurs could not maintain this self-representation without also systematically tailoring their conduct to fit these broader expectations. Thus conceptual change—in this case, the interjection of a conceptual category from one discursive realm into another—is constitutive in that it can actively shape how people behave, and hence, how the world actually is.[7]

---

[7] Skinner 1989: 20–22. Other political theorists have also contributed to this approach. Farr 1989 (in the same collection) argues that politics is linguistically constituted at the

The current study is deeply concerned with the relationship between social and conceptual change, as revealed in Roman aristocratic thinking and writing of the Julio-Claudian era. Aristocratic imaginings of the autocracy in which they live involve more than just the attempt to comprehend the new power structure: they are also attempts to affect that structure, to cause it to distribute power in ways that preserve, even enhance, aristocratic privilege and prestige. In part 1, I contend that both Lucan and Seneca portray received modes of ethical discourse as malfunctioning, or functioning in ways disadvantageous to the aristocracy at large, in the sociopolitical order of the principate; Seneca, however, argues that by adopting Stoic ethics the aristocracy can in certain ways reassert its traditional power and privilege against the power of the emperor. Again, in part 2 I argue that, among the familiar, long-standing authority figures in Roman society that are adduced as paradigmatic for the emperor—e.g., "dominant gift-giver," "father," "master"—one model or another may seem particularly appropriate at a given time because the emperor is behaving in a certain way. On the other hand, to propound one or another of these paradigms in a public manner is to invite others (including the emperor himself) to compare his behavior systematically to the model invoked, and thus to impose upon him a kind of social pressure to mold his behavior accordingly—much as the Elizabethan merchants found themselves constrained in unforeseen ways by the associations of the word "religious." Thus Roman aristocrats are attempting to guide and shape the new order —to constitute their social reality—even as they struggle to comprehend and articulate it.

The place of ethics in this study requires further discussion. Moral understanding was perhaps the most important mode of understanding in Roman culture, and almost all representations of social, political, or economic phenomena are at some level—often at the most obvious, surface level—also ethically significant. Ethics, then, is central to the conceptualizing and constructing that is the object of this study, and is a key concern throughout. In the first part, "Ethics and Imperial Ide-

---

same time that language is politically constituted. He suggests (p. 26) that conceptual change can be seen as an "outcome of the process of political actors attempting to solve the problems they encounter as they try to *understand and change* the world around them" (my emphasis). Thus he presents conceptual change as both reflective and constructive of political change. Ball 1988: 12, like Skinner, sees the cross-pollination of discourses as an important source of conceptual change that generates social change: "When the concepts and metaphors constituting the discourse of economics, for example—... or of any other discipline—enter the field of political meanings they alter the shape and structure of that field by altering its speakers' terms of discourse." Similarly, Bourdieu 1993 [1983]: 44.

ology," conflicting ethical systems take center stage as means of expressing the social and ideological tensions associated with the emergence of the emperor as a concentrated locus of power. Here I work with two specific authors, each treated in his own chapter, whose ethical engagements with the principate are particularly intense and sustained: the epic poet Lucan, whose poem on the civil war between Caesar and Pompey (49–48 B.C.) dates from the early 60s A.D. (the middle of the reign of Nero), and the younger Seneca, whose ethical treatises and letters were composed from the 40s to the 60s A.D., in the reigns of Claudius and Nero. These two chapters examine how, and on what grounds, these authors deploy crucial Roman value terms such as *virtus*, *pietas*, and *gratia*. I argue that both authors represent the new, concentrated locus of power in the Roman state (the emperor in Seneca's texts, and Julius Caesar in Lucan's) as spawning novel, disruptive ways of deploying these value terms—new modes of ethical discourse that are opposed to and compete with received, established modes. Specifically, as I contend in chapter 1, the ethical contradictions that fill Lucan's poem are his way of representing the competing, alternative views of the composition of the Roman community that emerged during the civil war and persist in Lucan's own day. For when Caesar takes up arms against the state, he creates a community of supporters who largely regard other Romans as enemies rather than as fellow citizens, and who deploy ethical language accordingly (e.g., it is right and proper to use violence against them). On the other hand, the Pompeians generally regard their Caesarian opponents as fellow citizens, which renders the use of violence against them problematic, if not impossible. The advent of the imperial regime therefore involves the creation of a faction within society—a subcommunity with a distinctive set of moral values—and consequently institutionalizes a persistent, unbridgeable cleft in aristocratic ethics. In chapter 2, I show that Seneca puts forth Stoic ethics, which locates moral value in mental dispositions, in a way that systematically engages with traditional, received aristocratic ethics, which locates moral value primarily in observed actions. Seneca urges his audience to accept the former in place of the latter, a move that (I argue) addresses specific, concrete social and cultural dislocations experienced by elite Romans in the face of the emperor's power—for example, a reduction of the opportunities and rewards for displaying military prowess, and a perceived aggravation of certain problems associated with flattery. In addressing these issues as he does, Senecan ethics offers a way of reestablishing aristocratic power and prestige, albeit in a transfigured form, in the new order.

Now, Seneca and Lucan, both writing quite late in the Julio-Claudian period, and being not only close relatives (Seneca was Lucan's paternal uncle) but also co-conspirators against Nero (both were forced to commit suicide in A.D. 65, upon the exposure of the Pisonian conspiracy), could be thought not to provide a representative sample of the conceptualizing and constructing of the new order that went on more widely in aristocratic society throughout this period as a whole. Indeed, their modes of framing in ethical terms the social and ideological conundrums of the new order are distinctly their own, unlike anyone else's. Nevertheless, I will show that these authors address the same problems that are revealed more broadly in Julio-Claudian sources, and address them in ways that intersect significantly with other contemporaneous modes of conceptualizing. It is these more widespread, more chronologically persistent modes of constructing autocracy that are the subject of the second part of this study, "Figuring the Emperor." The two chapters comprising part 2 range widely through authors and texts of the Julio-Claudian period, along with other texts (whether earlier or later) that discuss or bear upon this period. These chapters investigate how several longstanding, familiar types of authority relationship in Roman society—specifically the relationships of gift-creditor to gift-debtor, of father to son, and of master to slave—came to be used in the Julio-Claudian period as models by which to articulate and evaluate the emperor's relationship to his subjects, particularly aristocratic ones. In chapter 3, I examine the practices of the Julio-Claudian emperors as gift transactors; that is, as givers and receivers of objects and services in a society where such exchanges were a means of establishing hierarchical social relationships. I begin with a case study of the emperor at dinner among other diners, for the dinner party was a key social context in which hierarchical relationships were asserted and challenged through exchange. In this context and also more broadly, as I argue next, the emperor established his authority as legitimate through his relentless giving, or conversely delegitimated himself by failing to give and receive in the ways regarded as appropriate for someone with such resources. Furthermore, as a matter of practice and even policy, he conducted his exchanges so as to maximize his giving of gifts and minimize his receiving of them. Thus the emperor's authority was rendered socially and ethically comprehensible through its manifestation in this most familiar of cultural forms, giving and receiving. Chapter 4, finally, examines a pair of competing metaphors by which the emperor's relationship with his subjects, especially aristocratic ones, was widely modeled in the Julio-Claudian period, namely the relationships of master to slave and father to son. Each of these paradigms involves a particular set of expectations about the roles that the participants play in respect to one another, and hence about the ethical character of the relationship so modeled—the former being stereotyped as adversarial and exploitative, and the latter as warm and nurturing. There is no question of one or the other model winning out, or being more true than the other, in general or in any particular situation: their utility is precisely in their opposed ethical implications, hence their ability to impose specific behavioral expectations and pressures upon the emperor and his regime, as well as upon aristocratic subjects. The widespread, competitive setting and evaluating of paradigms for the emperor's authority, as discussed in chapters 3 and 4, along with the more idiosyncratic competing ethical discourses constructed by Seneca and Lucan, discussed in chapters 1 and 2, indicate the range and depth of aristocratic ideological activity, their constructing of the autocracy in which they lived, during the Julio-Claudian period.

PART ONE

ETHICS AND IMPERIAL IDEOLOGY

Chapter One

THE ETHICS OF CIVIL WAR: COMPETING COMMUNITIES IN LUCAN

1. Overview

THE IDEA that a society's moral values are linked in nonarbitrary ways with its sociopolitical arrangements, and that changes in sociopolitical arrangements are correlated to changes in values, is a familiar one to social scientists and political theorists. Yet this linkage, regarding the ancient world, has received only desultory scholarly attention. There exists a handful of relatively brief discussions of limited scope—journal articles or single chapters (or parts thereof) in book-length studies of other questions—along with a few larger-scale investigations. With a single exception, no sustained work has been done in the past three decades.[1] Yet, studies of the relationship between a society's structuration and its ethics have much to offer both social and intellectual historians of the ancient world. For an understanding of social conditions may illuminate why certain values or ethical problems take on particular importance at particular times, while an awareness of shifts in values may in turn reveal how social change was perceived by those who lived it. Here in part 1, I aim to exploit some of these possibilities for the cross-illumination of social and intellectual history. Specifically, I examine how two authors of the Julio-Claudian period, Lucan and Seneca, portray the entanglement of social and ethical issues in this era of significant social change for the Roman aristocracy. In so doing, I indeed hope to show some ways in which these aristocrats constructed autocracy—how they comprehended, in ethical terms, the sociopolitical order of the principate, and how these conceptions in turn participated in the structuring and formation of that order.

The readings I will offer here also intervene in a related but some-

[1] The earliest explicit discussion that I have encountered regarding the linkage of moral values and social structures in the ancient world is Fustel de Coulanges 1980 [1864], e.g., pp. 86–92. More recent large-scale studies include Ferguson 1958, Earl 1967, Adkins 1970, and Bryant 1996 (the latter a sociologist rather than a classicist, and heavily dependent on Adkins). Earl focuses on Roman society, Adkins and Bryant on Greek; Fustel de Coulanges and Ferguson discuss both. Briefer discussions particularly helpful for the current project are Smith 1976 [1947], Harris 1979: 10–41, and Minyard 1985: 5–32, which examine aspects of this linkage in the middle to late republic.

what broader debate that has developed over the past generation within the field of classics proper, as well as in other fields of the humanities. In response to certain midcentury modes of literary criticism that see literature as a highly autonomous realm following its own rules, analyzable on its own terms, and substantially insulated from (or at least transcending) the everyday preoccupations of its producer and the world in which he or she lived, some scholars have sought to bring the social engagement of literary texts into sharper focus; to look at these texts as products of the author's world that in various ways bring forth his or her concerns and anxieties as a member of a particular society at a particular time. Such scholars, in other words, are interested in the "politics" of literature. To see what such an approach to literature might be thought to involve, let us consider some important recent readings of Lucan's epic and of Seneca's ethical prose. As I discuss in chapter 2 in much greater detail, Seneca's letters and treatises address various ethical problems through the framework of a formal, philosophical ethical system. This system is largely Stoic, though it has eclectic elements as well. Seneca exhorts his (intended) audience of aristocratic readers to embrace this philosophical ethical framework in preference to the unphilosophical framework of traditional aristocratic ethics, and so to begin to move toward acquiring wisdom. In major studies of Seneca, two scholars — Miriam Griffin (1976) and J. P. Sullivan (1985) — have sought the "political" in these texts by asking the following questions: How does Seneca think an emperor ought to rule? How does he portray or respond to contemporary dynastic intrigues? What does the philosopher say about participation in public life? These questions seem to identify "politics" closely with governmental administration and its associated activities.[2] Now, while Seneca does address such questions in various ways, they are not among his primary concerns in most of these texts (perhaps excepting *De Clementia*). These questions arise only occasionally, as relatively minor byproducts of the overarching ethical exhortation; they are not (in my opinion) the reason for that exhortation.[3] While I believe that these scholars are correct in

---

[2] This view of the "political" is evident from the titles and some of the chapter headings in these books. Griffin's book, entitled *Seneca: A Philosopher in Politics*, contains the chapters "Seneca on the Fall of the Republic," "The Philosopher on the Principate," "The Philosopher on Political Participation." Sullivan's book, entitled *Literature and Politics in the Age of Nero*, contains the chapter "The Stoic Opposition? Seneca and Nero."

[3] Sullivan 1985, however, seems to imply that they are. He scrutinizes Senecan texts for hidden allusions to specific, identifiable contemporary events or circumstances such as palace intrigues or senatorial dissension, which he then contends are the stimuli for the production of these texts (see e.g., 122–43). Griffin 1976: 133–36 also makes such an argument regarding a Senecan treatise. Some of these connections are plausible, and it is unquestionably true that, in at least some cases, specific, identifiable events and circum-

seeking to understand literary texts as products of authors living in particular social environments, nevertheless to focus on what these texts can be interpreted to say about government, and furthermore to take these inferred positions as the very *raison d'être* of these texts, seems to me to mistake subordinate concerns for primary ones, to make the tail wag the dog. Similar readings have been offered of Lucan, as well. In his landmark 1976 study entitled *Lucan: An Introduction*, Frederick Ahl tries to link certain movements in Lucan's epic with attested details about the author's life. He argues that the first six books of the poem were written prior to Lucan's falling-out with the emperor Nero; that book 7 marks the poet's distraught response to this falling-out; and that the later books, particularly 9 and 10, display "greater confidence . . . [which] probably reflects his entry into the Pisonian conspiracy."[4] Here Ahl assumes too direct a connection between the author's role in public life and the production and content of his texts (so Masters 1992: 87–88). Moreover, this approach presents literary production as reactive — a response to political events and social conditions — though there is also good reason, as I suggested in the introduction, to scrutinize literary texts for the ways in which they constitute and seek to alter the social world in which they are embedded.

More recently, a different and broader understanding of "politics" has gained currency in classics and other fields. On this understanding, "politics" is taken to encompass a variety of structures and strategies by which power is distributed in society; it includes, but is by no means limited to, governmental activites. To illustrate how literary texts might be read in light of this broader view of "politics," I offer here examples of the work of just two scholars, though there are others. In an article entitled "'Augustan' and 'Anti-Augustan': Reflections on Terms of Reference" (1992), Duncan Kennedy argues that Horace in his *Satires* integrates himself into the new power structure established by Octavian, and invites his readers to do so as well, through his consistent use of a rhetoric of reconciliation and accommodation. This rhetoric is produced in part through Horace's careful demarcation of the range of references he allows to words like *amicitia* and *libertas*.[5] However, the

---

stances do spur literary production (Seneca's *Consolatio ad Polybium* and *Consolatio ad Helviam*, for example, overtly claim to be written, physically and conceptually, from exile). On the whole, however, I find strained and unpersuasive the causal links drawn by these scholars between specific contemporary events and the production of literary texts.

[4] Ahl 1976: 352–53; similarly Sullivan 1985: 146.

[5] Kennedy 1992: 30–35. I agree with Kennedy (and others) that the semantic fields of words are not merely received, but also constructed and contested discursively, and that such contestation is often the locus of ideological struggle. However, I cannot accept Kennedy's account of the semantics of *libertas* (p. 31) as it stands: see chapter 4.2 below.

political engagement of the *Satires* is not simply reflexive, a matter of the poet responding to or accomodating the pre-existing realities of the new power structure. For Horace actively constructs and submits to his audience for acceptance a social and ethical framework that legitimates this power structure. Along the same lines, Thomas Habinek, in a 1990 article entitled "The Politics of Candor in Cicero's *De Amicitia*," argues that Cicero presents an innovative ideal of aristocratic friendship in his treatise on this topic. Habinek contends that a candid friendship, in which one party may evaluate frankly the actions of the other or rebuke him outright if need be, was traditionally possible only between social unequals who therefore were not in direct social competition with one another. Cicero, however, presents candor as a desirable ideal for friendships between aristocrats who are social equals and do compete directly. This attempt to reconfigure established social practice, Habinek argues, is an effort to enhance elite solidarity in the face of the extraordinary challenges to traditional senatorial government during the 40s B.C. These two studies, then, and others in the same spirit,[6] locate the political engagement of literary texts not so much in their covert or even overt references to specific contemporary events in the area of governmental administration, as in their attempts to reorient and redeploy crucial social ideals and concepts in ways that serve specific interests in the broader political and social environment from which these texts emerged. This is the kind of engagement I seek to recover from Lucan and Seneca in this chapter and the next. I contend that the conflict and competition between alternative ethical systems and discourses, as represented in these texts, emerges from and gives form to the conflict and competition between the enduring but besieged sociopolitical structures and interests of the longstanding republican oligarchic order, and the emergent structures and interests of the new regime, the principate. That is, by placing differing and in some respects opposed ethical systems in conflict, these two authors and their audiences construct moral understandings of the new order and its relationship to what went before. In so doing, they actively articulate and evaluate roles that both they and the emperor play or may potentially play in society.

2. TRADITIONAL ROMAN ETHICAL DISCOURSE

As a basis for the discussions of Lucan and Seneca to follow, I begin by describing crucial features of an ethical system in which both authors were immersed: the traditional, received ethical system of the late re-

---

[6] See now Habinek 1998, a collection of new and revised essays that further develop this way of reading; also Roller 1998.

publican and early imperial aristocracy. I call this system "traditional" because aristocrats regarded it as passed down from their ancestors, the *maiores*, unchanged from time immemorial. Its values consisted in particular conceptions of proper behavior, closely linked with an interest in status and position: praise was bestowed for behavior that enhanced the position of the aristocracy with respect to other groups, and of individual aristocrats with respect to other aristocrats.[7] These behavior patterns and status concerns were encoded in the familiar moral vocabulary of the Latin language: *virtus, pietas, fas, ius, fides, laus, honor, gloria, nobilitas, dignitas*, and so on. All Roman aristocrats operated generally with regard to this mapping of ethical space: that is, all accepted that the terms *nobilis, pius, fidus*, etc., assign positive value in various moral categories, even though the content and boundaries of these categories were constantly subject to contestation.[8] The aristocracy's collective acceptance of this mapping—their judging of others according to these categories, and their own desire to be judged positively according to them—was part of their acculturation, hence partially constituted their identity, as aristocrats within Roman society and as Romans with respect to non-Romans. Looked at another way, the ethical categories defined by the traditional Roman moral vocabulary collectively provide a template for the structure of a community of persons (i.e., the Roman aristocracy) who embrace these crucial assumptions about what constitutes moral value and disvalue and how it is judged. These ethical categories mark out the boundaries of this community, articulate its internal relations, and define degrees of distinction within it; in other words, they define positions for people to occupy. Thus the use of these moral terms not only reflects social forms and structures, but also formalizes, confirms, and helps to reproduce those structures.[9]

---

[7] As Harris 1979: 10–41 shows, central aristocratic values had their origins and/or took on their distinctive forms in the context of the militaristic ethos of the middle Republic. Many features of Roman aristocratic ethics can also be paralleled in other complex agrarian societies: for a cross-cultural analysis of aristocratic values and ideology, see Kautsky 1982: 169–210 (esp. 169–77, 197–205).

[8] For example, Sallust, in the *Bellum Iugurthinum*, articulates a conception of *nobilitas* that serves the interests of *novi homines* such as Marius (and himself), and that opposes a conception held by the established aristocracy: he presents *nobilitas* as a function of one's *ingenium*, while aristocrats with long aristocratic heritages present it as a function of one's *genus*. See Earl 1961: 29–40, and Hellegouarc'h 1963: 476–83.

[9] Recently, the term "honor-community" has been applied to such groupings of persons who share crucial moral values: see Flower 1996: 12–15 on the *imagines* as judges of the behavior of members of the Roman aristocratic honor-community, and Lendon 1997: 237–66 on the Roman army as an honor-community distinct from that constituted by the aristocracy. Also helpful for understanding the sociopolitical function of traditional Ro-

One crucial feature of this ethical system is that moral value is heavily community oriented. Because the community as a whole, not its constituent individuals, is the basic unit of social organization, it is the community as a whole that is the ultimate source and reference point of moral value—the generator of incentives and sanctions for actions that reproduce its sociopolitical arrangements and ideologies. On the one hand, then, moral value is constructed externally, based on an agent's actions-in-the-public-eye that elicit evaluations of goodness or badness, rightness or wrongness from his peers and result in his having a reputation of a particular sort among them. On the other hand, when the agent himself endorses and subscribes to these values, when he judges himself as he foresees being judged by others and as he would judge them in turn, then this community-oriented value can also exist internally, as a disposition on his part to behave in socially valued ways and to evaluate himself, as well as others, according to these standards.[10]

These general features of the traditional Roman ethical system are manifested in the semantics of individual value terms. Here I briefly describe aspects of the semantics of two important ethical terms, *virtus* and *pietas*, in order to illustrate the communal orientation of value in this ethical system, and the capacity of the system's categories to articulate the community's relations both within itself and with other groups. Etymologically, as was recognized in antiquity, *virtus* indicates the distinctive or characteristic quality of a man;[11] the epitaph for Lucius Cor-

---

man values are Bourdieu's concept of a "field" (e.g., 1991: 171–202), a system of ideas that both structures and is structured by social practice; and Althusser's formulation of "ideology" as that which "interpellates" individuals as subjects, "hailing" them into particular social positions (e.g., Althusser 1971: 160–65, and 1969: 231–36).

[10] On the matter of internalizing community standards, see the discussion of "shame" by Cairns 1993: 14–18. Shame, on his presentation, requires the idea of a detached observer, an external judge of one's actions. However, this "other" need not be real; it can be wholly internalized, so that one is one's own external judge, so to speak. This internalized "other" may well represent the internalization of the community's standards, and so one who experiences a feeling of shame may indeed be judging himself just as real external observers would judge him. However, real external judges may or may not actually pass the same judgments that one's internalized "other" passes: one may disagree with their judgments, inasmuch as they represent the wrong kind of community and maintain the wrong standards, or because they judge without full knowledge, and so on. On this "internalized other," see further Williams 1993: 81–85; and chapter 2.4 below. Various scholars have examined the idea that the community is the origin and reference point of moral value generally (or particular values) in traditional Roman ethics. See Habinek 1998: 45–59; Kaster 1997: 10–13; Minyard 1985: 6–8, 10; Earl 1967: 19–26 (and ch. 1 *passim*); Earl 1961: 18–27 (especially 21); and Smith 1976 [1947]: 191–97.

[11] Cic. *Tusc.* 2.43: *appellata est enim ex viro virtus*. Ernout-Meillet 1959: 739, s.v. *vir*: "*Virtus* est avec *vir* dans le même rapport de dérivation que *iuuentus, senectus* avec *iuuenis, senex*. Comme ces deux mots, il marque l'activité et la qualité." Eisenhut 1973: 12–13: "Zustand des Mann-seins."

nelius Scipio Barbatus (*CIL* I² 7 = *ILS* 1), dating probably from the middle of the third century B.C.,¹² provides the earliest evidence for the sorts of actions that can be assigned to, and evaluated in, this category:

> Cornelius Lucius Scipio Barbatus
> Gnaivod patre prognatus, fortis vir sapiensque,
> quoius forma virtutei parisuma fuit,
> consol censor aidilis quei fuit apud vos
> Taurasia Cisauna Samnio cepit,
> subigit omne Loucanam opsidesque abdoucit.

> Lucius Cornelius Scipio Barbatus,
> sprung from his father Gnaeus, a brave and wily man,
> whose appearance was well matched to his valor,
> who was consul, censor, and aedile among you,
> took Taurasia and Cisauna in Samnium,
> subdued all Lucania and took away hostages.

If the actions catalogued in the last three lines of this text expand upon and substantiate the positive judgment, given in the second and third lines, that the deceased was *fortis* and displayed *virtus* (*fortis* is commonly used as the adjectival counterpart of the noun *virtus*), then his *virtus* consists in the magistracies that he held and the military victories he won—in both cases, performance in the public eye for the benefit of the community. He is also commended for his military cunning, his *sapientia*.¹³ A judging audience is explicitly invoked in line 4 (*apud vos*) as witness to Barbatus's actions, and thereby invited to confirm these positive evaluations.¹⁴ Centuries later, these patterns of action-in-the-public-

---

[12] The dating and relative chronology of the Scipionic epitaphs are much disputed, some scholars arguing (e.g., Van Sickle 1987: 42–43 and n. 9) that Barbatus's epitaph was composed as late as 200 B.C., and indeed postdates that of his son (*CIL* I² 8–9 = *ILS* 2–3). The most recent work, however, has tended to regard this inscription as roughly contemporary with Barbatus's death, probably toward the middle of the third century: see Flower 1996: 171–75 for discussion and bibliography.

[13] The correspondence between *fortis* and *virtus* is close, but not exact: see Moore 1989: 14–15 and Hellegouarc'h 1963: 247–48. That *sapientia*, in the 3rd and early 2nd centuries B.C., referred specifically to cunning or shrewdness in devising military stratagems, see Wheeler 1988 (esp. 182–88 on Barbatus).

[14] What is the composition of this audience? Since the sarcophagus was placed in a (usually) closed family tomb, the *vos* would in practice refer primarily to other Cornelii, the only ones to see the inscription regularly. However, the epitaph of Barbatus's son (*CIL* I² 8–9 = *ILS* 2–3), found in the same tomb, specifies an audience much wider than just members of the family: *honc oino ploirume cosentiont R[omani]* (or *R[omai]*); the epitaph of Atilius Calatinus attested at Cic. *Fin.* 2.116, also apparently dating from the third century, is similar. Moreover, the similarities between the tropes of the public funeral oration and those of the epitaph further suggest that the imagined audience for these epitaphs is Romans generally. See Van Sickle 1987: 49 and Flower 1996: 160–66, 177–79.

24 CHAPTER 1

eye remain major constituents of *virtus*. In Livy, for example, most occurrences of the word refer to soldiers' bravery or steadfastness in military operations, or to the abilities of a magistrate, whether in domestic politics or as a military leader on campaign.[15] In this early and persistent usage of the word, then, a person — usually a magistrate or soldier — is said to be *fortis*, i.e., to have displayed *virtus*, if his observed actions are judged to have rendered a beneficial service to the community, particularly in the military sphere.[16]

Together with these "enacted" usages of *virtus*, where the word is assigned to an agent by a judging audience of community members on the basis of his observed actions, there coexists a "dispositional" usage that marks a person as disposed to act in the ways described above, without implying that such action has in fact been observed.[17] The epitaph for L. Cornelius Cn. f. Scipio (*CIL* I^2 11 = *ILS* 7), dated to ca.

---

[15] See, for example, the cluster of occurrences of *virtus/fortis* in Livy 2.10–13, the account of the heroic military exploits of Horatius Cocles, Mucius Scaevola, and Cloelia. Each performs his/her exemplary deed before a large audience; each is praised and/or rewarded for that valor by the Roman community, the enemy, or both. For Livy's usage of *virtus* and *fortis* (etc.) more generally, see Moore 1989: 5–17. Hellegouarc'h 1963: 244–48 shows that these words have more or less the same range and distribution of usages in late Republican literature broadly.

[16] Although men are the expected agents of the actions to which *virtus* is ascribed, and although the etymology and contemporary understanding of the term suggests a specifically male activity and quality, it is nevertheless attributable to women as well: e.g., Livy 2.10.9–11 and the inscriptions cited by Eisenhut 1973: 210–11. Tension generated by this paradox is palpable at Sen. *Marc.* 16.2, where Cloelia's renown is said to be such that she is "all but counted as a man": *ob insignem audaciam tantum non in viros transcripsimus* (cf. Val. Max. 6.1.1, a similar judgment on Lucretia). Another tension is exposed at Sen. *Helv.* 19.6, where Seneca contends that, for women, being unknown is itself of positive moral value. He ascribes this value to his maternal aunt, asserting that she was renowned for this reason throughout Egypt (of which her husband was prefect) — famous, that is, for her laudable anonymity. Moreover, through this laudatory account Seneca seeks to immortalize her as an *exemplum virtutis* and thus present her to posterity for emulation. This tension is also present at Thuc. 2.45.2, where Pericles asserts that women whose κλέος is the least have the greatest δόξα. Rusten 1989: 177 calls this assertion "a deliberate oxymoron." The inconsistency he perceives, however, resides not so much in this specific passage, as in the overarching ethical imperatives that anonymity is morally valued in a woman, and that positive moral value warrants public praise.

[17] Cairns 1993: 10–11, discussing emotion terms such as "fear" and αἰδώς, distinguishes "occurrent" usages of these terms, which refer to a specific instance or experience of that emotion, from "dispositional" usages, which indicate a general vulnerability to such experiences. A distinction between specific manifestations and general inclinations also seems appropriate for ethical categories such as *virtus*, though with the alteration (suggested to me by Robert Kaster) of Cairns's term "occurrent" to "enacted." "Enacted" better describes the performance in the public eye that is valued according to the traditional Roman ethical categories, while "occurrent" seems more appropriate for the experience of having an emotion come over one.

180–70 B.C., points out that the deceased never held public office because he died young, aged twenty (*annos gnatus XX . . . / ne quairatis honore quei minus sit mandatus*, vv. 6–7), yet still insists that he was never surpassed in *virtus* (*. . . quei nunquam victus est virtutei*, v. 5). Absent any other relevant information about the young man's actions, the *virtus* here ascribed to him can only be a claim about how he would have discharged his magistracies had he lived; as such, this usage indicates a disposition.[18] Less ambiguously, when Cicero declares, *fuit, fuit ista quondam in hac re publica virtus ut viri fortes acrioribus suppliciis civem perniciosum quam acerbissimum hostem coercerent* ("there was, there was, this *virtus* once upon a time in our state, that brave men would summarily punish a destructive citizen with harsher penalties than the most bitter enemy," *Cat.* 1.1.3), the consecutive clause *ut . . . coercerent* marks the sort of action on behalf of the community to which the *virtus* of the *viri fortes* was expected to lead. This *virtus* is evidently dispositional, for it signifies a quality latent in the community at large and particularly in the minds of the brave men, a quality which could be translated into action when necessary. Similarly, Sallust says of Caesar, *sibi magnum imperium, exercitum, bellum novom exoptabat ubi virtus enitescere posset* ("he eagerly desired for himself a great command, an army, and a new war where his *virtus* could shine out," *Cat.* 54.4). Since in the dramatic setting of Sallust's text Caesar has not yet performed any military exploits in the public eye, it is merely his inclination to do so that is labelled by the term *virtus*. So, although the dispositional usage differs from the enacted usage in that it refers to an agent's state of mind rather than to his observed behavior, it signifies the same ethical orientation by the agent toward furthering the interests of the community through action (especially actions in the military and governmental arenas), and the same interest in having the community observe and evaluate such actions positively.[19]

---

[18] Eisenhut 1973: 209 similarly describes *virtus* here as marking "gute Eigenschaften" rather than "tapfere Taten." Earl 1967: 22–23 and Smith 1976 [1947]: 194–95 further discuss this inscription. It is quite possible that a twenty-year-old aristocrat in the early second century B.C. had already seen two or three years of military service as a military tribune (Harris 1979: 12–15) and might have displayed notable *virtus* in that context — though the inscription gives no hint of this.

[19] Other examples of the dispositional usage: Lucilius fr. 1326–38 Marx (esp. 1329–30 and 1337–38, on which see Eisenhut 1973: 35–37), Cic. *Mur.* 18. Despite the fairly close association of these two kinds of usages, in a couple of passages Cicero insists that only "enacted" *virtus* is really praiseworthy. At *Rep.* 1.2 he writes: *nec vero habere virtutem satis est quasi artem aliquam nisi utare; etsi ars quidem cum ea non utare scientia tamen ipsa teneri potest, virtus in usu sui tota posita est; usus autem eius est maximus civitatis gubernatio, et earum ipsarum rerum quas isti in angulis personant, reapse non oratione perfectio*. In comparing *virtus* to an *ars*, Cicero attributes an internality to it, for *ars* — an

In certain contexts—philosophical ones in particular—a much broader range of usages of *virtus* is apparent. In these usages, the word has little or no relation to be community-oriented modes of thought and action described above, and in fact refers exclusively to states of mind and not to action at all. Specifically, it is used as an umbrella term, either in the singular or in the plural, to encompass a collection of other terms that indicate positive moral value, and that stand in opposition to "vices" (*vitia*).[20] In part, at least, this extended semantic range arises from the usage of *virtus* to render into Latin the Greek term ἀρετή, which designates an ethical category of a different shape. For while notable service to the community may be included in the category of ἀρετή, this category is also much broader, including, e.g., the particular "excellence(s)" of an animal or object. Cicero draws attention to the tension between this broad usage of *virtus* and the narrower, community-oriented usage at *De Legibus* 1.45, where he mentions the "so-called *virtus* of a horse or a tree, in which we misuse the word." Here, presumably, he means that this usage of *virtus* does not fall within the word's familiar semantic field, indicating valued action (or the disposition toward such action) in the spheres of government or warfare.[21] Nevertheless, Cicero himself commonly uses *virtus* in this broader sense, and in Seneca's heavily Stoic ethical treatises this broader usage is sometimes opposed to, or made to engage with, the narrower politico-military one (see chapter 2.6 below).

The second ethical category of interest here, *pietas*, is also community oriented in that, like *virtus*, it marks out a set of valued roles for the individual to perform in society. The moral category defined by *pietas* and its opposite, *impietas*, encompasses the duties one owes toward

---

acquired skill or systematic body of knowledge—is a cognitive state: *cum ea non utare scientia tamen ipsa teneri potest.* (This formulation of *virtus* as an *ars* may owe something to the broader usage of *virtus* as a translation of ἀρετή, discussed below: for in certain Stoic formulations ἀρετή is said to be a τέχνη [*SVF* III 214, cf. 95]). But Cicero insists that to "have" *virtus* in this way (i.e., internally, as a form of knowledge) is insufficient, for its entire value lies in its public display, and the governance of the state is the most highly-valued form of this display. Thus, while *virtus* can lie latent as an *ars*, it cannot be recognized and praised unless it is manifested through community-oriented action in the public eye. See also *Off.* 1.19.

[20] E.g., Cic. *Inv.* 2.159: *virtus est animi habitus naturae modo atque rationi consentaneus. . . . habet igitur partes quattuor: prudentiam, iustitiam, fortitudinem, temperantiam*; also Sen. *Ep.* 113.1–2: *iustitia, fortitudo, prudentia ceteraeque virtutes . . . virtus autem nihil aliud est quam animus quodam modo se habens.* Cf. Cic. *Leg.* 1.44–45; *Cat.* 2.25. On the semantics of the plural form *virtutes*, see Moore 1989: 8–9, Eisenhut 1973: 42, Hellegouarc'h 1963: 245–46.

[21] The specific absurdity may be in attributing *virtus*, the "characteristic quality of a man," to something that is nonhuman. However, ἀρετή is attributable to such things, and it is as a translation of ἀρετή that *virtus* is used this way. On the relationship of *virtus* to ἀρετή, see Eisenhut 1973: 14–22; also Ferguson 1958: 161–64.

members of one's family, one's civic community, and the gods. These different relationships impose differing obligations: the bond between patron and client, for example, involves the exchange of objects and services; the status of citizen may require that one fight alongside other citizens (or, in the case of aristocrats, lead fellow citizens of lower status) on behalf of the state; differing degrees of kinship by blood or marriage are accompanied by differing social expectations; and religion, both in the public and domestic spheres, involves ritually prescribed exchanges between humans and divinities.[22] The category *pietas*, then, embraces a range of social behaviors that collectively provide a complex internal structure to the community, binding people more or less closely together within and among kinship groups, connecting them between social strata, and linking them to the divinities. Furthermore, for *pietas* as with *virtus*, it is possible to distinguish an "enacted" usage where judgment is passed on the basis of observed actions, and a "dispositional" usage that indicates the agent's inclination to act in ways that can be evaluated positively in this category. A person who is judged to be doing (or inclined to do) his share in binding society together in these ways is designated *pius*.[23] Significantly, though, the complex internal structure that the several aspects of *pietas* give to the community may also give rise to conflicting obligations. Obligations arising from civic association may, for example, be at odds with obligations arising from familial connection: the accounts of the severe fathers of the early and middle republic who execute their adult sons for treason or military disobedience show both the presence of conflicting obligations to family and state, and their resolution in favor of the latter.[24]

I have now argued that *virtus* (in the narrower, traditional sense) and

---

[22] On the semantics of *pietas*, see Hellegouarc'h 1963: 276–79, and especially 276–77 for this term's close association with fulfilling duties and obligations (*officia*). Moore 1989: 56–61 shows that this same pattern of usages holds in Livy. There is no necessary order of precedence for these various obligations: Wagenvoort 1924: 5–9 collects passages from Cicero in which one or another of the three components of *pietas* is privileged over the remaining two.

[23] Some instances of the enacted usage: Cic. *Rosc.* 66, where children who avenge the death of their father are called *pii*; Verg. *Aen.* 1.378, where Aeneas declares himself *pius* for bringing his *penates* from Troy; Ov. *Tr.* 1.2.37, where the poet labels his wife *pia* because she grieves for his exile; and Pliny *Ep.* 10.52, where the enthusiasm that the provincials display in taking the *sacramentum*, the oath of personal loyalty to the emperor, manifests their *pietas*. Instances of the dispositional usage: at *Planc.* 80, Cicero asks, *quid est pietas nisi voluntas grata in parentes?* — where *pietas* is portrayed as a state of mind through its equation with *voluntas*. Also, in Livy 6.34.8 one of the daughters of M. Fabius Ambustus hesitates to confess to her father that she is jealous of her sister's marriage, regarding this feeling as insufficiently *pia* toward her sister and her own husband.

[24] Harris 1986 conveniently collects the attested instances of fathers executing adult sons, though he is concerned with *patria potestas*, not *pietas*. Cf. ch. 4.3 and n. 40 below.

pietas are assigned both to actions that are seen as promoting the community's interests, and to pro-attitudes toward these interests and their advancement; moreover, these terms are at the community's disposal to allocate. But what sort of "community" is it that serves as the social basis and judge for the allocation of these terms? Above all, it is one whose boundaries are clear and widely agreed upon. For if the value terms *pietas* and *virtus* are to be deployed consistently, there must be general agreement regarding (1) who the outsiders are, against whom one may display *virtus* by fighting bravely, and (2) who the members of this community are, those to whom each member owes the various obligations and duties associated with *pietas*. In other words, these two categories of moral value, taken together, project a notionally unified, well-defined group which might be called a "community of moral obligation," and articulate consistently aspects of its inter- and intramural relations. In such a community the moral imperatives of *virtus* and *pietas* neatly overlap, for one who fights well or serves effectively as a magistrate (demonstrating *virtus*) thereby also defends and secures his family, fellow citizens, and gods (demonstrating *pietas*).

Civil war, however, by definition divides the civic community and turns it against itself, and may divide families as well—thus abolishing any notionally widely agreed social boundaries and bonds. Under these conditions, *pietas* and *virtus* become inconsistent, even contradictory: a soldier who demonstrates *virtus* by fighting the adversary effectively may also be judged *impius* for harming other members of his own civic community or family; likewise, if he refuses to fight (so as not to kill fellow citizens and family members), he fails his comrades-in-arms and may be accused of cowardice. For in civil war, the view that one's opponents are (at least) *cives*, i.e., fellow Romans, hence members of one's community of moral obligation, and the view that they are *hostes*, i.e., foreign enemies, therefore not members of this community, are available simultaneously.[25] These alternative conceptions of civil war—that it is

---

[25] The words *civis* and *hostis*, along with their cognates, are often marked terms (in Lucan and elsewhere) for delineating the boundaries of the community. Since a *hostis* is usually (1) an armed adversary, and (2) foreign, then to call another Roman a *hostis* (as Cicero sometimes calls Catiline and Antony) is to expel him from the civic community, insist he has no civic rights, and imply that war may justly be waged against him. *Civis*, on the other hand, designates a Roman citizen with full civic rights. On the semantics of *hostis* and *civis*, and their polemical deployment in the political struggles of the late republic, see Jal 1963 and Raaflaub 1974: 236–39. There is also a middle category, the *latro* (bandit) who comes from within the community but turns against it. We have abundant evidence that this term was used for labelling opponents in civil-war contexts throughout Roman history (see the discussion in Shaw 1984: 29–35), yet the term itself never occurs in Lucan, and the idea is scarcely hinted at. On these matters see section 7 and nn. 71, 81 below.

or is not a conflict within a single community of moral obligation—authorize competing ethical discourses, which in turn provide competing, often contradictory, value judgments on particular actions, and therefore motivate sharply divergent actions in a given situation.

And so it is in Lucan's *Bellum Civile*, whose subject matter is the civil war waged between Caesar and Pompey in 49–48 B.C. The poem is riven with ethical contradictions. It is not simply that different voices representing different interests—Caesar and Pompey themselves, for example—disagree about the proper moral evaluation of particular actions and patterns of behavior; such disagreement is widely present in ancient epic, as elsewhere in ancient society. Rather, these voices, including the narrative voice itself, are collectively trapped between two competing ethical discourses and irreconcilable modes of valuation, discourses based on and generated by the alternative views of the community in civil war just described. In this poem, actions are evaluated in both of these ethical frameworks—not only by different voices embracing alternative modes of valuation, but even by a single voice as it applies now the one evaluative framework and now the other. By examining Lucan's representations of *pietas* and *virtus*, I seek to demonstrate not only that these contradictions exist, but also that competing ethical discourses, and the contradictory moral judgments that derive from them, are necessary features of the condition of civil war as Lucan represents it. Finally, I consider the ideological ramifications of placing these two modes of ethical discourse in competition. For in so doing, Lucan makes the civil war a context in which he can participate in the ideological struggles of his own day by propounding, exploring, and evaluating a particular vision of the principate.[26]

3. The "Assimilating" Viewpoint

Of the two views of civil war articulated in Lucan, I first discuss what I call the "assimilating" view: one's opponent is more or less assimilated to oneself, with the result that the conflict is seen as taking place within a single community of obligation. Despite the presence of conflict, the community on this view remains fundamentally intact. The very term *bellum civile*, "civil war," privileges this view, implying as it does that the belligerants are all *cives*: fellow citizens, members of a single civic community. The poem opens by portraying the conflict from this point

---

[26] Several scholars in the past half-century have suggested that Lucanian paradoxes and contradictions are not problems to be condemned or excused, but effective literary strategies; this view has gained popularity in recent years. Proponents include Masters 1992, Henderson 1987, Martindale 1976, and Due 1962.

of view: the narrator describes the belligerants' behavior metaphorically as a person turning a sword against his own vitals (*populumque potentem / in sua victrici conversum viscera dextra*, 1.2–3), he apostrophizes both factions collectively as *cives*, "citizens" (1.8), and he portrays the opposing sides as identical and interchangeable ("kindred battle lines," "standards opposed to hostile standards, equal eagles, and javelins threatening javelins").[27] The narrator also condemns the conflict as a crime, as sacrilege, and as madness (*scelus* [1.2], *nefas* [1.6], *furor* [1.8]), for on this view the conflict involves grotesque impiety — slaughtering other members of one's civic community and family, thus massively violating the obligations and duties one owes fellow citizens and kin. Furthermore, on this view of civil war there is no place for *virtus* in the "traditional" military sense discussed above, for there is no foreign enemy against whom martial valor can properly be displayed. The assimilating view of the conflict thus makes violence against one's adversary ethically problematic, in ways we shall see.

The assimilating view is most clearly articulated and enacted throughout the poem by the Pompeian faction. Pompey himself is this view's most consistent advocate, though to various extents his troops and officers also assert and/or act upon this view. Consider Pompey's first words in the poem, the speech he delivers to his troops upon the outbreak of war (2.531–95). Here he systematically represents his clash with Caesar as a dispute within a single community of obligation. He begins by calling his soldiers the "truly Roman band" (*o vere Romana manus*) where the significance of the adverb "truly" is explained in the following clause: their war making is authorized by the Senate, while Caesar's weapons, lacking this authorization, are mere "private arms" (2.532–33). Thus Caesar and his soldiers are acknowledged as Romans but are placed outside the bounds of legality, lacking authoritative institutional sanction for their enterprise. A few lines later, Pompey denies that the looming conflict is a *proelium iustum*, a "proper battle" (2.539–40) — an expression I take to be equivalent to *bellum iustum*, "proper war," which is specifically associated with warfare against a *hostis*.[28] He insists, rather, that his own enterprise embodies the "anger

---

[27] 1.4–7: *cognatasque acies, . . . infestisque obvia signis / signa, pares aquilas et pila minantia pilis*. For the representation of the two sides as identical, see Henderson 1987: 150.

[28] *Proelium iustum* would normally mean a formal, set battle with squared battle lines, as opposed to raiding, surprise attacks, etc. (cf. Livy 5.49.5–6, with the other passages cited at *TLL* VII 2.721.6–18). But here, since this phrase is contrasted with "the anger of a vengeful fatherland" (indicating conflict within a single community), I take it to refer to "normal" external warfare against a *hostis*; also, lines 541–42 make a parallel distinction. Hence my view that it is equivalent to *bellum iustum*—perhaps used as a metrical variant

of a vengeful fatherland" — anger directed, implicitly, at a recalcitrant member of itself.[29] Elaborating this claim, he goes on to compare Caesar to other Romans who took up arms against their own state, naming Catiline, Lentulus, Cethegus, Cinna, Marius, Lepidus, Carbo, Sertorius, and even Spartacus as parallels (2.541–54). Likewise, at the end of the speech he explicitly calls the current conflict a *bellum civile* inasmuch as his own conquest of the world has brought all foreigners under Roman sway, leaving Caesar no war to wage *but* a civil one (576–95). Also, while Pompey mentions a "Gallic frenzy" (*Gallica rabies*, 535) entering Italy from the Alps, he does not compare Caesar himself to any specific foreign foe such as Hannibal, though other voices in the poem have already suggested this parallel (cf. 1.254–57, 303–305).[30] The assimilating view is evident in this speech in other respects as well. For Pompey repeatedly condemns Caesar as criminal, sacrilegious, and mad for assaulting his fatherland (*scelus* ([531], *pollutus* [536], *nefas* [538], *rabies* [544], *furens* [551], *furor* [573], *demens* [575]), precisely the terminology of madness and criminality that the narrator, manifesting the assimilating view, applies to civil war in the opening lines of the poem. Presumably these are not necessary characteristics of one who attacks an alien enemy, a project that few Roman aristocrats of the late republic and early empire found ethically problematic in principle. These terms present Caesar as someone who has turned against his community — a bad citizen, perhaps, but not a foreign foe.

Now, Pompey is addressing troops who have been levied to fight Caesar, and indeed Pompey explicitly appeals to them to "pray for a fight" (*votis deposcite pugnam* [2.533]). But if in his view the Caesarians are members of his (and his troops') community of moral obligation, is it consistent with this view to advocate violence against them? The answer

---

(see also Fantham 1992: 183). For the linkage of the phrase *bellum iustum* with external warfare, see Jal 1963: 77–78 and Shaw 1984: 6 and n. 10, along with the citations at *TLL* II 1847.79–1848.13.

[29] 2.538–42: *iam iam me praeside Roma / supplicium poenamque petat. neque enim ista vocari / proelia iusta decet, patriae sed vindicis iram; / nec magis hoc bellum est, quam quom Catilina paravit / arsuras in tecta faces.* Elsewhere in the poem as well the Pompeian cause is assimilated to the cause of the civic community as a whole. Earlier in book 2 Cato accepts Pompey as the standard-bearer of this community (*quin publica signa ducemque / Pompeium sequimur?* [2.319–20]), and in book 7 the narrator makes a similar identification, speaking of the Pompeian standards: *usque ad Thessaliam Romana et publica signa* (7.164). See also 2.519–21, 5.9–14.

[30] Cf. 1.475–84 for the idea that Caesar brings foreign enemies in his train. The reading *quoi . . . hosti* (2.554), if correct, refers to Crassus in relation to Spartacus and Caesar (Håkanson 1979: 36–38), which implies that Crassus and Caesar would have stood as foreign enemies to each other. But does *hostis* here encapsulate Pompey's view of the relationship, or what Pompey takes to be Caesar's view?

32 CHAPTER 1

seems to be yes. For in Pompey's presentation, Caesar and his troops, by taking up arms, have violated various obligatory bonds between themselves and their fatherland (*Roma, patria*: 2.538, 540) — violations that Pompey suggests should be punished, by himself and his soldiers, on behalf of the collective. On the one hand, then, Pompey and his troops face a conflict between two different sorts of obligations encompassed by *pietas*: those owed to those fellow citizens and family members who happen to be Caesarians, and those owed to the fatherland as a notionally collective entity that the Caesarians are attacking. In this speech, Pompey adjudicates this conflict by giving his *pietas*-obligations to the fatherland precedence over his *pietas*-obligations to the Caesarians. This I call a "weak" assimilating view, in that the assimilation of the opponent is only partial: he is not a foreign enemy, but is also not fully vested in one's own community of moral obligation.

Yet, as later episodes in the poem reveal, this conflict of *pietas*-obligation in fact hampers Pompey, and eventually his troops as well. Consider first the main confrontation between the Pompeian and Caesarian troops at Dyrrachium, narrated in book 6 (6.263–313). Here Pompey has surrounded a portion of Caesar's army, and could end the war on the spot if he annihilates these troops. Yet he restrains his men's swords:

> Totus mitti civilibus armis
> usque vel in pacem potuit cruor: ipse furentes
> dux tenuit gladios. felix ac libera regum,
> Roma, fores iurisque tui, vicisset in illo
> si tibi Sulla loco. dolet, heu, semperque dolebit,
> quod scelerum, Caesar, prodest tibi summa tuorum,
> cum genero pugnasse pio. pro tristia fata!
>
> (6.299–305)

All the blood in civil conflict could have been shed, even to the point of peace: but the leader himself restrained the furious swords. You would have been happy, free from kings and master of yourself, Rome, had Sulla conquered for you in that place. It grieves us, alas, and will always grieve us, that the pinnacle of your crimes benefits you, Caesar: you have done battle with a son-in-law who is *pius*. Oh, cruel fate!

The narrator here calls Pompey *pius* (305) — a positive evaluation — because he disallows the slaughter of the Caesarians (suppressing his own troops' martial valor in the process, we are told). So while Pompey earlier accepted that his *pietas*-obligation to the state entailed doing violence to the Caesarians (the "weak" assimilating view), here he does not follow through, but considers only his *pietas*-obligations to his father-in-law Caesar and to the Caesarian troops. This I call a "strong" assimilating view, in that the opponent here *is* regarded as a fully vested member of one's community of obligation; he is not now conceptually separated from a notional collective in such a way that his *pietas*-claims are distinguishable from those of the collective, as they are on the "weak" view. The narrator also contrasts this pious Pompey, who does not wage war, with Caesar, the apex of whose criminality is that he, in return, *does* wage war upon his (pious) son-in-law. Yet this is not an unqualified endorsement of Pompey's strong assimilating view and of the actions that arise from it, as the lamenting exclamation *pro tristia fata* signals. For a major consequence of Pompey's "pious" action is that the war will continue and the fatherland will eventually lose its liberty, subjected to a king's sway (*libera regum, / Roma, fores iurisque tui* . . . [301–2], also 306–13). Here, then, the narrator reassesses the conflict of *pietas*-obligation inherent in Pompey's assimilating perspective. He suggests that being *pius* in the short term, sparing the Caesarians to whom he regards himself obligated, is to be *impius* in the long term, ensuring further bloodshed in future battles and leading eventually to the destruction of the state itself (which Pompey, in his earlier speech, had presented as his primary *pietas*-obligation). Sulla, usually a byword for brutality and bloodthirstiness, is adduced here a particularly pointed way. For he behaved in precisely the opposite manner to Pompey: he ended his war quickly by wiping out his opponents in one great purge; he achieved what we are told Pompey failed to do, namely, "shed all the blood of civil war, to the point of peace" (299–300). Thus the narrator hints that Sulla's behavior, once all the debits and credits are tallied, might actually be more "pious" than Pompey's.

Pompey maintains this strong assimilating view into book 7, where the ethical difficulties entailed by this view are further elaborated. Here, on the morning of the battle of Pharsalus, we are told that Pompey's troops are overcome by a "dire frenzy" (7.51) and hence are eager to join battle. They accuse their leader of being "slow and cowardly" for pursuing a strategy of delay: *segnis pavidusque vocatur / ac nimium patiens soceri Pompeius* . . . (7.52–53). That is, they imply that his strategy betokens a lack of *virtus*, and that he is overly solicitous of his father-in-law (i.e., his decisions are governed by the specifically familial form of *pietas*-obligation). They themselves, it appears, do not feel these *pietas*-obligations, and do regard the Caesarians as appropriate targets for their *virtus* (more on this view below). Replying to these assertions Pompey concedes that battle can no longer be postponed, since the "prods of martial valor" are inciting his soldiers (*si modo virtutis stimulis iraeque calore / signa petunt* [7.103–4]). But he labels his soldiers' desire to fight as "madness for criminality," reasserting the usual terminology of the assimilating perspective, and suggests that victory without bloodshed is precisely what is wanted in civil war (*quis furor, o caeci, scelerum? civilia bella / gesturi metuunt ne non cum sanguine vincant* [7.95–96]). As in the Dyrrachium episode, then, Pompey seeks to avoid doing violence to the Caesarians—again manifesting the strong assimilating view.

The idea of "victory without bloodshed," Pompey's desideratum here, has appeared already in a brief episode within the Dyrrachium narrative in book 6 (118–39). In this episode, when Pompey first attempts to break through Caesar's encirclement—the first time Pompey himself sends his troops into battle—the sudden onslaught scares the Caesarians *literally* to death: "That his victory might owe nothing to the sword, fear had finished off his stunned enemies. They lay dead in the place they ought to have stood—the only thing their *virtus* had the strength to do. Already there was nobody left to receive wounds, and the storm cloud bringing so many weapons was being squandered" (*ne quid victoria ferro / deberet, pavor attonitos confecerat hostes. / quod solum valuit virtus, iacuere perempti / debuerant quo stare loco. qui volnera ferrent / iam derant, et nimbus agens tot tela peribat* [6.130–34]). The narrator expressly notes that Pompey remains undefiled by civil bloodshed because his victory is technically nonviolent: fear itself does the killing before Pompeian weapons can draw blood.[31] This is how civil war can be waged "without bloodshed" in accordance with the strong assimilating view; Pompey apparently hopes to win a similar sort of victory at Pharsalus.

The passages discussed so far, then, in various ways bring out some essential contradictions in Pompey's assimilating view of the conflict. Simply put, the different constituencies to which he considers himself bound by obligations of *pietas*—the Roman state, his own soldiers, Caesar's soldiers, Caesar himself—make conflicting, irreconcilable demands. For an action that appears pious in the short term may appear impious in the long term; also, there are justifications within the assimilating view for doing violence to the Caesarians as well as for not doing them violence. Furthermore, the strong form of this view that Pompey embraces in books 6 and 7—that considerations of *pietas* demand abstention from violence—finally brings him into conflict with his own soldiers, whose desire to be evaluated positively in the category of martial valor (*virtus*) urges them, for the moment, to seek battle.

But if his words and deeds have opened a gap between *virtus* and

---

[31] *Virtus* (132) here is used ironically of the Caesarians, since it is *pavor*, its opposite, that kills them. For given that they die of fright, their opportunities for displaying *virtus* are sharply limited—indeed, they display it only in "holding their ground," lying dead (and therefore not fleeing) where they should be standing.

pietas, Pompey attempts to close this gap in a speech to his soldiers just before the battle is joined (7.342–82). Here he seeks to motivate his troops to fight effectively precisely by invoking images of fatherland, wives and children left behind:

> "quem flagitat," inquit,
> "vestra diem virtus, finis civilibus armis,
> quem quaesistis, adest. totas effundite vires:
> extremum ferri superest opus, unaque gentis
> hora trahit. quisquis patriam carosque penates,
> qui subolem ac thalamos desertaque pignora quaerit,
> ense petat: medio posuit deus omnia campo.
>
> (7.342–48)

"The day your *virtus* demands," he says, "the end to civil conflict that you have sought, is at hand. Pour out all your strength: a final work of arms remains, and a single hour draws together all nations. Whoever longs for his fatherland and dear *penates*, whoever longs for his offspring and wife and relatives left behind, let him seek them by the sword: god has set everything in the middle of the battlefield."

Later he adduces still other images of his soldiers' community of moral obligation in need, asking his men to imagine Roman matrons urging them to battle from the walls of the city, Roman senators abasing themselves before them, and the city itself making an appeal (7.369–73) — that is, he appeals repeatedly to his soldiers' sense of *pietas*-obligation to family and civic community in an effort to motivate them to fight with valor (*virtus* [343]; *totas effundite vires* [344]). He even refers to the Caesarians as *hostes* (365), for once rhetorically ejecting them from this community. But can this rhetorical strategy succeed? How can his troops fight vigorously (demonstrating *virtus*) on the moral basis that Pompey has provided for them (that of piously preserving family and fatherland), when the purported *hostes* facing them are none other than the kin and fellow citizens to whom Pompey here declares them bound by *pietas*, and toward whom he himself has recently sought to avoid violence for this very reason, in accordance with the strong assimilating view? Pompey's framing of the upcoming battle does not permit these conflicting *pietas*-obligations to be resolved. Nor do his soldiers deal effectively with this difficulty on their own. For although we are told that his speech kindles their desire to display *virtus*,[32] it turns out (as we shall see) that their desire to be judged *pii*, upon which this desire for

---

[32] 7.382–84: *tam maesta locuti / voce ducis flagrant animi, Romanaque virtus / erigitur, placuitque mori, si vera timeret.*

virtus is presumably founded, will indeed undermine their will to fight as soon as they recognize their friends and relatives on the other side.

4. The "Alienating" Viewpoint

The Pompeian commander Petreius, in the fraternization scene in book 4, is the one Pompeian who systematically rejects the assimilating viewpoint, and so avoids the ethical contradictions that lumber Pompey. Some Caesarian and Pompeian soldiers pitch camp within sight of one another; they begin recognizing friends on the other side, eventually throwing down their weapons and going freely back and forth between the two camps. As the narrator describes these events (4.157–205), he assumes the assimilating perspective (as do the soldiers, presumably), heartily approving of the outbreak of concord (189) and peace (196). He also pronounces moral judgments in accordance with this view: for these soldiers to kill one another would be *nefas*, "wicked" (205, cf. 172), while the social bonds they forge are bonds of good faith and trust, *fides* (204). In lines 212–35, however, the narrator yields the floor to Petreius, who makes a bitter speech to his troops in exactly the opposite sense: he urges his men to kill the Caesarians who have peaceably entered the Pompeian camp. Rhetorically he excludes these visitors from his soldiers' community of obligation by calling them *hostes* (228), and insists that the Pompeian troops owe loyalty only to their own faction, which he identifies with the state as a whole: "heedless of your fatherland, forgetful of your own standards . . ." (*immemor o patriae, signorum oblite tuorum* [212]). His value judgments on their actions buttress his construction of this community of obligation: he calls his men's fraternization "wicked betrayal" (*proditio nefanda* [220–21]) and implies that they have acted in bad faith (*fides* [229–30]) in giving up the fight against the Caesarians—whereas the narrator had called the fraternization *fides*, and the prospect of further bloodshed *nefas*. Initially reluctant, the Pompeian soldiers are finally induced to abandon their own assimilating impulses and slaughter their Caesarian guests.[33]

Petreius's viewpoint, which I call the "alienating" view, is not "perverse"—an adjective sometimes applied to this line of thought—nor is

---

[33] In fact, Petreius has it both ways: for he also speaks of the Caesarians' *damnata signa* (217) and *sceleri iurata nefando sacramenta* (228–29), employing the language of criminality that typically accompanies the assimilating perspective. Thus he implicitly includes them in his community of obligation when he wishes to characterize them as criminal, but excludes them when he seeks to inspire his troops to kill them. See Jal 1963: 72–76 on sharp juxtapositions of the opponent-as-*civis* and opponent-as-*hostis* paradigms. On the two opposed uses of *fides* in this passage, see also Saylor 1986: 150 (and passim).

it merely a travesty or inversion of assimilating values: it has a systematic logic of its own. It is the view that one's opponent is an alien enemy, a *hostis*, who threatens one's own community of obligation yet is also utterly excluded from it. Therefore making war on him is both pious and valorous. On this view, the conflict at hand is not a *bellum civile* at all, but rather a *bellum externum*; it is essentially no different from a war against (say) the Parthians or a German tribe.[34] The alienating view is well represented throughout Lucan's poem and, notwithstanding its presence in Petreius's speech, is much more commonly associated with the Caesarians than with the Pompeians.

First, though, a word on Lucan's Caesar. In this poem, "Caesar" usually signifies the historical figure Gaius Iulius Caesar, who defeated Pompey and other rivals to establish himself as a dominant, unprecedentedly powerful individual in Roman society; this is the Caesar who laid the groundwork for the principate. On the other hand, "Caesar" is also assimilated, in some passages and in certain respects, to the Caesars who follow Iulius, the successors who assume his dominant position as well as his name. Lucan brings this assimilation about through various techniques, one of which is to exploit the polyvalence of the name "Caesar" itself. Thus, in book 1, "Caesar" twice refers to the emperor Nero (1.41, 59); and at the end of book 4 (4.823) Lucan speaks intriguingly of the *Caesareae domus series*—the "line of Caesar's house," or perhaps "one Caeser-house after another"—which has the "power of the sword" (*ius ensis*)[35] over "us," where the "us" presumably represents not only Lucan and his contemporary audience, but also earlier generations who were the contemporaries of each Caesar in the line. A second Lucanian technique for assimilating Iulius Caesar to his successors is to collapse the temporal distinction between the events narrated in the poem and the position from which they are narrated.[36] In

---

[34] On civil war vs. external war, see Jal 1962: 264–67, 384–85; also section 7 below. In this section (4), I discuss only passages in which *both* sides are said or implied to consist of Romans, but where the ethical discourse is that of a foreign war. I exclude passages in which one of the two sides is presented as non-Roman, e.g., the battles between Caesarians and Massiliote "Greeks" in book 3. In such passages, the belligerants regularly call one another *hostes*, acting and passing moral judgments accordingly: in Lucan such a conflict *is* a foreign war and lacks the moral complexity of a fight between Romans. Caesar himself makes this distinction in 7.269–76, assuring his troops before Pharsalus that very little of the fighting will actually be "civil" since Pompey's force is so heavily non-Roman: *civilia paucae / bella manus facient; pugnae pars magna levabit / his orbem populis Romanumque obteret hostem* (7.274–76).

[35] A metrical variant for *ius gladii*? Cf. ch. 4.3 and n. 53 below.

[36] Instances of collapsing temporal distinctions: see 7.207–13 and 9.980–86, where the narrator implicates himself and his audience in the factional struggles of the civil war. More subtly, it is sometimes impossible to establish the temporal location of the narrator's

such passages, the figure of Caesar literally encompasses the future of Rome, since he and his actions come to signify some or all of the emperors and their actions for the next 100 years. The figure of (Iulius) Caesar in this poem, then, is a prototype for other Caesars, and he might therefore be expected to encapsulate or bring in his train specifically imperial concerns. For the moment I merely suggest that alienating ethics, which Lucan typically associates with Caesar and the Caesarians, is also an important element of later Julio-Claudian ideology; this suggestion will be argued in greater detail in section 7 below.

The alienating view is first articulated at the initial crisis point of the poem, Caesar's arrival at the Rubicon. As Caesar stands on the bank of the river (1.185–86), a vision of the Roman state itself, the *patria*, appears to him and says, "Where beyond are you aiming? Where are you carrying my standards, soldiers? If you come with legal sanction, and as citizens, this far only is permitted" (*quo tenditis ultra? / quo fertis mea signa, viri? si iure venitis, / si cives, huc usque licet* [1.190–92]). This image of the fatherland embodies and enunciates the values of the civic community as a whole, telling Caesar that he will be violating the proper Roman way of doing things (*ius*), and hence will be excluded from the body of *cives*, if he crosses the river with his army: he will, in other words, alienate himself. Caesar responds (1.195–203) by forcefully asserting his membership in the civic community: he invokes the Trojan *penates* of his own house, the fire of Vesta, and Jupiter in two different forms — all symbols of the Roman community and his membership in it — asking them to favor his undertaking. In this way he affiliates his actions with the interests of the fatherland; he implies that he is *pius*. Indeed, he explicitly denies that he is attacking the fatherland (*patria*) itself: "It is not you I am harrying with furious arms" (*non te furialibus armis / persequor* [1.200–201]). Surprisingly, he concedes the application of the term *hostis* to himself, but insists that the blame for his behavior will ultimately fall upon his adversaries: "He, he will be guilty, who made me a *hostis* to you" (*ille erit, ille nocens, qui me tibi fecerit hostem* [1.203]). The violation of *ius* and *pietas* will then be theirs, not his, and his own claim to membership in this community will be vindicated.[37]

---

point of view (40s B.C. or 60s A.D.): see 4.189–92 with Masters's (1992: 88–89) discussion. Also, the poet occasionally makes the civil war the *aition* for modes of representation that were ideologically significant long afterwards: at 5.385–86, for example, he says that it was during the civil war that Romans first addressed lying words to their *domini*, a practice they continue to the present (see chapter 4.3–4 below on this "master" imagery). See also 7.638–46 (with Leigh 1997: 79–80) and 7.695–6.

[37] Shortly afterward Curio invokes a similar scenario. Urging Caesar to take up arms against his opponents, Curio says, *pellimur e patriis laribus patimurque volentes / exilium: tua nos faciet victoria cives* (1.278–79).

Caesar here resists being made the object of alienating discourse, though soon he will take up this discourse himself for use against the Pompeians. Initially, however, he makes no effort to exclude them from his own soldiers' community of moral obligation. Addressing his soldiers in book 1 (1.299–351), he justifies war by arguing that Pompey's extraordinary power must be abolished, and by claiming that he is looking out for his soldiers' welfare.[38] These arguments seem rather ad hoc; he fails to articulate a systematic moral basis for going to war—as he could do, for example, by tarring his opponents as *hostes*. For this reason, perhaps, his speech fails to persuade: "he finished speaking, but the crowd, doubtful, murmured to itself with indistinct mumbling. *Pietas* and their ancestral *penates* broke their determination, despite being fierce with slaughter, and their inflamed spirits" (*dixerat; at dubium non claro murmure volgus / secum incerta fremit. pietas patriique penates / quamquam caede feras mentes animosque tumentes / frangunt* [1.352–55]). His men feel themselves bound to their opponents by obligations of *pietas*, in particular perceiving them as kin and/or fellow citizens.[39] Thus the assault Caesar urges is precluded—though we are told that they nevertheless retain their fear of Caesar and their "grim love of the sword" (355–56).

But among Caesar's centurions is one Laelius, who wears an oak wreath indicating that he once saved the life of a fellow citizen in battle (1.357–58). This decoration, the *corona civica*, signifies the civic community's collective judgment that he has displayed both *virtus* and *pietas*—since his heroic action falls into the ethical categories of both "martial valor" and "service to the state."[40] As such he is an authoritative moral voice: it is he who provides a systematic moral basis for Caesar's war effort, and thus resolves the soldiers' concerns about *pietas*. Specifically, he grants Caesar the authority to define the community of Roman citizens as he wishes, simply by indicating whom his soldiers should attack: "nor is anyone a fellow citizen of mine if I hear

---

[38] Abolishing Pompey's power: 1.314–26, 333–40, 350–51. Welfare of soldiers: 1.340–46.

[39] The phrase *patrii penates* may imply specifically familial ties, i.e., the *penates* of the ancestral home (cf. Cic. *Ver.* 2.4.17: *deos penates te patrios reposcit*); or it may imply the tutelary divinities of the state as a whole (cf. Cic. *Sul.* 86: *di patrii ac penates qui huic urbi atque huic rei publicae praesidetis*), and so symbolize shared membership in the Roman civic community. There is irony if Caesar's troops are hindered from undertaking this war by the thought of these state *penates*. Supposedly brought from Troy by Aeneas, they were also claimed by *gens Iulia*, and it is these very *penates* that Caesar asks to favor his enterprise, and to which he stakes his claim to membership in the Roman community, at 1.196–97.

[40] On the symbolism of the *corona civica* in the early empire, see ch. 3.5 and n. 94 below.

your trumpets against him, Caesar" (*nec civis meus est, in quem tua classica, Caesar, / audiero* [1.373–74]). If the community so defined excludes the soldiers' blood relations and spouses, so be it, says Laelius: "I swear by your standards, successful in ten campaigns, and by your triumphs over whatever enemy: if you order me to bury my sword in my brother's breast or my father's throat or in the belly of my pregnant wife, even if my right hand is unwilling, I will nevertheless do it all" (*per signa decem felicia castris / perque tuos iuro quocumque ex hoste triumphos: / pectore si fratris gladium iuguloque parentis / condere me iubeas plenaeque in viscera partu / coniugis, invita peragam tamen omnia dextra* [1.374–78]). He also declares himself willing to plunder and burn the temples of the gods, and even to destroy the city of Rome itself, if Caesar requests it (1.379–86). In this oath Laelius disavows each significant aspect of *pietas* as normally understood: he forswears his obligations to the gods, to the state and community at large, and to his family. Family and fellow citizens are now valid targets of violent force, against whom one may appropriately display *virtus* at Caesar's command. Laelius obliquely acknowledges the normative force of the usual conception of *pietas* when he mentions the "unwillingness" of his right hand: he implies that, in such a situation, he would struggle to overcome an ingrained aversion to slaughtering members of his family. But this acknowledgment merely emphasizes the radical nature of the factionalized, alienating view he articulates. Those who participate in Caesar's enterprise constitute a community of moral obligation that supersedes considerations of kinship or membership in the Roman civic community; being a Caesarian is the one and only criterion for articulating claims to *pietas* and *virtus*.[41] It is striking, again, that Lucan places this prescriptive (re)definition of *civis* in the mouth of a wearer of the *corona civica*, who has thereby proved himself, and has been acknowledged as, an exemplary defender of his fellow citizens—though admittedly Laelius speaks as one who has campaigned with Caesar in Gaul for ten years (1.367–75) and thus, presumably, any fellow citizen whose life he saved was already also a Caesarian. At any rate, Laelius's alienating ethics is novel, overtly tailored to the needs of Caesar; it is indeed an ideology for the new order.[42] To judge from the soldiers' reac-

---

[41] The claim that in civil conflict factional allegiance trumps all other considerations, including kinship, obviously presupposes an alienating view, and is a literary topos in civil war contexts (which is not to say it is ahistorical: see section 7 below). Thucydides, for example, makes this very claim in the narrative of the Corcyrean *stasis* (3.82.6): καὶ μὴν καὶ τὸ συγγενὲς τοῦ ἑταιρικοῦ ἀλλοτριώτερον ἐγένετο διὰ τὸ ἑτοιμότερον εἶναι ἀπροφασίστως τολμᾶν.

[42] Helpful analyses of Laelius's speech and the problem of *pietas* can be found in Heyke 1970: 42–46, Ahl 1976: 200–201, and Leigh 1997: 206–10. There is some rhetorical variation (insignificant, I think) in Laelius's presentation of the claims of civic community

tions, Laelius's speech succeeds where Caesar's speech failed: now that Laelius has addressed their concerns about *pietas* by redefining the community of moral obligation, the soldiers pledge to follow Caesar into "any war to which he should summon them" (1.386–88).

In the next few books Caesar and the Caesarians regularly assert, and act in accordance with, this alienating view of the conflict. In a description of Caesar's march south through Italy at 2.439–46, we are told that Caesar rejoices in shedding blood continuously, in taking the towns by force, and in devastating the fields; he regards the defenders as *hostes* (440).[43] Furthermore, he is ashamed to go by an undefended route, lest he "appear to be a citizen" (*concessa pudet ire via civemque videri* [446]). In his actions, in his characterizations of the belligerants, and in the moral judgments on the action embedded in his emotional reactions (*gaudet* [440], *iuvat* [444], and *pudet* [446]), Caesar manifests the alienating view of the conflict: he and his opponents are foreign enemies in relation to one another; hence it is right, good, and a source of joy to destroy them violently.[44]

The behavior and ethical discourse of another of Caesar's centurions, Scaeva, are also rooted in the alienating view. Scaeva's *aristeia* is narrated at 6.140–262, where he singlehandedly holds off a Pompeian attack upon the Caesarian seige lines at Dyrrachium. The Caesarians are initially routed by the surprise attack, but Scaeva rallies them by speaking as follows: "'To what point,' he said, 'has impious fear, unknown to all the weapons of Caesar, driven you? . . . with *pietas* gone, young men, will you not stand your ground out of anger, at least?'" (*"quo vos pavor,"* inquit, *"adegit / impius et cunctis ignotus Caesaris armis? . . . non ira saltem, iuvenes, pietate remota / stabitis?"* [6.150–51, 155–56]). In accusing his fellow-soldiers of *pavor* (the opposite of *virtus*), which is also *impius* — i.e., of failing to fight well against a foreign enemy, and thereby neglecting their obligations to their community of moral obligation — he implicitly constructs a community of obligation consisting of Caesarians only, and excluding the Pompeians. Indeed, he

---

and family upon Caesar's soldiers. When he says *nec civis meus est*, he defines his opponents right out of the civic community; they are simply excluded, and their ineligibility for *pietas* follows automatically. But his description of killing parents and wife suggests that family is still family (he does not say "they are no longer family"): it is simply that *pietas* is not owed to them.

[43] In the *quod* clause at 2.440–43, the subjunctives *terat, inrumpat, perdat,* and *gerat* convey Caesar's own viewpoint, giving the reasons for his joy (see Fantham 1992: 165; also Woodcock 1959: 196–97 [§§240–41] on virtual *oratio obliqua*). Therefore the word *hostis*, embedded in this clause, is most easily read as Caesar's own conception of his opponents.

[44] The narrator, however, disapproves of Caesar's behavior and attitudes here, calling him *in arma furens* (439) and portraying his violence as excessive. For more such "hostile narration," see section 6 below.

refers to the Pompeians explicitly as *hostes* (156) and, once Scaeva has finished speaking, the narrator maintains this characterization of the Pompeians in the lines that follow (*hostes* [171], *hosti* [173], *hostem* [185, 206]). Thus Scaeva is the "focalizer" of the narrator's words: that is, the narrator adopts Scaeva's viewpoint, describing Scaeva's actions from within the alienating perspective through which Scaeva himself views the conflict and his own role in it.[45] Toward the end of his *aristeia*, however, Scaeva briefly adopts assimilating discourse and behavior in order to create a deception. We are told that his *virtus* subsides (*virtute remota* [229]) and he addresses the Pompeians as *cives* (230), asking them to spare him. When a Pompeian named Aulus draws near, Scaeva suddenly stabs him in the throat, reigniting his *virtus* (*incaluit virtus* [240]) and restoring the alienating pattern of action and valuation. His fellow Caesarians share the alienating view, and therefore, as members of his community of moral obligation and hence a valid judging audience for his spectacular public performance, they "praise him as the living image of outstanding Martial Valor" (*vivam magnae speciem virtutis adorant* [256]). They also dedicate his weapons to Mars (256–57), presumably a mark of their *pietas*. But again, his actions are valorous, and theirs are pious, only on the alienating view, in which the Pompeians are regarded as *hostes* and therefore violence against them is right, appropriate, and divinely sanctioned.[46]

The final strong statement of the alienating perspective occurs in Caesar's speech to his troops in book 7 (250–329), just before the battle of Pharsalus is joined. In the previous section I discussed the ineffectuality of Pompey's prebattle speech, his inability to articulate a consistent moral basis for killing Caesarians. Caesar, however, has no such difficulty. A crucial passage in his speech is the following:

> vos tamen hoc oro, iuvenes, ne caedere quisquam
> hostis terga velit: civis qui fugerit esto.
> sed, dum tela micant, non vos pietatis imago
> ulla nec adversa conspecti fronte parentes
> commoveant; vultus gladio turbate verendos.
>
> (7.318–22)

But this I ask you, young men, that no one be willing to strike the enemy in the back: consider anyone who flees a fellow citizen. But, while the weapons

---

[45] For more on the narrator and focalization (a term I borrow from narratology), see section 6 below.

[46] The narrator, in his exegetical frame to this episode (6.144–48, 257–62), passes moral judgments that are at odds with those passed by Scaeva's men. I discuss this matter in section 6 below. Marti 1966 offers a careful analysis of the Scaeva episode as a whole.

gleam, let no vision of *pietas* move you, nor your parents if you see them facing you: churn up with your sword those faces demanding reverence.

Here Caesar progressively nuances the notion of "enemy" (*hostis* [319]). First, opponents who flee are not enemies at all; on the contrary, he formally and explicitly defines those who flee as members of the civic community (*civis qui fugerit esto*). This definition provides a social, hence ethical, basis for sparing them: one should not seek to kill a fellow citizen; to do so would be impious.[47] Against those who stand and fight, however, Caesar urges his soldiers to fight vigorously. Even if they are your parents, he says, you must not let *pietas* move you; you must mangle their faces regardless (320–22). The claim that those who stand their ground do not warrant pious treatment, regardless even of kinship, effectively excludes them from his soldiers' community of moral obligation; it is this subset of the Pompeians who comprise the "real" *hostis* against whom martial valor may and must be displayed. In this passage, it is clear that Caesar has taken up Laelius's suggestion from book 1 (373–74), that the community of moral obligation be defined exclusively in terms of whom Caesar chooses to attack. Now, Caesar's language, like that of Laelius, also implicitly acknowledges the power of claims of kinship: for in speaking of parents as "demanding reverence" (*verendi*), he concedes that one might normally consider oneself bound to them by the obligations of *pietas*. But here too, in his explicit rejection of the traditional social bases for morally judging people's actions, Caesar emphasizes the innovativeness of his alienating view. By placing this assertion of the alienating moral outlook at the climactic moment of the epic, Lucan definitively attaches it to Caesar and his cause, strongly marking it as a distinctive new ethic that serves the interests of the eventual victor—indeed, it empowers that victory, as I will argue below—against the interests of the vanquished, those who represent the old sociopolitical order.

5. Ethics and Armies in Conflict

I have argued that the military and political competition between Caesar and Pompey also entails a competition between different articula-

---

[47] A few lines earlier (312–15) Caesar explains his *clementia* in terms consistent with this articulation of the community: *vincat quicumque necesse / non putat in victos saevum destringere ferrum / quique suos cives, quod signa adversa tulerunt, / non credit fecisse nefas*. It is those Pompeians who have ceased fighting (here, in defeat) whom Caesar regards as fellow citizens and therefore pardons (i.e., treats with due *pietas*). For a similar characterization of Caesar's *clementia*, see 9.272–76. This is an assimilating justification for *clementia*; for an alienating justification, see section 6 and n. 62 below.

tions of the community of moral obligation, and hence between two different ethical discourses regarding the conflict. Another passage from Caesar's speech in book 7 discusses the stakes of the latter competition in particular:

> haec [sc. est illa dies], fato quae teste probet, quis iustius arma
> sumpserit; haec acies victum factura nocentem est.
> si pro me patriam ferro flammisque petistis,
> nunc pugnate truces gladioque exsolvite culpam:
> nulla manus, belli mutato iudice, pura est.
>
> (7.259–63)
>
> This [sc. is the day] that certifies, with fate as witness, who took up arms more justly; this battle is going to make the loser guilty. If it is for me that you attacked your fatherland with sword and fire, fight savagely now and clear your guilt by the sword: no hand is pure, if the judge of the war is changed.

Caesar declares here that he is fighting Pompey for control of the content and application of the Roman ethical vocabulary. The victor, he says, will appropriate the (currently contested) term *ius* for his own cause, and assign the term *nocens* to the vanquished (259–60). Therefore he urges his soldiers to fight savagely (*nunc pugnate truces*), i.e., to display *virtus*: the blame incurred by their assault on the fatherland (*si ... patriam ferro flammisque petistis*), the impiety of attacking one's own civic community, will be cleared if and only if that attack is successful (*gladioque exsolvite culpam*). For the victor establishes himself as *iudex belli*, meaning that the allocation of value terms—including the very ones Caesar uses in this passage (*ius, nocens, culpa,* and *purus*)— will be entirely at his disposal. Only in victory, then, can Caesar enforce his own articulation of the civic community and thus make authoritative the ethical discourse based on that articulation. The definition of the community of obligation, and consequently the moral interpretation of history, belongs to the victor.[48] In the meantime, however, the moral interpretation of events is up for grabs. Contestation over the assignment of value terms is in fact a major theme of the poem, as the first sentence of the poem declares: "I sing ... of right conferred upon crime" (*iusque datum sceleri canimus* ... [1.2]).[49] Indeed, in many an-

---

[48] The idea that Caesar, in victory, will be able to enforce a particular definition of the community, hence an ethical discourse that serves his interests, is hinted at earlier as well: cf. Caesar's statement to the *imago patriae, ille erit ille nocens qui me tibi fecerit hostem* (1.203), and Curio's statement to Caesar, *tua nos faciet victoria cives* (1.279).

[49] On this phrase see Due 1962: 116–17. Figulus's prophecy also alludes to disputes over the moral valuation of actions in civil war (*scelerique nefando / nomen erit virtus* [1.667–68]); so does the narrator in his description of Scaeva (*pronus ad omne nefas et qui nesciret in armis / quam magnum virtus crimen civilibus esset* [6.147–48]).

cient civil war narratives, control of the ethical vocabulary is at stake: it is a commonplace that civil war produces multiple moral perspectives, resulting in contestation over the allocation of moral terms.[50]

We have seen that the assimilating view of the conflict strictly speaking admits no *hostis*, and that in Pompey's "strong" articulation of this view in books 6 and 7 (in contrast to his "weak" articulation in book 1) there is no social or ethical basis for displaying *virtus* at the Caesarians' expense: they are unconditionally owed the obligations of *pietas* as fellow citizens and family members. On the other hand, Caesar's predominantly alienating view, which excludes from the community of moral obligation all who actively oppose him, creates an ethical space in which his soldiers can display *virtus* as well as *pietas*. We now turn to the narrative of the battle of Pharsalus, to see how these differing social and ethical constructions of the war translate into action.

As the battle lines approach each other on the plain, the soldiers on both sides size up the opposition:

quo sua pila cadant aut quae sibi fata minentur
inde manus, spectant. vultus, quo noscere possent
facturi quae monstra forent, videre parentum
frontibus adversis fraternaque comminus arma,
nec libuit mutare locum. tamen omnia torpor
pectora constrinxit, gelidusque in viscera sanguis
percussa pietate coit.

(7.463–62, 464–68)

463–62 *hoc ordine* ΠΑ²PGV, *schol. Stat. Theb.* 6.760; *inverso* ZM, U *ex corr.*   463 *quae Håkanson* : quam ΠΩ : qua U   462 *manus* ZU : manum ΠPGVC, *Schol. Stat.*   *vultus* ΠZ²U : penitus *Håkanson* : tempus ΩC, *Schol. Stat.*   464 *parentum Housman* : parentes Ω[51]

---

[50] E.g. Thucydides 3.82.4, on the Corcyrean *stasis*: καὶ τὴν εἰωθυῖαν ἀξίωσιν τῶν ὀνομάτων ἐς τὰ ἔργα ἀντήλλαξαν τῇ δικαιώσει. τόλμα μὲν γὰρ ἀλόγιστος ἀνδρεία φιλέταιρος ἐνομίσθη, μέλλησις δὲ προμηθὴς δειλία εὐπρεπής, τὸ δὲ σῶφρον τοῦ ἀνάνδρου πρόσχημα, καὶ τὸ πρὸς ἅπαν ξυνετὸν ἐπὶ πᾶν ἀργόν (etc.). Cf. Martindale 1976: 48. Other examples: Plato *Rep.* 560D (a *stasis* situation: the *epithumiai* attempt to seize control of the oligarchic man's soul so as to turn him into a democratic man); Tac. *Hist.* 1.37.4, Sal. *Cat.* 52.11, Sen. *Ben.* 5.15.4–6, and two poems about civil war attributed to Seneca (Shackleton Bailey, *Anthologia Latina* I 460–61; see e.g., 460.19: *quod fuerit virtus, factum est scelus* . . . ; also 460.28: *impius hoc telo es, hoc potes esse pius*). For further discussion and references, see Lebek 1976: 233 and n. 6; Barton 1993: 157 and n. 65.

[51] The transposition of lines 462 and 463 is universally accepted, but the text of 462–64 is doubtful. Housman 1926 prints *quam . . . manum* (463–62) and *vultus . . . parentum* (462–64), while Shackleton Bailey 1988, following Håkanson 1979: 43–45, prints *quae . . . manus* and *penitus . . . parentes* respectively. However, the conjecture *penitus*

46 CHAPTER 1

> ...they look to see where their weapons will fall, or what hands threaten doom against them from the other side. That they might know what terrible deeds they were about to do, they saw the faces of their parents confronting them opposite and the weapons of their brothers close at hand, and they did not see fit to shift their ground. Nevertheless, a numbness froze all their breasts, and their blood congealed cold in their vitals because of the outrage to *pietas*.

When they see their brothers and fathers opposing them, they realize the violence they are doing to *pietas* (*percussa pietate* [468]): their breasts go numb, their blood runs cold, and the start of the battle is deferred. For the moment, the claims of familial obligation prevail — despite the fact that Caesar (and Laelius earlier) expressly denied the validity of those claims, and that Pompey's speech kindled his soldiers' desire to display *virtus*.[52] But soon Crastinus hurls the first lance (7.470–75) and the battle is on. The Pompeians quickly have difficulties: they are too crowded to wield their weapons effectively; they can only hide behind a wall of shields (7.492–95). Meanwhile, Caesar's troops attack furiously (7.496–98). An extremely one-sided battle ensues, in which the Caesarians do all the killing: "One battle line endures civil war, the other wages it; from that side the sword stands cold, but from Caesar's every guilty blade is warm" (*civilia bella / una acies patitur, gerit altera; frigidus inde / stat gladius, calet omne nocens a Caesare ferrum* [7.501–3]). This one-sidedness is emphasized again thirty lines later: "what followed was no battle, but war is waged on one side with throats, on the other with the sword; nor does this battle line have as much strength to kill as that one has capacity to perish" (*nulla secutast / pugna, sed hinc iugulis, hinc ferro bella geruntur; / nec valet haec acies tantum prosternere quantum / inde perire potest* [7.532–35]). Throughout the narrative of the battle, the emphasis is on Caesarians killing (e.g., 7.557–85) and Pompeians dying (e.g., 578–85; cf. 597–616, 669–72, 728–31); there is little indication of the reverse happening, except possibly for a description of Caesar stanching wounds, presumably those of his own men (566–67).[53] Ultimately, then, the soldiers

---

(Håkanson 1979: 45) seems unnecessary, since the reading *vultus . . . parentum* not only makes good sense, but is also attractively parallel with *fraterna . . . arma* in 465. I am indebted to Charles Murgia for his suggestions on this text.

[52] Similar moments occur elsewhere too in the poem, when adversaries first meet face-to-face: cf. 4.26–28, when Pompeians and Caesarians first see one another at Ilerda (*piguit sceleris; pudor arma furentum / continuit* [26–27]); also 4.169–72, another confrontation in the same campaign (*deprensum est civile nefas* [172]). This latter instance starts a cycle of mutual recognition and greeting, followed by full-fledged fraternization; in book 7 Crastinus disrupts that potential trajectory.

[53] Lines 617–30 contain a generic description of hand-to-hand combat and kin slaugh-

on each side act in accordance with the ethical frameworks that their commanders provided them in advance. Pompey's soldiers seemingly do not fight at all; they do not commit the impiety of killing family members and countrymen, the people whom Pompey, in his speech before the battle, urged them to defend. In the end their performance in battle accords with a strong assimilating view of the conflict. Meanwhile Caesar's troops fight effectively, displaying *virtus* by killing those who, on Caesar's definition, are utterly excluded from their community of moral obligation.[54] As Lucan presents this battle, Caesar's victory is not just a triumph of armed force, but also of an ethical viewpoint. The new order owes its victory in large part to its novel, alienating ethics, and with victory these ethics are presumably established (as Caesar suggests at 7.259–63, discussed above) as the valorized framework in which to evaluate actions—especially those of the victors, whose interests and agendas this ethical system underpins, and the vanquished, whose interests it opposes and undermines.

6. The Narrator

In my discussion of conflicting definitions and discourses, I have not yet examined the most authoritative voice in the poem, the narrative voice. Like all narrators in ancient epic poetry, Lucan's is, at one level, omnipotent and omniscient: this narrator can move the narrative instantly from one location to another, expand or compress time at will, and so on. But other narrators, particularly those of Homer and Vergil, generally do not put forward strong opinions: they tend to remain ethically and emotionally detached from the events they narrate, and gain credibility precisely by virtue of their self-effacement.[55] Lucan's narrator, on

---

ter where no partisan affiliations are given, and might therefore be understood as describing the actions of both sides. But even here it seems more likely that the Caesarians are doing the killing. Compare, for example, 7.626–30 with Laelius's words at 1.373–78; also, it is the Caesarians who later have nightmares about kin slaughter (764–80).

[54] On the Pompeians' *pietas* in the battle, cf. Heyke 1970: 85–86. The are also hints of a vestigial assimilating perspective among the Caesarians, for as they kill kin and countrymen their reactions sometimes suggest that they feel qualms (see e.g., 7.560–65, 626–30); they also have nightmares afterward (764–80) in which they perceive their actions as a *saevum scelus* (766).

[55] For the narrative voice's "special powers" and "privileged knowledge of events" (specifically in Homer), see Richardson 1990: 109–11. For the relative self-effacement of the narrative voices in Homer and Vergil, see respectively Richardson 1990: 158–66 and Lyne 1987: 1–2, 217–24. Heinze 1915: 370–73 is the classic discussion of the "subjectivity" or "objectivity" of the narrator, in Vergil and elsewhere. On Lucan's control over his narrative (e.g., the narrative techniques he uses to obstruct Caesar), see Masters 1992: 1–10.

the other hand, as many scholars have remarked, is deeply engaged emotionally and ethically with the poem's action. He often takes obtrusive, partisan stances on the events he narrates, and therefore seems scarcely less opinionated than the voices of Pompey, Caesar, and other characters. Accordingly, the ethical stances he takes, and the value judgments he passes, may seem no more (or less) credible and authoritative than those of the other characters.[56]

This claim that Lucan's narrator is an active, partisan spectator of the events he narrates is unquestionably true in certain respects. However, an exclusive focus on overt interventions misses subtler, less obtrusive, but equally important ways in which the narrator can present and manipulate his own narrative. For instance, the narrator may be completely subsumed in someone else's viewpoint, adopting the ethical stance and worldviews of the character or group whose story he is narrating at the moment: that is, the character or group in question focalizes the narrator's description of its actions. One such passage, discussed in section 4 above, is the narrative of Scaeva's deeds (6.165–257): here the narrator regularly refers to Scaeva's Pompeian foes as *hostes* (171, 173, 185, 206), just as Scaeva does (156); also, the taunting address to the Pompeians (196–202), denying that ordinary weapons can stop him, could be seen as Scaeva's own boast, though it is in the narrator's voice.[57]

At a more visible and self-assertive level, the narrator sometimes

---

[56] On the Lucanian narrator's involvement in his own narrative, and how this affects his authority within the poem, see Masters 1992: 5–6 and n. 14, also 88–90. On the narrator's obtrusive, judgmental stance (i.e., his intrusions into the narrative *in propria voce*) see Syndikus 1958: 39–43 and Seitz 1965: 216–32 (comparing the Lucanian narrator's interventions with those of the Vergilian and Homeric narrators).

[57] Fowler 1990: 42–43 (and passim) describes this phenomenon (which he calls "deviant focalization") in some detail. Many other examples from Lucan could be adduced; the narrative of the Spanish campaign at the start of book 4 provides a sampling. For the most part the narrator accompanies Caesar and his men, giving their view and telling their story: as they race the Pompeians for possession of a hill (4.24–47), pursue them to the mountains (148–69), and eventually surround them (254–65), the narrator regularly calls the Pompeians *hostes* (4.30, 34, 42, 160, 167, 263)—a word that represents the focalization of the Caesarians, with their alienating view. But in the fraternization scene (169ff.), as the soldiers begin to recognize one another, the narrator calls the (erstwhile) opponents *hospes, propinqui,* and *consortes* (177–78); line 179 (*nec Romanus erat qui non agnoverat hostem*) explicitly marks the perceptual transformation of *hostis* into *Romanus* and *agnatus* (cf. 194). The vocabulary of madness and criminality, indicative of the assimilating view, now appears in the narrative (*scelus, sceleratus, nefas, nocens* [172, 193, 205, 207]). Here it is the soldiers collectively, with their newly acquired assimilating perspective, who focalize the narrator's language. But when Petreius breaks up the fraternization, suddenly the narrator refers to the Caesarians as *hostes* (208)—Petreius's point of view (cf. 228)—and the Pompeians adopt his alienating perspective, butchering the unarmed Caesarians in their camp (235–53).

adopts an ethical stance at odds with that of the character or group whose actions he narrates—a situation I call "hostile narration." For example, he heaps contempt upon the Caesarians as he relates their occupation and plundering of the Pompeian camp after the battle of Pharsalus (749–86). He emphasizes in particular the civic and kinship bonds that they have violated (760–63, 772–76), employing the characteristic vocabulary of madness and criminality that, as we have seen, typically accompanies the assimilating view. But from the Caesarians' own alienating perspective, of course, they have seized an enemy camp, and on that view their actions are sane, just, and generally ethically sound.[58] Here, then, the narrator adopts an assimilating ethical stance as he relates actions done in accordance with an alienating view.[59]

At his most obtrusive—the narrative mode that scholars have repeatedly noted and discussed—the narrator actually interrupts the narrative and gives a more or less extended evaluative commentary on the action *in propria voce*. A striking case is 6.257–62, where the narrator, in a direct address, tells Scaeva that his alienating view of the conflict is false. For while Scaeva calls the Pompeians *hostes* (156), vigorously fights them, and deploys ethical language accordingly (e.g., *pietas* is owed only to fellow Caesarians [151, 155]), here the narrator insists that they are not a foreign enemy such as the Teutoni or Cantabri (258–59: evidently "true" *hostes*); hence there can be no triumph, and no proper dedication of spoils to Iuppiter Tonans (260–61). Consequently Scaeva's *virtus*, grotesquely misdirected, has gained him nothing but a "master" (*dominus*, 262).[60] A final example of this most assertive obtrusion of the narrative voice is his denunciation of the consequences of the battle of Pharsalus:

maius ab hac acie quam quod sua saecula ferrent
vulnus habent populi; plus est quam vita salusque
quod perit: in totum mundi prosternimur aevum.
vincitur his gladiis omnis quae serviet aetas.
proxima quid suboles aut quid meruere nepotes
in regnum nasci? pavide num gessimus arma
teximus aut iugulos? alieni poena timoris

---

[58] The narrator's moral condemnation of the Caesarians here resides in words such as *scelus* (750, 757, 766), *nocens* (751, 763), *impius* (760), *infandus* (762), *vaesanus* (764), *furens* (764), etc.

[59] Other examples of "hostile narration": 4.235–52 (the actions of Petreius and the Pompeians as they violently break up the fraternization) and 7.545–85 (Caesar's actions in the battle of the centers).

[60] On the disjunction between the judgments passed on Scaeva by the internal Caesarian audience and the external audience of narrator and (perhaps?) readers, see Leigh's acute observations (1997: 232–33).

in nostra cervice sedet. post proelia natis
si dominum, fortuna, dabas, et bella dedisses.

(7.638–46)

The peoples of the world have a wound from this battle greater than their own age could bear; it is more than life and safety that passes away: we are laid low for the whole eternity of the universe. Every age is conquered by these swords, and will be slaves. Why did the next generation, or the one after that, deserve to be born into tyranny? Did we ply our weapons in a cowardly manner, or shield our throats? The penalty for someone else's cowardice sits upon our necks. Fortune, if you gave a master to those born after the battle, you might also have given them a war to fight.

This passage indicts both parties: the Caesarians for seeking to impose a "master" (*dominus* [646]) upon the state and thus to "enslave" everyone else (*serviet* [641], *in nostra cervice* [645]); but also the Pompeians for their cowardice, their failure to fight that enabled the Caesarian victory. In condemning the Pompeians for *pavor* and *timor* (7.643–44)—i.e., a lack of *virtus*—the narrator adopts an alienating view, and so rejects the inevitable consequences of the strong assimilating perspective. His judgment here implies that the Caesarians *are* a valid target for martial valor (hence are *hostes*) and that the Pompeians should have taken this view themselves.

I have selected these examples of the narrator's moral evaluations of the actions he narrates so as to demonstrate his inconsistency, on several axes, in the face of competing ethical discourses and competing articulations of the community of moral obligation. First, as in the Scaeva episode, at one level the narrator may implicate his own viewpoint with that of a character (see section 4 above): thus Scaeva focalizes the narrator's alienating narration of events. At another level, however, he sharply distinguishes his own viewpoint from the character's, as when he explicitly rejects Scaeva's alienating view and embraces an assimilating outlook instead (see the previous paragraph). Second, he can enthusiastically reject each faction's characteristic viewpoint: by lamenting the Pompeians' cowardice (7.638–46, quoted above), he indicts the strong assimilating perspective that underlay their collapse; then, just one hundred lines later, he provides a hostile narration of the Caesarians' plundering of the Pompeian camp—embracing an assimilating ethical stance—and in so doing rejects the alienating perspective that justifies the Caesarians' actions. Finally, he can equally enthusiastically embrace each faction's characteristic viewpoint. In an apostrophe to Pompey after the battle, the narrator tells the defeated general "it was worse to win" (*vincere peius erat*, 7.706)—presumably endorsing a strong assimilating perspective that regards killing as criminal in civil war.[61] And even Caesar's alienating perspective is praiseworthy, under the right circumstances: when the Pompeian general Afranius surrenders a Pompeian army in Spain (4.337–401), Caesar sends these troops home unpunished and unconscripted. For in his alienating view, these men, being *hostes*, have committed no moral crime in fighting, nor do they owe any military duty to their conquerors.[62]

The narrator, then, is inconsistent in that he does not systematically endorse one or the other of the competing conceptions of the community of moral obligation and their corresponding ethical discourses. Rather, he moves back and forth between them, at one point or another judging the actions of each side by the moral standards of each ethical discourse. Masters, discussing the narrator's vacillation between the Pompeian and Caesarian causes, speaks of Lucan's "fractured voice" and suggests (rightly, I think) that its inconsistency necessarily follows from the poem's subject matter. The present discussion reveals a similar connection between subject and form, for we have seen that the cleft in the civic community — the defining contradiction of civil war, which also extends into families — is reproduced first in a divided ethical discourse, and second in the narrator's conflicting moral evaluations.[63] Conse-

---

[61] For similar statements that victory in civil war is worse than defeat, see 7.123 and 4.258–59. This claim is a topos in civil war narratives: see Ahl 1976: 145 and 245 n. 16. To his citations add Sen. *Ben.* 4.32.2, and one of Seneca's poems (Shackleton Bailey, *Anthologia Latina* I 461). The poem opens: *sicine componis populos, Fortuna, furentis / ut vinci levius, vincere sit gravius?* It tells of a soldier who kills an "enemy" in civil war, only to discover that he has killed his brother. He then exhorts himself to suicide with the following argument: *eripuit virtus pietatem, reddere virtus / debet: qua rapuit, hac reparanda via est* (15–16). Here winning is apparently worse because, in the soldier's assimilating perspective, *virtus* precludes *pietas* altogether (unless the *virtus* is directed against oneself, avenging one's prior *pietas*-transgression.)

[62] Afranius too, in the surrender scene (4.337–62), represents his own troops and the Caesarians as *hostes* relative to one another: see 339, 344, 355. The only hint of a problem with this picture is his passing comment (360–61) that Caesar could not exhibit these defeated troops in a triumph (on which see section 7 below). I am not persuaded by Leigh's contention (1997: 53–67) that Caesar's clemency in this scene is "odious," or that his *serenitas* (4.363) has "unpleasant implications." Indeed, Caesar's position that armed resistance is no crime (cf. 7.314–15) is consistent with the alienating perspective, for the war is criminal only if regarded as civil. Thus his *clementia* here has an alienating justification (cf. the assimilating one, n. 47 above).

[63] Masters 1992: 90: "The poem, the civil war, is and takes as its subject the internal fracturing of authority. It is a world where what should be one is many, where the unity of the Roman state is painfully divided. . . . It is, therefore, mimicry of civil war, of divided unity, *concordia discors*, that has produced this split in the authorial, dominating, legitimising persona" (see also pp. 10 and 87–90 generally). Masters's claim that the narrator is not consistently pro-Pompeian and anti-Caesarian overlaps with, but is not identical to, my claim that he does not consistently privilege either ethical discourse. One further inconsistency in the narrative voice (also observed by Ahl 1976: 197): the narrator does not

quently, in failing to adopt one view over the other, the narrator not only narrates the civil war, but performs it as well: he allows the alternative ethical discourses and views of community to compete through his own voice just as they compete through the words and actions of the characters. This unresolved competition also suggests that neither discourse, and neither conception of the community of moral obligation, by itself can adequately embrace the conflict that is the poem's subject.[64]

But despite these contradictions, the narrator is not without direction: through the poem as a whole he does seem to adopt (and praise) the assimilating view, and engage in its corresponding ethical discourse, more often than he embraces the alternative. Perhaps we should reflect this differential preference by labeling assimilating discourse "dominant" or "normative" in the poem, and alienating discourse "oppositional" or "subversive." But the latter is not thereby swept under the rug. It remains a coherent, visible, persistent, and powerful discourse, emerging repeatedly in the statements and actions of many characters—Pompeians as well as Caesarians—and in the narrative voice. Indeed, the battle of Pharsalus brings victory to the Caesarians, who are the main exponents of the alienating view. Nevertheless, the narrator does not reflect or echo that de facto triumph in his narration, for he holds the ethical conflict in suspense, maintaining an overall preference for the losing mode of discourse. I also see little evolution: there is no move toward a reconciliation of these discourses, nor does either one seem to become more favored or prominent, or less so, over the course of the poem. These discourses simply coexist, in somewhat unequal authorial favor, ever competing and conflicting with each other. They are inesca-

---

even accept unflinchingly the view that nonparticipation in the conflict is good and desirable. Cato, whom the narrator portrays sympathetically in book 2, chooses participation over nonparticipation (2.286–95, 319–23), and the narrator claims at 7.645–46 that participation in civil war is preferable to suffering a *dominus* (cf. 1.669–72). Yet the narrator elsewhere suggests that nonparticipation *is* preferable: 4.382–401, with Saylor 1986: 155–56.

[64] Indeed, the opening phrase of the poem, "war more than civil" (*bella . . . plus quam civilia* [1.1]), may also suggest that both available ethical frameworks are inadequate to the subject. For if the phrase *bellum civile* conveys specifically the assimilating view on the conflict, then the phrase "more than civil" may imply that the assimilating view is inadequate. However, this phrase may also imply "less than (or not exactly) external," in which case the alienating view is also inadequate. On this reading, the words *plus quam*, like the aporetic competition between ethical discourses, marks the lack of a comprehensive view, and the need for a third way. I thank an anonymous reader for the journal *Classical Antiquity* for this interpretation of this notorious phrase. Obviously, such a reading of the first line of the poem must be retrospective, since it presupposes a knowledge of themes and conflicts that unfold over many books.

pable artifacts of civil war, the necesary consequence of the military and ethical eruption of Caesarism into aristocratic ethics.[65]

A possible third way does appear in book nine (9.1–949), where Cato is at the center of an entirely different mode of ethical discourse. Here Cato and *virtus* are closely associated. But his *virtus* seems to have little to do with martial valor, for there is no fighting in this section of the poem; nor is it ever in tension with *pietas*, as it often is elsewhere. Rather, it is linked repeatedly with suffering, endurance, and toil. Now, it is a commonplace of imperial Stoicism that moral virtue, while in no way dependent upon "indifferent" externals such as pain, suffering, and death, is best displayed—and may even be strengthened—by being exercised in their presence.[66] In this and other respects, the ethical discourse centered on Cato is strongly Stoic. In chapter 2.6 below, I discuss this Stoic conceptualization of *virtus*, and its relationship to the "traditional" usage of the word to indicate military valor, in greater detail.

But Stoic ethics differs radically from both alienating and assimilating ethical discourse. The latter two are fundamentally the same, being alternative versions of the traditional, external, community-oriented mode of evaluation. They operate identically with respect to the underlying conception of the community of moral obligation and differ only insofar as that underlying conception differs. In Stoic ethics, however, moral value is regarded as internal to an agent, residing in states of mind and intentions that are not readily accessible to others. The actual, observable results of these states of mind and intentions—the agent's overt success or failure at achieving his aims—are regarded as largely beyond his control and therefore without moral value. It follows that the community, which observes an agent's actions, is no longer an authoritative moral judge: for in this ethical system, it has no unmediated access to the states of mind that are the "true" objects of moral evaluation.[67] Instead, the moral standard invoked in Stoicism is that of *natura*

---

[65] Recent work on the *Aeneid* has shown how oppositional points of view coexist with the dominant, teleological Aenean/Augustan point of view: see Fowler 1990: 57, Lyne 1987: 217–38, and Conte 1986: 152–84. The latter, for example, speaks (183) of "[viewing] the form of the content in the *Aeneid* as the ideal locus of a clash between values that individually lay claim to all-inclusiveness in their own milieu but together make irreconcilable claims." This is part of the argument I have tried to make in regard to Lucan's epic.

[66] Cato's *virtus* is associated with words like *durus*, *labor*, and *patientia* at 9.381, 403, 407, 445, 506, 562, 570. For (Stoic) *virtus* becoming stronger and more visible when surrounded by *adversa*, see e.g. Sen. *Prov.* 2.1–4, 2.7, 2.12, and passim; Lucan's Cato makes a similar claim at 9.402–407. See Eisenhut 1973: 153–56 on the distinctively Stoic character of Cato's *virtus*; also Morford 1967 on Cato's endurance of pain and death in book nine.

[67] Cato asserts the moral irrelevance of observable outcomes at 9.570–71, as does the narrator at 9.593–96. The latter passage is as follows: *si veris magna paratur / fama bonis*

or *deus*, the Stoic deity that is immanent in all things at all times. Embodied in Lucan's Cato, then, Stoicism potentially offers an escape from the competing, irreconcilable discourses discussed above: it provides a universal moral standard, invariant over all conditions of peace and war, unity and disunity, as the basis for a reconstituted, unitary ethical discourse. However, at 9.950 the narrator turns his attention back to Caesar; Cato and his Stoic ethics do not reappear in the poem. How Lucan might have developed this alternative system subsequently, and how it might have interacted with the poem's other ethical discourses, we will never know.

7. Lucan and Early Imperial Aristocratic Ideology

Several times in the poem Caesar articulates an ideological reconstruction of the Roman community and its ethical discourse. This reconstruction, which he can impose if he wins, will establish his alienating view of the community as the normative basis for ethical valuation, thereby (he says) removing any moral opprobrium from himself and depositing it upon his adversaries.[68] Yet within the poem itself no such reconstruction occurs. As noted above, Lucan at no point allows Caesar's alienating view and its ethical discourse to dominate, despite its success in battle; also, voices that move toward Caesar's view in the last three books (after Pharsalus) are presented unsympathetically.[69] The historical Iulius Caesar, however, did attempt such a reconstruction, and we can recover its general outlines. Once we have done so, we will be able to consider the ideological consequences of Lucan's disallowing that reconstruction, and of his projecting the particular image of civil war that he does from the cultural context of Neronian Rome.

---

et si successu nuda remoto / inspicitur virtus, quidquid laudamus in ullo / maiorum, fortuna fuit. Here the narrator confirms my point: in Cato's ethical system, where actual outcomes have nothing to do with moral value, traditional external evaluation has no morally significant object; the deeds of our ancestors that we praise are in fact due only to fortune. On the location of moral value in Stoicism, and the difficulties of judging others on the basis of observed actions, see ch. 2.2–5 below.

[68] See 7.259–63 and the discussion of that passage in section 5 above; see also 1.203 and 1.279.

[69] For example, a deserting Pompeian soldier urges Cato to stop resisting Caesar, now that Pompey is dead, with the following words: *Pompeio scelus est bellum civile perempto, / quo fuerat vivente fides. si publica iura, / si semper sequeris patriam, Cato, signa petamus, / Romanus quae consul habet* (9.248–51). He thus identifies Caesar's cause with that of the community as a whole (*publica, patriam, Romanus consul*), which in turn necessitates a reconfiguration of ethical discourse (what was *fides* is now a *scelus*). But Cato defeats this argument by portraying Caesar as a *dominus*, who intends to enslave the community and therefore does not have its interests at heart (9.256–83).

Raaflaub 1974, in his minute examination of the rhetoric of the civil war, argues — largely on the basis of letters preserved in the Ciceronian corpus dating from 50–48 B.C. — that the historical Pompeians did indeed generally claim to be defending the commonwealth (*res publica*). They called Caesar and his followers such things as "depraved citizens," "bandits," and "condemned criminals" (*perditi cives, latrones, damnati*), and remarked upon the madness and criminality (*furor, amentia, scelus*) of those who would attack their own country. There is little evidence that they called them *hostes*, at least not commonly.[70] This portrayal of the Caesarians as people who have turned against their state from within appears to be close to Pompey's weak assimilating view of them in his initial speech (2.531–95, section 3 above): they are not foreign enemies, yet are nevertheless legitimate targets of violent force from the state's representatives.[71] However, no evidence suggests that the historical Pompeians ever took the strong assimilating view, as Lucan's Pompey and then his troops come to take, that the civic and familial bonds between the two sides make violence against the Caesarians virtually impossible.[72] On the other hand, the historical Caesar and his followers generally labeled the conflict a "civil disagreement," "secession" (*civilis dissensio, secessio*), or the like; they labeled the Pompeians "personal enemies" or "opponents" (*inimici, adversarii*) rather than using the alienating term *hostes*.[73] They too, then, seem to

[70] For the attested terminology see Raaflaub 1974: 192–200; he infers the use of *hostis* largely on the basis of (better-attested) Ciceronian invective against Catiline and Antony (id. 77 n. 313; 234–35). He suggests, however (p. 238), that even without explicit use of the term *hostis* Pompeian rhetoric effectively presented Caesarians as foreign foes.

[71] The figure of the bandit (*latro*), though absent from Lucan, looms large in civil war contexts throughout Roman history. A bandit comes from within society, yet turns against it, or inverts it, creating a sort of "antistate" or opposing locus of authority that may command considerable support in the areas where the bandits operate. "Legitimate" authorities may well direct violence against bandits, as against foreign enemies: but bandits are not insurgents, and there is sometimes the possibility they can be reintegrated into society. All these issues are discussed in a Roman context by Shaw 1984; see also Habinek 1998: 69–87 on one instance of a polemical deployment of the figure of the *latro* in a civil-war context (Cicero in his Catilinarian speeches).

[72] Our scanty evidence for the rhetoric of the historical Pompeians after Pharsalus, however, suggests that the familial form of *pietas*-obligation was particularly privileged. Pompey's sons asserted *pietas* as a moral basis for continuing the fight against Caesar: Gnaeus used *pietas* as a battle cry at Munda (Appian *B.C.* 2.104), while Sextus adopted *pius* as a cognomen (Crawford 1974: I 486–87, 520 [nos. 477–79, 511] and II 739; see also Powell 1992: 151–57 on Sextus). Cicero glosses the sons' *pietas* as a (laudable) effort to avenge their father's death (*Phil.* 5.39; cf. Lucan 9.147), though presumably they would have claimed to be promoting the civic and religious interests of the broader Roman community as well.

[73] See Raaflaub 1974: 234–39; esp. 236–38 on Caesar's careful deployment of the terms *hostis* and *adversarius* so as to construct the conflict as a dispute within a single commu-

have embraced an assimilating view—contrary to Lucan's presentation—and in fact to have spoken more gently of the Pompeians than the Pompeians spoke of them. The evidence for the Caesarian viewpoint is plentiful, coming from Caesar's *Commentarii*, Hirtius's *Bellum Gallicum* 8, and portions of Cicero's Caesarian speeches (especially *Lig.*, *Marc.*, *Deiot.*). But these sources, in contrast to the Pompeian ones, postdate the bulk of the civil war, and therefore must be seen, whatever their truth value, as re-presentations of the conflict that serve Caesar's interests in the aftermath. Indeed, the advantages for Caesar of presenting his cause this way, for public consumption and for posterity, are manifest: by embracing an assimilating ethical discourse, he can seek (or claim to seek) reconciliation with the vanquished and to reintegrate them into the community of which, on this view, they have always been a part. This, then, is the historical Caesar's ideological reconstruction of the civil war, the history he as victor gets to write that allows him to mobilize support and consolidate power. Why Lucan might have so strikingly inverted the character of the ethical discourse historically associated with the Caesarians, while softening that associated with the Pompeians, I will discuss shortly.

Another means of access to the historical Caesarians' re-presentation of their cause following their victory is through the symbolism of Caesar's triumphs. It is a commonplace, in Lucan and elsewhere, that a triumph ought not to be celebrated for a victory in civil war,[74] and there are at least two reasons, inherent in the ceremony's form and symbolism, why this is so. First, the triumphal procession symbolically subjects the non-Roman to the Roman: it includes a display of spoils, pictures of towns captured, and a parade of notable prisoners led in chains before the *triumphator*'s chariot.[75] Second, the triumph is inherently expansionist in its celebration of military conquest. Valerius Maximus, writing a generation before Lucan, asserts (2.8.4) that a victory won in reconquering territory previously conquered but subsequently lost does not qualify for a triumph.[76] A victory in civil war is incompatible with a

---

nity. The designation *secessio* perhaps points to the conflict of the orders—a dispute within the community that, however bitter and intermittently violent, was eventually resolved—as the paradigm for the current conflict.

[74] E.g., Lucan 1.12, 3.79, 6.257–61; Tac. *Hist.* 4.4; Hist. Aug. *Sev.* 9.10.11; Val. Max. 2.8.7: *verum quamvis quis praeclaras res maximeque utiles rei publicae civili bello gessisset, imperator tamen eo nomine appellatus non est, neque ullae supplicationes decretae sunt, neque aut ovans aut curru triumphavit, quia, ut necessariae istae, ita lugubres semper existimatae sunt victoriae utpote non externo, sed domestico paratae cruore.* See also Campbell 1984: 138.

[75] For description and testimonia, see R. Cagnat in Daremberg-Saglio 1875: V 488–90.

[76] Similarly in later authors: Suet. *Cl.* 17 implies that a *iustus triumphus* presupposes the conquest of new territories; cf. Tac. *Ann.* 12.20.2, with Campbell 1984: 137–38 (but read

triumph on both these counts, for neither are the vanquished non-Romans, nor does the victory expand the empire. Now, the historical Caesar sent no word of his victory at Pharsalus to the senate—a normal preliminary, along with being proclaimed *imperator*, for a commander who hopes for a *supplicatio* or triumph. Indeed, says Dio (42.18.1), Caesar not only did not triumph, but did not wish to appear to take pleasure in this victory.[77] His actions are consistent with an assimilating viewpoint, such as is attested for him in literary sources other than Lucan—the view that the battle of Pharsalus was part of a properly civil war, a conflict within a single community of moral obligation.

This interpretation of Caesar's nontriumph for Pharsalus is confirmed by an analysis of the triumphs Caesar did celebrate. In his quadruple triumph of 46 B.C., celebrating victories in Gaul, at Zela, at Alexandria, and at Thapsus, Caesar mixed conflicts that could generally be accepted as "external" (the first two) with those that were widely considered civil—yet to celebrate triumphs was to portray all four alike as *bella externa*.[78] Our sources point out that the triumph for Thapsus involved a systematic manipulation of symbolism: for although his principal military opponents in Africa were Cato and Metellus Scipio, his triumphal procession prominently displayed the younger Juba, son of the Numidian king who supported Cato and Scipio. Thus Caesar emphasized the foreignness of the force opposing him and so constructed Thapsus symbolically as a battle between Romans (his own troops) and non-Roman Africans.[79] After his victory at Munda, however, Caesar went even fur-

---

"Valerius Maximus" for "Valerius Flaccus" at p. 138 n. 88). The expansionist subtexts of the triumph are also implicit at Plut. *Pomp.* 45, who notes that Pompey's three triumphs, for victories in Africa, Europe, and Asia (the three known continents), could be seen as a symbolic conquest of the world. Similar representations of Pompey's triumphs appear in a set of poems attributed to Seneca: Shackleton Bailey, *Anthologia Latina* I 396–400; also Vell. Pat. 2.40.4.

[77] Dio 42.18.1: οὔτε γὰρ ὁ Καῖσαρ τῷ κοινῷ τι ἐπέστειλεν, ὀκνήσας δημοσίᾳ χαίρων ἐπὶ τοιαύτῃ νίκῃ φανῆναι, διόπερ οὐδὲ ἐπινίκια αὐτῆς ἔπεμψε. See Weinstock 1971: 60–61 and n. 8 on the preliminaries usual for a triumph or lesser honor. For Caesar's triumphs generally, see Weinstock 60–79, along with Gelzer 1968: 284–85 and 308–309. In a similar vein, Dio says (41.52.1) that Pompey did not report his success at Dyrrachium to the senate despite being proclaimed *imperator*, on the ground that he had defeated fellow citizens.

[78] Cicero, however, objects even to the Gallic triumph on the ground that longtime ally Massilia (reduced in the campaign against Pompey) was included among the conquered cities—the crowning instance, he says, of Roman *nefaria in socios* (*Off.* 2.28). Similarly, Campbell 1984: 139 says of Octavian's triple triumph in 29 B.C. for Dalmatia and Pannonia, Actium, and Egypt, "[h]is propaganda represented these campaigns not as part of a civil war, but the destruction of a foreign foe."

[79] Plut. *Caes.* 55: ἔπειτα θριάμβους κατήγαγε <τὸν Κελτικόν,> τὸν Αἰγυπτιακόν, τὸν Ποντικόν, τὸν Λιβυκόν, οὐκ ἀπὸ Σκιπιῶνος ἀλλ' ἀπ' Ἰόβα δῆθεν τοῦ βασιλέως. Here,

ther: according to Plutarch (*Caes.* 56.7–9), he caused outrage by triumphing unambiguously over other Romans. For (says Plutarch) he had previously avoided seeking recognition for victories in civil war, and his fellow countrymen were grieved that he now celebrated a triumph for destroying Pompey's family rather than for defeating foreigners.[80] Caesar, then, used triumphal imagery to represent each conflict *after* Pharsalus as a *bellum externum*, and to exclude those opponents from his, and the Romans', community of obligation. These representations may not have been widely persuasive; certainly Cicero (and later Plutarch) is dubious. But the point is that Caesar made the attempt, and in the most public and visible way: we must regard these performances as part of his attempted ideological reconstruction.[81]

Lucan, however, disallows this Caesarian ideological reconstruction in two ways. First, the poem portrays no systematic remobilization of ethical discourse to Caesar's advantage, before or after Pharsalus: it insists on presenting an endlessly divided community, forever bollixed up in competing, irreconcilable discourses. In this respect Lucan differs from other Augustan and Julio-Claudian authors (like his uncle Seneca: see chapter 2 below) who implicitly or explicitly acknowledge that many ideological resources have been organized in support of the imperial regime. Second, and more striking, is Lucan's alteration of the modes of discourse that each faction embraced historically: Lucan's Caesarians take a radically factionalized, exclusive view of their community of obligation, while the historical Caesarians apparently did not; and Lucan's Pompeians, especially in the latter books of the poem, are so much more inclusive than the historical Pompeians that they cannot

---

δῆθεν implies that Caesar's sleight-of-hand was not persuasive. Cf. Appian *B.C.* 2.101. Tac. *Hist.* 4.4 is equally cynical about the alleged grounds for a bestowal of triumphal honors in A.D. 69: *Muciano triumphalia de bello civium data, sed in Sarmatas expeditio fingebatur.*

[80] Dio (43.42.1) also comments on the contemporary perception that this triumph was inappropriate.

[81] Cicero explicitly asserts the power of these public celebrations to prescribe a novel form for the civic community, rather than merely to reflect a familiar form. In *Phil.* 14.21–25 (postdating Caesar's triumphs by just two or three years) he says that if a *supplicatio* is granted for Hirtius and Pansa's victory over Antony at Mutina, this very action will define Antony as a *hostis*, thus excluding him from the civic community, and define the battle itself a *bellum externum* rather than a *bellum civile* (*supplicationem modo qui decrevit, idem imprudens hostis iudicavit; numquam enim in civili bello supplicatio decreta est. decretam dico? ne victoris quidem litteris postulata est* [*Phil.* 14.22]; see also *Phil.* 14.24). That one of Caesar's contemporaries could make this argument lends at least circumstantial support to my claim here, that Caesar exploited triumphal imagery for the same ends. On Cic. *Phil.* 14.21–25 and the conditions for a *supplicatio*, see Halkin 1953: 92–93.

even fight.[82] This alteration enables Caesar's victory within the poem, but also precludes him from duplicating the historical Caesar's ideological reconstruction.

Lucan's resistance to Caesarian ideology must itself be ideologically important. What interests does Lucan's construction of civil war serve, given that its ethical structuring substantially contradicts that of the dominant (i.e., Caesarian) historical tradition? Moreover, what is the ideological significance, within the social and political context of Neronian Rome, of a Roman aristocrat's evincing so powerful an interest in fractured communities and competing, irreconcilable ethical discourses? One way of illuminating this question requires us to revisit the alienating rhetoric of Laelius's oath (1.373–86), in turn appropriated by Caesar (7.318–22), discussed in section 4 above. This rhetoric asserts (1) that opponents of Caesar are the opponents of all his followers; (2) that those who oppose Caesar count as foreign enemies (*hostes*) who must be confronted militarily; and (3) — a corollary of (2) — that the obligations of *pietas* bind the Caesarians exclusively to one another, overriding all other possible claims: wherefore they must kill even their own kin (wives, fathers, children) if the latter happen to oppose Caesar. These alienating assertions of Laelius and Caesar bear a striking resemblance to surviving texts and descriptions of imperial "oaths of loyalty," which were administered at the beginning of an emperor's reign, and regularly thereafter, to various groups, especially to soldiers and residents of towns and regions. A good deal of evidence for the content and character of these oaths survives: in addition to brief mentions and descriptions in literary texts, we have six inscriptions (three largely complete) recording the actual texts of these oaths.[83] One such inscription (*CIL* II 172 = *ILS* 190 = Herrmann 1968 no. 1 p. 122), dating to shortly after the accession of Caligula (A.D. 37), records the oath sworn to the new emperor by the residents of Aritium, in Lusitania. It begins as follows:

ex mei animi sententia, ut ego iis inimicus   5
ero, quos C. Caesari Germanico inimicos esse

---

[82] As a parallel for Lucan's alteration of Pompeian and Caesarian rhetoric, consider his treatment of the battle of Massilia: here he makes Caesar the aggressor and the Massiliotes the aggrieved, reversing the roles that Caesar and other sources assign to the parties (Masters 1992: 17–22); see also Lounsbury's analysis (1975: 212) of how Lucan in book 7 inverts Caesar's presentation of Domitius and Crastinus. Lounsbury, Masters, and others have shown that Lucan's *Bellum Civile* engages and responds to Caesar's *Commentarii*, and that this engagement often involves strategically distorting Caesar's account.

[83] These oaths of loyalty have been studied in great detail by Premerstein 1937: 13–116 and Herrmann 1968. The latter conveniently collects the six epigraphic texts, with full bibliography and apparatus, on pp. 122–26. Only four of these were known to Premerstein: see pp. 45–51.

```
cognovero, et si quis periculum ei salutiq(ue) eius
in[f]ert in[f]er[e]tque, armis bello internecivo
terra mariq(ue) persequi non desinam, quoad
poenas ei persolverit, neq(ue) me <neque> liberos meos    10
eius salute cariores habebo, eosq(ue) qui in
eum hostili animo fuerint, mihi hostes esse
ducam . . .
```

(I swear) sincerely that I will be ill-disposed toward those whom I recognize as being ill-disposed toward Gaius Caesar Germanicus, and if anyone brings or will bring danger to bear upon him or his safety, I will not cease to pursue (him) by force of arms in murderous war by land and sea, until (he) has paid him the penalty, nor will I hold either myself or my children dearer than (I hold) his safety, and those who oppose him with hostile spirit, I will regard as my own enemies. . .

In particular, this oath involves the claim (1) that the emperor's opponents (*inimici, hostes*) are one's own;[84] (2) that one will pursue such opponents with military force; and (3) that the emperor's safety ranks higher in one's estimation that the well-being of one's self and children. These three claims correspond closely to the three enumerated above as being present in the oath of Laelius and speech of Caesar. Another inscription records the oath sworn by the inhabitants of Paphlagonia in 3 B.C. to Augustus and his descendents (*ILS* 8781 = Herrmann 1968 no. 4 pp. 123–24):

```
            . . . [φί]λους ἡγού[μενος]                      12
οὓς ἂν ἐκεῖνοι ἡγῶντα[ι] ἐχθρούς τε ν[ομίζων]
οὓς ἂν αὐτοὶ κρίνωσιν, ὑπέρ τε τῶν τ[ούτοις]
διαφερόντων μήτε σώματος φείσεσθ[αι μή]τε           15
ψυχῆς μήτε βίου μήτε τέκνων, ἀλ[λὰ παν-]
τὶ τρόπωι ὑπὲρ τῶ[ν] ἐκείνοις ἀνηκό[ντων]
πάντα κίνδυνον ὑπομενεῖν· . . .

. . . οὕς τε ἂν ἐχθροὺς αὐτ[ο]ὶ κρίν[ωσιν, τού-]       23
τους κατὰ γῆν καὶ θάλασσαν ὅπλο[ις τε]
καὶ σιδήρωι διώξειν καί ἀμυνεῖσ[θαι.]                  25
```

[84] The designation of such opponents first as *inimici* (ll. 5–6) and second as *hostes* (l. 12) may or may not be significant. Herrmann 1968: 50–51 and n. 1 sees this as simple *variatio*, since the terms are not always sharply distinguished (cf. Hellegouarc'h 1963: 188–89), and he suggests that *mihi . . . hostis* has the same force as *inimicus*. Conversely, Premerstein 1937: 50–51 sees this distinction as important, in that (in his view) it represents a fossilization of elements of the oath for Octavian in 32 B.C., where Octavian's *inimicus* (Antony) stood together with the state's *hostis* (Cleopatra).

. . . regarding as friends whomsoever they regard (as friends) and considering as enemies whomsoever they (so) judge and, on behalf of their kinfolk, to spare neither my body nor soul nor life nor children, but to endure every danger in every way on behalf of those connected to them . . . and whomsoever they judge as enemies, (I swear) to pursue these and ward them off by land and sea, with armor and sword.

Here again, the three elements identified above are present: the swearer claims to observe the imperial household's distinctions between enemies and friends; to spare nothing, not even his own life and children, in the defense of the household; and to engage its enemies militarily. These three elements are all present together only in the two epigraphic texts quoted here. However, one or two of these elements can be found in each of the other inscriptions, and they are also found in the literary testimonia for loyalty oaths in the early empire.[85] It seems clear, then, that Lucan has retrojected these three crucial elements onto the civil war of 49–48: he makes Laelius offer such an oath to Caesar in book 1, and makes Caesar urge that his soldiers act on similar terms in book 7. Thus he makes this particular manifestation of the ethics of the principate present at the very foundation of the new order. Moreover, I surmise that Lucan's contemporary readers would have recognized in these passages the sort of loyalty oath with which they were familiar from their own experience. Whether the rhetoric of these oaths did historically emerge, in whole or in part, from the context of the factional strife and civil wars of the late republic is uncertain;[86] I claim here only that Lucan presents the key stipulations of these oaths as consistent with,

---

[85] That one's friends and/or foes are the same as the emperor's: Herrmann 1968 no. 2 pp. 122–23 (*CIL* XI 5998a); Herrmann no. 3 p. 123 (Cagnat 1906: IV 251); Herrmann no. 5 pp. 124–25 (*Année épigraphique* 1962: 248). That one will pursue any such foes with military force: Herrmann nos. 2 and 6 fr.3 (restored) p. 126; Plut. *Galba* 26.1. That one holds the emperor's interests or safety above those of oneself or one's own family: Suet. *Cal.* 15.3; Dio 59.9.2; cf. Epict. *Diss.* 1.14.15, Dio 63.14.1, Sen. *Polyb.* 7.4 (the latter two are not certainly oaths). Cf. Premerstein 1937: 76–78, Herrmann 50–54.

[86] The origins of the imperial oath of loyalty have been much debated. The first and third elements of the oath, as defined above, appear in an oath ascribed to the followers of M. Livius Drusus in 91 B.C. (Diodorus Siculus 37.11): ὄμνυμι . . . τὸν αὐτὸν φίλον καὶ πολέμιον ἡγήσεσθαι Δρούσῳ, καὶ μήτε βίου μήτε τέκνων καὶ γονέων μηδεμιᾶς φείσεσθαι ψυχῆς, ἐὰν [μὴ] συμφέρῃ Δρούσῳ τε καὶ τοῖς τὸν αὐτὸν ὅρκον ὀμόσασιν. The historicity of an oath in these terms in 91 B.C. has been doubted; Premerstein 1937: 27–30 and Herrmann 1968: 55–58 suggest that the terms of this oath as given in Diodorus were fabricated later by opponents of Livius. Perhaps; but the similarity of these particular elements of the oath to those found in imperial oaths, along with the association of alienating rhetoric with civil strife and factional violence, makes plausible the conjecture that such elements were already appearing in oaths of loyalty in the late republic. For other late republican oaths, see Premerstein 30–56 and Herrmann 58–89.

indeed already present in, the alienating language that he associates primarily with the Caesarians.[87]

But regardless of its historicity, Lucan's presentation is ideologically significant. For by implying that these oaths of loyalty, these familiar features of the Julio-Claudian political landscape, are grounded in the alienating language of the Caesarians, he invites his readers to infer that these oaths perpetuate in contemporary society the divisiveness of the Caesarians' alienating view. In short, the civil war never ends, though military conflict may cease. For in exacting oaths of loyalty on these terms, the *princeps*, himself a(nother) Caesar, institutionalizes himself as the leader of a permanent Caesarian faction. He retains the authority (according to the stipulations of the oaths) to define the boundaries of the community exclusively with reference to who supports or opposes him, and to disregard the civic and familial ties — the traditional social bases of *pietas* — that assimilating ethics respects. Now, we have seen that the historical Caesar attempted to reconstitute a unitary community of obligation in the wake of the civil war both through the use of assimilating language in literary texts and through the symbolism of his triumphs. On Lucan's presentation, however, not only do the Caesarians generally embrace an alienating discourse, but this discourse survives and indeed defines the very essence of the imperial regime.[88]

Lucan thus presents Caesar's alienating ethical discourse in the civil war as the ideological foundation of the principate as it is experienced by himself and his audience. His examination of divided communities and competing discourses in the framework of the civil war, which is at once the origin of the principate and also a moment at which these issues are particularly prominent and sharpened, is therefore one respect in which his work engages with contemporary concerns. By refusing to allow his Caesar to mimic the historical Caesar's ideological reconstruction, Lucan resists the reorganizations of community and discourse to

---

[87] Premerstein 1937: 50: "Die den Hauptinhalt bildende Verpflichtung, die Widersacher des Prinzeps zu Wasser und zu Lande mit allen Waffen bis zur endlichen Züchtigung für ihr verbrecherisches Verhalten zu bekämpfen, das Heil des Prinzeps über alles andere— selbst über das eigene Leben und das der Kinder—zu stellen, führt uns in die blutige Atmosphäre des herannahenden Bürgerkrieges, in eine kritische Lage, wie sie später weder unter Augustus selbst, noch unmittelbar nach dessen Tod beim Antritt des Tiberius und insbesondere nicht bei dem des Gaius gegeben war." The claims made here, namely that the rhetoric of the imperial oaths of loyalty had its origins in the civil wars, and that these oaths therefore perpetuated and institutionalized civil-war rhetoric, are rejected by Herrmann 1968: 88–89. But whether these claims are right or wrong historically, they are precisely what Lucan implies by putting such words in the mouths of Laelius and Caesar.

[88] For another respect in which the principate can be seen as an institutionalization of civil war, see Barton 1993: 146; for a rather different view of the "endlessness of civil war," see Masters 1993: 251–53.

Caesar's advantage. Yet in the end, he suggests, it is his own Caesar's alienating discourse that is institutionalized in the loyalty oaths of Julio-Claudian Rome. Lucan may generally resist Caesar and Caesarism, in part by manipulating aspects of the received historical tradition, but he concedes its success and calls attention to its enduring incursion into aristocratic ethics. Thus he leaves competing articulations of the community and competing discourses forever in conflict, with no resolution in sight. His is, I think, a dark view of the position of the Julio-Claudian aristocracy: Caesar and the principate ensure a perpetual, irreparable fracturing of their community and destroy even the possibility of talking meaningfully (i.e., morally) about the regime itself or any other matter.

Lucan's bleakness in this respect, however, contrasts with the relative optimism of his uncle and contemporary, the younger Seneca. As I argue in the next chapter, Seneca, like Lucan, is preoccupied with competing and conflicting ethical discourses in Julio-Claudian Rome, conflicts that he presents as rooted in a power struggle between the *princeps* and the aristocracy as a whole. However, in Seneca's case these conflicts among ethical discourses are of his own making: throughout his ethical prose he places Stoic ethics in dialogue with traditional ethical discourse, urging his audience to embrace the former and reject the latter. For it is in Stoic ethics that he sees the salvation of the aristocracy, its release from the ethical traps that have infested traditional ethics since the advent of the principate. So where Lucan represents endlessly competing, irreconcilable ethical discourses as the hallmark of the principate, Seneca promotes a new, reconstituted, Stoic ethical discourse that, he suggests, can resist any and all threats posed to elite privilege by the emerging imperial sociopolitical order.

Chapter Two

ETHICS FOR THE PRINCIPATE: SENECA, STOICISM, AND TRADITIONAL ROMAN MORALITY

1. Overview

LIKE LUCAN'S *Bellum Civile*, Seneca's prose treatises are filled with competing moral judgments based in competing ethical systems. Indeed, one might argue that these competing judgments are the *raison d'être* for the texts that contain them. For the works entitled *De Providentia, De Vita Beata, De Beneficiis, De Clementia* ("On Providence," "On the Happy Life," "On Benefits," "On Clemency"), and so on are constructed as dialogues in which alternative sets of moral views regarding the nature of providence, happiness, benefits, etc., are made to engage one another dynamically. This characterization of Seneca's prose writing holds too for the *Epistulae ad Lucilium* ("Letters to Lucilius"), inasmuch as the formal conceits of the epistolary genre — the second-person address, and the claim to be both responding to points raised by the addressee in a previous letter and soliciting a further letter from him in turn — help to structure and sustain a dialogical exchange, in this case regarding the nature of moral value.[1]

Unlike Lucan, however, the competing ethical discourses in Seneca's treatises and letters do not arise from alternative conceptions of the community: they arise rather from alternative conceptions of the very foundation of ethics, the bases of the kind of value that we would call "moral." For "morality" has to do with rules and obligations, with what one "ought" to do in light of impartial, objective criteria that are broadly indifferent to one's particular interests and relations to particular persons. Indeed, it involves a degree of abstraction from particulars, requiring one to place oneself and one's interests on par with others and their interests, regarding all alike as equally subject to those broader principles that frame what one "ought" to do or aim for.[2] In traditional Roman ethics, as discussed in chapter 1.2 above, the objective external

---

[1] The dialogical form of Seneca's ethical prose — relatively unsystematic moral exhortation directed at a quasi-anonymous or generic interlocutor — has been regarded as a Romanized form of the Greek philosophical "diatribe" (Stückelberger 1980: 133–36). However, the character and even the existence of the "diatribe" as a genre is disputed.

[2] On the distinctive features of the "moral" point of view, in contrast with other points of view, see Williams 1981: 1–5.

criteria that underpin moral value are supplied by one's community of moral obligation, which passes judgments regarding how effectively an individual's observed actions serve its interests. Traditional ethics is well represented in Seneca, as in Lucan. In Seneca, however, we find in addition an altogether different kind of ethics, namely Stoic ethics, which articulates a basis for moral value in the context of a formal, systematic philosophy. In Stoic ethics, as I discuss below in greater detail, the objective criterion underpinning moral value is supplied by positing a human end, namely "living in accordance with nature." Now, one's behavior as a member of various human collectivities, such as one's family and city, is highly relevant to this end, for such affiliations are in some sense "natural." But the appeal to "nature" also provides grounds for dismissing the value judgments passed by such collectivities on the basis of their own interests, and even for regarding such judgments as morally wrong, at least in some cases.[3] And so it is in Seneca, in whose prose treatises and letters these two ethical systems are made to engage one another. He himself, or rather his authorial persona, usually serves as an advocate of Stoic ethics, while his interlocutor or addressee, who usually stands in for the reading audience as a whole, is made into the mouthpiece for traditional Roman ethics. Usually Seneca presents his philosophically formed judgment on the matter at hand as different from and superior to the "traditional" position attributed to the interlocutor (hence audience, in most cases). Even when Seneca claims that his Stoic views do not depart far from "common conceptions," and even in those cases where he overtly appeals to traditional ethical views to validate his argument, it remains (I contend) his primary rhetorical aim to differentiate Stoic from traditional ethics, and to privilege the former over the latter.

This chapter, like the previous one, broadly falls into two parts. First, I describe the confrontation that Seneca engineers between Stoic ethics and traditional Roman ethics, showing how he deploys certain elements of this highly elaborated, formal philosophical ethical tradition to ground or critique aspects of the relatively informal, unphilosophical traditional Roman ethical system. In particular I examine how Seneca problematizes, by applying Stoic ethics, traditional Roman conceptions of "good" and "bad," of *gratia* (gratitude) and proper modes of reciprocity, and finally of external evaluation—that is, the positive or negative judgments that members of an individual's community pass on him (or her) based on observing his or her actions in the public eye, and

---

[3] This is not, of course, to imply that within traditional ethics there are no conflicts of obligation, or situations where majority or collective judgments can be considered wrong. Conflicting obligations within this system generated by civil war are amply illustrated in chapter 1 above.

expressed verbally so that these evaluation can circulate within the community (sections 2–5). I subsequently argue that Seneca's advocacy of Stoic ethics, in place of or as a modification of traditional Roman ethics, addresses real and pressing conflicts of sociopolitical interests in Julio-Claudian Rome: Seneca suggests to his aristocratic readers that, if attentive to his ethical reforms, they stand to reclaim certain privileges and powers traditionally exercised by the aristocracy but recently monopolized by the *princeps*. Two specific points of political contestation to which Seneca's proposed ethical innovations may be seen to offer resolutions are, first, the unavailability of independent military commands for most aristocrats, along with the disappearance of the concomitant military honors (section 6); and second, the changing status of flattery as a political and ethical concern for early imperial aristocrats (section 7). In later chapters I will argue that Seneca's ethical innovations are relevant to still other areas of competition between aristocracy and *princeps*.

2. Stoicism's Two Regimes of Value

I begin with a sketch of the two regimes of value in Stoic ethics: for, as we shall see, the distinction between these different kinds of value is useful to Seneca in constructing a critique of traditional ethics. As noted above, Stoic ethics posits a human *telos*, or end, namely happiness, which is completely and exclusively constituted by "living in agreement with nature." This nature, regarded externally, is the rational principle that organizes the universe—the objective state of affairs that is outside of our control but frames all that we can and should do, and the principles of which are to be grasped through physics, logic, and grammar. It is commonly designated "nature," "god," "providence," and "fate" more or less interchangeably in Stoic sources.[4] Regarded internally, it is

[4] Though broadly interchangeable, these term (and others as well) can be made to pick out a particular, distinguishable aspects of this rational, universal organizing principle. First and foremost, it is *divina ratio* (*Ben.* 4.7.1, cf. *Nat.* 1 pr. 14) or *mens universi* (*Nat.* 1 pr. 13), terms that mark its rational, intentional governance of the physical material of the universe (cf. *Ep.* 65.2, 12, 23–24). Yet it can also be identified with the physical universe itself: *quid est deus? quod vides totum et quod non vides totum* (*Nat.* 1 pr. 13), and thus called *mundus* (*Nat.* 2.45.3). It is also associated with beginnings: in the guise of *fatum* it is the original cause from which the causal nexus issues (*Ben.* 4.7.2, *Nat.* 2.45.2), while as *providentia* (*Nat.* 2.45.2) it is the entity that both originally set up the laws of the universe and sees to it (through the causal nexus) that everything happens in accordance with those laws for all time; as *natura* (*Ben.* 4.7.1, *Nat.* 2.45.2) it is the originary force that gives rise to living things. *Fortuna* is something different: see ch. 4.6 and n. 101 below. All of these Latin terms also have Greek equivalents, and are widely attested in Stoic sources: see e.g., *SVF* I 102; II 913, 933, 945 (p. 273 ll. 25–26), 1076.

the rational principle within each adult human being that governs our impulses and so enables us to pursue our various individual goals, and which, if and when perfected, empowers us to organize our aims and motives in such a way that they harmonize completely with external nature: this is, indeed, "living in agreement with nature." For the rational principle in adult humans is a small fragment of the overarching rationality of the universe; our particular nature(s) and universal nature are fundamentally the same. Therefore the life in agreement with nature, in addition to being identified with "happiness," is also a *morally good* life, since "nature" supplies the objective external standard of evaluation that characterizes the moral. Furthermore, this morally good life is lived only by the good or wise man—who is said to be vanishingly rare, with the consequence that no actual persons are technically "happy" or "good."[5]

Thus the terms "good" and "bad" (by which Anglophone scholars commonly render the Greek terms ἀγαθόν and κακόν, and their standard Latin translations *bonum* and *malum*) pick out a specifically moral kind of value. One common Stoic definition of the "good" glosses it as "benefit": presumably, what benefits a person as a rational being, and so contributes toward the end of living in agreement with nature, is therefore good.[6] In practice, "good" and "bad" are predicated by Stoics only of an agent's mental dispositions, or of processes closely associated with these dispositions. These terms are not properly applied to a person's actions or the consequences of those actions, nor to any of the material or physical circumstances of a person's life. For these, say the Stoics (e.g., Diog. Laert. 7.101–103), admit of being used either well or badly, hence do not have the necessary relationship to benefiting that the "good" requires; they are instead labeled "indifferent" in regard to the achievement of happiness, or alternatively "middle"—neither good nor bad. Most important among the things properly labeled "good" or

---

[5] The formulation of the end as "living in agreement with nature" goes back to Zeno; the crucial description of it is Diog. Laert. 7.85–89. This passage, and the question of the relationship between internal nature and external nature in the early Stoa, has recently been the subject of debate between Long 1996 [1983] and Engberg-Pedersen 1990: 36–44 (to whom Long responds in his "postscript" to the 1996 reprint of the 1983 article, pp. 177–78). My brief summary here follows Long. Seneca gives a similar definition of the human end at *Ep.* 66.39–40; see also 66.12 for human rationality as a piece of the divine rational structure of the universe. On the rarity of the wise man (*tamquam phoenix semel anno quingentesimo nascitur*, Sen. *Ep.* 42.1), see further citations and discussion at Engberg-Pedersen 1990: 139–40 and 252 n. 65.

[6] For definitions of the good in terms of benefiting, see Diog. Laert. 7.94, Sextus *Adv. Math.* 11.22, Sen. *Ep.* 87.36. Diog. Laert. 7.104 defines benefit as "to set in motion or sustain in accordance with virtue," and harm (the opposite of benefit) as "to set in motion or sustain in accordance with vice"; for discussion see Tsekourakis 1974: 68–75 and, more generally, LS I 374–76.

"bad" are the particular mental states designated as "virtues" or "vices,"[7] where moral virtue is understood to be a particular kind of knowledge (namely, the awareness that the good and happy life consists in living in agreement with nature, and furthermore some understanding of what specific actions accord with nature in any given situation), and vice is the absence of this knowledge.[8]

The second regime of value in Stoicism operates among the "indifferent" or "middle" things. For while Stoics deny that things such as wealth, health, good looks, and good reputation are consititutive of happiness (hence lack the moral value associated with the predicate "good"), they are in some sense better than poverty, sickness, ugliness, and ill repute. But what precisely is this sense? At the foundation of this value difference is the nature of human beings as rational animals: for nature has so designed us as to wish, for example, to preserve ourselves physically, and to associate with our fellow humans. Thus health, good repute, and so on have value in regard to what we seek or avoid by our very nature, and their opposites have disvalue in this respect; it accords with our constitution as humans to select the former and reject the latter. Consequently, Stoics speak of health, wealth, etc., as being things "according to nature," and designate them as "preferred" or "to be selected" among the class of indifferent things. Their opposites are "contrary to nature" and are designated as "dispreferred" or "to be rejected." It must be stressed, however, that these states are not constitutive of happiness or unhappiness; particular states or actions "according to nature" do not immediately imply a life "in agreement with nature": a wealthy, healthy, beautiful person is still "unhappy" and vice-ridden if his or her mental states are not properly arranged—for then he or she would make ill use of these preferred indifferents—while an ugly, sickly, poor person could still be, in Stoic terms, virtuous and therefore happy, on account of making good use of his or her allocation of dispreferred indifferents (by enduring them bravely, for example).[9]

---

[7] On the content of the categories "good" and "bad," and their relationship to the categories "virtue" and "vice" (the former pair has wider extension, though virtue is said to be the "primary" species of good), see LS I 376 (with 60G, J-M). On the location of moral value proper in Stoic ethics, see in general LS I 354–59.

[8] There is some scholarly debate about what sorts of knowledge, according to the Stoics, constitute moral virtue (which is to say, what precisely the Stoic wise man knows): compare the weaker claim of Kerferd 1978 with the stronger claim of Engberg-Pedersen 1990: 128–31. Some virtues, including the four canonical primary virtues, are presented by the Stoics as forms of knowledge or science (ἐπιστήμη or τέχνη), while others are not: see Diog. Laert. 7.92–93, LS 60K, 61D.

[9] LS I 354–59 provides a set of key texts and discussion; in Seneca, a typical passage is Vit. 24.4–25.8. E.g., 24.5: *divitias nego bonum esse; nam si essent, bonos facerent: nunc, quoniam quod apud malos deprenditur dici bonum non potest, hoc illis nomen nego.*

But there are important connections between these regimes of value. In the first place, those things "according to nature," i.e., the preferred indifferents, though not constitutive of the (happy) life "in agreement with nature," are nevertheless foundational for that life. For in view of a human's constitutive nature, to choose a preferred indifferent over a dispreferred one is in general more likely to be what universal nature requires than to do the reverse. Crucially, though, Stoics acknowledge that in any particular case one may nevertheless be wrong to choose a preferred indifferent. For every life involves a greater or lesser amount of pain, illness, sorrow, disgrace, and the like; an allocation of these "dispreferred" things is itself part of the life in agreement with nature. The wise man, who lives in agreement with nature and is therefore happy, will therefore choose these dispreferred things in the particular circumstances in which they are required, even though, since they are contrary to his own nature as a human being, he reasonably seeks to avoid them in general.[10] Second, it is precisely through this selecting and rejecting of indifferent things (whether preferred or dispreferred) that the human being exercises his moral faculties: by striving to do this rationally he can progress toward a morally virtuous state. Also, if he is already a wise man, it is in his consistent, rational, unerring choosing of what the life in agreement with nature requires that his perfect moral virtue is made apparent.[11]

This broad outline of the two regimes of value in Stoic ethics effaces many complexities and glosses over divergences on various points among the Stoics themselves, not to mention considerable diversity of

---

ceterum et habendas esse et utiles et magna commoda vitae adferentis fateor. Also *Ep.* 66.14–23, 85.38–40 on how favorable and adverse circumstances admit equally of the exercise of virtue; *Prov.* 2–3 (and passim) for examples of men exercising and manifesting moral virtue under conditions of military defeat, poverty, condemnation, exile, torture, etc., and who are therefore not unhappy. By "according to nature" and "in agreement with nature" I render the Greek expressions κατὰ φύσιν and ὁμολογουμένως (τῇ φύσει), respectively (though the end is variously formulated in our sources: see LS I 400).

[10] For discussions of this situation, in which the right action (i.e., what is required by universal nature) would be to choose something normally dispreferred (i.e., contrary to a person's individual nature), see Kidd 1978, Engberg-Pedersen 1990: 136–39, Tsekourakis 1974: 32–34 and, much more briefly, LS I 400. I discuss "proper functions" in section 5 below.

[11] Diog. Laert. 7.104: "One can be happy even without these things [sc. wealth, reputation, health, strength], the manner of their use being conducive either to happiness or unhappiness" (also Sen. *Ep.* 66.38: *id aliquando contra naturam est in quo bonum illud existit*). Also, at Plut. *Mor.* 1069E, a Stoic is made to assert that nature and the things in accordance with nature are the ἀρχαὶ τοῦ καθήκοντος and ὕλη τῆς ἀρετῆς. See also the lengthy discussion of the "material of right actions" by Tsekourakis 1974: 30–37, along with his remarkable sketch of the two spheres of Stoic value, and their interconnections, on p. 9.

opinion among modern scholars. Nevertheless, the material I have presented here is fairly well attested in our sources, both Greek and Latin, and many specific assertions here can be corroborated or nuanced, directly or indirectly, by passages of Seneca himself (as I have indicated in the notes). This, then, is more or less the ethical framework that serves as the basis for Seneca's Stoic challenge to traditional Roman ethics. It is by means of the distinctions between and interrelations among these two regimes of Stoic value that Seneca engages the (more or less) traditional ethical understandings that he causes his interlocutors to voice, and so seeks to make a case for giving Roman aristocratic ethics a Stoic inflection. The character of this engagement will, I hope, begin to emerge in the next few pages.

3. Where Does Moral Value Reside? Stoic and Traditional Ethics

To begin to show how Seneca causes Stoic ethics to confront traditional ethics, I turn first to the treatise *De Providentia* ("On Providence") in which he discusses the significance of the fundamental moral evaluative terms *bonum* and *malum* ("good/good thing," "ill/bad thing"). This dialogue opens with an interlocutor (identified initially as the addressee, Lucilius) posing the question why, if *providentia* governs the universe, bad things happen to good men (§1.1)—"providence," again, like "god" and "nature," being among the generally interchangeable terms by which Stoics label the rational governing principle of the universe. The answer, for which Seneca argues in the course of the dialogue, is that bad things do not in fact happen to good men; people wrongly believe so because they do not properly understand what is "good" and what is "bad." While he grants that people sometimes experience things they would rather not experience, he denies that these experiences are correctly designated as "ills," *mala* (e.g., §§3.14, 5.1), and he refers to them instead as *adversarum impetus rerum* ("onslaught of adverse things," §2.1), *quaedam dura* ("certain difficulties," §6.2), *incommoda* ("dispreferred things," §§1.1, 3.2),[12] or the like. He reserves the word

---

[12] *Incommoda* is a regular Senecan translation of ἀποπροηγμένα, the Stoic technical term commonly rendered in English by "dispreferred" (as a species of the category "indifferent"), while *commoda* translates προηγμένα, "preferred": see e.g., *Ep.* 87.36–37 (on the relationship between *commoda* and *bona*), 92.14–16 (on the relationship between *commoda*, *incommoda*, and happiness). Cicero's usage (*Fin.* 3.45, 69) is slightly different. In the current passage, then, the word *incommoda* contributes to the Stoic coloring of the argument as a whole. Further discussion in Griffin 1976: 295–96.

malum for an entirely different class of things. At §6.1 he contrasts the "proper" usage of the word with his interlocutor's improper usage:

> "quare tamen bonis viris patitur aliquid mali deus fieri?" ille vero non patitur. omnia mala ab illis removit, scelera et flagitia et cogitationes inprobas et avida consilia et libidinem caecam et alieno imminentem avaritiam; ipsos tuetur ac vindicat: numquid hoc quoque aliquis a deo exigit, ut bonorum virorum etiam sarcinas servet? remittunt ipsi hanc deo curam: externa contemnunt. (*Prov.* 6.1)

> "But why does god allow anything bad to happen to good men?" But he doesn't allow it. He has removed all bad things from them, crimes and sins and wicked thoughts and covetous plans and blind lust and greed that threatens other people's goods; he protects and delivers the men themselves: does someone ask this too of god, that he guard even the baggage of good men? They themselves release god from this care: they despise externals.

Here Seneca explicitly constructs an opposition between things that are "external" to a person ("baggage," "externals") and the person himself (*ipsos*) or the things internal to him, the mental states and emotions specified in the list "crimes and sins and wicked thoughts...." It is specifically these internal things, the negative states of mind and emotions given in this list, that Seneca calls *mala* and that he denies are experienced by the good man. With his usage of *mala* in the third sentence of the passage quoted, then, Seneca corrects his interlocutor's usage of *malum* in the first sentence, where we are to understand that the word is being used incorrectly to describe the state of the good man's "externals."

The relationship between goods and ills, externals and internals is further articulated in the next few sections of the dialogue. Just as all things that are correctly called *mala* are states internal to a person, so too all things that are correctly designated as *bona* (presumably including the opposites of the states listed as *mala* in §6.1) are internal states, as god himself (*deus*) explains at §6.5: "all your goods are turned inward.... I have placed every good within" (*bona vestra introrsus obversa sunt.... intus omne posui bonum*). On the other hand, the good man gives no moral consideration whatsoever to externals (*externa contemnunt*, §6.1): these, he knows, are irrelevant to virtue and hence are not proper loci for moral value judgments one way or the other. Thus, god insists at §6.3 that wealth, luxury, and so on are actually "false goods" (implying that many people wrongly believe them to be goods), contrasting them with the implicitly "true" *bona* that are internal: "I have surrounded others with false goods ... I have bedecked them with gold and silver and ivory, but there is nothing good within" (*aliis bona falsa circumdedi . . . auro illos et argento et ebore adornavi, intus boni nihil est*). These externals, these false goods, are merely a veneer that block our view of the true moral value that lies within (§6.4).[13] Finally, at §6.6, Seneca once again assures his interlocutor that the things he regards as grim, fearful, and hard to bear (*tristia, horrenda, dura toleratu*) do not have any moral significance whatsoever: "despise poverty, despise pain, despise death, despise *fortuna*" (*contemnite paupertatem . . . contemnite dolorem . . . contemnite mortem . . . contemnite fortunam*).

Three aspects of Seneca's exposition here are noteworthy and significant for the argument I develop in this chapter. The first aspect is the strongly Stoic character of Seneca's argument: for in distinguishing two regimes of value, in only one of which can the terms *bonum* and *malum* properly be applied, he articulates the standard Stoic ethical position traced in section 2 above. Only his terminology is slightly unorthodox, inasmuch as he uses adjectives and adverbs of interiority (*intus, introrsus*) to indicate the realm of moral value proper, in which the terms *bonum* and *malum* are operative, and he uses the noun *externa*, "externals," or related ideas (e.g., what "surrounds" you, your "baggage") rather than *indifferentia*, "indifferents," to label things such as wealth, poverty, health, pain, etc., to which no moral value attaches but which admit of being evaluated positively or negatively in other terms (*commoda, incommoda, dura,* etc.). Elsewhere Seneca clarifies his terminology by identifying that which is "internal" as the soul, which (he says) is the only thing that is truly one's own and under one's control; only the soul's dispositions admit of moral evaluation as good or bad.[14] He correspondingly identifies the "external" as everything else, none of which is one's own or under one's control because it is subject to the vicissitudes of *fortuna*.[15] Seneca does sometimes use the term *indifferentia* (ἀδιάφορα) or *media* ("middle" things, i.e., neither good nor bad)

---

[13] The same idea occurs at *Ep.* 115.6–7: to see virtue hidden within a person, we have to look through many things that cloak that virtue—poverty, lowliness, and ill repute, for example. Conversely, if we look through the dazzling cloak of riches, high standing, and power, we may perceive a soul filled with vice.

[14] Thévenaz 1944 discusses the moral value of internals and moral valuelessness of externals in Seneca, arguing (191–92) that Seneca causes *suum* and *se* to collapse together, so that being and having become identical; thus oneself is one's only secure possession. He also notes the broader philosophical contexts (Stoic and other) in which the internal/external distinction is articulated (cf. n. 16 below).

[15] E.g., *Ep.* 82.5: *philosophia circumdanda est, inexpugnabilis murus, quem fortuna multis machinis lacessitum non transit. in insuperabili loco stat animus qui externa deseruit et arce se sua vindicat; infra illum omne telum cadit.* Similarly *Epp.* 66.35, 74.6, 94.72; *Vit.* 8.4, *Tranq.* 14.2. *Fortuna* is not identical to *deus / natura / providentia*: see ch. 4 n. 101 below.

for those things that do not admit of moral evaluation, but these terms are less common.[16]

The second important point is that, as we can see from this passage, the ethical conceptions held by Seneca's interlocutor are generally the values of traditional Roman ethics. This interlocutor's persistent attempts to label externals as good and bad indicates that he understands moral value to be inherently community oriented, constructed ultimately under the gaze of others on the basis of observed actions, status symbols, and other visible signs. Moreover, in attempting to sway his interlocutor, Seneca frequently deploys figures from the Roman past as models for action in the present (e.g., *Prov.* 3.4–14) — the heavy use of such historical exempla being a distinctively Roman ethical discursive idiom. In section 5 below I discuss Seneca's use of historical exempla at greater length. Thus Seneca is not expounding Stoic ethics in a vacuum. On the one hand he puts Stoic ethical views in dialogue with (more or less) traditional, received ethical views held by Roman aristocrats generally, and voiced in this text by the interlocutor; on the other hand, through his heavy use of historical exempla, Seneca employs a venerable mode of moral argumentation that would be familiar, and presumably persuasive, to his audience.

The third crucial feature of Seneca's argumentation is its sustained engagement with the interlocutor's traditional view — the "common conceptions" he holds — about the nature and location of moral value. From the beginning of *De Providentia* to the end, Seneca is in constant contact and dialogue with this traditional view. To be sure, he argues forcefully that it is mistaken: he corrects the interlocutor's own (mis)usages of the terms *bonum* and *malum* by distinguishing the "truly" bad and good from the indifferents, and insisting that the words *bonum* and *malum* are applicable only to the former. Yet this very process of correcting, which involves introducing the ethically crucial distinction between externals and internals, and then comparing the usages of *bonum*

---

[16] Notably *Epp.* 82.10 (and ff.), 117.8–9; *Vit.* 22.4. By using the term *externa* (etc.) to designate everything except the soul, Seneca reduces to two categories the threefold division of soul, body, and externals (ψυχή, σῶμα, ἐκτός) that we find in other Stoic sources (though this division is originally Peripatetic: see Sextus *Adv. Math.* 11.44–45, Ar. *Nic. Eth.* 1098b12). Likewise, his firm restriction of moral value to the soul is at odds with other sources' assertions that both moral value proper and the preferential value of indifferents can be found in several of these realms. Thus, just as conditions of the body and of externals (in this narrower sense) may be "indifferent," so may certain conditions of the soul: see *SVF* III 127, 136. Conversely, moral goodness and badness can inhere in certain external things as well as in the soul: see *SVF* III 96, 97a. See also LS I 376 on the rather wide range of phenomena — some of the soul, others external — admitted as "goods" in our sources. Seneca does offer a threefold division of "goods" at *Ep.* 66.5, 36–39, but this is an altogether different kind of classification (cf. *Ben.* 5.13).

and *malum* in Stoic and traditional ethics, makes clear that Seneca is at pains to show exactly how the Stoic view of moral value that he advocates is related to the interlocutor's uninspected, common conceptions. This dialogical engagement is itself entirely consonant with the Stoic pedagogical tradition: for Stoics regularly accepted (or claimed to accept) common, everyday understandings of words, at least as a starting point for discussion. Often they ended up arguing for understandings remote enough from that starting point that they were accused of paradox mongering. Yet even then, they could defend themselves by insisting that their apparently paradoxical positions were deduced by impeccable logic from common conceptions—ethical propositions to which even those who lack philosophical training would readily assent[17]—and they themselves formulated a number of paradoxes of this sort as pedagogical devices. Indeed, Seneca's *De Providentia* itself takes a paradoxical proposition as its starting point: it proposes to demonstrate that, in a world governed by *providentia*, bad things do *not* happen to good men, even though they suffer sickness, exile, and so on. The impulse to resolve this paradox provides the occasion for introducing Stoic ethical concepts over against traditional ones, and it is here that the pedagogy begins.[18]

---

[17] So the Stoic Cato is made to argue at Cic. *Fin.* 3.48: *haec mirabilia videri intellego, sed cum certe superiora firma ac vera sint, his autem ea consentanea et consequentia, ne de horum quidem est veritate dubitandum*. On this passage and Stoic argumentation in general, see Long 1996 [1971]: 139; also id. 1996 [1983]: 170–72 and n. 15, and Inwood 1995: 248–50. Nevertheless, the opponents of Stoicism still attacked them for contradicting even the common conceptions that they claimed to accept: this is the polemic of Plutarch's treatise *De Communibus Notitiis adversus Stoicos* (*Mor.* 1058E–1086B).

[18] That the Stoics themselves embraced propositions that they called παράδοξα, "things contrary to common opinion" (Cic. *Parad.* 4), indicates the delicacy of the balance they tried to strike between common ethical conceptions and radical ones. One typical Stoic paradox, presented here *exempli gratia* and further discussed in chapter 4.6 below, is the proposition "only the wise man is free and all fools are slaves" (Cic. *Parad.* 33, Dio Chr. *Or.* 14, Epict. *Diss.* 4.1). Given the Stoic position that wise men are vanishingly rare and that all who are not wise are fools, it follows that, at any given moment, everyone (or virtually everyone) living in the world is a slave—a paradox, for this usage of "slave" and "master" is remote from the default understanding of these terms as "chattel" and "legal owner of chattel." Yet Stoics contend that these usages are in one crucial respect very close to common conceptions. For they deduce the paradoxical conclusion from the commonly held views that freedom is, on the one hand, the condition of not being a slave, and on the other, the ability to do as one pleases. The key move is to interpret the latter criterion, the "ability to do as one pleases," not as meaning that freedom implies significant scope for discretionary action, but as meaning that one's wishes must accord with actual possibilities and constraints. On this understanding, the "free" man never perceives any hinderances to doing as he pleases, because he only pleases to do what is unhindered (e.g., Sen. *Ep.* 61.3, cf. 54.7; also Brunt 1988: 311). Then indeed only the wise man, who lives in full agreement with nature, is "free," and all others, who do sometimes feel constraint because their minds are not perfectly in accord with *deus*, are "slaves."

However, the rigorous distinctions between Stoic and traditional Roman ethics that Seneca articulates throughout *De Providentia* are by no means systematically maintained elsewhere in his ethical prose. Consider a second discussion of the terms *bonum* and *malum*, and how they are correctly to be understood and used, in *Ep.* 85.24–29. Here a hostile interlocutor insists that the good man must surely fear the bad things (*mala*) that threaten him — things such as torture, imprisonment, poverty, and death. As he does in *De Providentia*, here too Seneca corrects his interlocutor's usage by asserting that the threats in question are merely so-called *mala*, but not *mala* in fact: the only "true" *malum* is *turpitudo* ("shameful character"), which (apparently) consists precisely in yielding to these so-called *mala*.[19] Later in this letter, however, Seneca's usage becomes inconsistent. In §§38–41 he develops the argument that the Stoic sage has the opportunity to exercise his virtue even in the midst of poverty, pain, exile, and so on. In the course of this argument, he on the one hand refers to these undesirable conditions of life in terms that accord with the Stoic view, articulated earlier in this letter, that such conditions are morally insignificant: he calls them *necessitates* ("things that are inevitable," §38), matters of bad *fortuna* (§§ 38, 40), and *adversae* ("difficulties," §39). Yet intertwined with these expected usages are some unexpected, even contradictory ones: in §38 Seneca describes the sage as "controller of goods, conqueror of ills" (*bonorum rector, malorum victor*), and in §40 asks, "you think he is oppressed by ills? He makes use of them" (*tu illum premi putas malis? utitur*) — applying the terms *malum* and *bonum* to precisely the externals that, both here and elsewhere, he insists do not carry moral value and cannot have these terms predicated of them. Now, one way to save Seneca from a charge of inconsistency would be to attribute these usages to the interlocutor; to regard the interlocutor as (in narratological terms) the focalizer of these words. Such an understanding is particularly attractive in the case of the question at §40 ("you think he is oppressed by ills?"), where Seneca could be seen as repeating the interlocutor's question back to him in the interlocutor's own words. Yet earlier in this letter (§§24, 26), as well as in *De Providentia*, Seneca is at pains to correct his interlocutor's (mis)usage of value terms: he does not parrot back such errors or tacitly let them pass. Moreover, the letter concludes (§41) by explicitly predicating the term *malum* of a series of undesirable externals: "thus the sage is an expert at subduing ills: pain,

---

[19] *Ep.* 85.25: "*at enim dementem puto qui mala inminentia non extimescit.*" *verum est quod dicis, si mala sunt; sed si scit mala illa non esse et unam tantum turpitudinem malum iudicat, debebit secure pericula aspicere et aliis timenda contemnere.* . . . (§26) "*quid ergo?*" *inquit, "mortem, vincula, ignes, alia tela fortunae non timebit?*" *non; scit enim illa non esse mala sed videri.* . . . (§28) *quaeris quid sit malum? cedere iis quae mala vocantur.*

poverty, disgrace, imprisonment, exile, which everywhere inspire terror, are gentle when they reach him" (*sic sapiens artifex est domandi mala: dolor, egestas, ignominia, carcer, exilium ubique horrenda, cum ad hunc pervenere, mansueta sunt*). As the concluding assertion of the letter, the view communicated is unquestionably Seneca's own, authoritative one; it seems quite impossible that the usage of *malum* here could represent the interlocutor's (discredited) ethical stance rather than Seneca's own stance. In these sections of *Ep.* 85, then, Seneca labels these undesirable conditions of life both by terms appropriate to a Stoic ethical framework (*necessitates, adversae*), and also by the moral predicates (*bonum, malum*) that reflect common usage, the traditional ethical views of "the many." Thus he neither simply abandons the distinctions he rigorously defends earlier in the letter (and elsewhere) between correct and incorrect ways of using *bonum* and *malum*, nor does he scrupulously maintain those distinctions.

How are we to account for such inconsistencies? Seneca himself frequently distinguishes, implicitly or explicitly, between the specialized, technical usages of ethical terminology in philosophical ethics, and the everyday, common usages that typify traditional Roman ethics. In a well-known passage at the beginning of *Ep.* 59, for example, Seneca defends his usage of the ethical term *voluptas* in its "customary" or "public" sense rather than in its Stoic sense; also at *De Beneficiis* 2.35.2 and 4.26–27 he discusses crucial distinctions between "ordinary" and Stoic usages of words. Thus he distinguishes two linguistic registers, technical and Stoic vs. commonsense and familiar.[20] Given Seneca's overt articulations of this distinction and his generally diligent maintenance of it, I would be disinclined to attribute his inconsistent usages of *malum* at the end of *Ep.* 85 to inadvertence; he must be aiming here for a particular rhetorical effect by employing the traditional, "commonsense" understanding of *malum*. Here, where his point is to insist upon the good man's virtuosity—his ability to exercise *virtus* under any condition of life—it is perhaps not central to the argument to insist that difficult conditions of life are not *mala*; Seneca's point is made equally well whether he uses the morally implicated designations *bonum* and *malum* in their common, everyday way (a usage which, from a Stoic

[20] Seneca's use of different modes of discourse, the "technical" and "common" modes that I describe here, has been observed and commented on by several scholars—in the greatest detail, by Habinek 1989: 241–45, who maps Seneca's distinction between *decreta* and *praecepta* in *Epp.* 94 and 95 onto "two modes of ethical discourse: one scientific, abstract, and professional; the other hortatory, concrete, and popularizing" (243). In the same vein, Griffin 1976: 153 argues that Seneca's language in book 1 of *De Clementia* adheres largely to "common usage," while in book 2 a more careful, precise use of language signals a technical philosophical argument (cf. Faider et al. 1950: 143). See also Inwood 1995: 262–63 and, for other kinds of discursive variation in Seneca's prose, Edwards 1997: 34–35.

ethical viewpoint, is strictly inappropriate to this situation), or designations such as *necessitates* and *adversae res* which are strictly more appropriate (in the Stoic view) because not morally implicated. Earlier in the letter (§§24–29), where Seneca argues that the good man cannot fear what is not morally bad, it is central to his argument to insist that imprisonment, illness, etc., are not *mala*. But at the end of the letter, where his argument requires no such strict distinction, he can employ *bonum* and *malum* in their "commonsense" ways without detriment. Indeed, his argument may be all the more persuasive to a potentially hostile audience, such as the interlocutor constitutes: for with these usages he appeals to the kinds of ethical views most people have about the world, and so, taking common conceptions as his starting point, helps his ultimately Stoic argument to "get off the ground."[21] For if Seneca broadly aims to persuade his aristocratic audience to see the world in Stoic ethical terms, it is perhaps not surprising that he appeals, at least now and then, to his audience's usual understandings about where moral value resides in the world and how it is allocated, as part of an argumentative strategy that seeks ultimately to nuance or even displace these very views. Thus Seneca's engagement with the traditional Roman values of his interlocutors and addressees is complex, ranging in tone from hostile to conciliatory: yet in typically Stoic style there is always an engagement, always contact with the common conceptions that Stoic ethics seeks to appropriate, or ground, or modify, or supplant.[22]

4. Who Judges and How? Dilemmas of Internal and External Evaluation

We have seen how Seneca seeks to attach the basic moral value terms *bonum* and *malum* to the internal states (i.e., states of mind or soul) of agents, a move generally in accordance with Stoic ethics, and detach

---

[21] This is the phrase used by Long 1996 [1971]: 139 and Inwood 1995: 250 to describe the Stoic aim in taking common conceptions as the premises from which they deduce their main ethical propositions, some of which are so far removed from common conceptions as to be paradoxical (see n. 18 above).

[22] This engagement takes on a variety of forms within the Stoic tradition generally. LS I 436 trace an evolution: they regard statements attributed to Zeno (e.g., Diog. Laert. 7.32–33, 121–22) as indicating that the founder of the school regarded conventional usages as "completely misguided" and "quite incorrect." They note, however, that Chrysippus made certain concessions to ordinary usages (Plut. *Mor.* 1048A), and they see a further rapprochement between Stoic and "common" ethical views in the Roman period. Along the same lines, Brunt 1975: 12–16 suggests that Panaetian Stoicism, far from challenging traditional Roman ethical conceptions, actually provided a philosophical grounding for them; he also seems to regard Senecan Stoicism as adhering closely to (and underpinning) received common conceptions (22). But I will argue below (sections 6–7) that Seneca is more radical than this.

them from the agents' exterior circumstances (i.e., conditions of the body, or their social, economic, or political circumstances), where "common opinion" would locate them. As noted above, this "common opinion," the view often voiced by Seneca's interlocutor, represents traditional Roman ethical discourse in crucial respects, particularly in its preoccupation with passing judgment on others on the basis of observed, community-oriented actions and visible status markers. Manifestly, to remove moral value from such actions and visible markers, and to locate it instead in the agent's mental states, is to deprive the external observer of his grounds for passing moral judgment on the agent. Who, then, *is* in a position to judge an agent, if moral value is internal, and how does he go about doing it? How, in short, does ethical discourse work in a Stoic ethical universe? There is much in Seneca's ethical prose pertinent to these questions, and I begin my examination of them by considering his treatment of the ethical category *gratia*.

In traditional ethical discourse this category is quintessentially community oriented, for its field of reference is the social bonds forged within the community by the exchange of objects and services. The adjective *gratus* and noun *gratia* carry the active senses "(suitably) thankful/grateful (for a favor received)" and "the feeling or offering of goodwill (to another)," respectively. These active senses are my main focus here. However, these words also have passive senses, respectively, "received with pleasure" and "favor (in which one is held)"; both the active and the passive senses are used regularly in the context of social exchange.[23] Moreover, these terms and their negations display the the familiar semantic split into enacted and dispositional usages, discussed in chapter 1.2 above. On the one hand, a person may be judged *gratus* if he observably presents himself as thankful for an object or service received; generally this entails making a public, visible return.[24] On the other hand, he can call himself *gratus* upon receipt of a favor, or apply

---

[23] On the semantics of these words see Hellegouarc'h 1963: 202–208, and Saller 1982: 21. At greater length, see *TLL* VI 2.2206–16, 2260–61. David 1992: 146, 151–53 suggests that the expressions *gratiam habere* and *gratiam referre* reveal an important slippage between attitudes and objects in Roman thought (i.e., between internality and externality, in the terms I use here); he consequently suggests that *gratia* is a conceptual unity, combining activity and passivity. For more on gratitude and reciprocity, see ch. 3 passim (but especially section 5) below.

[24] Representative examples of the enacted usage: *Rhet. Her.* 4.57 (people are revealed as *ingrati* toward the state if they flee dangers that must be faced on its behalf); Livy 2.10.12 (the state is *grata* toward Horatius Cocles in return for his heroic exploit: it erects a statue and gives him land); Tac. *Hist.* 4.3 (Vespasian's failure to give Capua financial support, though the town was loyal to him, proves that *gratia* is regarded as a burden). In each of these cases, the terms (*in*)*gratus/gratia* are assigned with reference to specific, observable actions done or not done in return for prior services.

this adjective in its passive sense to the favor itself ("pleasing"), thus declaring his positive feelings toward his benefactor and toward the favor received, and marking his intention to make an appropriately public, observable return at some later time. Indeed, in these dispositional usages, a grateful attitude is often indicated precisely by a declaration of intent to make a specific, publicly observable return. In the *Oratio Cottae*, a surviving fragment of Sallust's *Histories*, the speaker Cotta tells his senatorial colleagues that, in return for the benefits they have bestowed upon him, he could scarcely seem sufficiently *gratus* if he were to give his life for each of them individually (§5). It is precisely his declared wish to act on their behalf in the future that indicates his (current) grateful attitude; the fact that the specific acts of reciprocation that he envisions are impossible merely underscores the depth of his gratitude, his awareness of the difficulty of reciprocating appropriately. Such an immediate, well-defined connection between attitude and community-oriented action is also expressed in Cicero's formal definition of *gratia* at *De Inventione* 2.66: "they call *gratia* that which keeps a deferential regard for dignity and friendships in the memory and repayment of services" (*appellant . . . gratiam quae in memoria et remuneratione officiorum et honoris et amicitiarum observantiam teneat*). *Gratia*, then, is said here to have regard for social position (*honor*) and friendships—hence is explicitly concerned with one's relations to one's community—and this regard is maintained through *both* memory of *and* concrete reciprocation for services rendered: that is, both the mental state and the overt act of reciprocation are central, inseparable aspects of this value.[25] Sometimes, however, no action that would constitute reciprocation is specified, as in letters of recommendation, whose conclusions often contain the formulaic promise "if you take care of the person I am commending to you, I (or he) will be *gratus*." Yet even a usage such as this may imply, in addition to a certain attitude on the author's part, that a concrete act of reciprocation will be forthcoming—though this is not certain.[26]

Throughout his treatise *De Beneficiis* ("On Benefits"), a work utterly

---

[25] Again at *Inv.* 2.161 Cicero links *memoria* and *remuneratio* as central aspects of *gratia*. For another example of this immediate linkage between a (current) grateful attitude and a (future) concrete act of reciprocation, see Pliny *Ep.* 8.12.2–3: here Pliny assumes that the gratitude of a reciter to those who attend his recitations would naturally result in his attending their recitations in return; cf. *Ep.* 1.13.6. For perversions of this linkage, e.g., a benefit reciprocated with hatred or enmity, see ch. 3.6 below.

[26] For such promises in *commendationes*, see e.g., Cic. *Fam.* 13.6, 13.8.3, 13.9.3, 13.13, 13.15.3, 13.16.4; Pliny *Ep.* 3.2.6; Cotton 1981: 28. Similarly vague assurances appear at Pl. *Merc.* 105 (the youth says he will be *gratus pro meritis* if the owner of his love interest sells her to him), and at Cic. *Off.* 2.66 (nothing surpasses eloquence in regard to the *gratia* it inspires in those it defends).

preoccupied with the protocols of social exchange, Seneca denies the significance of action, whether actual or projected, in the ethical category of *gratia*.[27] The basis of his objection is the now familiar claim that internal states, which are morally significant, must not be confused with external behavior, which is morally insignificant. At *Ben.* 4.21 Seneca articulates his position particularly clearly. First he describes the semantics of the word *gratus* as follows: "There are two types of grateful person: one is called grateful who gives back something in return for that which he received; he perhaps can swagger around, and has something to brag up and show off. Another is called grateful who receives a benefit in good spirit, and owes it in good spirit; this man is closed up within his conscience" (*duo genera sunt grati hominis: dicitur gratus qui aliquid pro eo, quod acceperat, reddidit; hic fortasse ostentare se potest, habet quod iactet, quod proferat. dicitur gratus qui bono animo accepit beneficium, bono debet; hic intra conscientiam clusus est*, §21.1). Though brief, this description accords generally with the semantics of the *gratus/gratia* cluster as described above: the first usage describes one who makes a concrete return and, in so doing, presents himself to an external judging audience for approval (the "enacted" usage); the second indicates a disposition involving no concrete return or external judgment. Indeed, by his use of *dicitur* Seneca alleges that both usages are widespread, and thus he presents his semantic analysis as describing common conceptions. At the end of the sentence quoted, however,

---

[27] My discussion of Senecan *gratia* in the next few pages is often in implicit dialogue with Inwood 1995, who demonstrates that Seneca makes his Stoic articulation of gratitude engage closely with common conceptions—showing, for example, that Seneca makes the figure of the sage relevant to the actual decisions normal moral agents must make in ordinary social exchange situations. This work is a major contribution to our understanding of the social engagement of Senecan Stoicism. My differences with Inwood are matters of emphasis, but are nevertheless significant. While I cannot venture a full-scale crititique of his argument here, I think it is fair to say that Inwood's Seneca is first and foremost a Stoic philosopher, who presents the system's ethics as similar in crucial respects, and therefore relevant, to the moral dilemmas faced by his implied audience; it helps the ordinary Roman aristocrat deliberate and ground his everyday choices as a moral agent. I, on the other hand, see Seneca as a Roman aristocrat in the first instance, who presents Stoic ethics to his social peers (the implied audience) as a way out of certain contemporary ethical binds (secs. 6–7 below). Put another way, Inwood's Seneca engineers a rapprochement between the abstract ideals of the sage and the moral dilemmas of ordinary social actors, while my Seneca puts forth Stoic ethics as something significantly *different* from traditional Roman aristocratic ethics, and preferable by virtue of addressing more effectively certain pressing contemporary problems. I agree with Inwood that Seneca makes his Stoicism engage closely with the ordinary ethical views and problems of Roman aristocrats: but I see the project as one of differentiation and ultimate displacement, not assimilation and reconciliation.

Seneca breaks off the *dicitur* construction and resumes his own persona, signaling his disagreement with these common conceptions: he continues, "and yet this [second] man, even if he can do nothing further, is *gratus*. He loves, he owes, he desires to repay the favor; whatever more you want, he himself is not lacking" (*atqui hic, etiam si ultra facere nil potest, gratus est. amat, debet, referre gratiam cupit; quidquid ultra desideras, non ipse deest*, §21.2). Here Seneca presents *gratia* as a disposition, yet he implies that there is no immediate connection between this disposition and any publicly observable reciprocation. That is, he denies that the validity of someone's claim to being *gratus* depends upon making concrete remuneration in the sight of an external, judging audience; rather, being *gratus* requires only the desire or wish to act reciprocally. Seneca reiterates these points a few lines later: "I want to repay the favor: after this something is left for me to do—not to be grateful, but to be released; for often he who has returned a favor is an ingrate, and he who has not is grateful" (*volo referre gratiam: post hoc aliquid superest mihi, non ut gratus, sed ut solutus sim; saepe enim et qui gratiam rettulit ingratus est, et qui non rettulit gratus*, §21.3). The point of the final paradoxical clause, presumably, is that "true" gratitude, being entirely vested in mental states, is in no way correlated with making or failing to make a concrete return.[28]

Thus Senecan *gratia* differs strikingly from the common conception. On the one hand, Seneca not only eliminates the enacted usage—declaring in §21.3 that concrete remuneration is not *gratia* but "release," and indeed has no correlation at all with *gratia* (since this is exclusively a mental state)—but he also diverges from the dispositional usage. For while §21.2 shows that Senecan *gratia* is a mental state, it is not articulated with respect to a future, concrete, visible act of reciprocation. It is simply a warm feeling toward the benefactor, an awareness of obligation which arises with no apparent reference to an external judging community. It continues to mark something valuable in the economy of social exchange, but the value is no longer that of reinforcing social bonds through reciprocal exchange of objects and services. On the other hand, this articulation of gratitude accords with Seneca's usual, Stoic articulation of the ethical differentiation between internal conditions and external circumstances. For to have something concrete to give in return, and to have an occasion for so doing, are matters of external circumstance that are subject to the whims of *fortuna*, the unknown cause that is *ex hypothesi* outside of one's own control. Gratitude cannot be a moral virtue available to everyone if it is not completely under

---

[28] Seneca makes similar arguments at *Ben.* 2.24.4–25.1, 2.31–35, 3.7.6, 4.9.1, 4.10.4.

the agent's control; hence the necessity to limit it to the mind, the one realm that is (on the Stoic view) exempt from *fortuna*.[29]

Several consequences follow from this reorientation, which Seneca summarizes in *Ben.* 4.21.5 as follows:

> est aliquando gratus etiam qui ingratus videtur, quem mala interpres opinio contrarium tradidit. hic quid aliud sequitur quam ipsam conscientiam? quae etiam obruta delectat, quae contioni ac famae reclamat et in se omnia reponit et, cum ingentem ex altera parte turbam contra sentientium adspexit, non numerat suffragia, sed una sententia vincit.

> Sometimes a person is in fact grateful who appears ungrateful, whom opinion, a bad spokesman, says is the opposite. What does this man follow other than his conscience itself? which even when it is crushed gives him delight, which shouts out against the mob and rumor and relies entirely upon itself and, when it sees a huge throng of people who think otherwise on the other side, does not count the votes but wins by its single vote.

First, the ultimate arbiter of a person's goodness or badness in regard to *gratia* is his own *conscientia* ("conscience" or "moral self-knowledge"), which is in a position to judge his internal state.[30] The community at large is in no position to judge because, being able to observe only actions, it has no immediate access to that internal state. It follows that external judgments of moral value are unreliable at best, lacking any necessary relationship with the "real" moral value that resides unobservably within.[31] Therefore, the good man regards all such ethical judgments as mere *fama* and *opinio*, and pays them no heed. Not only does he not care how the community at large judges him for actions already taken, but he also will not choose his future actions with any thought

---

[29] At *Ben.* 2.31.1 Seneca asserts that his claim "whoever receives a benefit gladly has reciprocated it" is a Stoic paradox (cf. *Ep.* 81.11 for another paradox involving gratitude); he also here classifies gratitude as a moral virtue that shares with *pietas*, *fides*, and *iustitia* the property of being "perfect within itself, even if the agent cannot lift a finger." At 2.31.4 he explicitly exempts *gratia* from the effects of *fortuna*.

[30] In Seneca, the word *conscientia* generally designates one's knowledge or awareness of oneself as a moral agent; *bona conscientia* and *mala conscientia* designate one's self-awareness as a good or bad moral agent, respectively. In some cases, however, *conscientia* seems to indicate not moral self-awareness per se, but rather the locus of that awareness, or the capacity by which that awareness is achieved—i.e., something like the English term "conscience." See also *Ira* 1.14.3, *Clem.* 1.15.5, *Ep.* 81.20, and *Vit.* 20. 4–5 (discussed below). For a different view of Senecan *conscientia*, see Grimal 1992: 157–59.

[31] *Ben.* 3.9 provides a variation on this theme. In the midst of an argument that *ingratia* cannot and should not be actionable, Seneca imagines a series of accusations cast by benefactors against putatively ungrateful recipients; in each case he suggests that the recipients are not in fact ungrateful (similar guesswork about the recipient's mental disposition is implied at *Ben.* 4.33.1). For the benefactor has no more privileged knowledge of the recipient's true moral state than does any other external judge.

for the *fama* that they may be foreseen to generate. He will never, for example, choose to repay a benefit out of concern for what people will say if he does not, as Seneca's exchange with his interlocutor shows: "'but I am afraid that people will speak ill of me.' The person does ill who is grateful because of reputation rather than conscience" (*"at vereor ne homines de me sequius loquantur." male agit, qui famae, non conscientiae gratus est, Ben.* 6.42.2; cf. *Vit.* 26.4–5, *Ep.* 81.20). With such statements, traditional Roman ethics and its external modes of moral evaluation, at least regarding *gratia*, would seem to be definitively renounced.

Similar claims are made for other ethical categories, and are also made in general: Seneca insists that moral value resides in states of mind that are not necessarily manifested in action that the community at large can observe; nor do these states of mind even look toward such observable action in the future. In *Ep.* 113.32, he contends that the value of being *iustus* ("just") is in no way enhanced by having a reputation for it; in fact, *iustitia* ("justice") may be accompanied by a bad reputation (*infamia*), which should actually be a cause for pleasure provided it is "well-earned."[32] Again, in *De Ira* 3.41.1–2 he says that the person who has banished the vice of anger from his soul may be thought (wrongly) by others to be *iners* ("idle," "feeble"); this man too should be content with his ill repute (*mala fama*), provided his *conscientia* is satisfied.[33] In general, *conscientia* has access to internal states that outside observers lack. In his *Exhortationes*, lost but for a few fragments preserved by Lactantius, Seneca asks, "why do you choose a hidden place and banish onlookers? Suppose it is granted that you escape the eyes of everyone, madman: what good does it do you to have nobody privy, when you have your moral self-knowledge?" (*quid locum abditum legis et arbitros removes? puta tibi contigisse ut oculos omnium effugias, demens: quid tibi prodest non habere conscium habenti conscientiam?* Lact. *Inst.* 6.24.17 = fr. 14 Haase; cf. *Ep.* 43.3–4, 97.15–16). Here the pointed, punning contrast between *conscius* and *conscientia* suggests that *conscientia* is a more authoritative judge than outside observers: for it knows one's true moral viciousness, even if other people are successfully kept in the dark. Seneca also argues more

---

[32] *Ep.* 113.32: *nihil ad rem pertinere, quam multi aequitatem tuam noverint. qui virtutem suam publicari vult non virtuti laborat sed gloriae. . . . saepe iustus esse debebis cum infamia, et tunc, si sapis, mala opinio bene parta delectet.*

[33] *Ira* 3.41.1–2: *pacem demus animo. . . . conscientiae satis fiat, nil in famam laboremus; sequatur vel mala, dum bene merentis. "at vulgus animosa miratur et audaces in honore sunt, placidi pro inertibus habentur"* (cf. section 5 and n. 52 below). For the same idea, see *Helv.* 13.4: *ignominia tu putas quemquam sapientem moveri posse, qui omnia in se reposuit, qui ab opinionibus vulgi secessit?*

generally that actions chosen out of concern for one's reputation will surely be inappropriate. In *Ep.* 99.16–18, he analyzes the behavior of the person who, upon the death of a family member, grieves more loudly and profusely in the presence of others than he does in private. In his public behavior, Seneca says, this person engages in imitation and is following *exempla* ("examples," "models [of moral behavior]") by comporting himself in accordance with others' expectations. But by looking to what is customary rather than to what is proper, he deviates from *natura* and *ratio* ("nature" and "reason")—that is, his actions are not in accordance with nature—and is merely cultivating his reputation (*fama*) among the many, even though their judgments are based on no good authority.[34] Likewise, Seneca notes (*Ep.* 94.69–71) that luxurious clothing, tableware, and so on are brought out only when there is a crowd to admire them, and that one does not bother with such things when one is alone. Therefore he recommends solitude as a means for controlling vicious impulses, to remove the temptation to cultivate external appearances.[35] In these respects too, then, Seneca insists that value conferred by external observers, on the basis of actions done in the public eye, is conferred on the wrong basis.

Yet even as external evaluation is shown out the front door, it creeps in again through the back. For in a number of passages Seneca appeals to traditional, community-oriented, external modes of evaluation—i.e, to the everyday moral views of his Roman aristocratic audience—in the course of arguments that overtly deny the validity of precisely these views. I have already discussed several passages in which Seneca declares that *conscientia* is the only authoritative moral judge and is superior to any external judges. Yet in some passages where Seneca describes at greater length the superior authority of this internal judge, the imagery and metaphors he employs to articulate that authority are themselves drawn from the traditional mechanisms of external, community-oriented moral evaluation. In another passage of the *Exhortationes* quoted by Lactantius, Seneca claims that the eye of the omniscient Stoic divinity is upon everyone, and that even if one conceals an ill deed from all humans, it is nonetheless visible to this god (*Inst.* 6.24.11–12). He

---

[34] *Ep.* 99.16: *permittamus illis* [sc. *lacrimis*] *cadere, non imperemus; fluat quantum adfectus eiecerit, non quantum poscet imitatio. nihil vero maerori adiciamus nec illum ad alienum augeamus exemplum.* . . . (§17) *sequitur nos, ut in aliis rebus, ita in hac quoque hoc vitium, ad plurium exempla componi nec quid oporteat sed quid soleat aspicere. a natura discedimus, populo nos damus nullius rei bono auctori.* . . . (§18) *omnia itaque ad rationem revocanda sunt. stultius vero nihil est quam famam captare tristitiae.* Similarly, see *Tranq.* 15.6.

[35] *Ep.* 94.69: *ubi testis ac spectator abscessit, vitia subsidunt, quorum monstrari et conspici fructus est.* See also *Ben.* 6.43.3: *opinionem quidem et famam eo loco habeamus tamquam non ducere sed sequi debeat.* Similarly, Martial 1.33, Plut. *Mor.* 528A–B.

then declares, "for it does no good that one's moral self-knowledge is secret: we lie open to god" (*nam nihil prodest inclusam esse conscientiam: patemus deo*, = fr. 24 Haase). It is reasonable for Seneca to picture this divinity as having access to one's mental states, since Stoic dogma holds that adult humans partake in rationality along with god, and that the human mind is a piece of the rational divine principle of the universe (see section 2 above). Nevertheless, the divinity is presented here as external to oneself, like any human judge from within the civic community. This is a significant choice: for Seneca might simply have said, as he does in the passages discussed in the previous paragraph, that *conscientia*, which as a part of our mental makeup partakes of universal rationality, *is* our judge—thus representing the divinity as an internal, rather than external, principle. This presentation of the judging function of *deus* in terms of the human community's judging function is still clearer in *De Vita Beata* 20.5, where Seneca systematically maps the pillars of Stoic ethics onto the institutionalized vectors of traditional Roman ethics: "may I know that the universe is my fatherland and the gods are my guardians, and that they stand above and around me as censors of my deeds and words" (*patriam meam esse mundum sciam et praesides deos, hos supra me circaque me stare factorum dictorumque censores*). Seneca here models his moral universe as the fatherland, with the gods in the role of censors—traditionally the most authoritative judges and defenders of the community's morals. As such they stand "above" Seneca, but also "around" him, scrutinizing him like a judging audience composed of community members.

Similarly, Seneca's Stoic articulation of the well-lived or badly lived life draws upon the traditional ethical assumption that morally valued action welcomes, even demands, external witnesses to judge it accordingly, while agents who act viciously may seek to avoid witnesses, lest they be judged negatively. An example showing the place of this assumption in traditional ethics can be found in Velleius Paterculus (2.14.2). Following his account of the tribunate and death of Livius Drusus, whom he characterizes as "a man most noble, eloquent, and hallowed" (*vir nobilissimus eloquentissimus sanctissimus*, 2.13.1), Velleius describes an exchange between Livius and an architect whom he has retained to build him a house. The architect says that he can make the house intensely private, so that nothing within is open to external scrutiny and judgment: *ita se eam aedificaturum ut liber a conspectu immunisque ab omnibus arbitris esset neque quisquam in eam despicere posset*. Livius replies that he would prefer a house in which all his actions are visible to the public: *siquid in te artis est, ita compone domum meam ut quidquid agam ab omnibus perspici potest*. This, says Velleius, is proof of his good morals (*argumentum morum*, 2.14.3). Along the same lines, at *Ep.* 43.5 Seneca asserts that one who lives an upright life should welcome the public scrutiny that the morally vicious person shuns: "a good conscience summons a crowd, but a bad one is anxious and worried even when alone. If what you do is honorable, let everyone know; if shameful, what does it matter that no one knows, when you know?" (*bona conscientia turbam advocat, mala etiam in solitudine anxia atque sollicita est. si honesta sunt quae facis, omnes sciant; si turpia quid refert neminem scire cum tu scias? Ep.* 43.5; cf. 97.12–13, *Ben.* 7.1.7, fr. 14 Haase). But on Seneca's own account the presence or absence of witnesses to one's actions should be beside the point, for actions do not reliably exteriorize internal moral states such that observers can infer the latter from the former; besides, "the many," who by definition value externals, are poor moral judges and cannot be relied upon to praise virtue and blame vice even if they are witnesses to it.[36] These contradictory elements in Seneca's position regarding external judgment come together most jarringly in *De Vita Beata* 20.4, a passage in which the man striving for virtue enumerates the ideals he embraces. Among these is the following: "I will do nothing by reason of *opinio*, everything by reason of my moral self-knowledge. Whatever I do to which I alone am privy, I will regard as done under public scrutiny" (*nihil opinionis causa, omnia conscientiae faciam. populo spectante fieri credam quidquid me conscio faciam*). The first sentence here makes the familiar Senecan claim that the good man employs his moral self-awareness as his only ethical guide and rejects the ethical views of misguided external judges. The second sentence asserts that the good man's moral self-awareness discharges precisely the same judging function as external judges would provide. Thus, it seems, Seneca invokes the authority of external moral evaluation to support his assertion that external moral evaluation has no authority.[37]

Again, what do we make of such passages? For whether Seneca invokes the Stoic deity as a witness of one's moral state using metaphors that are derived from the civic community, or whether he invokes members of the civic community itself as witnesses of one's moral state, in either case the appeal is implicated in traditional external evaluation, while the moral state that is being submitted for approval is precisely the view that the external mode of evaluation should be rejected. One possible approach is to argue that, in these passages, Seneca's project collapses into incoherence; that he is unable to maintain a rigorous sep-

---

[36] On the relationship between one's "internal judge" and actual external judges, see ch. 1 n. 10 above.

[37] Cf. *Ben.* 7.1.7, a description of the virtuous man, for a similar apparent circularity: *conscientiam suam dis aperuit semperque tamquam in publico vivit se magis veritus quam alios.*

aration between the Stoic ethical views he advocates and the traditional, community-oriented ethics he ostensibly rejects. Indeed, Seneca can be shown in other respects to undermine stated positions with the rhetoric of those statements: as Habinek 1992: 202–203 demonstrates, the rhetorical strategies by which Seneca argues that philosophy is available to everyone, regardless of status or origin, are themselves elitist in privileging certain kinds of origins, and in this respect undermine the very point in support of which they are adduced.[38]

In this case, however, I would not wish to maintain that Seneca somehow loses control of the distinction between Stoic and traditional ethics, given the number of passages in which he articulates this distinction forcefully and maintains it rigorously. Indeed, in several of the passages in which this distinction seems to collapse—especially *De Vita Beata* 20.5, where the Stoic cosmos is modeled as a *patria* and the gods as censors—the very systematicity of the mapping precludes any inadvertence on Seneca's part. Rather, I would appeal again to common conceptions and their foundational role in getting Stoic ethics off the ground. Thus one may see these passages as moments when Seneca, quite consciously, chooses to present the evaluative structures of Stoic ethics precisely *in terms of* the "commonsense" evaluative structures of traditional Roman ethics, which are familiar to and accepted by "the many." A passage like *De Vita Beata* 20.5 can then be regarded as a kind of translation, for it systematically lines up conceptions of community, moral authority, and the process of judging in the two systems for comparison. Stoic ethical principles are translated into the more-or-less corresponding traditional principles, even as the former are privileged over the latter. Even in *De Vita Beata* 20.4 (discussed above: "I will do nothing by reason of *opinio*, everything by reason of my moral self-knowledge. Whatever I do to which I alone am privy, I will regard as done under public scrutiny"), one can choose to see not a jarring incoherence or circularity in Seneca's argumentation, but rather a compressed, elliptical expression of the mapping spelled out in a more leisurely fashion elsewhere (e.g., in §20.5, just a few lines below). An aphorism quoted by Quintilian, *conscientia mille testes* ("moral self-knowledge equals a thousand witnesses," *Inst.* 5.11.41), may also lend support to this interpretation. For while this aphorism has no context— it may or may not be necessary to infer a philosophical one such as we find in Seneca—it evidently expresses in a highly compressed fashion

---

[38] On this rhetorical strategy in Seneca, see chapter 4.6 below. Habinek 1992: 191 also suggests (following Edward Said) that new beginnings, inevitably and necessarily, are fashioned out of elements that they purport to supersede or overturn.

the internal judging mechanism in terms of the external one and marks the internal one as more authoritative.

5. THE PROBLEM OF EXEMPLA

Seneca's rejection of traditional, external moral evaluation also calls into question that most familiar and ubiquitous form of Roman moral argumentation, the use of exempla.[39] For if external evaluation is suspect, then the ethical status of exemplarity—the presentation of historical figures as positive or negative models for action—also becomes uncertain. How can figures from the past, any more than one's contemporaries, be praised and blamed as moral agents on the basis of their observed and recorded actions, if such actions are not a reliable guide to the internal dispositions in which alone moral value resides?

To illuminate some of the difficulties raised by Seneca regarding the moral interpretation of historical exempla, I turn first to a letter (*Ep.* 94) in which he claims to reevaluate a group of famous *imperatores*—successful generals whom, he asserts, people praise as *magni* and *felices* ("great" and "happy," §60). The first two commanders he discusses are Alexander and Pompey, each of whom is commonly called "the great" (§§62–65); he concludes with Julius Caesar and Gaius Marius (§§65–66).[40] Essentially, Seneca denies that the military success experienced by these four generals is the product of *virtus* (§§64, 66), and attributes it instead to *ambitio, cupiditas, crudelitas,* and *furor* ("ambition," "greed," "bloodthirstiness," "frenzy," §§61, 62, 65, 66), vices that he suggests drove on and subjected these men just as mercilessly as they themselves subjected other peoples. In a lengthy discussion of Alexander (§§62–63), he points to a perversity of action ("he snatched away what was best from each people: he bid the Spartans to be slaves, and the Athenians to be silent") and a general superfluity or transgressiveness ("he surrounded the whole world with arms . . . cruelty in the manner of giant beasts, which bite more than hunger requires . . . he goes beyond the ocean and the sun . . . he does violence to nature itself") to support the argument that his military successes correlate with vice, not virtue. He even provides an invidious interpretation of Pompey's hon-

---

[39] The significance of historical exempla in Roman ethical argumentation hardly needs illustration, but for an explict assertion of its importance, see Quint. *Inst.* 12.2.29–31 (cf. 12.2.23–28).

[40] While the canonical *felix*, Sulla, is missing here, Seneca calls Alexander *infelix* (unhappy) because a *furor aliena vastandi* drove him on. Seneca also links Alexander's unhappiness with his greatness (*magnitudo*) at *Ep.* 91.17: he is *infelix* because, upon learning the true size of the world, he realizes how small his empire really is, hence perceives his cognomen *magnus* to be false.

orific cognomen *magnus*, "the great": he declares it an index of Pompey's mad ambition rather than a measurement of the value of his services to the state (§64: "insane love for false greatness" [*insanus amor magnitudinis falsae*]; §65: "unbounded lust for growing larger, when only to himself did he seem insufficiently 'great'" [*infinita . . . cupido crescendi, cum sibi uni parum magnus videretur*]; cf. *Brev.* 13.7). By asserting that these commanders' demonstrated martial prowess is actually a manifestation of vices within, he at a stroke converts a ground for praise (according to traditional ethics) into a ground for blame, and positive exemplarity into negative exemplarity.

At the same time, Seneca implies that the key moral category *virtus* should now no longer be understood to refer to martial valor visibly displayed, but rather to a mental disposition. This implication is particularly clear in the description of Marius. In §66 he writes, "Do you suppose that when Gaius Marius slaughtered the Teutoni and Cimbri, when he hounded Jugurtha through the deserts of Africa, he pursued such dangers at the prodding of *virtus*? Marius commanded his army, ambition commanded Marius" (*quid tu C. Marium . . . cum Teutonos Cimbrosque concideret, cum Iugurtham per Africae deserta sequeretur, tot pericula putas adpetisse virtutis instinctu? Marius exercitus, Marium ambitio ducebat*). In posing this question, Seneca purports to challenge his interlocutor's mode of ethical understanding by giving him grounds for answering "yes": for in traditional Roman ethics, spectacular military success of the sort that Marius achieved is precisely what constitutes *virtus* (see ch. 1.2 above). But then Seneca implicitly answers "no" to his own question (thus correcting the interlocutor's presumed "yes") by invoking the vice *ambitio*. Indeed, by opposing *ambitio* to *virtus* Seneca makes it possible to understand *virtus* as now referring to philosophical virtue, the umbrella term that stands in opposition to vice generally.[41] Finally, wrapping up his discussion of these *imperatores*, Seneca claims a general validity for the kind of reanalysis he practices upon these four specific exempla (§68): "all these exempla that are stuffed into our eyes and ears must be unwoven, and our breast, which is full of evil speech, must be emptied of it" (*omnia ista exempla quae oculis atque auribus nostris ingeruntur retexenda sunt, et plenum malis sermonibus pectus exhauriendum*). As he does in his treatment of gratitude (section 4 above), then, here too Seneca rejects the idea that moral value

---

[41] On this passage Bellincioni 1979: 213 writes, "*virtus* è da intendere qui naturalmente non nel senso romano, ma filosofico." This is true—at the end. But Seneca's point is precisely to make *virtus* slip from the traditional to the philosophical conceptualization. For the social stakes of this reconceptualization of *virtus*, see section 6 below. On *virtus* as a philosophical umbrella term, see chapter 1.2 above.

resides in the recorded or observed actions of agents and locates it instead in their mental dispositions.

Now, one might object that Seneca simply replaces one set of a priori assumptions about the relationship between moral value and action in the public eye (that military success carries positive moral value) with another set of a priori assumptions (that it carries negative moral value, since it manifests vicious mental states); therefore his transformation of the famous generals from positive to negative exempla lacks persuasive force. But there is a further element in Seneca's argument here, as his lengthy discussion of Alexander shows. For to corroborate his claim that vices (not virtue) drove Alexander to world conquest, Seneca adduces a variety of other actions—forcing the Athenians to be silent, going beyond the bounds of nature—that suggest unsound mental states (". . . or do you think a man is sane who . . .", §62). Here Seneca is drawing upon a well-established tradition that Alexander, in addition to being a military genius, was often cruel, ungrateful, drunk, inadequately loyal to his native Macedonian traditions, and otherwise culturally transgressive. Indeed, Seneca misrepresents received ethical opinion on Alexander by attributing to his interlocutor the simple view that Alexander is praiseworthy because of his military success: this neglects the other side of received opinion, that Alexander is blameworthy in other respects. Yet the success of Seneca's argument actually depends upon the true ethical complexity of this figure. For unless his readers already accept that there are grounds for morally condemning Alexander, Seneca's contention that he should indeed be condemned would probably fall flat; it would seem arbitrary and unfounded. Thus Seneca is arguing that the one basis on which Alexander is conventionally praised, namely his military valor, is but a part of a broader, more comprehensive pattern of blameworthy actions—i.e., actions from which one can more readily infer a vicious disposition than a virtuous one. These same observations also hold for Seneca's treatment of Marius, Pompey, and Caesar. While he does not provide detailed descriptions of these generals' blameworthy behavior, all three, like Alexander, are ethically complicated figures in the received historical tradition, their laudable military successes tempered by blameworthy displays of cruelty, lust for power, and the like. In these cases too, Seneca requires his audience to supply, out of its preexisting knowledge, a pattern of blameworthy action into which to fit the proposed devaluation of these generals' military successes. Again, then, the position that Seneca attributes to his interlocutor, that these figures are simply praiseworthy for their military success, is only a partial image of the received tradition regarding these figures; indeed, Seneca's own argument presupposes that the tradition is more complex.

Seneca's argument here also has an implicitly philosophical dimension, which requires a brief look at the technicalities of the Stoic concept of the "proper function" (Greek καθῆκον, Latin *officium*). In Stoic ethics, "proper functions" are activities conforming to a creature's natural constitution; for adult humans, who partake of rationality, they are activities for which a rational justification can be given.[42] Like the "indifferents" discussed above (section 2), proper functions admit of degrees, designated "intermediate" (that is, *merely* in conformity with nature) unless they are modified by an adverb indicating that the agent has a virtuous or vicious disposition. If modified by an adverb indicating virtue, the proper function becomes a "perfect proper function" or "right action" (Greek κατόρθωμα, Latin *recte factum* or *perfectum officium*), done in accordance with "right reason." Since perfect proper functions require virtue, they can be done only by the wise man, who alone has full and comprehensive knowledge of what must be done in every circumstance and why.[43] An action that is less than perfect (i.e., every action done in the real world) may either fail to be a proper function, or may be a proper function that lacks "right reason."[44] Now, Roman Stoicism often articulates proper functions with reference to the agent's social roles. It has long been recognized (e.g., Brunt 1975: 15) that translating καθῆκον as *officium* facilitates this connection, since *officium* is commonly used of the duties incumbent upon a magistrate, senator, etc. In the first book of his *De Officiis* Cicero discusses at length the behavior appropriate to a variety of social roles—not only aristocratic public offices, but also various kinship relations, friendships, and different stages of life.[45] Cicero's contemporary, Marcus Brutus, is also attested (Sen. *Ep.* 95.45) as having written a treatise entitled "On Proper Function," giving advice on the behavior appropriate to parents, children, and brothers. Two generations after Seneca,

---

[42] Conformity with natural constitution: LS I 365 (citing a number of passages). Rational justification: Diog. Laert. 7.107, Stob. 2.85–86 WH (= LS 59B), Cic. *Fin.* 3.58; discussion by Tsekourakis 1974: 25–30, Engberg-Pedersen 1990: 133–36.

[43] "Intermediate" and "perfect" proper functions: Cic. *Fin.* 3.58–59, with discussions by LS I 365–67, II 359; Engberg-Pedersen 1990: 132–36. For example, "walking about" is said to be a (sc. intermediate) proper function under most circumstances (Diog. Laert. 7.109 = LS 59E): presumably it accords with our nature as two-legged creatures, and often admits of rational justification. But "walking about prudently"—i.e., in a manner conditioned by the cardinal virtue "prudence"—is a perfect proper function (Stob. 2.96–97 WH = LS 59M).

[44] On perfect vs. less-than-perfect actions, see LS I 367 (also Long 1996 [1983]: 168–69), Engberg-Pedersen 1990: 134–36.

[45] Cic. *Off.* 1.32, 53–56, 122–25, 149. See also 1.107–118 on the four *personae* that make up what each individual is; the third and fourth of these pertain to one's social roles. Long 1996 [1983]: 164–66 discusses the connections between this passage and the Stoic theory of proper functions.

Epictetus examines the duties demanded by one's familial and civic roles.[46] While no systematic discussion of the duties associated with particular social roles survives in the Senecan corpus, Seneca does nevertheless address such matters in his ethical prose, considering for instance whether, and how, a slave can benefit his master (*Ben.* 3.18–28) or an aristocrat his ruler (e.g., *Ben.* 6.29–34; *Ira* 3.14–15: see sec. 7 below).

The Stoic doctrine of proper functions creates a potential difficulty for Seneca's revaluation of the four generals in *Ep.* 94. For it might be argued that the military functions discharged by kings, consuls, and dictators are among the duties incumbent upon these social roles, wherefore the actions of these generals may admit of rational justification, the key criterion for the proper function. Moreover, to do proper functions consistently is an essential element in the progression toward wisdom and happiness.[47] These generals' actions qua generals, however, are wrong not necessarily on the criterion of omitting a proper function, but on the criterion that their dispositions are vice-ridden, as evidenced by their behavior in other contexts. For even if they act appropriately in this one sphere, they do not in others, and so lack the consistency that marks the virtuous disposition; they are far indeed from doing truly praiseworthy "right actions." Once again, what is morally significant is not any specific action in itself, but the disposition of the agent.

The problem of assessing an agent's moral state on the basis of (potentially misleading) observable actions and other signs receives a more thorough discussion in *Ep.* 120.[48] Near the beginning of this letter, Seneca trots out a pair of hoary *exempla virtutis:* the incorruptible Fabricius who refused Pyrrhus's gold, and then alerted him to a poisoning plot; and the valiant Horatius Cocles, who secured his comrades' retreat by defending a bridge alone until it collapsed around him, and then swam ashore triumphantly (§§6–7). Here Seneca is not presenting these figures and their actions to his readers for emulation, for their actions per se are not to the point in this letter. Rather, he is concerned with how internal moral qualities are inferred from external actions and ap-

---

[46] E.g., *Diss.* 2.10 passim (see Long 1996 [1983]: 162–64); *Ench.* 30; also Brunt 1975: 12–14, with his valuable collection of passages at 32–35, and Bonhöfer 1894: 90–97.

[47] On discharging the duties incumbent upon generals, see Cic. *Off.* 1.144; Epict. *Diss.* 3.24.99, *Ench.* 30. Engberg-Pedersen 1990: 138–40 gives an account of the complex way in which progressing toward wisdom is related to the ever more complete and consistent execution of proper functions; also LS I 366–68.

[48] Lengthy selections of this important letter are quoted by LS (60E) in regard to "good" and "bad" in Stoicism; they also cite it regarding proper functions at I 367. Yet they omit from their quotation, and consequently do not discuss, the exempla of Fabricius and Horatius, which are integral to Seneca's argument. Thus they cloak the dialogical character of Seneca's discussion—its engagement with the common conceptions of the intended audience, hence its essential Romanness.

pearances. Fabricius and Horatius, being well-known exempla with pat, established moral interpretations, serve as typical instances of the standard mode of inferring moral value — that is, they are adduced here as examples of traditional exempla. What is this standard mode of inference? Originally, Seneca says — for he frames his explanation as an historical evolution — moral value was inferred "by analogy" (*conlatio, analogia*) from the condition of the body and the quality of its actions. Bodily health and strength, which are evident to the eye, authorized observers to infer mental health and strength (§§4–5). Through their actions, then, figures like Fabricius and Horatius allowed observers to form a "picture of virtue" (*haec et eiusmodi facta imaginem nobis ostendere virtutis*, §8).[49]

As in the earlier letter, however, here too Seneca identifies shortcomings in this mode of inferring value. The brilliance of someone's deeds may conceal underlying vices (§5); and worse, vices may masquerade as virtues to which they are closely related, thus presenting a false appearance of the good (§§8–9).[50] These two assertions, bracketing the exempla of Fabricius and Horatius, seem to aim not at overturning the conventionally positive evaluations of these two figures, but rather at casting doubt upon the entire mode of judging instantiated by these conventionally positive evaluations. For again, the problem is not with the specific actions done, which may well admit of justification in Stoic terms as proper functions, but with inferring moral value on the basis of just one or two such deeds. As Seneca says in §9, "while we watched those whom an outstanding deed had made noteworthy, we began to mark who had done some deed with a lofty spirit and great vigor, but just once. We saw one man brave in war, but cowardly in the forum;

[49] That the conception of the good arises through analogy with things that are not good but resemble it in crucial respects, cf. Cic. *Fin.* 3.33–34 (= LS 60D: the mind first recognizes things that accord with nature, and "climbs up" from these to form a conception of the good); also Diog. Laert. 7.53 (= LS 39D), 91. See also LS's commentaries on these particular passages, and in general LS I 375, Brunt 1975: 12. For those who correctly understand the location of moral value, however, the analogy goes the other way. At *Ben.* 2.34.3–5 Seneca defines the virtue *fortitudo* as a state of mind or type of knowledge (*scientia* = τέχνη) — a philosophical definition — and says that when gladiators or slaves are called *fortes viri*, it is due to a "lack of words" (*inopia sermonis*), implying that this usage is an inexact metaphorical extension. He argues similarly that philosophical usages of *parsimonia* and *beneficium* are primary, and their common usages are secondary, inexact extensions. Cf. Inwood 1995: 261.

[50] *Ep.* 120.8–9: *mala interdum speciem honesti obtulere et optimum ex contrario enituit. sunt enim, ut scis, virtutibus vitia confinia, et perditis quoque ac turpibus recti similitudo est: sic mentitur prodigus liberalem, cum plurimum intersit utrum quis dare sciat an servare nesciat. . . . imitatur neglegentia facilitatem, temeritas fortitudinem. haec nos similitudo coegit adtendere et distinguere specie quidem vicina, re autem plurimum inter se dissidentia.* See also *Ep.* 95.43, 65.

enduring poverty with spirit, but ill repute abjectly: we praised the deed, but despised the man" (*dum observamus eos quos insignes egregium opus fecerat, coepimus adnotare quis rem aliquam generoso animo fecisset et magno impetu, sed semel. hunc vidimus in bello fortem, in foro timidum, animose paupertatem ferentem, humiliter infamiam: factum laudavimus, contempsimus virum*). One or a few admirable actions, then, or admirable actions in just one sphere of human enterprise, are not diagnostic of an agent's moral condition. For while proper functions are in the power of anyone, consistency is the mark of the wise man, the truly virtuous disposition. Specific actions must therefore be separated from moral character as objects of evaluation ("we praised the deed, but despised the man"). An accurate assessment of moral character requires that we observe a broad slice of the agent's life, to see if his actions are praiseworthy across the board.

Consequently, Seneca continues (§9), a new mode of evaluating has emerged, one that attends to consistency and patterns of behavior. In the wise man, the man in whom all moral virtues are present simultaneously, that pattern consists of moderation and good order consistently and invariably displayed at all times and under all circumstances. It is from this pattern, described in detail in §§10–13 and 18–19,[51] that external judges can infer that perfect virtue resides within (*intelleximus in illo perfectam esse virtutem*, §10), whereas prior judging audiences misperceived moral value because they inferred it on the basis of just a few praiseworthy deeds (§5: *aliqua benigna facta, aliqua humana, aliqua fortia nos obstupefecerant: haec coepimus tamquam perfecta mirari*). Conversely, as Seneca argues elsewhere, the failure to display this consistent pattern authorizes a judging audience to infer the presence of vices. We have already seen such an argument in his revaluation of Alexander, where he invokes a broad pattern of blameworthy behavior as the proper ethical context for interpreting Alexander's military successes (which thus become manifestations of vice, not virtues). Likewise in *Ep.* 114.4–8 Seneca explores in detail the relationship of poetic and oratorical style to the moral qualities of the poet/orator. He uses Maecenas as an exemplum, contending that the latter's stylistic vices, together with

[51] Part of this description of the *vir bonus* is as follows (*Ep.* 120.11–12): *ex quo ergo virtutem intelleximus? ostendit illam nobis ordo eius et decor et constantia et omnium inter se actionum concordia et magnitudo super omnia efferens sese. hinc intellecta est illa beata vita secundo defluens cursu, arbitrii sui tota. quomodo ergo hoc ipsum nobis apparuit? dicam. numquam vir ille perfectus adeptusque virtutem fortunae maledixit, numquam accidentia tristis excepit . . . quicquid inciderat non tamquam malum aspernatus est et in se casu delatum, sed quasi delegatum sibi.* Other Senecan *descriptiones* of good men and their bearing occur at *Ep.* 95.65–73, 104.27–34; *Const.* passim. The consistency of virtue, hence of the virtuous man, is a philosophical commonplace; see LS I 383 for further references and discussion.

his eccentric dress and behavior, reveal dubious *mores* (§§6–7). Other aspects of one's external bearing can also reveal one's internal states. In *De Ira* 2.35–36, Seneca describes the unattractive physical appearance of an angry person, from which he infers that the soul within is even more unattractive and vice-ridden.[52]

In providing these detailed descriptions of the behavior patterns that signify moral value, Seneca implies that his audience — the aristocratic community at large — can be trained to analogize properly, to infer moral value correctly. Elsewhere too he suggests that this new ethical system can be inculcated into a broad audience. In *De Ira* 3.41.2, Seneca's interlocutor points out that a man who displays consistent and moderate behavior, and who therefore is praised as *placidus* ("calm," "tranquil") according to Seneca's ethical standards, is condemned by the crowd (i.e., on a traditional ethical standard) as *iners* ("feeble"), for the crowd, he says, confers positive value on bold people whose actions are spirited. Seneca concedes that most people will judge the calm, tranquil man negatively "on first sight" (*primo aspectu*), yet he predicts that they will come to recognize this man's positive moral value, and will then praise him as Seneca does.[53] Toward the end of *Ep.* 94 Seneca describes the form that the necessary training could take. Here he suggests two ways in which a person can root out his vices: one way is to isolate himself, thus avoiding the temptation to engage in mutual external evaluation and cleave to community standards of behavior (§§69–71; cf. *Ep.* 104.20–21). But if such isolation is impossible, an alternative is to engage someone, alternatively called an *advocatus* (§§52, 59), *custos* (§55), and *monitor* (§§8, 10, 72) ("counsellor," "guardian," "advisor"), who will ceaselessly remind one how to evaluate correctly what one sees: "Therefore, if we are placed in the middle of the tumult

---

[52] *Ep.* 95.65–66 also refers briefly to a process, designated *ethologia* or *characterismos*, that describes the external marks of each interior virtue and vice, and enables an external judge to distinguish between the virtues and vices that resemble one another. According to Plutarch (*Mor.* 1042E–F), Chrysippus too asserted that peoples' mental states were perceptible to external observers. On what the souls of tyrants look like, see Tac. *Ann.* 6.6, Plato *Gorgias* 524E. Graver 1998: 607–14 examines Seneca's characterization of Maecenas in detail, showing that Seneca has virtually a physiognomic view of prose style: stylistic features, like aspects of demeanor and appearance, offer insight into the condition of the author's soul.

[53] *Ira* 3.41.2: "*at vulgus animosa miratur et audaces in honore sunt, placidi pro inertibus habentur.*" *primo forsitan aspectu; sed simul aequalitas vitae fidem fecit non segnitiem illam animi esse sed pacem, veneratur illos populus idem colitque.* Similarly, at *Ep.* 79.13–15 Seneca asserts that *gloria*, the public recognition of one's virtue, is the "shadow" of virtue and, like any shadow, sometimes precedes and sometimes follows the object that casts it (cf. *Ben.* 6.43.3). He then adduces *exempla* of men whose *gloria* came late or even after death. But in each case it did come eventually — further evidence that the *vulgus* can learn to recognize the marks of inherent virtue.

of cities, let an advisor stand at our side and, against those who praise enormous estates, let him praise the person who is weathy with little and measures riches by their utility. Against those who extol influence and power, let him esteem leisure given over to literature and the spirit that is turned back from externals to its own things" (*itaque si in medio urbium fremitu conlocati sumus, stet ad latus monitor et contra laudatores ingentium patrimoniorum laudet parvo divitem et usu opes metientem. contra illos qui gratiam ac potentiam attollunt otium ipse suspiciat traditum litteris et animum ab externis ad sua reversum*, §§72–74; cf. §§50, 55, 59–60). This advisor, then, would praise the person who despises externals, as the advisor himself presumably does (e.g., §59), and would thereby counter the moral valuation of externals by those who engage in traditional ethical discourse.[54]

Instances of Seneca himself playing this role of moral instructor—of evaluating certain men as good or as bad against the opinion of a crowd believing the opposite—occur throughout his ethical prose. He presents his revaluation of the four generals in *Ep.* 94.60–67 as precisely such an instance. Similarly, in the *Consolatio ad Helviam* he adduces three exempla of good men who may be thought to have suffered disgrace or harm at the hands of their fellow-citizens (13.4–8). The first of these is Socrates. The sentence imposed upon Socrates, if read in the framework of traditional ethics, signifies the community's negative evaluation of his actions ("corrupting the youth"), which it regards as contrary to its interests; his imprisonment and death sentence reify that negative judgment. But Seneca insists that, on the contrary, his presence dissipates the prison's power to stigmatize at all: "Socrates entered the prison with that very expression by which he had once, by himself, brought thirty tyrants back into line, intending to remove the disgrace from the place itself; for if Socrates was in the place, it could not seem a prison" (*Socrates tamen eodem illo vultu quo triginta tyrannos solus aliquando in ordinem redegerat carcerem intravit, ignominiam ipsi loco detracturus; neque enim poterat carcer videri in quo Socrates erat, Helv.* 13.4).[55] The second exemplum is the younger Cato, whose electoral defeats, Seneca says, confer *ignominia* on the offices themselves, rather than on Cato (*Helv.* 13.5); third, Aristides' sharp reply to a man who spat upon him amounts to "insulting insult itself" (*hoc fuit contumeliam ipsi contu-*

---

[54] The idea that one's rationality can be perverted by keeping bad company or by the attraction of externals (τὰ ἔξωθεν πραγματεία) is articulated in a Stoic context at least as early as Chrysippus: Diog. Laert. 7.89.

[55] Socrates is also said to confer positive value upon the prison (or at least to remove its ability to confer negative value upon him) at *Vit.* 27.1 and *Ep.* 24.4. For the same idea in declamation, see Sen. *Cont.* 9.1.10 on Miltiades' imprisonment: *nullus tunc erat locus Athenis honestior quam qui Miltiaden habuerat* (cf. *Cont.* 9.1.12–13).

meliae facere). Elsewhere in the same essay, Seneca insists that Marcellus's departure for Mytilene after Caesar's victory at Pharsalus could indeed be termed "exile"—for all those in Rome who thereafter had to do without Marcellus (*Helv.* 9.4–6).[56] Now, we have seen that in Senecan Stoicism imprisonment, death, exile, electoral defeat, and the like are "externals" which carry no moral value in and of themselves (cf. *Prov.* 3.4–14). Socrates and the others incur no (moral) harm from the *incommoda* that they experience. On the contrary, Seneca in each case makes the stigmatizing mark of the community's negative judgment redound upon the judges and stigmatize *them* instead. In these cases Seneca probably has no hard sell, for he draws on a preexisting historical and rhetorical tradition in which Socrates, Aristides, and Cato are generally represented as good men who were victims of injustice. Thus Seneca's implied audience is already predisposed to accept his argument. But to give these cases a philosophical twist—declaring that these men suffer no harm, but their judges do—is a crucial move rhetorically and pedagogically, for it brings home to his audience the importance of learning for themselves the proper way to judge, lest they too suffer harm from misrecognizing and misjudging the (true) moral value that resides in others. By overtly playing the role of moral advisor in these examples, Seneca carries out precisely the pedagogical program that he advocates throughout his ethical prose.

6. Ethics in Julio-Claudian Society: Military Glory and Senecan *virtus*

In the discussion above, I have shown some of the ways in which Seneca causes Stoic ethics to engage and critique traditional Roman ethics, particularly in problematizing received ideas about the nature and location of moral value and the process of evaluating others. I turn now from the "how" of this engagement to the "why." To reiterate the view expressed in the Introduction and in chapter 1.1 above, I believe that scholars who have sought to understand conceptual change in various societies by linking it with political change have gained interesting and compelling results. As in chapter 1.7, then, so here I will seek to identify some distinctive social and ideological features of the Julio-Claudian principate that can be linked to Senecan ethical stances discussed so far

---

[56] Along the same lines, see *Tranq.* 17.9: *Catoni ebrietas obiecta est: facilius efficiet, quisquis obiecit, crimen honestum quam turpem Catonem.* This trope can be found elsewhere too in Julio-Claudian prose, e.g., Val. Max 7.5.6: *ergo, si vere aestimare volumus, non Catoni tunc praetura sed praeturae Cato negatus est.* Similarly Dio 37.26.1–2: those who banished Cicero are exiles, while Cicero creates his own *patria* wherever he goes.

in this chapter. Now, to seek such links is not to deny that Seneca is also working in a well-defined philosophical tradition; I have already indicated his relationship with that tradition in number of respects. It is a tradition, moreover, whose own rules and boundaries give it a degree of autonomy from the social realities of the specific societies in which it was practiced: thus Seneca and Chrysippus are both recognizably Stoics, despite living in radically different societies some three centuries apart. Nevertheless, I believe that the particular philosophical problems within this tradition upon which Seneca dwells, as well as his manner of articulating these problems and presenting them to his readership, are intimately connected to the particular social and ideological configurations of the culture—Julio-Claudian aristocratic culture—that he and his audience inhabit. My aim in this section and the next is to demonstrate two such connections.

A very broad application of this approach already can be found in classical scholarship. It has long been asserted that the first two centuries of the Roman principate witnessed an intensified engagement with Stoicism by the ruling elite. Brent Shaw, in an article entitled "The Divine Economy: Stoicism as Ideology," draws parallels between this Roman cultural phenomenon and the emergence of Stoic philosophy in the Hellenistic world in the late fourth and early third centuries B.C. He contends that, in both Hellenistic and Roman imperial society, Stoicism served as an ideology underpinning an emergent monarchic political order; it provided the ruling elites in each society with "signposts on the road to the exercise of novel forms of political power and the social relations inherent in them."[57] Along the same lines, Michel Foucault identifies an emergent "individualism" and emphasis on "cultivation of the self" in Roman elite society of the first two centuries A.D., of which Stoicism was one manifestation. This phenomenon, he argues, is connected to the changed conditions for exercising power under the imperial regime.[58] Now, these arguments (as Shaw indicates) are closely connected to a similar set of arguments, advanced by an earlier generation of scholars, regarding the emergence of Hellenistic philosophies in the Greek world. This is the view that, once the successor kingdoms were established following the death of Alexander the Great, the civic institutions and activities of the *polis*, and the moral values associated with it, were devitalized and superseded. The various Hellenistic philosophical

---

[57] Shaw 1985: 23–30, 51–52; quotation from p. 52.

[58] Foucault 1986 [1984]: 41–43, 83–95. He argues that this self-cultivation by aristocrats is not so much an act of withdrawal from the political arena as a way to "define the principle of a relation to self that will make it possible to set the forms and conditions in which political action . . . will be possible or not possible, acceptable or necessary" (p. 86).

systems, including Stoicism, provided values appropriate to this new world of empires, specifically offering "compensation" or "consolation" to those who were politically and ethically disoriented by the eclipse of the *polis*.[59] This view, however, has not withstood closer scrutiny. For more detailed studies have shown that the *polis* remained the primary and vital focus of political and social life for most people in the Hellenistic period; the nature of the bond between city and citizen did indeed change, but was enhanced in certain respects even as it was undermined in others.[60] In the Roman context too, the broad explanatory frameworks of Shaw and Foucault will be confirmed, refuted, or nuanced only through finer-grained examinations of particulars. I examine two relevant particulars in this section and the next. I begin by pursuing Seneca's treatment of *exempla virtutis* (hence the content of the category *virtus* in Senecan ethics) in light of the changing conditions for achieving military glory in the Julio-Claudian period; I go on to examine the contemporary aristocracy's pervasive view that ethical discourse itself is subverted by flattery, especially in the vicinity of emperors. In each case, I suggest that Seneca presents Stoic ethics as offering solutions to these perceived problems. Moreover, I contend that Seneca's Stoic ethics does not merely attempt to adapt aristocratic ethics to new social realities; it also seeks actively to shape those realities to the advantage of the aristocracy.[61]

First, then, for aristocratic military activity in the Julio-Claudian period. A body of scholarship has argued convincingly that, as Augustus and his successors brought the military apparatus of the Roman state increasingly under their direct, personal control, the elites in general found decreasing opportunity for gaining glory and enhancing status through military achievement. For although those who directly commanded the troops—military tribunes and legionary commanders, primarily—were drawn from the ranks of the senators or equestrians (as they had always been), and although aristocrats commonly (though not inevitably or necessarily) held one or more such posts in the course of their public careers, nevertheless the military honors that were tradi-

---

[59] E.g., Adkins 1970: 213–16, 232–40; also Ferguson 1958: 135–37. This view has recently been reasserted by Bryant 1996: 427–65, esp. 450 and 455.

[60] Roisman 1997 (reviewing Bryant 1996), following his reference to Davies 1984: 304–20.

[61] My discussion here is not assisted by the body of scholarly work investigating the "Stoic (or Senecan) stance regarding the principate," e.g., Brunt 1975: 16–21, Griffin 1976: 202–21, 315–66: should the Stoic participate in politics? If so, under what conditions? These questions have to do with Stoic political theory, ideas of the best kind of constitution, and the like. In contrast, I here am formulating elements of a social history of imperial Stoicism: what are the social and historical circumstances that might have made Stoic ethics appealing to Julio-Claudian aristocrats in the first place?

100 CHAPTER 2

tionally highest and most prestigious were rapidly monopolized by the emperor himself and by members of the imperial family.[62] The last full-scale triumph celebrated by someone who was not a member of the imperial family occurred in 19 B.C., and the last such *ovatio* occurred in A.D. 47; the year A.D. 22 marked the last time that a nonmember of the imperial family was proclaimed *imperator* for a victory won while fighting under his own auspices; and only two such aristocrats under the empire received *cognomina* from the name of a conquered nation.[63] Now, other, less spectacular military honors, such as *ornamenta triumphalia* and statues in military dress, continued to be available through the Julio-Claudian period and beyond. Moreover, military achievement remained a source of prestige. For in addition to the public display entailed by the honors themselves, their attainment—and the victories they honored—were further celebrated, publicized, and transmitted to posterity in dedicatory inscriptions, and in the works of historiographers, biographers, and poets.[64] Thus one must not understate the importance of military achievement in aristocratic competition of the Julio-Claudian period. By the same token, one must not overstate its importance in the Republic: for while the social, economic, and political

---

[62] For a description of the senatorial career in the early empire, see Talbert 1984: 13–22. On the restriction of military honors generally, see Talbert 1984: 362–64, 425–30; Campbell 1984: 348–62.

[63] For the triumph of L. Cornelius Balbus in 19 B.C., attested only in the *Fasti Triumphales*, see Ehrenberg-Jones 1955: 36; also *Inscrr. Ital.* v. 13.1, pp. 86–87. For the *ovatio* of A. Plautius in A.D. 47, see Tac. *Ann.* 13.32, Suet. *Cl.* 24; for the proclamation of Q. Iunius Blaesus as *imperator* in A.D. 22, see Vell. Pat. 2.125.5, Tac. *Ann.* 3.74; on the *cognomina* of Lentulus Gaetulicus and P. Gabinius Secundus Cauchius (honors received in A.D. 6 and sometime in the reign of Claudius, respectively), see Vell. Pat. 2.116.2, Dio 55.28.4, Florus 2.31, Suet. *Cl.* 24. See also Talbert 1984: 362–64, Campbell 1984: 358–62.

[64] Dedicatory inscriptions detailing military achievements and honors received by senatorial aristocrats of the Julio-Claudian era include *ILS* 939 and 986. The former, as restored by Buecheler, celebrates the *virtus* of the dedicator and his father, both named L. Apronius Caesianus, in a campaign against the Gaetuli in A.D. 20: (*filius Aproni . . . effigiem . . . genitoris . . . locavit*) *armaque quae gessit: scuto [per volnera fracto] / quanta patet virtus! ens[is ab hoste rubet] / caedibus attritus, consummatque [hasta tropaeum] / qua cecidit [f]os[s]u[s] barbar[us ora ferus]* (ll. 15–18). By associating *virtus* with victory in battle, and by its concern to put evidence of this *virtus* before the public eye (*patet, tropaeum*), this inscription locates itself and the actions of its dedicand in the context of traditional Roman ethical discourse. Such achievements, of course, are also described in literary texts: note, for example, the historical tradition's highly positive portrayal of Domitius Corbulo, whose high standing and reputation was built mainly upon military success. Similarly, though beyond the end of our period, note Tacitus's celebration of Agricola's military success (e.g., *Ag.* 39–40; 39.2 claims superior prestige for military achievement over other, non-military aristocratic activities). See also Campbell 1984: 321–24, 352–53.

rewards that accrued to militarily successful aristocrats in the middle and late Republic have been well documented, it has also been shown that the failure to achieve this kind of success did not necessarily correspond to reduced prospects for success in public life; for example, defeated generals went on to hold higher magistracies at the same rates as other aristocrats.[65] Nevertheless, the traditionally highest honors were out of reach for most aristocrats by the middle of the Julio-Claudian period. They themselves perceived this and recognized that, consequently, their ability to enhance their status relative to other aristocrats (not to mention the *princeps*) by pursuing military glory was significantly curtailed. Velleius Paterculus writes that Marcus Aemilius Lepidus, thanks to his victories in Pannonia in the winter of A.D. 8/9, would have received a triumph had he fought under his own auspices; as it was, he received *ornamenta triumphalia* (2.115.3). While Velleius here seems not to be lamenting the unavailability of the higher honor, he nevertheless indicates an awareness of changed circumstances: he praises Lepidus by comparing his actual reward to the one he once would have had. Likewise, Domitius Corbulo is said (Tac. *Ann.* 11.20) to have lamented the diminished autonomy of military commanders under the Julio-Claudians—implying that they could no longer pursue glory for themselves as they once did.[66] Furthermore, numerous complaints are attested, in texts dating from or referring to the Julio-Claudian period, that still other traditional aristocratic status symbols—enrollment in the senate, the ornaments of various senatorial ranks, and even the lesser military honors—were cheapened by being dispensed prodigally and to the undeserving.[67]

Seneca's selection and deployment of *exempla virtutis*, I suggest, takes on particular significance in view of the reduced social stakes of military

---

[65] On the militaristic ethos of the middle-to-late republican aristocracy, including the interpenetration of military succes, political success, social standing, and moral value, see Harris 1979: 10–41; on the election rates of defeated generals, see Rosenstein 1990: 6–7 and passim.

[66] Tac. *Ann.* 11.20: Claudius orders Corbulo back across the Rhine; Corbulo obeys but exclaims, *beatos quondam duces Romanos!*—implying that in the good old days commanders had greater control over the prosecution of their campaigns. See also Tac. *Ag.* 40.1, dismissing as second rate the honors that Agricola received for his military exploits in Britain: *igitur triumphalia ornamenta et inlustris statuae honorem et quidquid pro triumpho datur . . . decerni in senatu iubet*. These honors are contrasted with Domitian's fraudulent triumph over the Germans, described at *Ag.* 39.1.

[67] On the devaluation of even the lesser military honors, see Campbell 1984: 351, 361 citing (e.g.) Tac. *Ann.* 4.23, 11.20; Dio 60.23.2. Also Suet. *Nero* 15.2. Complaints about the diminished honor of the senate when Caesar enrolled his allies: Dio 43.47.1, Sen. *Cont.* 7.3.9 (cf. Barton 1993: 156–57 and n. 61). Disapproval of the various honors—some military, some senatorial—that Claudius bestowed upon his freedmen: Suet. *Cl.* 28 (discussed in ch. 4.5 below).

achievement for early imperial aristocrats. For in characterizing the *virtus* of the figures he adduces as exemplary, Seneca commonly insists — in typical Stoic fashion — that the successful execution of military operations is irrelevant to "true" moral virtue, and hence is neither a necessary nor valuable end for aristocrats to pursue. We have already seen, in Seneca's revaluation of the four famous generals (*Ep.* 94.61–67, discussed in section 5 above), that these commanders are not credited with *virtus* on account of victories won, as his audience might suppose: rather, they are blamed for the vices that drove them to grasp for power at all costs, thus afflicting the world with war and suffering. We also saw that this argument depends partly upon repositioning the term *virtus* by rejecting the traditional frame of moral reference, with its emphasis on observed actions and external judging, and embracing instead a Stoic ethical framework in which moral value resides only in mental dispositions. In the preface to the third book of his *Naturales Quaestiones*, Seneca offers a similar interpretation of the military achievements of Philip, Alexander, and Hannibal. Here too these commanders are presented not as positive exempla on account of victories won, but as negative exempla for the scale of their murder and plundering.[68] As he says in §10, with a glance at Alexander, "what is the most important thing in human affairs? Not to have filled the seas with fleets, nor to have planted your standards on the shore of the red sea, nor, when the land has run out of things for you to harm, to have wandered over the ocean seeking things unknown: but rather to have seen everything with your mind and to have defeated your vices, the greatest victory of all" (*quid praecipuum in rebus humanis est? non classibus maria complesse nec in rubri maris litore signa fixisse nec deficiente ad iniurias terra errasse in oceano ignota quaerentem, sed animo omne vidisse et, qua maior nulla victoria est, vitia domuisse* . . .). This interpretation again calls into question any potential attribution of *virtus* to Alexander on account of his military success (which, as noted above, is part — but only part — of the traditional ethical position), by pointing to a broader set of transgressive and ruinous actions as indicative of the lurking vices, the vicious mental dispositions, that are the proper targets of one's aggression (the Stoic ethical position).

Elsewhere too, Seneca diminishes the worth of traditional Roman military valor relative to other kinds of achievement. In *Ep.* 67, a discussion of whether the brave endurance of torture or other afflictions can be a "good" (*bonum*), and is therefore "choiceworthy" (*optabilis*),

---

[68] E.g., *Nat.* 3 pr. 5: *quanto satius est sua mala extinguere quam aliena posteris tradere? quanto potius deorum opera celebrare quam Philippi aut Alexandri latrocinia ceterorumque qui exitio gentium clari non minores fuere pestes mortalium quam inundatio* . . . ?

he cites the Decii as men who, in particular circumstances, intentionally selected an evidently unpleasant course of action:

> Decius se pro re publica devovit et in medios hostes concitato equo mortem petens inruit. alter post hunc, paternae virtutis aemulus, conceptis sollemnibus ac iam familiaribus verbis in aciem confertissimam incucurrit, de hoc sollicitus tantum, ut litaret, optabilem rem putans bonam mortem. (*Ep.* 67.9)

> Decius offered himself as a sacrifice on behalf of the state and, having spurred his horse, went headlong into the midst of the enemy, seeking death. Another Decius after him, rivalling his father's *virtus*, having uttered the solemn and now kindred formula, ran headlong into the thickest part of the battle line, anxious only about constituting an acceptable offering, regarding a good death as something to be selected.

On this account, the Decii chose to offer themselves as sacrifices in battle (*devovit, litaret*) on behalf of the community (*pro re publica*), thus dying a "good death" (*bonam mortem*) and presenting themselves not only as examples of *virtus* to others but also, in the son's case, as an imitator of his father's example (*paternae virtutis aemulus*). Seneca's emphasis on their spectacular valor on behalf of the state seemingly locates them, and their *virtus*, in the traditional Roman ethical universe. But Stoic ethical concerns are also evident, for these *exempla* are framed as situations in which someone chooses to pursue something—here death—that, while in the regime of "indifferents," is contrary to nature (since humans have a natural impulse to self-preservation), hence is ordinarily "dispreferred." That right action sometimes involves selecting things that are ordinarily dispreferred is a familiar conundrum in Stoic ethics, and is in fact the topic of this very letter (*Ep.* 67).[69] In the continuation of the passage quoted, Seneca brings forward this philosophical dimension. He says, "do you doubt whether the best thing is to die memorably and in some work of *virtus*? When someone endures physical agony bravely, he uses all the *virtutes*" (*dubitas ergo an optimum sit memorabilem mori et in aliquo opere virtutis? cum aliquis tormenta fortiter patitur, omnibus virtutibus utitur*, §§9–10). He goes on to enumerate several specific *virtutes* that are evident when one endures torture: *fortitudo* (with its subsets *patientia, perpessio,* and *tolerantia*), *prudentia*, and *constantia* (§10).[70] Here again, then, Seneca interprets a

---

[69] On selecting dispreferred things, see the discussion in section 2 and nn. 9–10 above. In the current passage, *optabilis* appears to translate ἐκλεκτέος ("to-be-selected"), the usual term in Greek Stoic sources for how one normally views preferred indifferents (e.g., LS 58B, D; 64C6). Elsewhere in this letter, though (e.g., §§4–5), *optabilis* is also predicated of moral goods, and thus translates αἱρετός ("to-be-chosen") as well, the Greek term of art for how one should view moral goods.

[70] On the relationship between *virtus* and *fortitudo*, see Eisenhut 1972: 41–43.

traditional exemplum in a Stoic evaluative context, and the content of the term *virtus* shifts accordingly: the proper arena for exercising *virtus* is now not warfare, but the endurance of ill fortune. At the same time the exemplary quality of the Decii also shifts. For Seneca accepts that they are exemplary, but not for the reasons that his implied audience might think. Their *virtus* resides not in their valorous exploits in battle, but in choosing to suffer pain and death—the choice that preconditioned those exploits. Seneca then presents two further figures, Regulus and Cato, who by choice submitted themselves to excruciating pain: "don't you think that Regulus *chose* to pass into the hands of the Carthaginians? . . . gaze upon Marcus Cato, bringing his perfectly undefiled hands toward that hallowed breast of his, and opening up the wounds that were not deep enough" (*ita tu non putas Regulum optasse ut ad Poenos perveniret? . . . aspice M. Catonem sacro illi pectori purissimas manus admoventem et vulnera parum alte demissa laxantem*, §12–13, cf. §7). Cato and Regulus are authoritative here as *exempla virtutis* for the same reason as the Decii: at critical moments, they too realize that to choose something unpleasant/dispreferred may nevertheless be a moral good, and they choose accordingly.

The value of Cato and Regulus as *exempla virtutis*, however, goes beyond their mere embodiment of a Stoic understanding of *virtus*. A further, crucial aspect of their exemplarity is that these two figures directly contradict the traditional understanding of *virtus* as brilliant valor displayed in battle. For each suffered exemplary pain and death as an eventual consequence of suffering a catastrophic military reverse. In short, they are counterexamples to the traditional understanding: here, Seneca declares, are two figures who displayed *virtus* not just despite, but because of, their failure on the battlefield. Their inability to achieve their military aims (in contrast to the Decii, who did achieve their aims and therefore are rhetorically less effective, for Seneca's purposes) throws the question of their mental dispositions into the highest relief: thus Seneca celebrates Cato's military defeats on the ground that his endurance of them proves his (Stoic) *virtus*. Against overwhelming odds (*Ep.* 104.29–30; *Prov.* 3.14), he fought for the cause of *libertas*, never swerving in his aim despite suffering reverse after reverse (*tam infeliciter quam pertinaciter, Prov.* 3.14; cf. *Ep.* 104.30)—thus demonstrating the consistency of action and intention characteristic of the wise man. These repeated defeats were merely blows of *fortuna* that he successfully overcame (*Prov.* 2.9–10; *Epp.* 71.8–11, 104.29), and his failure to join battle himself earns praise on the ground that he did not defile his sword with the impious bloodshed of civil war (*Prov.* 2.10, *Epp.* 24.7, 67.13).[71] Still more striking as a celebration of military defeat is Seneca's

---

[71] On military defeat and *virtus* see also *Ben.* 5.3.2: *ideo nemo trecentos Fabios victos*

description of the death of Metellus Scipio (*Ep.* 24.9–10). On the brink of capture in Africa by the Caesarians, Scipio transfixes himself with his sword. His last words, to those inquiring where he is, are *imperator se bene habet* ("the general is well situated"). On this statement Seneca comments as follows (§10): "this utterance made him equal to his ancestors and did not permit that the glory destined for the Scipios in Africa be interrupted. It was a great deed to conquer Carthage, but a greater one to conquer death" (*vox haec illum parem maioribus fecit et fatalem Scipionibus in Africa gloriam non est interrumpi passa. multum fuit Carthaginem vincere, sed amplius mortem*). According to this judgment, Scipio rivals and even surpasses the glory of his two triumphal ancestors despite his utter military failure. He too is worthy of bearing the cognomen "Africanus," for his *virtus* in "conquering death" — that is, the fortitude, displayed in his dying words, with which he confronts death and endures his self-inflicted wound — surpasses theirs in conquering Carthage.[72]

A final exemplum of the same sort is Mucius Scaevola, as described in *Ep.* 24.5. Frustrated in his attempt to assassinate the enemy king Porsenna, he inflicts exemplary punishment upon himself by incinerating his right hand. Of this famous action, Seneca says, "you see a man neither learned nor supplied with any precepts against death or pain, but equipped only with a soldier's strength, exacting punishment from

---

dicit, sed occisos; et Regulus captus est a Poenis, non victus, et quisquis alius saevientis fortunae vi ac pondere oppressus non summittit animum. The point of these (apparent) paradoxes, again, is to emphasize both the moral insignificance of military outcomes per se, and the moral significance of the agents' mental dispositions.

[72] For similar praise of Scipio's death, see *Ep.* 70.22, Val. Max. 3.2.13; also Mayer 1991: 154–55. In contrast, see *Ep.* 71.10: . . . *et Scipionem in Africa nominis sui fortuna destituat* (i.e., he conspicuously fails to emulate his ancestors' glory). Note that Seneca again resorts to a traditional mode of acknowledging moral value in order to articulate the character of Stoic moral value: he assigns the honorific cognomen "Africanus", a traditional military honor, to Scipio to commemorate the (philosophical) *virtus* he manifests in defeat.

The "good death" is perhaps the only single action to which Seneca grants a priori exemplary force in its own right. As discussed above, he generally contends that single actions are not necessarily correlated to virtue and vice; only long-term patterns of action are diagnostic for the agent's moral condition. But often he implies that one's manner of facing death somehow balances the moral value of one's entire life as lived up to that point; that is, it has equal or even superior diagnostic value for one's moral condition. See e.g., *Ep.* 13.14: *fortasse . . . mors ista vitam honestabit. cicuta magnum Socratem fecit. Catoni gladium adsertorem libertatis extorque: magnam partem detraxeris gloriae* (cf. 71.16: *non est ergo M. Catonis maius bonum honesta vita quam mors honesta* . . .). Also 24.9 (on Scipio): *non fortes tantum viros hoc momentum efflandae animae contempsisse sed quosdam ad alia ignavos in hac re aequasse animum fortissimorum*; cf. *Ep.* 77.20, 82.12. The idea of the good death making up for a bad life is well attested elsewhere in imperial prose: Vell. Pat. 2.87.1 (of Antony), Plut. *Cato Minor* 73.2–3L (of Cato's son), Dio 64(63L).15.2a–2[2] (of Otho).

himself for his unsuccessful attempt" (*vides hominem non eruditum nec ullis praeceptis contra mortem aut dolorem subornatum, militari tantum robore instructum, poenas a se inriti conatus exigentem*). Seneca here marvels that Scaevola acted as he did without any philosophical training, when he was equipped merely with "a soldier's strength": for this, presumably, could scarcely be expected to generate so virtuous an action. Here again Seneca suggests that the tools that equip one to embody and manifest *virtus* are provided by philosophical training,[73] and not by military training, even as he concedes that Scaevola may be an exception to this principle. For *virtus*, again, consists not in the success or failure of a military undertaking, but in one's dispositions regardless of outcome—though, as always, the relevant states of mind are thrown into higher relief in the case of failure: as Seneca further says of Scaevola (§5), "he could have done something more successful in Porsenna's camp, but nothing more brave" (*facere aliquid in illis castris felicius potuit, nihil fortius*, cf. *Ben.* 7.15.2). Seneca's treatment of Scaevola, Cato, Regulus, Metellus Scipio, and even the Decii therefore not only illustrates the particular content with which the term *virtus* is invested by Seneca's Stoic ethics, but also pointedly emphasizes the irrelevance of military success per se—the traditional content of *virtus*.[74]

Here, then, is one significant cultural rupture that Seneca's deployment of *exempla virtutis* addresses. We have seen that the opportunities for winning high military honors—historically, an important route to enhanced prestige and standing for Roman aristocrats—were sharply reduced with the advent of the principate. By presenting an ethical system in which military achievement emphatically lacks moral significance, yet in which *virtus* is still attainable because it resides elsewhere, Seneca offers his audience a new set of ethical signposts to orient thought and action, new means by which aristocrats can pursue familiar

---

[73] This causal link is articulated elsewhere: see e.g., *Ep.* 24.6 for Cato armed with his sword and his Plato, and *Ep.* 89.8 for the mutually entailing relationship between *philosophia* and *virtus*. There may also be an implied contrast with Lucilius, whom Seneca in this letter urges to await with fortitude the potentially devastating verdict of a certain legal case (24.1–3). For Lucilius *is* fortified with philosophy: if Scaevola could do as he did without such fortification, the more easily can Lucilius.

[74] Busch 1961: 146–48 also discusses some of these *exempla*, arguing that *virtus* on Seneca's articulation belongs equally to deeds done in battle and to wisdom/proper states of mind. But I believe she overlooks the rhetorical strategies whereby Seneca privileges the latter sort of *virtus* over the former, even as the former serves as a model for the latter. Some of Seneca's favored *exempla virtutis*, however, enact and illustrate Stoic *virtus* without obviously contradicting traditional moral values. The brave suffering for which he praises Socrates and Rutilius, for example, in neither case stems from military failure on their part.

cultural imperatives (e.g., "associate the ethical category *virtus* with yourself!") in a world in which the old signposts increasingly fail to point the way. *Exempla virtutis* are among the most important of these ethical signposts. Now, some of Seneca's favored exempla are familiar, longstanding members of the canon: Regulus and Scaevola are entirely congenial to his project in their traditional form. Other ancient exempla, such as the Decii, require a degree of reworking to draw the necessary contrast between outcomes and mental dispositions; such exempla are also supplemented by figures of more recent vintage, such as Cato, Metellus Scipio, and Iulius Canus (*Tranq.* 14; see below).[75] Still others who might be admired at least for their military success—Alexander, Marius, and the like—are presented only as negative exempla. This culling, supplementation, and reinterpretation of the canon of *exempla virtutis*, along with explicit redefinitions of *virtus*, are the central strategies by which Seneca seeks to give this ethical category a Stoic orientation. In so doing, he adapts old aristocratic impulses to the new imperial order. Yet this adaptation is not merely reactive: it may also be seen as a move to reconstitute the traditional aristocratic privilege of monopolizing moral value. For Senecan ethics does not so much concede to the imperial regime the old aristocratic monopoly on *virtus*, as much as it shifts the arena of competition, insisting that "real" *virtus* resides in a location that remains accessible to aristocrats in general.[76] I do not

---

[75] The earliest surviving attestations of the sufferings of Scaevola and Regulus date from the mid-to late second century: for Scaevola, see Cassius Hemina fr. 16 Peter; for the torture of Regulus see Sempronius Tuditanus (cos. 129 B.C.; fr. 5 Peter) *apud* Gellius 7.4.1. I assume, however, that exemplifying accounts of both figures were in circulation much earlier. The same assumption holds for the Decii, for whom the first surviving attestations are in Cicero (see Barton 1993: 40ff). Cato, and Metellus Scipio to a lesser extent, do make it into the empire's canon of exemplary figures. But as Litchfield 1914: 53–62 shows, the canon virtually closed with the civil wars of the 40s-30s B.C., and other than emperors virtually no imperial figures achieved and maintained exemplary status. Seneca aggressively seeks to augment the canon with imperial figures, but even he engages in special pleading: e.g., *Canus Iulius, vir imprimis magnus, cuius admirationi ne hoc quidem obstat quod nostro saeculo natus est* (*Tranq.*14.4); for other figures see *Marc.* 2.2, *Ep.* 27.5, 83.12–15, *Ben.* 3.26–28; on this matter see Alewell 1913: 109 and n.1. However, these figures generally do not stick. Iulius Canus (*PIR*[1] I 165; not in *PIR*[2]) is mentioned by Plutarch fr. 211 Sandbach, which would suggest that this exemplum survived at least for a couple of generations. However, no other attestation of Canus survives, unless he is identified with the "Canius" of Boeth. *Cons.* 1.3. The advantage of using more recent figures, presumably, is that enough is known about them that one can speak usefully of patterns of action. This is not the case for the very ancient exempla (Horatius, Fabricius, Scaevola), who are known for only one or two actions.

[76] Other ways in which the sites of aristocratic competition shift from republic to empire: the arena, in which aristocrats begin to appear as gladiators, is one locus in which glory can still be won for conspicuous displays of valor (Barton 1993: 28); the centumviral court becomes the privileged locus for advocacy with the disappearance of the repub-

claim that the reduced scope for military glory, and the possibility of locating *virtus* elsewhere, is the main reason, or even an important reason, why Seneca advocates Stoic ethics. It is, however, one respect (another will be suggested in the next section) in which his ethics might have seemed attractive and resonant to his intended audience. Whether Senecan ethics actually did strike a chord is unknown, but it is plausible that Seneca laid out his system under the assumption that it might, or should, engage his audience's attention in part by addressing the social dislocations they perceived.

7. Ethics in Julio-Claudian Society: Flattery and Stoicism

Another contemporary aristocratic concern with which Senecan ethics engages is the matter of flattery—"flattery" being the term by which Anglophone scholars conventionally translate the Latin words *adsentatio, adulatio,* and in some circumstances *blanditiae* ("saying yes," "fawning," "blandishments"), along with the Greek κολακεία. These terms mark characteristic features of "speaking to power"—features of the speech of those who have fewer economic, political, and/or cultural resources to those who have more. Specifically, they mark an effort by the subordinate party to please the superior so as to obtain resources from him, or to avoid suffering or punishment that he has the power to inflict.[77] Indeed, a number of early imperial texts imply or state outright that targets of flattery are usually people of high social standing, wealth, and ambition,[78] and there is ample evidence that Roman aristocrats of the late republic and early empire regarded *assentatio/adulatio* as a constant and normal (if insidious) feature of their everyday interactions with their social subordinates. Most tellingly, Cicero reveals that—at least during the late republic—a standard topic of certain progymnastic rhetorical exercises was to identify and describe the characteristic fea-

---

lican *quaestiones*; and activities such as declamation and recitation become more prominent in the early empire as means by which standing is constructed.

[77] I borrow the phrase "speaking to power" from Scott 1990, a stimulating cross-cultural study of the ways in which subordinates speak to their superiors, and of how subordinates and superiors speak among themselves when members of the other group are absent. Bartsch 1994: 22–31 emphasizes the degree to which flattery of the *princeps* was initiated by, and was a resource for, the aristocracy (contra the Tacitean view that flattery of the *princeps* by aristocrats is a reactive, coerced performance); see also Konstan 1997: 93–108 on flattery in a Hellenistic court context.

[78] E.g., Vell. Pat. 2.102.3: *etenim semper magnae fortunae comes adest adulatio*. Likewise, Val. Max. 4.7 pr., Sen. *Ira* 2.21.7, *Vit.* 2.4, *Ben.* 6.30.3–6. Also Plut. *Mor.* 49B–D, 53B, 58C–E.

tures and strategies of the flatterer.⁷⁹ Now, the many and varied exercises that formed the backbone of rhetorical education were one channel by which elite children and adolescents were exposed to complex social issues and thereby required to think consciously and abstractly about their own social roles: that is, these exercises were important devices for acculturating elite children *as* elites. Therefore, the fact that characterizing the flatterer was a topic for such exercises implies that the ability to detect flattery by inferiors was regarded as a useful skill for aristocrats to possess, and proves that aristocrats were required from an early age to think about this feature of their own social existence in a conscious, structured manner. Furthermore, three sustained discussions of flattery—its characteristics, aims, and consequences—survive in literary texts of the late republic and early empire. Their very existence suggests the continuing importance of this matter in the lives of elites from Cicero's day onward.⁸⁰ There are many different types of power-laden interactions that late republican and early imperial texts portray as involving flattery; many involve elites who are targets of flattery by their inferiors, or Greeks (sometimes other foreigners) who flatter the kings or tyrants who rule or threaten them.⁸¹ Interestingly, Roman aristocrats are seldom portrayed as flatterers (though they are often targets of flattery) in texts of the republican period. Even the

---

⁷⁹ Cic. *Top.* 83 gives *qualis sit assentator* as an example of the sort of topic on which one would produce a *descriptio* (a standard rhetorical exercise); likewise, at *Top.* 85, a topic for the rhetorical exercise *comparatio* is *quid intersit inter amicum et assentatorem* (cf. *De Or.* 3.117, Sen. *Ep.* 45.7).

⁸⁰ These three discussions are Cic. *Lael.* 89–99, Sen. *Nat.* 4A pr., and Plut. *Mor.* 48E–74E (= *Quomodo adulator ab amico internoscatur*). The latter in particular may be regarded as a highly polished, adult, literary version of the student exercises discussed above. A briefer treatment of flattery also appears in Dio Chr. *Or.* 3.12–24, roughly contemporary with Plutarch. Though later than the Julio-Claudian era, these two texts have much in common with the portrayals of flattery in Seneca and Cicero. Collectively, all of these texts show both the conventionality of the topos "characterize the flatterer," and also the continuity of the issue of flattery as a concern for elites. Philodemus's Περὶ παρρησίας, being concerned with frank criticism among members of an Epicurean community, has little to say about flattery and free speech in the context of sharply inegalitarian social relations; see however cols. XXIIb–XXIVa.

⁸¹ For flattery of aristocrats by parasites (a comic trope) and other dinner guests: e.g., Sen. *Ira* 3.8.6, *Ep.* 47.8; [Quint.] *Decl. Min.* 296.7; Plut. *Mor.* 50D, 54B; discussion in Damon 1997: 80–85, 99–101. By the residents of the province one is governing: Cic. *Q. Fr.* 1.1.15–16, 1.2.4; Sen. *Nat.* 4A pr. 3 and passim. By other inferiors for other (or unspecified) reasons: Cic. *Clu.* 36, Cic. apud Asc. *Corn.* 79C; Sen. *Ira* 2.21.7, *Tranq.* 1.16, *Ep.* 123.8. For flattery of foreign kings/tyrants by subjects, courtiers, etc.: e.g., Cic. *Tusc.* 5.61; Livy 31.15.2, 31.25.10, 45.10.11; Sen. *Suas.* 1.6; Plut. *Mor.* 52D, 56E. Curiously, I have found no instances of slaves described as flatterers of their masters, though *adulatio/assentatio* is sometimes characterized as or associated with "slavish" behavior (Cic. *Q. Fr.* 1.1.16; Vell. Pat. 2.83.1; Sen. *Ira* 3.17.1; Tac. *Hist.* 1.1).

powerful warlords of the late republic are almost never said in contemporary texts to be targets of flattery by other elites (but cf. Cic. *Att.* 13.28.2, and perhaps Caes. *B.C.* 1.4.3). In a few texts dating from or referring to the republican period, however, some aristocrats are derisively called "flatterers of the plebs"—a rare situation in which flattery is said to be directed down the socioeconomic scale, from those of high status to those of low status.[82] With the advent of the principate, however, our sources begin to speak of aristocrats themselves as flatterers of the emperor, or of other members of the regime's inner circle. For ordinary aristocrats now stand to gain and lose status, wealth, and even their lives at the whim of members of the regime, rather than through the workings of electoral assemblies, senatorial politics, criminal and civil courts, etc.[83] I will argue that Seneca's pervasive concern about the grounds for praising and blaming, as traced in sections 3–5 above, intersects in a number of ways with these looming elite anxieties about flattery: the necessity for aristocrats themselves to "speak to power," since there now exist persons of transcendent weath and status, while at the same time they remain targets of flattery by their own inferiors. I begin, then, by replicating the declamatory topos just discussed: I describe the characteristic features of the flatterer, and of the discourse of flattery, as it is portrayed in late republican and early imperial texts—texts produced, of course, by elites who are themselves likely targets of flattery. It will be apparent that these characteristics are fairly conventional: specific details found in any one account are usually paralleled in at least one other. This I take as evidence that the basic problems flattery was thought to pose remained much the same throughout this pe-

---

[82] "Flatterers of the plebs": Cic. *Lael.* 93–96, *Off.* 2.63; Livy 3.68.10, 3.69.4, 45.18.6, 45.23.9; similarly, 23.4.2. On the one hand, these usages point to the real power that the republican plebs as a group wielded—e.g., in the tribal assembly, through the tribunes, and through public displays of pleasure and displeasure—over the political fortunes of elite Romans, which is why some elites thought it desirable or necessary to seek the plebs' favor. In this respect these elites are indeed "speaking to power" in addressing the plebs as they do. On the other hand, the derisive tone of these passages implies the view that such behavior by elites is inappropriate and degrading (see e.g., Cic. *Lael.* 94; Livy 3.69.4). Konstan 1997: 102–103 and n. 14 discusses those Athenian politicians who were called "flatterers of the demos."

[83] Flattery of *principes* by senators in the Julio-Claudian period is widely represented in literary sources: e.g., Suet. *Aug.* 53.1–2 (flattery of Augustus); Plut. *Mor.* 60C–D, Suet. *Tib.* 27 (Tiberius); Tac. *Ann.* 12.41 (Claudius); Tac. *Ann.* 14.10, 15.59 (Nero). Other close associates of the emperor or members of the imperial household as targets of *adulatio/adsentatio* by elites: Livia (Tac. *Ann.* 1.14), Germanicus (Tac. *Ann.* 2.12), Domitius (who will become Nero upon adoption by Claudius: Tac. *Ann.* 12.26). Cf. Dio 61.10 on the hypocrisy of Seneca himself, who denounces flattery even as he flatters the freedmen of Claudius's wife Messalina.

riod, and consequently, specific ways of articulating those problems also endured.

The flatterer's aim, according to these texts, is to please the target and so to ingratiate himself. His primary strategy is to present the target to himself as a person of superior status, achievement, capabilities, and moral authority relative both to the flatterer and to others. That is, he tells his target things that he believes the target wants to hear and believe about himself, and so encourages him to follow his own preexisting inclinations.[84] Now, our sources regularly characterize flattery as "false" in two distinct but related ways. First, if the flatterer is consistently agreeable (as the term *adsentator*, "yes-man," suggests) in an attempt to please, he inevitably makes knowingly false moral evaluations: that is, he praises or accedes to actions or intentions of the target that he actually believes are blameworthy and should be rejected. Flattery, then, is ethical perjury, for it opens a gap between speech and thought, between praise overtly conferred and blame which is not declared to the target. Awareness of this gap, indeed, may cause the various audiences for flattering speech—the target included—to scrutinize the speaker's words for a subtext, an implication beyond their surface meaning, that can be taken as conveying his "true" judgment, which is otherwise not overtly indicated.[85] This leads to the second kind of falseness. For because the target is told only what he wants to hear, and has his own inclinations confirmed to him as morally correct, he may come to hold an unduly positive valuation of his own actions and intentions, a view much more positive than the actual valuation held by others (including

---

[84] Many passages can be adduced that corroborate and nuance each point in this discussion; this note and the next several provide a few representative citations. Flatterers insist on the target's superior status relative to others: Cic. *Lael.* 99; Sen. *Ira* 2.21.7; Plut. *Mor.* 54B–D, 58B–D. Flatterers say what they believe the target wants to hear about himself: Cic. *Lael.* 91, 98; Sen. *Ep.* 77.5, *Ben.* 6.33.1; Plut. *Mor.* 51E–52A. The target is pleased by flattery, and is eager to believe this view of himself: Cic. *Lael.* 97–98; Sen. *Tranq.* 1.16–17, *Ep.* 59.11 (similarly, *Tranq.* 1.16, *Ben.* 5.7.4: one may be one's own *adsentator*).

[85] Bartsch 1994: 63–69 (also chs. 4 and 5 passim) discusses this phenomenon, which she calls "doublespeak." In Scott's terms, such utterances by subordinates on one level conform to the "public transcript," the dominant party's official view of itself, while on another level they contain an oppositional claim, a "hidden transcript," that in some way voices the true views of the subordinate party (Scott 1990: 1–16, 18–19, 152–66 and ch. 6 passim). The awareness by *princeps* and aristocracy that much of the latter's praise may be insincere causes *laudatores* to insist more and more obsessively on the sincerity of the praise they bestow, as Bartsch masterfully demonstrates regarding Pliny's *Panegyricus* (148–87). The same concern is already evident, however, in Seneca's *De Clementia*, addressed to the young emperor Nero (e.g., 1.13.5, 14.2, 19.7) and in other Julio-Claudian texts. The word *dissimulatio* is also sometimes used in early imperial texts to describe the action of cloaking true judgments under insincere words: see Sen. *Ben.* 6.32.4, *Ira* 2.33.5; also Rudich 1993: xxi–iii, xxxi–ii, 252.

the flatterer). Deceived by this false view of himself as a moral agent, he may embark on a potentially disastrous course. Passages from Cicero's *Laelius* bring out many of these points:

> virtute enim ipsa non tam multi praediti esse quam videri volunt. hos delectat adsentatio, his fictus ad ipsorum voluntatem sermo cum adhibetur, orationem illam vanam testimonium esse laudum suarum putant. nulla est igitur haec amicitia, cum alter verum audire non volt, alter ad mentiendum paratus est. (§98)

> sed obsequium multo molestius, quod peccatis indulgens praecipitem amicum ferri sinit; maxima autem culpa in eo qui et veritatem aspernatur et in fraudem obsequio impellitur. (§89)

> Not so many men wish to be endowed with virtue itself as wish to *appear* so endowed. Flattery delights these men, and when speech molded to their wishes is applied to them, they regard that empty speech as proof of their praiseworthiness. This, then, is no friendship, when one party is unwilling to hear the truth, and the other is prepared to lie. . . . but complaisance is much more harmful (sc. than truth), because by indulging a friend's sins it permits him to be carried headlong; but the greatest fault is in him who both rejects truth and is urged on to mischief by complaisance.

Cicero asserts that the flatterer's evaluative statements are "false," tailored to what the target wants to hear (*fictus ad ipsorum voluntatem sermo; peccatis indulgens veritatem aspernatur et in fraudem impellitur*) — noting that the target does not want to hear the "truth." Indeed, the target takes the flatterer's statements as external confirmation of his preexisting belief in his own praiseworthiness (*testimonium laudum suarum*). As a result, he may come to grief (*praecipitem ferri*). A passage in Seneca (*Ben.* 6.30.4–5) similarly links false declarations of value by the flatterer and a false self-image by the target, but emphasizes more strongly the target's destructive behavior resulting from this deception.[86]

The linkage of flattery and falseness just discussed is often contrasted with another linked pair of terms, namely "friendship" and "truth" (or "frankness"). Cicero's lengthy discussion of *adulatio/adsentatio* is itself embedded in the treatise entitled "On friendship" (*De Amicitia*), and the relevant essay by Plutarch is conventionally titled "How to distinguish a flatterer from a friend" (*Quomodo adulator ab amico internoscatur*). Furthermore, the friend and flatterer are formally opposed in

---

[86] Other passages attesting the falseness of the flatterer's stated judgments, the deception of the target, or his ensuing ruinous behavior, include Cic. *Lael.* 91–92, *Off.* 1.91; Sen. *Ira* 2.21.8, *Nat.* 4A pr. 13, *Ben.* 5.7.4, *Ep.* 123.9; Plut. *Mor.* 56E–F; Tac. *Ann.* 1.1, 6.38. Occasionally it is claimed that the target knows he is being lied to, yet takes pleasure in these lies nonetheless: Sen. *Ep.* 59.11; Dio Chr. *Or.* 3.19.

the progymnastic rhetorical exercises attested by Cicero (*Top*. 85: *quid intersit inter amicum et assentatorem*, cf. *De Or*. 3.117). The contrast between these categories is constructed as follows. A flatterer masquerades as a friend of his target, but in fact *adulatio/adsentatio* is inconsistent with *amicitia*, for an *amicus* tells the truth frankly. He gives praise when appropriate, but also reproaches and rebukes if he disapproves of a friend's actions or intentions, and consequently does not allow him to hold a false moral valuation of himself. Now, since the flatterer is regularly understood to be of lower social status than his target, these passages that develop a distinction between flatterer and friend would seem to imply that the sort of friend under consideration is also one of lower status. Indeed, it is clear that Roman elites embraced the social ideal of the *amicus minor*, a friend of lower status who speaks frankly and gives useful advice, at least as early as the mid-second century B.C. Polybius (31.24.4–5) describes how he undertook to teach the youthful Scipio Aemilianus how to behave in a way "worthy of his ancestors"; also the "good friend" fragment of Ennius as contextualized by Gellius (*NA* 12.4 = *Ann*. fr. 278–86 Sk.) describes the characteristics that make a man of lower status a resourceful, helpful adviser for an aristocrat. The flatterer, then, is no *amicus*. In fact, he is an *inimicus*, or possibly something even more harmful, for he causes these very categories to become confused, so that his target — in addition to holding a false valuation of himself — may misrecognize friends as foes and vice versa. Consequently, the mere knowledge that flattery exists may cause potential targets to suspect the motives of anyone who praises them. Thus flattery not only undermines ethical discourse, but also damages the fabric of society by confounding social relations.[87]

A flatterer, then, deploys value terms so as to enable — even encourage — his target to act contrary to widely held values, thus subverting ethical discourse, while a friend communicates and upholds these values. The mechanics of the flatterer's subversion of ethical discourse are of interest particularly (but not exclusively) to Seneca. He describes the flatterer's deployment of value terms at *Ep*. 59.11:

---

[87] *Amicitia* and flattery are incompatible, yet difficult to distingiush: Cic. *Lael*. 89–92 (e.g., 92: *simulatio amicitiae*); Sen. *Ep*. 45.7; Plut. *Mor*. 50A–51E (and passim). *Amici* are frank, speak the truth, and give blame as well as praise: Cic. *Lael*. 90–92, 97; Sen. *Ben*. 6.34; Plut. *Mor*. 50B, 55A–B. (Often, however, the words for "frank" or "candid" speech — *libertas* or παρρησία — implicitly or explicitly emphasize the blame-aspect of ethical discourse: e.g., at Plut. *Mor*. 66B, the verb παρρησιάζομαι is grouped with ἐλέγχω and ψέγω, all three in opposition to ἐπαίνω and κατευλογέω.) For a discussion of the figure of the *amicus minor* in the texts of Polybius and Ennius (and elsewhere), see Habinek 1990: 171–76. Flatterers are not *amici*, but *inimici*: Sen. *Ep*. 45.7. Flatterers are worse than *inimici*: Cic. *Lael*. 90. The existence of flattery may cause all praise to be viewed with suspicion: Sen. *Nat*. 4A pr. 18–19, Plut. *Mor*. 49E–50B.

non sumus modica laudatione contenti: quidquid in nos adulatio sine pudore congessit tamquam debitum prendimus. ... adeoque indulgemus nobis ut laudari velimus in id cui contraria cum maxime facimus. mitissimum ille se in ipsis suppliciis audit, in rapinis liberalissimum et in ebrietatibus ac libidinibus temperantissimum; sequitur itaque ut ideo mutari nolimus quia nos optimos esse credidimus.

We are not content with moderate praise: whatever shameless fawning has heaped upon us we seize upon as our due. ... and to such an extent we make allowances for ourselves that we wish to be praised for something whose opposite we are just then doing. Someone hears himself called most gentle in the very act of inflicting punishment, or utterly generous while he plunders, or thoroughly moderate in bouts of drunkenness and lust; it therefore follows that the reason we are unwilling to change is that we believe ourselves the very best.

Crucially, Seneca here posits that certain actions done or characteristics manifested by the target carry negative moral value, but that the flatterer labels them with ameliorative terms. Plutarch too (*Mor.* 56B–C) warns that flatterers "cloak wickedness with the names of virtue" (τὰ τῆς ἀρετῆς ὀνόματα τῇ κακίᾳ περιτιθέντες) and, like Seneca, lists some ameliorative terms by which a flatterer may dissimulate his target's vices.[88] Thus flattery, as these passages present it, involves creating a uniform front of praise where (our sources posit) blame is appropriate, and so leading the target to believe (wrongly) that his own positive self-assessments are correct. But the flatterer may be even more insidious. For while our sources overwhelmingly focus on the (false) praise he bestows, they occasionally observe (Cic. *Lael.* 99; Plut. *Mor.* 51C–D, 59A–60D) that a skillful flatterer may also strategically deploy blame, criticizing the target in such a way as to further ingratiate himself, yet perhaps causing his flattering aims to be misrecognized. Thus Plutarch

---

[88] See also Sen. *Ep.* 45.7, *Nat.* 4A pr. 8, Dio Chr. *Or.* 3.18, 20–22. The "misuse" of value terms described in these passages is reminiscent of the contestation over allocating value terms in civil war contexts, discussed in chapter 1.5 above. Indeed, Plutarch *Mor.* 56B–C quotes the famous passage of Thucydides on the shifting of value terms during the Corcyrean *stasis* (Thuc. 3.82.4, also cited above, ch. 1 n. 50) in conjunction with his discussion of how flatterers redesignate vices as virtues. These phenomena differ fundamentally, however. The competition over how value terms are allocated in civil war results from the cleaving of the judging community into rival factions, whose interests (and consequently their ways of deploying ethical language) are systematically opposed. However, the redesignation of vices as virtues in the discourse of flattery appears to occur within a unified judging community, whose members share a single value system, and involves the ad hoc negation or inversion of the actual value judgments that the flatterer (internally) forms regarding the target's actions.

notes (51C) that a flatterer's blame is no more "true" or useful to the target than is his praise.

In the passages discussed so far, our sources—Seneca included—address themselves implicitly or explicitly to elites who are subject to flattery by their inferiors, describing its characteristics from the superior party's point of view and warning of its dangers. But as Seneca shows elsewhere, it is not only as targets that elites may be involved in flattery: for when confronted by people of even greater power and higher status, they potentially become flatterers themselves. Consider, for example, *De Beneficiis* 6.29–34. Here Seneca discusses whether one can return a benefit, and show oneself *gratus*, to a benefactor who is significantly more favored by fortune (i.e., more wealthy and powerful) than oneself. The answer, he says, is yes. For even if one can provide such a benefactor no material benefit, one can be his *amicus* in the sense described above—refraining from flattery, speaking frankly, and offering good advice: "for what keeps you from showing your gratitude even when [your benefactor's] affairs are prosperous? How many things there are through which we can repay whatever we owe even to those who are prosperous: trustworthy advice, constant familiarity, conversation that is affable and pleasant without flattery. . . . Success has placed nobody so high that he does not require a friend all the more because he lacks nothing" (*quid enim prohibet referre gratiam prosperis rebus? quam multa sunt per quae, quidquid debemus, reddere etiam felicibus possumus: fidele consilium, adsidua conversatio, sermo comis et sine adulatione iucundus. . . . neminem tam alte secunda posuerunt ut non illi eo magis amicus desit quia nihil absit*, Ben. 6.29.2). Seneca goes on to describe how this powerful, fortunate man can ruin himself and others if he hears only lies and flattery. He comes to be deceived about his own powers; in his ignorance he initiates destructive wars, perpetrates slaughter, and brings his kingdom crashing down around himself (§30.3–6). Note that what began as a generalized representation of a man favored by *fortuna* (or more favored, at any rate, than Seneca's implied reader) slides over into a representation of a ruler or *princeps* in particular. Seneca's next two exempla confirm that this slippage has occurred, for he cites Xerxes (§31) and Augustus (§32) as powerful men in need of a friend. In the latter case, Augustus is said to lament the loss of Agrippa and Maecenas, whom he believes (but Seneca doubts) told him the truth rather than flattering lies. Nevertheless, Seneca goes on (§33.1), the truth and good advice are precisely what an aristocrat should communicate to a king or emperor: "tell them . . . not what they want to hear, but what they will always wish they had heard; let a truthful voice one day enter those ears that are full of flattery; give useful advice" (*dic illis* [i.e., *felicibus et in summo humanarum opum positis] non quod volunt audire, sed quod audisse semper volent; plenas aures adulationibus aliquando vera vox intret; da consilium utile*). In this passage, then, Seneca is concerned generally with how one "speaks to power," whether as an *adulator* or as an *amicus:* that is, he is interested in the viewpoint of the inferior party. Specifically, he considers the ways in which aristocrats speak to their rulers, a situation obviously relevant to the Julio-Claudian aristocracy even though some of his exempla are drawn from other cultures.

If an aristocrat stands to gain or lose much depending on whether he hears frank or flattering speech from his inferiors, Seneca also shows in a number of passages that the stakes are just as high for him depending on whether he speaks frankly or flatteringly to his ruler. Some aristocrats, to be sure, speak frankly and are rewarded. At *De Beneficiis* 6.31, Demaratus alone among Xerxes' advisors—the rest of whom encourage the king to pursue the invasion of Greece as he had conceived it (§§1–3)—tells him that he has planned badly and will be defeated (§§4–10); when this prediction is borne out, Xerxes rewards Demaratus because he alone spoke the truth (§11). However, others who speak frankly are horribly punished for saying things the ruler does not wish to hear—or, after suffering abuse at his hands, revert to flattery in order to avoid further punishment. At *De Ira* 3.14, the passage with which my book began, the Persian courtier Praexaspes tells Cambyses that he should drink less heavily; Cambyses angrily proves himself unimpaired by shooting an arrow through the heart of Praexaspes' son. Thus, says Seneca (§14.6), Praexaspes "was added to the number of those who, by great disasters, have shown how much good advice costs the friends of kings," noting also here that Praexaspes might have done better *not* to give such advice. In the next section (3.15), yet another Persian courtier, Harpagus, gives unspecified good advice to his ruler, in return for which his children are cooked up and fed to him. Asked how he likes the meal, he replies "all meals are pleasant at a king's table." By such *adulatio*, says Seneca, he avoided having to eat the remainder of the dish.[89] So despite his pronouncement (*Ben.* 6.33.1) that aristocrats should address their rulers without flattery and give useful advice, and despite his more general concern that flattery subverts ethical discourse, Seneca appears to concede in these passages (*Ira* 3.14–15) that giving good advice to one's ruler may not always be the best course of action, and that even flattery may serve a worthy, expedient purpose under certain circumstances.

---

[89] Two other passages, *Ira* 2.33 and *Tranq.* 14, portray in detail similarly disastrous interactions between aristocrats and their ruler. The latter passage is further discussed below. See also *Ira* 3.17.1.

How is an aristocrat to negotiate such a minefield? In speaking to power, where can security be found if flattery is in general ethically unacceptable? For Seneca, the answer is philosophy, which appears in several passages as a versatile tool for avoiding the damage associated with flattery. It not only helps aristocrats defeat the flattery of their inferiors—a longstanding problem, as we have seen—but also offers them signposts for negotiating their relationship with the *princeps* and the imperial regime, without engaging in flattery themselves.

At *Ep.* 77.5–6 Seneca relates an anecdote that reveals the value to an aristocrat of a frank inferior who is also philosophically astute. The aristocrat, one Tullius Marcellinus, suffers from a troublesome disease and is contemplating suicide. Seneca writes,

> convocavit complures amicos. unusquisque aut, quia timidus erat, id illi suadebat quod sibi suasisset, aut, quia adulator et blandus, id consilium dabat quod deliberanti gratius fore suspicabatur. amicus noster Stoicus, homo egregius et, ut verbis illum quibus laudari dignus est laudem vir fortis ac strenuus, videtur mihi optime illum cohortatus. sic enim coepit: "noli, mi Marcelline, torqueri tamquam de re magna deliberes. non est res magna vivere: omnes servi tui vivunt, omnia animalia. magnum est honeste mori, prudenter, fortiter. cogita quamdiu iam idem facias: cibus, somnus, libido, per hunc circulum curritur. mori velle non tantum prudens aut fortis aut miser, etiam fastidiosus potest."

> He summoned a number of friends. Each one of them either, out of timidity, recommended to Marcellinus that which he [the friend] would have recommended to himself, or, because of being fawning and complaisant, gave such advice as he suspected would be most pleasing to the man deliberating. Our Stoic friend, an outstanding person and (to praise him in words by which he is worthy to be praised) a brave and energetic man, in my view exhorted him the best. For he began thus: "Do not rack yourself, my dear Marcellinus, as though you are deliberating about a great matter. To live is no great matter: all your slaves live, as do all animals. What is great is to die honorably, with foresight, bravely. Consider how long now you have been doing the same thing: food, sleep, lust; one goes around in this circle. Not just the man of foresight or the brave man or the wretched one can wish to die; even the sated man can."

The Stoic's advice is explicitly said here to be preferable to that of the others, either those "flatterers" who seek to guess Marcellinus's real desires, or the "timid" who simply advise him as they would choose themselves. The content of the Stoic's advice is a set of philosophical commonplaces on death, which apparently have the effect of confirming Marcellinus in his intention: for in the next section Seneca declares, "he needed no persuader, but an assistant" (*non opus erat suasore illi sed adiutore*, §7). Now, this story is illuminated by Seneca's discussion in *De Beneficiis* 6.33 regarding how an aristocrat may show gratitude to a higher-status benefactor, i.e., a king or *princeps*. As discussed above, Seneca says in this passage that the aristocrat need only fulfil the imperatives "let a truthful voice one day enter those ears that are full of flattery" and "give useful advice" (§33.1) and thereby become his benefactor's *amicus* rather than his *adulator*; for to give oneself as an *amicus* is a great gift indeed (§33.3). Seneca also illustrates the content, or possible content, of such advice (§33.2): "teach him not to trust his good fortune. . . . Will you have bestowed too little on him if you dislodge his stupid faith in everlasting power, and teach him that the gifts of chance are inconstant, and flee with greater speed than they come, nor does retreat happen by the same degrees by which the summit was reached, but often there is no interval between the height of fortune and its nadir?" (*effice ne felicitati sua credat. . . . parum in illum contuleris si illi stultam fiduciam permansurae semper potentiae excusseris docuerisque mobilia esse quae dedit casus, et maiore cursu fugere quam veniunt, nec iis portionibus quibus ad summa perventum est retro iri, sed saepe inter maximam fortunam et ultimam nihil interesse?*). Useful and true advice for a ruler, then, includes these philosophical commonplaces on the mutability of fortune.[90] Both here and in the Marcellinus story, Seneca implicitly invokes the old social ideal of the *amicus minor* who speaks frankly and gives helpful advice to his superior, with the twist that the *amicus minor* is a Stoic. The advice that he gives his superior in each case therefore consists of philosophical commonplaces carefully selected and tailored to fit the latter's circumstances. The implication of these passages seems to be that, if the inferior party in a relationship of unequal power is philosophically trained, he will not flatter but will speak out his true, philosophically inflected judgments; thus the stronger party will not be deceived and believe false things about himself. Both the utility and the truth of the inferior's advice to

---

[90] The idea that one should remind powerful people of the mutability of fortune has Stoic credentials: Cicero (*Off*. 1.90) says that Panaetius approved of a statement made by Scipio Aemilianus, to the effect that men who are excessively confident in their good fortune need to be led, like overly spirited horses, "into the training ring, so to speak, of *ratio* and *doctrina*" that they may learn the weakness of human affairs and fickleness of *fortuna*. According to this simile, it is philosophy that teaches these men what they need to know (i.e., that their position is precarious), and the Stoic Panaetius recounts it presumably because he approves. See also *Nat.* 3 pr. 7–9, where Seneca insists that one should teach others about the mutability of *fortuna*, while narrating the military victories of foreign kings (§§5–6: an activity presumably associated with traditional ethics) are mere *vana studia* (§2).

the superior are therefore assured, and so, consequently, is his status as *amicus* rather than *adulator*.[91]

It therefore appears that one way for a Roman aristocrat to avoid suffering and inflicting the damage that results from flattery is to seek out Stoic friends among his inferiors (such as Marcellinus's friend), and to be a philosopher himself in dealing with his superiors, especially the *princeps*. Moreover, such an aristocrat also has the tools to avoid deception and harm when he himself faces flatterers. Lucilius, at any rate, who shares Seneca's philosophical investment in Stoicism, is able (on Seneca's characterization) to regard the praise that the Sicilians bestow upon him during his governorship as nothing more than a token of his magistracy, just as the lictors are (*Nat.* 4A pr. 13). He regards their praise as flattery and dismisses it, because he knows that it does not convey frank value judgments: "I neither wish to deceive nor can I be deceived; I would prefer to be praised by you, if you were not also praising bad men" (*ego nec decipere volo nec decipi possum; laudari me a vobis, nisi laudaretis etiam malos, vellem*).[92] Thus on Seneca's account, philosophy (especially Stoicism) seems to offer an island of evaluative stability in a sea of ethical discourse roiled by flattery. For Stoic mouths produce only frank value judgments, while Stoic ears are able to recognize flattering statements, dismiss them as false, and so avoid deception.

But what of the difficult cases mentioned above, where aristocrats are punished for speaking unwelcome truths to tyrannical rulers? What tools does philosophy provide aristocrats who must operate in an environment where frankness is extremely dangerous? Seneca addresses this situation most directly in *De Tranquillitate Animi* 14. At the beginning of this section (§§1–2) he makes the familiar Stoic claim that tranquillity of mind is best secured by attaching moral value only to inter-

---

[91] This implication may receive further confirmation at *Brev.* 15.2 Here Seneca says that the great philosophers themselves are available, through their works, to give advice. Of the person who consults them, Seneca writes, *habebit cum quibus de minimis maximisque rebus deliberet, quos de se cotidie consulat, a quibus audiat verum sine contumelia, laudetur sine adulatione*. Seneca seems to be presenting these philosophers as *amici minores* who, by reason of their philosophical astuteness, necessarily speak frankly and are worthy of consultation (though moments before, in §§14.5–15.1, he has presented them in entirely the opposite position, as the social superior upon whom one calls early in the morning).

[92] In this passage (*Nat.* 4A pr. 13) Seneca does not directly attribute Lucilius's view of flattery to his philosophical training. But throughout *Nat.* 4A pr., Seneca implies the value of this training to Lucilius as he discharges his duties as governor. He urges him, for example, to separate himself from the crowd (§§1–3), and to put credence in his own evaluations of himself rather than in others' evaluations of him (§§14–18)—the familiar topoi of Seneca's Stoic moral exhortation. Thus I see the attitude toward flattery attributed to Lucilius as informed by the Stoic principles that otherwise are said to inform his behavior.

nals: for one cannot then be disquieted by blows of fortune, which can affect only one's external circumstances. To illustrate the tranquillity of mind that accompanies this pattern of valuation, Seneca adduces three exempla. The first (§3) is Zeno himself, the founder of the Stoa, who receives with suitable aplomb the news that he has lost everything in a shipwreck; the second (also §3) is a philosopher named Theodorus, who is unimpressed when a tyrant threatens to kill him and leave him unburied. The third and longest exemplum (§§4–10) is the Roman aristocrat Iulius Canus, put to death by Caligula. Seneca describes at length Canus's calm, Stoic bearing in the days and hours prior to his execution: "It beggars belief what that man said, what he did, what a tranquil state he maintained" (*verisimile non est quae vir ille dixerit, quae fecerit, quam in tranquillo fuerit*, §6; cf. §10). He is playing a board game at the moment the executioner comes, thus "mocking" death, and he explains as he is led away that he will soon learn the answers to philosophical questions about the immortality of the soul and its sensation as it departs the body (§§7–9). In thus seeking to learn something from death itself, Seneca says admiringly, "no one ever did philosophy longer" (*nemo diutius philosophatus est*, §10).[93]

In this context, then, let us consider Seneca's description and interpretation of the fateful exchange with the *princeps* that earned Canus his condemnation:

> Canus Iulius . . . cum Gaio diu altercatus, postquam abeunti Phalaris ille dixit "ne forte inepta spe tibi blandiaris, duci te iussi," "gratias," inquit, "ago, optime princeps." quid senserit dubito; multa enim mihi occurrunt. contumeliosus esse voluit et ostendere quanta crudelitas esset in qua mors beneficium erat? an exprobravit illi cotidianam dementiam? — agebant enim gratias et quorum liberi occisi et quorum bona ablata erant. an tamquam libertatem libenter accepit? quidquid est, magno animo respondit. dicet aliquis, "potuit post hoc iubere illum Gaius vivere." non timuit hoc Canus; nota erat Gai in talibus imperiis fides. (*Tranq.* 14.4–6)

> Iulius Canus, having quarreled at length with Gaius, after that Phalaris said to him as he was leaving, "lest you by any chance comfort yourself with foolish hope, I have ordered you executed," replied, "I give you thanks, O best of emperors." What he meant I am not sure, for many possibilities occur to me. Did he wish to be insulting and show how great was his cruelty if death was a benefit? Or was he rebuking him for his everyday insanity? — for those whose children were killed and whose goods had been taken away used to thank

---

[93] While Seneca does not explicitly identify Canus as a Stoic, his disposition, inferred from his consistency of bearing and behavior, coincides with the Stoic good man's *constantia animi*. Plutarch, however, calls him "one of the Stoic philosophers," and provides a slightly different account of his actions as he is led to execution (fr. 211 Sandbach).

him. Or was it as if he was receiving freedom willingly? Whatever it is, he responded with greatness of spirit. Someone will say, "Gaius might, after this, have ordered him to live." Canus did nor fear this; the trustworthiness of Gaius in such orders was well known.

Remarkable here is Seneca's implication that Canus's reply to Caligula upon being told of his death sentence ("thank you, most excellent emperor") does *not* constitute flattery. For in other instances, Seneca unequivocally labels as "flatterers" aristocrats who praise or thank their ruler after suffering injuries at his hands. At *De Ira* 3.14 the Persian courtier Praexaspes, whose son has just been shot by Cambyses, praises the king's aim; Seneca condemns this praise as a shocking example of the lengths to which flatterers will go, and the opportunities they will seize, in an effort to work their wiles (§3). Seneca is more forgiving of Harpagus (*Ira* 3.15), who is fed the flesh of his children and declares the meal pleasant. Seneca says that Harpagus thereby achieves the worthy goal of not having to eat the leftovers—but calls Harpagus's words *adulatio* nonetheless (§1; cf. *Ira* 2.33). Regarding Harpagus Seneca seems to be working with the understanding of flattery described at the beginning of this section: that it is an effort to please someone powerful so as to avoid suffering (further) injury at his hands.[94] Indeed, Seneca concedes (in the last two sentences quoted above) that Canus's reply to Caligula might be interpreted in a similar way—i.e., Canus hopes that Caligula will change his mind if flattered. But Seneca expressly rejects this line of interpretation. Why? I take it, because Canus's subsequent actions prove his philosophical distinction: given the contempt he later shows for death, he cannot be seen here as trying to evade it by flattery. More generally, as noted above, on Seneca's account a philosophically astute inferior necessarily speaks frankly to a superior, telling him hard truths and avoiding *adulatio*. It is therefore impossible that Canus intended to flatter, or in any way to cloak his actual judgments, so his reply to Caligula ("thank you . . .") cannot be taken as seeking to please. On the contrary, it must overtly speak out Canus's condemnation of Caligula. Seneca confesses his puzzlement regarding *how* it condemns (*quid senserit dubito*), and he gamely suggests three possible interpretations. But he remains certain nevertheless that the reply was "great spirited" (*quidquid est, magno animo respondit*).[95] What philoso-

---

[94] In the cases of both Praexaspes and Harpagus, Seneca suggests that these men did not say what they really thought; that they chose words that cloaked their true feelings (*Ira* 3.14.5: *potest dici merito devorasse verba*; §15.3: *necessaria ista est doloris refrenatio*). In Scott's (1990) terms, Seneca infers a hidden transcript of condemnation behind the public transcript of praise.

[95] Thanking the *princeps* at the end of an interview may have been a conventional

phy provides Canus, then, is the tools by which he can speak the truth to power, and then die well. Flattery—even expedient flattery of a tyrant—is apparently impossible for one who is so trained. The stability of ethical discourse therefore remains assured, even if it imperils the life of the speaker. As compensation, however, Canus is apotheosized into the exemplum par excellence for proper aristocratic behavior when confronted by a tyrant: this account's overt relevance to the situation of Seneca's implied audience (it strikes particularly close to home, since it involves a Roman aristocrat and his *princeps*, and not a foreign courtier and his king), its position as the final and climactic exemplum in a sequence of three, its extraordinary length, and finally the framing devices that draw explicit attention to the exemplary quality of Canus's behavior[96]—all of these features mark this exemplum out as particularly worthy of the reader's attention, admiration, and emulation.

In one way, Canus is a difficult exemplum for Seneca to embrace. For if it is accepted that Stoics praise and blame appropriately—speaking their true judgments without flattery—and if Canus establishes his philosophical credentials by facing death as he does, then the fact that his words to the emperor, on the surface at least, do not appear to communicate an appropriate value judgment, requires that Seneca engage in special pleading and interpretive gymnastics. In other words, Seneca's own philosophical postulates and axioms, combined with the particularities of this situation, require that Canus's words be interpreted as conferring blame, no matter what those words actually are. It would have been easier for Seneca if Canus had said nothing at all, for then he could be argued to have left his condemnation tacit, to be inferred (correctly) by people who understand things rightly. In a remarkable passage of *Ep*. 102 (§§11–17), Seneca grasps this nettle unflinchingly and argues that, in a community consisting entirely of good men, value judgments would no longer need to be verbalized at all. While his argument is intricate and too long to be quoted here in full, it rests fundamentally on a parallel pair of semantic distinctions: specifically, Seneca distinguishes *laus* from *laudatio*, on the one hand, and

---

practice: cf. Tac. *Ag.* 42.2, *Hist.* 2.71.2, *Ann.* 14.56.3. In each of these cases, however, Tacitus is at pains to suggest that the thanks offered are insincere, part of a scripted performance demanded of subordinates by the *princeps*. Seneca's interpretation of Canus' thanks is entirely at odds with this Tacitean view.

[96] The exemplum is introduced by a pair of clauses attesting Canus' personal greatness and his appropriateness as an object of attention by subsequent generations: *Canus Iulius, vir in primis magnus, cuius admirationi ne hoc quidem obstat quod nostro saeculo natus est* (§4). It concludes with a dramatic apostrophe to the deceased, making the same points: *dabimus te in omnem memoriam, clarissimum caput, Gaianae cladis magna portio* (§10).

claritas from *fama* and *gloria* on the other. *Laus* and *claritas*, as defined here, refer exclusively to states of mind: *laus* indicates a positive value judgment about another person that forms in the mind of the good man, and *claritas* designates the condition of a person about whom all good men have (internally) formed positive value judgments. Good men all necessarily form the same judgments, because each one's judgment is firmly imbued with truth (*si de me bene vir bonus sentit, eodem loco sum quo si omnes boni idem sentirent; omnes enim, si me cognoverint, idem sentient. par illis idemque iudicium est, aeque vero inficiscitur,* §12).[97] The counterparts to these words, *laudatio* and *fama/gloria*, refer to the verbal expression of value judgments, but not just those of the "good men"; rather, these are the verbalizations of the many as they (inconsistently and often wrongly) judge value in contemporary society.[98] Verbalization is a feature of the discredited ethical discourse of the many. Good men need not communicate their judgments verbally at all; they all know the content of one another's minds because that content is the same for all. If good men form a positive judgment of someone, they can remain silent, yet the person they have evaluated is nonetheless *clarus*. So in a society of good men, the process of morally evaluating others therefore continues (or praising does, at any rate, since blaming is presumably no longer necessary), but that process is completely autonomous from verbal communication. Praise and good repute exist only internally as *laus* and *claritas* (which are mutually entailing in this community), not in verbal form as *laudatio* and *fama*.[99] The real world, of course, does not consist entirely of good men. But Seneca's interpretation of Canus's words, divorced as it is from their surface meaning, perhaps adumbrates in this real-world instance the irrelevance of verbalized judgments that achieves its extreme form in the imagined society of good men. Seneca presents himself as a privileged interpreter of

---

[97] For the consistency of the good man's judgment and its foundation in truth, see also *Ep.* 95.57–59. For the inconsistency and mutability of the judgments of the many, see e.g., *Epp.* 95.57–59 and 102.13.

[98] E.g., §§14–15. With these distinctions and definitions, Seneca corrects and nuances the interlocutor's usage of these terms in §§8, 9, and 12.

[99] The essentially averbal nature of the society of good men is exposed again at *Ben.* 5.25.3. In discussing how and when to request reciprocation for a *beneficium* that one has given, Seneca notes in passing that, in a community of good men, one should remain silent and wait: *tacendum erat et expectandum, si inter sapientes viveremus*. The point is that a wise man would inevitably realize the appropriateness of the current situation, and would reciprocate without prompting (or at any rate, I presume, conceive the *wish* to reciprocate). On the ὁμόνοια of good men, see *SVF* III 625, 661. Erskine 1990: 18–27 discusses Zeno's assertion, in his *Politeia*, that in a community of wise men many normal institutions would be absent because otiose: lawcourts, gymnasia, temples, etc. Seneca's suggestion that speech itself is otiose in such a society is therefore in the spirit of Zeno's reasoning.

Canus's words, because he knows what the content of Canus's mind had to be; the fact that Canus's words seemed to express something else is somewhat beside the point, just as among good men it is of small account whether and how value judgments are verbalized.

The Canus exemplum, along with that of Tullius Marcellinus and his Stoic friend, show some of the tools that Stoicism supplies aristocrats for stabilizing ethical discourse that has been destabilized by the presence or threat of flattery. On the one hand, the damage aristocrats stand to suffer through being flattered by their subordinates—having false views of themselves as moral agents—is eliminated if these subordinates are Stoics, who will articulate their true judgments; on the other hand, Stoicism also empowers aristocrats to speak frankly to their own superiors, namely the *princeps* and his close associates. So if speaking one's mind at will is a privilege of power, as Scott suggests, then Senecan Stoicism purports to offer Julio-Claudian aristocrats a means of reclaiming this traditional privilege, even in their disempowered relationship vis-à-vis the *princeps*, albeit in an altered form. They are not rendered immune from corporal or other punishment at his hands, but they can regard any such suffering as morally indifferent (though "dispreferred"). Indeed, they can seize the opportunity provided by such adversity—as also in the case of military defeat, discussed above—to exercise the moral virtues of endurance, fortitude, and the like. In these respects, then, I agree broadly with Brent Shaw's assessment (see section 6 above) that Stoicism provided Roman elites of the early empire a set of "signposts on the road to the exercise of novel forms of political power and the social relations inherent in them." I have difficulty, on the other hand, accepting Foucault's suggestion that the prominence of Stoicism in early imperial society adverts to an efflorescence of "individualism." For while Stoicism may well involve an intensification of one's relations with oneself, the material I have discussed in the last two sections (6–7) suggests that this intensification occurs in the service of sustaining or altering relations among persons. For Seneca, Stoicism's ultimate utility is in its social effects.

8. Conclusion

My major aim in this chapter and the previous one has been to illuminate aspects of the engagement of Seneca and Lucan with sociopolitical phenomena of concern to themselves and their peers, the late Julio-Claudian aristocracy. The particular phenomena that have received detailed discussion—the institutionalization of the imperial oath of loyalty, the changing conditions of military command, the problems posed by flattery — can all be connected to the changing distribution of power and transformed modes of exercising it, upon the advent of the principate. These authors, moreover, chose to examine these phenomena largely in light of their ethical implications: the content of moral value terms, and the ways in which moral value is allocated. These particular issues are not the only issues of contemporary importance that were or could have been addressed in ethical terms (for a further instance, see chapter 4.5–6 below). Nor is ethics the only arena in which these authors, or aristocrats in general, confronted issues of contemporary importance. Indeed, in part 2 of this book I will argue that another way in which Julio-Claudian aristocrats sought to comprehend the novel power structure of the principate, understand its ramifications for the contemporary aristocracy, and manipulate it to their own advantage, was to articulate the *princeps'* authority in terms of culturally familiar authority relationships, such as that of gift-giver to gift-recipient, or master to slave, or father to son. Such paradigm setting has strong ethical implications, but is not itself an ethical discursive mode in the sense of being primarily concerned with how moral value is allocated and where it resides, or with the content of value terms. Finally, it is assuredly not the case that the several particular sociopolitical phenomena discussed in these chapters somehow caused or generated the competing modes of ethical discourse that I have traced in each author; that these authors constructed works containing competing ethical discourses precisely in order to address these particular problems. Such a claim would, again, be to make the tail wag the dog.

What I *do* wish to maintain, as the conclusion to be drawn from these two chapters, is this: the particular ethical discourses that are made to compete in the works of Lucan and Seneca, and the ways in which they are made to compete, constitute an engagement with and exploration of the possibilities for and limits of exercising power in the new sociopolitical order. In Lucan's poem, two different versions of traditional ethical discourse, based on different views of the constitution of the Roman community, are placed in competition. The assimilating view, the ethical discourse based on the received understanding of the shape of the community, turns out to be less effective in motivating military action that the alienating view, the ethical discourse based on a new, radically exclusive, factionalized conception of the community; the latter, embraced by the Caesarians, brings them victory. The institutionalization of alienating discourse in the imperial oath of loyalty indicates the continuing dominance of Caesarism and the marginalization of traditional aristocratic views and values even late in the Julio-Claudian period, more than a century after the battle of Pharsalus. Seneca, meanwhile, confronts traditional ethical discourse with Stoic ethics, showing (inter alia) that the latter provides better resources than the former for reasserting traditional aristocratic privileges in crucial areas, against the challenges posed to those privileges by the *princeps* and his regime. On the one hand, then, these works respond to shifts in the distribution of power in Roman society under the principate, while on the other hand they actively seek to shape that distribution of power and contemporary perceptions of it. So even when governmental structures and institutions receive no explicit discussion, these works can be seen as socially and politically engaged: for the competing ethical discourses that they contain serve specific interests in the social and political context in which these works were produced. Ethical modes of understanding were fundamentally important in Roman aristocratic culture, and the aristocracy was always inclined to cast social and political developments in moral terms. But when the ethical frames the social or political in Roman culture, it does not thereby conceal or efface it. I hope to have shown here some of the ways in which this framing occurs.

PART TWO
FIGURING THE EMPEROR

Chapter Three

THE EMPEROR'S AUTHORITY:
DINING, EXCHANGE, AND SOCIAL HIERARCHY

1. Overview

IN THE PREVIOUS two chapters I examined certain ethical conundrums associated with the emergence of the principate, as represented in two specific Julio-Claudian authors. Now I shift my focus to the figuration of the emperor himself, the keystone of this new social, political, and moral order. After five centuries of the oligarchic regime that later came to be called the "republic," the emergence of an autocrat posed difficulties of comprehension not only for Roman aristocrats, but for everyone else in Roman society, including the emperor himself: how to understand the unprecedented concentration of power in the hands of one person, and how to articulate the relationships that such a person could and should have with others. In this chapter and the next, I examine how the figures of the gift giver, the master, and the father — three longstanding, familiar authority figures in Roman society, all with strong ethical overtones — serve in the Julio-Claudian period as paradigms for the authority that the emperor exercises over others. Because of their ethical overtones, to model the emperor's authority according to one or another of these paradigms is implicitly to make evaluations of his rule as good or bad, presenting his exercise of power as legitimate or illegitimate. On the one hand, then, I seek to show how Romans of this period adduced familiar precedents in an effort to comprehend the relatively novel and constantly evolving phenomenon of the *princeps*; that is, how they conceptualized and constructed the new order from familiar pieces of the old. On the other hand, I aim to expose the dialogical aspect of this activity of representation. For not only do these paradigms make conflicting claims about the character of the emperor's authority — inviting acquiescence or resistance from his subjects — but they also implicitly impose constraints, differing in each case, upon the emperor's own behavior, constraints which he himself may accept or resist. The emperor's authority receives form and meaning from these alternative paradigms, the competition among them, and the debates that circulate around them.

Here in chapter 3, I examine the emperor as a giver of gifts. In many societies, giving and receiving is central to the establishment and maintenance of social relations, especially relations of unequal power. One manifestation of this linkage, familiar to students of both the modern and ancient Mediterranean worlds, is the social institution of patronage. The difficulties entailed in any attempt to define patronage, particularly but not uniquely with respect to ancient Roman society, are well known: in antiquity we find no single term or set of terms to encompass the range of relationships that modern scholars include under the rubric of "patronage" (i.e., the Roman terms *patronus* and *cliens* have a more restricted semantic range than do the terms "patron" and "client" as used by modern scholars); also, the relationships that are accepted, or have been argued, to be classifiable as "patronage" are so diverse and multifarious as virtually to defy definition. Nevertheless, recent work on Roman patronage has more or less converged to define a set of characteristics usually present in relationships classified as "patronal": they are ongoing personal relationships between social unequals, which are established and reproduced through the reciprocal exchange of goods and services; moreover, this exchange is typically asymmetrical, with the socially dominant party giving more than he receives. A further characteristic sometimes asserted is that these relationships are voluntary, hence (at least in theory) formed and dissolved at the transactors' convenience.[1] The social and economic centrality of such relationships in Roman society, from the darkest beginnings to the end of antiquity, is widely accepted, even though virtually every aspect of the characterization just given is debated—e.g., what constitutes "reciprocity"; what degree of social intimacy is required to qualify a relationship as "personal"; whether voluntarism is a legitimate cri-

---

[1] For this definition of patronage, see Saller 1982: 1, followed by Wallace-Hadrill 1989a: 3–4, Konstan 1995: 328, and others. In contrast, Johnson and Dandeker 1989: 222–28 (and passim) urge a shift of focus from exchange in strictly dyadic relationships to the reciprocities that operate across broader system of interlinked relationships. Such a shift in focus may, as they suggest (225), cast new light on the socially integrative and controlling functions of patronage, as well as illuminate the true movement of objects and services. Yet their argument does not obviate the need to understand dyadic exchange relationships better, especially in their ideological dimensions, since Roman writers themselves articulate the social consequences of exchange in terms of relationships between pairs of individuals. On the usages of the terms *patronus* and *cliens* in the late republic and empire, see e.g., Saller 1982: 8–11; Saller 1989; David 1992: 163–69. On voluntarism (or its lack), see Johnson and Dandeker 1989: 223, 228–34; Wallace-Hadrill 1989b: 76 (arguing that the relationship between the freedman and his former master should be regarded only as a special case of patronage, because of its obligatory, nonvoluntary nature—despite the fact that a standard usage of the term *patronus* in Roman society is to designate the former master in relation to his freedman). Millar 1984: 17 objects to modern usages of the vocabulary of patronage that diverge from ancient usages; the broader modern usages are defended by Saller 1983: 255–56 and n. 56, and White 1993: 32–33.

terion, and if so, what kinds of bonds could plausibly be called "voluntary."

Among the other points of contention, classicists have debated whether and to what extent the authority of the Roman emperor may be understood in the framework of patronage. Anton von Premerstein, in the first major section of his work *Vom Werden und Wesen des Prinzipats* (1937: 13–116), was the first to argue in detail for such an understanding of the principate. Although his argument that the patronal relationship between the emperor and his subjects rested upon the annual swearing of loyalty oaths is now rejected, his basic contention that patronal relations are central to the operation of the imperial regime has been highly productive: this idea implicitly or explicitly underpins virtually all subsequent discussion of imperial power and its legitimation. Paul Veyne's important study *Bread and Circuses* (1990 [1976]) argues, contra Premerstein, that the emperor's gifts are in most cases quasi-automatic and do not create personal relationships with the recipients (e.g., 341–51), despite the use of "language of the kingly style" (347) that may be taken to imply otherwise; he argues that the emperor gives as an agent of the state, and is merely discharging necessary, expected services. On the other hand Richard Saller, in *Personal Patronage under the Early Empire* (1982), defends a modified form of Premerstein's thesis (esp. 33–39, 73–75): after a thorough survey of the emperor's giving (41–78, 119–143) he argues that imperial largesse does generally constitute patronal behavior. Millar's monumental study *The Emperor in the Roman World* (1977), and recently Lendon's *Empire of Honour* (1997), while not directly addressing this debate, have further documented the emperor's enormous and varied resources for giving, as well as the social, political, economic, and ideological significance of his distributions.

Central to all of these studies is the idea—whether affirmed or denied—that the emperor's authority is constituted at least partly through exchange: that relations of domination are created, sustained, and challenged by giving and receiving in particular ways under particular circumstances and over periods of time. I will soon begin examining the connection between exchange and social hierarchy in early imperial society generally, and as it relates to the Julio-Claudian emperors in particular. I anchor my investigation in a body of anthropological work that inquires into the connection between exchange and hierarchy in other preindustrial societies. For while the idea of the emperor as patron has been productive, I suggest that his authority can be more fully comprehended by placing the "patron" and "client" in the background, and taking transactors of exchanges as the central object of analysis.[2]

---

[2] White 1993: 14–34 (esp. 34), discussing the relationship between poets and their

This move has several advantages. First, several terminological difficulties disappear: the divergence of the usages of *patronus* and *cliens* in antiquity from the usages of "patron," "patronage," and "client" by modern scholars, which has caused much confusion (see n. 1 above), is no longer an issue. Second, and more significantly, a number of new arenas appear in which hierarchy-establishing transactions occur: for example, an emperor's grant of "clemency," *clementia*, emerges as an important tool for establishing and maintaining power relations, yet imperial clemency has not been examined in this light, perhaps because it has not been considered a "patronal" activity. Third, a focus on "exchange" rather than "patronage" illuminates the ideological importance of transactions that do *not* establish hierarchical relationships, which are strategically useful alternatives to the transactions that do, and also reveals the significance of offerings that are resisted or declined, in contrast to those that are willingly accepted with a view to immediate or eventual reciprocation.[3]

It is convenient for the discussion that follows to adopt the longstanding, though contested, anthropological concepts "gift-exchange" and "commodity-exchange," in a somewhat expanded form and with modifications for the Roman social context. These terms signify different ways in which objects and services can circulate in a society, and are associated with different kinds of relations between transactors. A gift is something that, when bestowed upon one person by another, creates or reinforces a personal relationship between giver and receiver. Specifically, it imposes a "gift-debt," an obligation by the receiver to reciprocate by bestowing a gift of his own, at some later time, upon the original giver. In the meantime, the recipient's gift-debt renders him socially subordinate and inferior to the giver. He is not acquitted of this obligation, and its concomitant subordination, until such time as he reciprocates on a level at least equal to that on which he has received. This mode of exchange therefore involves a high degree of sociability between the transactors. The gift-exchange relationship is perhaps normatively

---

richer friends, similarly avoids the terms "patron" and "client," which he regards as ill defined and often inappropriate, and instead analyzes "structures of exchange." Indeed, one may co-opt the concepts of patron and client entirely into an exchange framework, as does Lendon 1997: 66–69 (and 156). He describes clientage as the condition of chronic gift-debt, of being "limited to returning gumballs for diamonds" under most circumstances (66).

[3] Saller 1982: 1 excludes "commercial transaction[s] in the marketplace" from the ambit of patronage, insisting that the latter relationship be "a personal one of some duration" (implying that the former is not). The distinction made here between two modes of exchange is real and important, but it is crucial to recognize that they coexist as viable alternatives in many exchange situations (see the next two paragraphs).

warm, amicable, and mutually beneficial: yet the recipient may not want the object or service given, or its accompanying social obligation; nor may the giver always bestow a gift with the recipient's good in view. It is possible, in other words, for such a relationship to be hostile and mutually antagonistic, at least for a short while; indeed, a given exchange relationship may move from an amicable phase to a hostile one, or vice versa. I use the terms "amicable reciprocity" and "hostile reciprocity" to designate these opposed phases.

"Commodity-exchange," on the other hand, designates transactions wherein two persons simultaneously exchange objects or services that they regard as quantitatively or qualitatively equivalent, but do not themselves enter into a personal relationship. Commodity-exchange is a price-forming process, creating a relationship between the things exchanged (any purchase of an object or service for a specified amount of money is an exchange of this sort), while the transactors themselves remain mutually independent. This kind of exchange, then, entails a low degree of sociability between the transactors. Objects, not their transactors, are placed into a relationship by commodity exchange, while gift exchange places the transactors and not the objects into a relationship. Yet gift-exchange and commodity-exchange are entirely compatible: they can and do exist side-by-side in many societies, including Roman elite society. For an object or service may move as a gift at one time, and as a commodity at another; indeed, in a single transaction one party may deem that an object has been bestowed as a gift, while the other party regards it as a commodity. Now, in adopting this scheme of gift-exchange (with its alternative modes of amicable and hostile reciprocity) and commodity-exchange, I do not maintain that all exchanges in Roman society can usefully be schematized in this way, nor do I fancy that this scheme provides anything but the roughest approximation of the social implications of exchange in Roman society. But I do see the modes of exchange defined here, and the tensions that exist between them, as corresponding empirically with various Roman articulations of how exchange is used to establish, buttress, or undermine power relations not only between elites and nonelites, but also within the elite — especially between emperor and aristocracy. Thus I suggest that these categories, though derived from the anthropological study of premodern societies of the nineteenth and twentieth centuries, nevertheless may be useful for grasping one contemporary Roman mode of understanding power and authority generally, and the emperor's in particular.[4]

---

[4] Mauss 1990 [1924] is the seminal discussion of the gift; though here I draw primarily on Gregory 1982: 10–28, 41–55 (and passim). Also helpful is Sahlins 1972: 191–205,

At the core of my analysis of social hierarchy and exchange in this chapter is the convivium, the Roman dinner party. In section 2 I argue that power relations suffused these gatherings, and that social hierarchies were established, challenged, and generally negotiated through the exchanges that occured in this context. In section 3 I contend that speech is one of the most important elements to be factored into the complex exchange of goods and services that took place at the convivium; I then go on (section 4) to discuss in detail how representations of the convivial behavior of the emperor (or a stand-in for him) — especially his reception and reciprocation of the speech of other aristocratic diners — served to legitimate or delegitimate him as an authority figure. In the final two major sections (5 and 6) I extend some of the results gained from the case study of the convivium, examining the social ramifications of the emperor's distribution of other goods and services, and also the social consequences of his reception of the goods and services offered to him.

---

who posits a "reciprocity continuum." One pole of this continuum, which he calls "generalized reciprocity," involves giving to close social connections in such a way that the return is unspecified and left indefinite; this pole roughly corresponds to what others call "gift-exchange." The other pole, "negative reciprocity," occurs between people who are unconnected: this is the unsociable extreme of trying to get a lot in return for a little — e.g., cheating the tourists. In the middle is "balanced reciprocity," where similar amounts of things are exchanged with people at a moderate social distance; this roughly corresponds to the traditional category of "commodity exchange" (a similar exchange continuum is positied by Bourdieu 1977 [1972]: 173–74). Sahlins's "negative reciprocity," wherein exchange may be used as a weapon, is the inspiration for my category of "hostile reciprocity," though his negative reciprocity is utterly impersonal while my hostile reciprocity involves wounding exchanges between people well known to one another, who might at other times exchange gifts amicably, or exchange commodities. My categories may not cover every possible mode of exchange: Humphrey and Hugh-Jones 1992: 1–19 argue that barter cannot be subsumed under gift or commodity exchange and therefore is a distinct mode; cf. Appadurai 1986: 10 (and 3–16 more generally on gifts and commodities).

Anthropological work on exchange is of course already familiar to Roman social historians and has been handled by them in varying ways. In some cases this work is acknowledged in passing, e.g., White 1993: 14–27 ("modern exchange theory"), and Saller 1982: 22. Other scholars engage and discuss this material more systematically: e.g., Veyne 1976: 67–84 (material not included in the abridged 1990 translation, which consequently gives a distorted view of Veyne's engagement with Mauss, Bataille, etc.), Konstan 1997: 3–6 (arguing that friendship in the ancient world is disinterested and disembedded from economics, against the view that gift-exchange precludes such a relationship); David 1992: 121–45 (arguing that the *lex Cincia de donis et muneribus* exposes a tension between gift-exchange and commodity-exchange in the relationship between judicial patrons and clients in the middle and late republic); also Dixon 1993b.

2. Giving a Dinner: The Convivium as Object of Exchange

The Roman dinner party, the convivium, creates groupings of individuals of (usually) differing social status, places them together in one room and for a certain amount of time, and causes them to interact socially face-to-face. While the idea of equality is sometimes asserted, in practice the convivium is not generally a socially egalitarian event: it tends to function as an arena in which status distinctions and power relations are established, confirmed, or challenged. I will argue that this function is discharged substantially through the dynamics of gift-exchange and its tension with commodity-exchange. For many elements of this social occasion, including the issuing of an invitation, its acceptance or rejection, the arrival of the guests, the host's provision of food, drink, and presents for the guests, and the conversation itself, can be seen as offerings and counter-offerings of gifts that forge hierarchical social bonds, either friendly or unfriendly, between host and guests; yet it is sometimes possible for at least one party to choose to regard these exchanges as commodity-transactions, and thus to deny that any social bond is created. Dining is central to Roman culture as to all human cultures, and a great many accounts of convivia, or references to events that occur at convivia, are found in literary texts dating from or referring to the Julio-Claudian period.[5] The emperor himself, or a stand-in for the emperor, figures in a number of these accounts; in these cases, the focus is invariably on this figure's words and deeds, on his conduct in relation to the others who are present. By examining the flow of power through the convivium, and the different modes of exchange that structure and mediate that flow, I show how representations of the emperor at dinner confirm or undermine him as a legitimate bearer of authority, as one who gives and receives (or fails to do so) in ways that are deemed appropriate for so powerful a figure. Thus, observing the emperor's behavior in the power-laden context of the convivium is one way in which Romans of the early empire could render him comprehensible as a locus of concentrated power. At the same time, the emperor himself used the convivium as a stage on which to display himself and his power in particular ways and to particular ends.

I begin by examining the convivium itself as an element in a gift-

---

[5] While I focus on Julio-Claudian convivial practice and representation, I adduce earlier and later evidence when it exposes enduring practices and understandings. Indeed, in this section (2) I range more widely over late republican and early imperial sources that I do in later sections, as I develop a sociology of the power relations of the convivium in general.

exchange economy. In the context of a preexisting relationship, a dinner invitation could be regarded as confirming friendly bonds that already exist, while its absence might be taken as a slight. Thus, in *De Ira* 2.24, Seneca lists a series of perceived social slights that may cause one to grow angry: "He greeted me in a less-than-friendly manner; he did not cling to my kiss; he abruptly cut me off as I began to speak; he did not invite me to dinner; his expression seemed rather distant" (*ille me parum humane salutavit; ille osculo meo non adhaesit; ille inchoatum sermonem cito abrupit; ille ad cenam non vocavit; illius vultus aversior visus est*). The speaker here sees himself as entitled to receive a dinner invitation from the offender in view of their (apparently preexisting) relationship, just as he is entitled to a certain kind of kiss, a certain tone of greeting, and so on. Now, while a dinner invitation could no doubt be offered in the context of any relationship at almost any time, it seems commonly to have filled a particular position, with specifiable exchange value, in a sequence of alternating gifts that forge a new relationship. Juvenal, early in *Satire* 5, describes such a sequence in detail (vv. 12–23). Here the protagonist Trebius is invited to dine as a guest of a wealthy man named Virro. The poem's speaker, who describes to Trebius what his experience at this dinner will be, declares that this single invitation will constitute Trebius's entire repayment for having courted Virro for two months with regular *salutationes*—early-morning visits to a superior's house that display one's deference. He implies that this invitation is paltry recompense (12–15), and alleges that Virro's motives in inviting Trebius are not primarily to honor him (16–17); he also explicitly calls Trebius the *cliens* (16) of Virro, marking him as the subordinate party in this relationship: nevertheless, the speaker concedes, this invitation is exactly what Trebius was seeking (*"una simus," ait. votorum summa. quid ultra / quaeris?* 18–19).[6] Seneca too discusses this mode of establishing hierarchical relationships in *Ep.* 19.11, scrutinizing the superior party's aims and means. He declares to his interlocutor (putatively the addressee Lucilius, but as usual this interlocutor stands in for any member of Seneca's intended audience of fellow aristocrats) that he is wrong to suppose that he will find friends among those early-morning callers whom he subsequently invites to dinner: "You will have dinner guests whom your naming-slave has pulled from the

---

[6] This passage also illuminates a consequence of the incommensurability of gift-exchange: the various observers of an exchange can all reckon the current balance of the exchange differently. Thus, according to the speaker, Trebius regards the account as balanced (*quid ultra quaeris?*), while the speaker himself thinks that Trebius has given more than he will receive. Virro, presumably, would consider the dinner a munificent return and count himself ahead. See Konstan 1995: 336–38 on the actual and imagined positions of the various parties in this poem, and Damon 1997: 179–84 on its exchange dynamic.

crowd of *salutatores;* but the man is mistaken who looks for a friend in his reception area and puts him to the test in the convivium. The busy man beseiged by his own possessions has no greater ill than that he thinks people are his friends when he is no friend to them; that he fancies his benefactions effective at winning over people's minds, when for some people, the more they owe, the more they hate. A small debt obligates someone to you; a large one makes him your enemy." The interlocutor then responds with surprise: "What, benefactions don't win you friends?" (*quid ergo? beneficia non parant amicitias?* §12). His presupposition, which Seneca rejects, is that *beneficia* of the sort just discussed—specifically, hosting a selection of one's *salutatores* at a dinner party—will make these guests well-disposed toward their host, and hence make them his friends. Seneca points out that, on the contrary, the guests may resent and hate their host precisely *because* of the debt they owe.[7] Both Seneca and Juvenal, then, depict an exchange trajectory in which one party appears (perhaps repeatedly) as a *salutator* of the other, who eventually reciprocates by providing dinner; this relationship moreover is hierarchical, the first party inferior to the second. But dinner is not the only possible reciprocation for the *salutator*,[8] nor does this trajectory encompass the only role a dinner can play in an exchange relationship. The poet Martial suggests that a person may be seeking a dinner invitation when he praises someone's recitations or forensic speeches (2.27), flatters someone he meets in a bath (12.82), or sends a flattering poem (9.19); again, in all of these instances the target of praise is presented as the social superior.[9] Thus a dinner invitation by a superior can reciprocate a wide variety of objects and services offered by an inferior.

[7] My analysis here tacitly accepts the conclusions of Konstan 1995: against the view that *amicus* is often a euphemism for *cliens* or (more rarely) *patronus,* Konstan contends (p. 329 and passim) that *amicus* means "friend" in much the modern sense, someone in whose company one takes pleasure and toward whom one has warm feelings; one's client or patron may well be one's *amicus,* but this does not make *amicus* a synonym for "client" or "patron." White 1993: 30–31 (with notes) argues for a similar distinction. In the passage of Seneca under discussion (*Ep.* 19.11), the argument's point depends precisely on the distance between the idea of the socially subordinate guest/*salutator* and the (true) friend, the *amicus.*

[8] The objects and services a *salutator* receives in return vary inter alia with his status. Thus Martial complains at 12.29(26) that he, a mere equestrian, has his *salutationes* reciprocated only by the occasional invitation to dinner, while his addressee, a senator who also makes morning rounds, stands to receive in return a consulship or provincial governorship. On high-ranking aristocrats as *salutatores,* cf. Sen. *Ben.* 3.28.5–6. On the *salutatio* as an institutionalized occasion for interaction between persons of differing social status, see Saller 1982: 61–62, 128–29; Millar 1977: 141–42.

[9] Similarly in 1.44 Martial solicits dinner invitations by offering poems to his patron Stella. See Gowers 1993: 225 on the poetry-for-food exchange; also Petr. *Sat.* 5 v. 5.

This is not, of course, the end of the exchanges. The provision of dinner elicits still further objects and services in return, confirming and strengthening the personal relationship between the two transactors. In poem 10.19(18) Martial suggests that hosting convivia, along with gift giving generally, providing loans, and standing surety, are the sorts of offerings by which one acquires a crowd of "friends" who solicitously attend upon one (*turba . . . quae curet amicum,* v. 3) — though the Marius who is the subject of this poem makes no such gifts, yet absurdly has a multitude of cultivators nonetheless. In poem 9.100, Martial is invited to dinner by one Bassus and offered three *denarii* in addition, on the expectation that he will attend his host as a *salutator* the very next morning and accompany him on his daily rounds (see below).[10] A host may also look for a more material return for the meal he provides, such as a gift of silver plate or a new cloak (Mart. 7.86; cf. 10.15(14), 10.57).[11]

In the passages discussed so far, the host is the dominant partner in the relationship: his provision of dinner either (in his view) establishes his social superiority over his guests on the ground that this offering outweighs their *salutationes* or other offerings, or it presents such a hierarchical relationship as the status quo. Now, of course, men of lofty status also dined as guests of humbler men, and the status relations between them were not thereby reversed; several such situations are discussed below. Nevertheless, the vast majority of representations of early imperial convivia present a socially dominant host and subordinate guests; it was doubtless an economic reality that wealthier men could sustain the cost of providing more frequent and elaborate meals than poorer men. These status distinctions, moreover, were commonly asserted or displayed within the convivium itself. The host who pointedly distinguishes himself from his guests by serving them lower-quality foods and wines than he serves himself, or by expounding at length the

---

[10] Similarly at Hor. *Epist.* 1.7.46–95: the humble auctioneer Mena declines the aristocrat Philippus's invitation to dinner. Greeted first by Philippus the next day (a great honor, since normally an inferior greeted his superior first in this kind of street meeting: see Hall 1998), Mena apologizes for not having reciprocated with a morning visit to Philippus's house, and for not having greeted him first (68–69). After this exchange he cannot fail to come to dinner that night, whereupon he is ensnared into clientage, and the *salutatio*-for-dinner exchange that he initially resisted is regularized: *mane cliens et iam certus conviva* (75).

[11] Damon 1997: 146–71 offers a rich analysis of the nuances of exchange between superiors and inferiors in some 20 epigrams of Martial involving convivia. She, like Cloud 1989, teases detailed social-historical information out of epigram and satire, while pointing out the potential perils of working historically with such sources. See also Saller 1983: 251–53 and White 1993: 14–27 on the movement of objects and services between social unequals. Whether these ordinary exchanges were economically significant for either transactor is debated (e.g., Saller and White loc. cit.); my focus here is on their symbolic significance as tokens of social bonds.

exotic origins and great cost of the comestibles, furniture, or decor, is a topos of satirical writing in the early empire. The guests, in turn, may be vexed, abashed, and/or infuriated by being subjected to this humiliating presentation of the social status quo. Hosts may also make distinctions among their guests, giving to some higher-quality food and wine than to others; also, since in the standard nine-person triclinium the locations on the couches were themselves coded for status, the host inevitably created a social hierarchy among his guests simply by assigning them places to recline.[12] There is also some evidence that, in larger gatherings where more than one triclinium was used, different tables could be allocated to different status groups.[13] Satirical treatments of the invitation-to-dinner theme (such as Juvenal's *Satire* 5, discussed above) suggest that, for these reasons, convivia hosted by rich men often fail to repay the effort required to get invited. That is, the guests (or some of them) consider that, thanks to the insults and humiliation they suffer, the convivium as a whole does not measure up to, much less exceed, the gift-weight of their own client services. Conversely, passages that describe humble meals served with little elaboration also tend to insist that no invidious status distinctions are made,[14] and imply that the expected social bond formation does occur.

The host may also undermine this binding function if he makes the

---

[12] D'Arms 1990 discusses some of these features of the Roman convivium. Although his evidence is primarily Flavian, many of the phenomena he identifies are also attested for the Julio-Claudian period and earlier. Hosts serving themselves better food and wine than they serve their guests: Pliny *Ep.* 2.6; Mart. 1.18, 1.20, 1.43, 2.43, 3.49, 3.60, etc. (all from the guest's point of view), 12.27(28) (host's point of view); Juv. *Sat.* 5 passim (with Gowers 1993: 211–19); D'Arms 1990: 309, 315. For a Julio-Claudian instance see Petr. *Sat.* 34 (quality of wine tied to status of guests). Also, Plut. *Cato Minor* 6.1 attests (perhaps anachronistically) for the late republic the throwing of dice for the first choice of portions for a meal: this may be an equalizing gesture, implying that the portions themselves will not necessarily be equal. (On the lot-distribution of portions of food and other items in the early empire as "a mechanism for mitigating envy," see Barton 1993: 135). Hosts bragging about their food, furniture, etc.: Hor. *Serm.* 2.8.6–7, 42–53, 90–93 (with Gowers 161–79); Sen. *Tranq.* 1.7, *Ben.* 7.9.2–4; Mart. 8.6. Guests annoyed or awed in the face of such display: Hor. *Serm.* 2.8.26–33, 93–94; Petr. *Sat.* 41.1–5. Guest flattering host by praising his furniture: Plut. fr. 180 Sandbach.

[13] On hierarchical reclining arrangements, see D'Arms 1990: 315–16; the locus classicus is Plut. *Mor.* 615E–619F. Passages attesting or implying such arrangements for the Julio-Claudian period or late republic include Sal. *Hist.* 3.83M, Hor. *Serm.* 2.8.21–26, Sen. *Suas.* 7.13, Sen. *Const.* 15.1 (cf. *Brev.* 12.5, *Ep.* 47.5), *Ira* 3.37.4, Petr. *Sat.* 65.7, Plut. *Brut.* 34.8, *Ant.* 59.3–4. Different tables for different status groups: Cic. *Att.* 13.52.2, Suet. *Caes.* 48, Tac. *Ann.* 13.16; cf. D'Arms 309–11.

[14] Observed by D'Arms 1990: 318–19. See e.g., Mart. 5.78.22–25: *parva est cenula, quis potest negare? / sed finges nihil audiesve fictum / et vultu placidus tuo recumbes, / nec crassum dominus leget volumen* (etc.); similarly 10.47.7–8, 10.48.21–24, Pliny *Ep.* 1.15.4. Cf. Suet. *Tib.* 34.1, where the emperor is said to serve leftovers to encourage frugality by his own example.

expectation of reciprocity too overt. In poem 9.100, Martial is invited to dinner by one Bassus, and offered three *denarii* as well,[15] on the clear expectation that he will appear at Bassus's house the next morning as a *salutator* and attend him on his daily rounds. Martial declines this invitation, declaring "my toga is indeed worn and cheap and old: but I don't buy it for three *denarii*, Bassus" (*trita quidem nobis togula est vilisque vetusque: / denaris tamen hanc non emo, Basse, tribus*, 9.100.5–6). The toga here represents the condition of clientage (as often in Martial and elsewhere); Martial's claim that he did not get it for three *denarii* suggests that Bassus cannot have it (i.e, the client-services it represents) at that price, either. Thus Martial implies that Bassus has commodified this exchange: to offer food and money in return for specified services the very next day too overtly sets a price on those services, whereupon the invitation—ordinarily regarded as a gift—admits of being regarded as a commodity, thus losing its social binding force. Once it is commodified, Martial can reject the suggested exchange as a bad bargain, contending that the payment is too low.[16] Similarly, a passage in the anonymous poem entitled *Laus Pisonis* ("Praise of Piso"), which probably dates from the Claudian or Neronian period,[17] reveals a subordinate's anxieties about potential commodification of his relationship with a high-ranking aristocrat. The speaker declares (122–27) that many men surround themselves with companions gained through "morally bankrupt fee-for-service" (*impia merces*) rather than through "morally blameless love" (*purus amor*, 123): for example, a lowly person is invited to dinner, and paid a sum of money in addition, to suffer verbal abuse (126–27). Thus the collapse of the ideally amicable personal

---

[15] 3 *denarii* = 192 *quadrantes*, almost twice the regular amount of the *sportula* (100 *quadrantes*) given by private individuals to their *salutatores*. Martial (3.30, 60; 4.68, 10.27) indicates that this *sportula* was at least sometimes conjoined with a *cena recta*: cf. Hug, *RE* 3A.1885–86, and Duncan-Jones 1982: 138–40, esp. 139 n. 7. The *Laus Pisonis*, if it dates to the mid-first century, attests for the Julio-Claudian period a similar exchange of a dinner and money for specified services (vv. 126–27, and see below).

[16] Cf. Mart. 7.86: Sextus has stopped inviting his old friend Martial (*vetus sodalis*, 5) to his birthday dinner. Martial surmises that Sextus has broken their personal bond because Martial has not reciprocated with gifts such as silver plate, or a new toga or lamp (6–8). Martial concludes by declaring, *non est sportula quae negotiatur: / pascis munera, Sexte, non amicos* (9–10): that is, he accuses Sextus of regarding his invitations as commercial transactions whose aim is to elicit material recompense rather than to nurture personal bonds. In short, the relationship collapses because Sextus has commodified the exchanges it rests upon. See also Juv. *Sat.* 10.44–46, Epict. *Ench.* 25.

[17] This dating rests on the (uncertain) identification of the Piso in question with the conspirator of A.D. 65. Most manuscripts attribute the poem to Lucan, while the florilegia place it after Calpurnius Siculus's Bucolics (perhaps implying Calpurnius's authorship), and other stylistic and thematic parallels with the Bucolics have been adduced. On these matters see Amat 1991: vii-viii, xiv, 71–79.

bond is attributed to a process of price setting—i.e., commodification—which is manifested in the fee-for-service exchange at the dinner party.

These passages from Marital and the *Laus Pisonis* seem to privilege gift giving over commodity-exchange, the former idealized as entailing a warm personal bond between host and guest, and the latter stigmatized as involving only calculations of crass self-interest. In other texts, however, commodity-exchange appears as an attractive alternative to accepting a dinner invitation and its concomitant social subordination. In Martial 12.48 the speaker, who has been invited to a magnificent dinner, refuses to attend because he does not want to be bound into a hierarchical relationship (1–4, 15–16); he declares a preference for attending dinners he can reciprocate on the same scale (*haec mihi quam possum reddere cena placet*, 18). On the one hand, by declining this invitation, he avoids being "captured," i.e., subordinated in gift-debt.[18] On the other hand, to reciprocate a dinner with another dinner, in fairly short order, and on about the same level of munificence, as the speaker imagines doing, is to commodify the exchange (or is it rejecting the gift?) by returning precisely what he received. Indeed, this strategy is used by wary antagonists or rivals who would regard as intolerable the subordination imposed by an unreciprocated gift. Thus the rival warlords Sextus Pompeius, Antony, and Octavian host each other for dinner on successive days when meeting at Misenum in 39 B.C. (Dio 48.38.3, Plut. *Ant.* 32, App. *B.C.* 5.72–73); likewise for Octavian and Antony at Tarentum in 37 B.C. (Plut. *Ant.* 35, Dio 48.30.1); for Antony and Cleopatra when they first meet in Tarsus in 41 B.C. (Plut. *Ant.* 26.3–27.1); and for Augustus's adoptive son Gaius and the Parthian king Phraataces on the Euphrates in 1 A.D. (Vell. Pat. 2.101.3).[19]

A further variation on the linkage of dinner invitations and social

---

[18] *Convivas alios cenarum quaere magister, / quos capiant mensae regna superba tuae* (Mart. 12.48.15–16). Cf. Hor. *Epist.* 1.7.73–74, where Mena, having finally accepted Philippus's dinner invitation, is said to be hooked like a fish into the latter's clientela. In these poems, then, the social inferior regards the freedom associated with commodity exchange as preferable to the binding subordination imposed by gift exchange.

[19] Even in this situation, greater honor may accrue to the person hosting first: thus the three who met at Misenum cast lots to determine the order (so Pelling 1988: 190). Several passages from Seneca support my suggestion that the point of these mutual feastings is for all parties to avoid incurring gift-debt: for Seneca notes situations in which the recipient of a gift avoids obligation by reciprocating in kind, quickly, and on the same scale. At *Ben.* 2.21.1–2 Seneca posits a situation in which a disreputable man gives one money with which to buy one's freedom. In this case, says Seneca, one should accept the money *tamquam creditum, non tamquam beneficium*: one should repay it, but not enter into *amicitia* with him. To regard this money as a loan is to regard the exchange as a commodity-transaction, whereupon one can deny that any personal bond is forged. Also *Ben.* 4.40.4: *reiciendi genus est protinus aliud invicem mittere et munus munere expungere*. Similarly 6.35.3–4, 6.40.2–41.2, 7.19.7. For more on strategies to avoid incurring gift-debt, see section 6 below.

142 CHAPTER 3

subordination occurs when the inviter is of much lower status than the invitee. While examples illustrating this situation are few, all (somewhat counterintuitively) seem to imply that the host does not in this situation obligate his guest, but rather is obligated by him. Such a situation is described in detail in one of the minor declamations ascribed to Quintilian (301), in which a rich man, who has come to dinner at the house of a poor man, rapes the man's freeborn daughter (who brings in the food) upon being falsely told that she is a slave. The daughter then demands that the rich man marry her, and he in turn brings against the poor man a change of entrapment (*circumscriptio*). The poor man, speaking for himself in court, declares himself greatly honored that the rich man appeared at his humble board: *ago gratias: venisti, habuisti honorem, et illud humile limen intrasti* (§10)—though he also, in the fashion more typical of a host, declares that his invitation was an attempt to win his guest's favor (*quare tamen invitavi? quoniam promerenda nobis est vestra potentia*, §11). A bond has indeed been created, as the poor man presents it, for he later invokes the "prerogatives of our shared table" (*ius mensae communis*, §11) as a ground for claiming the rich man's aid, and he suggests more generally that this dinner put their relationship on a new footing (*cum mihi tecum coepisset novus usus*, §14). But both parties seem to agree that, in view of the wide social gap between them, the debt of obligation here resides with the host simply because the lofty guest has deigned to appear, rather than (as is usual) with the guest because he has received an invitation, food, entertainment, and perhaps other presents from the host. This text certainly postdates the Julio-Claudian period, since the minor declamations are Flavian at the earliest. However, the social dynamic articulated in this declamation allows us to make sense of an otherwise puzzling passage of Seneca. In his *De Tranquillitate Animi*, Seneca asserts that one must carefully evaluate the people one encounters in life, to decide whether they are worth expending one's time upon (7.1–2). Of the unworthy, Seneca writes, "some people even reckon up our services against us. Athenodorus [a philosopher] says that he will not even go to a dinner if the host will not be indebted to him for this" (*quidam enim ultro officia nobis nostra imputant. Athenodorus ait ne ad cenam quidem se iturum ad eum qui sibi nil pro hoc debiturus sit*). I take it that Athenodorus speaks here with the perverse elitism that sometimes characterizes the utterances of philosophers, inverting the usual expectation that the guest will be indebted to his host: he presents himself as a man of such lofty status that he confers honor on any host simply by deigning to accept the invitation.[20] Yet Seneca seems to approve of

[20] I mean "perverse elitism" literally: e.g., the case of Diogenes the Cynic who, as a slave

Athenodorus's stance, for in the next sentence he lends it support by deriding people who think they adequately reciprocate their friends' services just by hosting them at dinner. Such people, it seems, are unworthy of your expenditure of time for the very reason Athenodorus gives: they reckon against you the services you do for them—that is, they, as hosts, imagine they obligate you, the guest, when on this account the obligation actually flows the other way; and it flows that way presumably because of your own lofty status relative to them. Cicero too describes this sort of inversion (though he is critical of it) in a well-known passage of his *De Officiis* (2.69): he complains that lofty aristocrats not only do not regard themselves as obligated by benefits received, but believe that they have conferred a benefit just by accepting a benefit, however great it is. Yet Cicero himself, as D'Arms points out (1990: 315), reports that he squashed one Gnaeus Octavius, who badgered him with dinner invitations, by asking, "I say, who are you?" (*oro te: quis tu es? Fam.* 7.16.2). Cicero underscores Octavius's insignificance at *Fam.* 7.9.3, where he claims not quite to recall the man's name: "There's a Gnaeus Octavius—or maybe it's Gnaeus Cornelius . . . he is constantly asking me to dinner" (*Cn. Octavius est an Cn. Cornelius quidam: . . . is me . . . crebro ad cenam invitat*). While Cicero does not stoop to accept this invitation, one may conjecture that, had he eventually accepted, he would have regarded his presence as a gift outweighing the food, drink, etc., provided by the host; Octavius might well have agreed. Undoubtedly aristocrats did dine sometimes, perhaps often, as honored guests of lesser men, and it seems likely that under such circumstances both parties might regard the aristocrat as conferring the greater benefit simply by showing up.[21] This social dynamic is worth keeping in mind, since it

---

for sale upon the scaffold, tells the auctioneer to hawk him to anyone who wants a master for himself (Diog. Laert. 6.29–30). Here, as in the statement of Athenodorus, the philosopher is invoking an aristocracy of virtue, in which he is a high-ranking member of the elite, that trumps the conventional aristocracy of birth and wealth. Yet, in these cases at least, the philosopher's position in this (novel) aristocracy of virtue is articulated by invoking the traditional symbols of social status, such as slaveholding or the obligations incurred by attending a dinner party. Cf. Sen. *Ben.* 5.6.2–7 on how a philosopher can top a king in transacting gifts.

[21] See also Horace's modest tone in his invitation to Maecenas (*Carm.* 3.29.1–16), along with the observations of Lendon 1997: 65: "If a man is grand enough, to have him as a guest is honorific: he is doing you a favour." Again 69: "The honour consequences of a favour cannot be determined without estimating the disparity of prestige between the men." On 96 Lendon discusses people so lowly as to be beneath aristocratic notice, and to be ignored because to give them any attention at all (even negative) is to dignify them too much. Similarly, David 1992: 167–68 argues that, in the late republic, the character of the relationship established between a (judicial) patron and a client he has defended depended both upon the magnitude of the patron's service and upon the relative status of the two parties.

may be germane to situations where the emperor dines as a guest of someone else. Specifically, it may illuminate the dynamics of the convivium in which the equestrian Vedius Pollio hosts the emperor Augustus (section 4 below).

The emperor, like any other aristocrat, exploits the structural features of the dinner-party and its gift-exchange dynamic (including the tension with commodity-exchange), in order to bind and subordinate his guests to himself. Three Julio-Claudian examples will suffice for the discussion here. The simplest is first: Suetonius (*Vesp.* 2.3) reports that the young Vespasian, holding a praetorship under Caligula when this emperor was hostile to the senate, once gave thanks before that body that the emperor had invited him to dinner. Now, Suetonius adds that Vespasian also decreed that conspirators be left unburied, and requested that extra games be added to Caligula's German triumph—suggesting that Vespasian was a flatterer, seeking to differentiate himself from the mass of senators whom Caligula disliked. Nevertheless, Vespasian's thanksgiving for the dinner marks him publicly as a willing gift-debtor to the emperor, one contentedly bound into a subordinate relationship by virtue of having dined as his guest. For Seneca argues at length that the recipient of a benefit should broadcast his benefactor's generosity to the widest possible audience (*Ben.* 2.11.2–3, 2.22–25), thus indicating his warm feelings, making a beginning of reciprocation, and acknowledging the bond formed between them. Thus, whatever Vespasian's motives and Suetonius's opinion of them, the surface of this exchange displays in simple, ideal form the construction of the emperor's authority as legitimate by virtue of his gift giving.[22]

The second example, also from Suetonius, involves Augustus's convivial practices: Suetonius says (*Aug.* 74), "He held dinner parties constantly, always with full formality, and always with careful discrimination among men and ranks. Valerius Messalla reports that no freedman was ever invited to dinner by him except for Menas, but in his case only when he was granted freeborn status after betraying Sextus Pompeius's fleet" (*convivabatur assidue nec umquam nisi recta, non sine magno hominum ordinumque dilectu. Valerius Messala tradit neminem umquam libertinorum adhibitum ab eo cenae excepto Mena, sed asserto in ingenuitatem post proditam Sexti Pompei classem*). The claim that Menas was the only freedman ever to dine with Augustus is presented

---

[22] Pliny's *Panegyricus*, a speech to the senate thanking Trajan for making him consul, presents itself similarly as a simple avowal of subordination and gratitude for the emperor's benefactions. See §§90–92 for Trajan's benefactions to Pliny, and passim for the latter's subordination. Similar is Dio 59.27.1, where a senator gives a speech of thanks for receiving a kiss from Caligula. On speeches of thanks as a mode of reciprocating imperial favors, see Lendon 1997: 156–57 and n. 256, with further references.

here as the exception proving the stated rule, that this emperor discriminated carefully among men and social classes when arranging his dinner parties: for Menas, one of Sextus Pompeius's admirals, was granted freeborn status, a gold ring, and enrolled as an equestrian, in return for having gone over to Octavian in 38 B.C., delivering to him Sardinia, Corsica, ships, and men (Dio 48.45.5–7, App. *B.C.* 5.78–80). This signal service, without which Octavian might never have defeated Sextus at all, also earned Menas a place among Octavian's dinner guests. In this case, however, amicable reciprocity was not maintained. For Menas considered all of Octavian's honors to him inadequate since he was not given a command in the fleet; he therefore defected back to Sextus in 36 — apparently revoking his service, at least symbolically. Shortly thereafter he returned to Octavian but was now regarded with outright suspicion; he died the following year.[23] Whatever the complexities of Menas's actual exchange relationship with Octavian, the Suetonius passage portrays a *princeps* who issues invitations appropriately, violating his principle of honoring exclusively aristocratic guests only in order to reciprocate a major gift he had previously received. This scrupulous reckoning of his gift-debts, and their display and reciprocation in convivial contexts, is of a piece with his dining practices more generally, as Suetonius describes them (*Aug.* 74): for Augustus generally arrived late and left early (whereas decadent convivia began early and ran late); he provided relatively few courses of no great luxury, but was extremely companionable, drawing out the reticent in conversation. Such affability and unpretentiousness in the convivium, as noted above, is associated with the absence of onerous displays of social hierarchy.

The third example, once more from Suetonius, again involves the emperor Caligula. Toward the end of A.D. 39, having spent all the money at his disposal (*Cal.* 37.3), Caligula transported all manner of goods from Rome to Lugdunum (modern Lyon) and auctioned them there to the provincials, in an effort to raise money. In the course of the auction, Suetonius reports the following (§39.2): "He had learned that a wealthy provincial had paid out 200,000 sesterces to the slaves who issued his invitations, in order to be seated at a convivium by deceit. Caligula was not at all annoyed that the honor of his table was valued so highly; on the next day, as this man was sitting at the auction, the emperor sent someone to deliver him some trifle for 200,000 sesterces, and to tell him that he would dine with Caesar at Caesar's personal invitation." Strik-

---

[23] Menas returns to Sextus: Dio 48.54.7, App. *B.C.* 5.96. He deserts again to Octavian: Dio 49.1.3–4, App. *B.C.* 5.101–102. He dies in 35: Dio 49.37.6. The *ius ingenuitatis* was later in the emperor's power to bestow: see Saller 1982: 42, with *Dig.* 40.11. For the connections among the *anulus aureus*, free birth, and equestrian status, see ch. 4 nn. 89, 98 below.

ing here is the provincial's overt commodification of the dinner invitation: he set a price of 200,000 sesterces on a single evening's presence at the imperial board. Now, had this situation not come to the emperor's attention, presumably the slaves would have been paid and the provincial would have come to dinner, but perhaps not regarded himself as obligated and subordinated in gift-debt, inasmuch as he had purchased his place there. Nor, presumably, would Caligula himself ever have known of this transaction. Once apprised, however, the emperor arranged instead to take the man's money through a transaction at the auction, a commodity-exchange context in which no gift-obligation is incurred by either party (even if, on this account, the provincial did not receive value for his money). Caligula could not have simply accepted the money as a gift, were it offered, lest he incur a gift-debt in turn, hence the importance of the commodity-exchange armature. Then he sent a personal invitation to the man to dine with him—presumably a more intimate, and binding, gesture than leaving the invitation to the discretion of a slave—thereby imposing a gift-debt upon him.[24] If this analysis is correct, Caligula is portrayed here as exploiting brilliantly the different ways in which objects circulate and in which sociability is constructed in the regimes of gift-exchange and commodity-exchange: he maximizes both his monetary profits and the gift-debts owed him.[25]

3. Speech and Power: Amicable and Hostile Reciprocity in the Convivium

So far, I have considered how the provision of dinner, or even merely issuing an invitation, functions as one object of exchange among other objects and services in the larger world. Next I examine the offerings

---

[24] Hurley 1993: 152 comments on this passage, "Gaius, now reduced to the level of his bribe-taking staff, auctions off the pleasure of his own company. The trifle (*nescio quid frivoli*) is a pretense that the Gaul's cash outlay was for merchandise, not for an invitation." True, provided one recognizes that this pretense is economically and ideologically central to the whole transaction. Also, there is probably no such thing as a "bribe" in the context of a patrimonial administrative system: for the idea of the bribe—the offering of money to create a special social bond that has a view toward some sort of future reciprocation—is precisely the aim of the gift. Alternatively, one may say that "bribe" is another word for "gift," but from the viewpoint of someone accustomed to rational-legal administrative systems. See e.g., Saller 1982: 126 and n. 45; Garnsey and Saller 1987: 152, Dixon 1993a: 62.

[25] See Millar 1977: 168 for a Trajanic parallel. For more on Caligula's strategies as a transactor of gifts and commodities, and on his handling of auctions in particular, see section 6 below.

and exchanges, particularly verbal ones, that take place within the convivium itself. For through their verbal sallies and other actions, guests may please their host and so elicit further gifts, perpetuating a cycle of amicable reciprocity, or they may offend him and suffer retaliation, initiating a cycle of hostile reciprocity. Indeed, a guest's speech in the convivium can be regarded as at least partial reciprocation for the food and drink itself, provided such speech is deemed appropriate. In Petronius's *Satyricon,* for example, the host Trimalchio twice reproaches silent guests by saying, "you used to be pleasant at dinner gatherings" (*solebas suavis esse in convictu*, 61.1–2, 64.2) — exposing the expectation that guests should speak so as to give pleasure to the assembled company, and alluding to these particular guests' success in speaking thus at prior dinners (in the first case he elicits a werewolf story; in the second a song). The exchange-aspect of convivial speech is clearer in Martial 9.35, where a guest named Philomusus is said to earn his dinner (*cenam mereris*, v. 1) by telling fantastic "news" during the meal; and it is manifest in a passage of Plutarch's *Quaestiones Conviviales*, where a guest, after intervening in the discussion at hand, declares to the host, "This is my contribution, counted over to you in return for these festivities."[26] As even these few passages indicate, verbal interventions of many sorts were possible in convivial contexts: singing, storytelling, joking, and conversations on literary, philosophical, or other theoretical topics all might have their time and place.[27] For a guest dining at the invitation of someone of higher status, then, the pressing problem was to identify the specific form and content with which to endow his utterances so as to give pleasure to the assembled company, and especially to the host, in the immediate convivial situation. It seems unsurprising that lower-status guests might construct their utterances (of whatever form) to include flattery of their higher-status hosts; our sources provide many representations of flattering speech by guests. Perhaps more surprisingly, however, our sources also indicate that abusive, insulting speech by guests was common — indeed, abuse seems to have been no less usual, appropriate, and desirable in the convivium than flattering, deferential speech, provided it was deployed appropriately. Deployed inappropriately, on

---

[26] Plut. *Mor.* 682A: αὗταί σοι, εἶπον, ὦ Φλῶρε, συμβολαὶ τῆς εὐωχίας ἀπηριθμήσθωσαν. Similarly 664D, 668D. On social behavior more generally as an object of exchange, and for the implication of such exchange in the construction of social hierarchies. See Homans 1958.

[27] The topics treated in Plutarch's *Quaestiones Conviviales* (*Mor.* 612C–748D) are varied; all purport to be discussions at dinner, and several topics concern dining itself. Cf. Hor. *Serm.* 2.6 (the mouse fable told at dinner); also Gell. 19.9 and Suet. *Tib.* 56 for literary topics. Serious discussions are sometimes called inappropriate (or at least atypical) to convivial contexts: Cic. *Off.* 1.144; see also below on convivial *urbanitas.*

the other hand, either mode of speech could give offense, triggering retaliation and thus turning the convivial exchange hostile.

A guest who seeks to please the host and so to perpetuate the amicable social bond forged by his acceptance of the invitation may well choose to speak in a complimentary, deferential manner. Such speech, of course, may not represent the guest's actual judgments: literary descriptions of dinner parties represent guests applauding the host with more enthusiasm than they feel, or suppressing laughter (Petr. *Sat.* 47.7, 48.7; Hor. *Serm.* 2.8.77–78, 82–83)—types of self-misrepresentation that I identified above (chapter 2.7) as characteristic of the discourse of flattery. The payoff, however, is that hosts may be pleased and give further gifts in return for such speech. Seneca (*Ep.* 47.8) describes a hypothetical convivium in which guests who engage in flattery (*adulatio*), or display "immoderation in eating or speech" (*intemperantia aut gulae aut linguae*), are rewarded with another invitation for the following evening; similarly, in Petronius's *Satyricon* (52.7), the declaimer Agamemnon enthusiastically applauds a joke of Trimalchio's, for "he knew by what services he might be invited again to dinner."[28]

Yet, vituperation and mockery also occur regularly in convivial speech—a mode of speaking that our sources call "free."[29] Coming from a guest, such speech is often directed against the host or other guests, though sometimes also against people who are absent. Like praise, abusive speech is sometimes said to be appropriate and even desirable: Quintilian twice specifies the convivium as an important social context in which jokes are delivered and *urbanitas* displayed (*Inst.* 6.3.14, 105). Thus, perhaps counterintuitively, such speech may in certain respects strengthen and confirm friendly social bonds at this occasion, contributing to a cycle of amicable reciprocity; descriptions of convivial speech in the Julio-Claudian period bear this out. In *Ep.* 122.12–13 Seneca relates a pair of jokes delivered by an equestrian named Varus at the expense of a certain wastrel, Acilius Buta: Seneca describes Varus as a "pursuer of good dinners, which he used to earn by the outrageousness of his speech" (*cenarum bonarum adsectator, quas improbitate linguae merebatur,* §12). It is unclear whether the jokes related here are made in the context of a dinner party, but if so, Buta is not the host, nor apparently is he present; he is merely a convenient target. Nevertheless, Varus's witty insults exemplify the "outrageousness of speech" that gives pleasure and thus wins him invitations to dine at the houses of men richer and more powerful than he. The convivial

---

[28] Damon 1997 analyzes some of the rhetorical strategies by which parasites flatter their hosts, especially confirming or reiterating his assertions with amplification: see pp. 81–85 (on Terence), 177–79 (on Juvenal).

[29] Cf. ch. 2.7 and n. 87 above.

setting is more certain at *Ep.* 27.6–8: Seneca relates two jokes made by Satellius Quadratus, described as "one who nibbles at stupid rich men, and consequently, one who smiles at them and, what follows from both of these, one who mocks them" (*stultorum divitum adrosor et, quod sequitur, adrisor et, quod duobus his adiunctum est, derisor*). The butt of these jokes is his host Calvisius Sabinus, who both here and earlier in this letter is characterized as precisely such a "stupid rich man" (§§5–6).[30] The jokes presumably show Satellius in his role as "mocker" (*derisor*), but the causal linkage by which Seneca connects the roles of "nibbler" (*adrosor*), "smiler" (*adrisor*), and "mocker" (*derisor*) suggests that delivering witty insults with an ingratiating smile is precisely a strategy for cadging dinner invitations.[31] Horace too portrays an abusive dinner guest who readily insults everyone at the party:

saepe tribus lectis videas cenare quaternos,
e quibus unus amet quavis aspergere cunctos
praeter eum qui praebet aquam; post hunc quoque potus,
condita cum verax aperit praecordia Liber:
hic tibi comis et urbanus liberque videtur.

(*Serm.* 1.4.86–90)

You can often see foursomes dining on the three couches, among whom one person will love to insult everyone in any way possible, except for him who serves the water [i.e., the host]; but once he is drunk, he insults the host too, when truthful wine has revealed the things hidden in the heart. This man seems to you refined and urbane and free.

The host himself becomes a target once this abusive guest has drunk sufficient wine (*verax Liber*). Horace himself is condemning this behavior, but presents his putative addressee, a generic Roman (v. 85), as regarding such speech as entirely suitable in context—"refined," "urbane," and "free" (*liber*) like the wine itself (*Liber*). The inevitable presence of wine is a key reason why such speech is presented as usual,

---

[30] Calvisius Sabinus: cos. A.D. 26; *PIR*² C 354. Satellius Quadratus: *PIR*¹ S 145; otherwise unknown.

[31] Saggese 1994: 54 (and n. 8) compares this passage to Mart. 6.44.3–4: *omnibus adrides, dicteria dicis in omnis / sic te convivam posse placere putas*. Here too the addressee, a dinner guest, believes (wrongly, in Martial's view) that mocking and smiling makes him a pleasant dinner companion (see also Damon 1997: 149–50 on this poem). Still, such passages suggest that abusive speech could be expected to please at least some members of the party: Plut. *Quaest. Conv.* 2.1 (*Mor.* 629E–634F), on the art of making pleasant conversation at dinner, discusses how to make jokes so exquisitely urbane and calibrated as to gratify even the person who is their target (629F, 631C), without ever inspiring resentment.

appropriate, and even desirable in the convivial context, enabling skilled practicioners of such speech earn a return invitation.[32]

But other, greater rewards are also possible. Plutarch (*Ant.* 28.7–12) tells of a Greek physician named Philotas, dining as a guest of Marc Antony's son Antyllus in Alexandria in the 30s B.C., who uses a rhetorical trick (σόφισμα) — in this case, an absurd enthymeme whose conclusion is identical to its major premise — to flummox and silence a tiresome, long-winded fellow guest. Delighted at Philotas's wit, Antyllus gives him a quantity of valuable drinking vessels.[33] Such a gift far outstrips a mere dinner invitation. Yet even a rich gift of valuables, which is presumably in the power of any aristocrat to bestow upon a dining companion of lower status, pales in comparison to the uniquely valuable gifts that may be had from the emperor when he is present himself at a convivium. Suetonius reports (*Tib.* 42.1) that Tiberius, at some unspecified time early in his reign, was so pleased with the good fellowship of two dining companions, Pomponius Flaccus and Lucius Piso, during a two-day, one-night debauch, that he appointed the former

---

[32] Abusive speech at convivia may have been institutionalized to some degree. Barton 1993: 107–108 (and ch. 4 passim) suggests that the terms *derisor* and *scurra* do not merely describe the behavior of certain participants, but indicate a role to be filled. It may be filled either by a guest (as in the examples cited above), or by a slave, for there is some evidence that certain slaves were specially trained to deliver abuse, targeting the host (their own master) as well as the guests. At *Const.* 11.2–3, for example, Seneca claims that we take pleasure in the abusive speech of slaves because they are socially far inferior to us (*contemptissimi*), yet we regard the very same speech as *contumelia* or *maledicta* if it comes from one of our *amici*. The implication is that invective only threatens our status if it comes from someone whose status is sufficiently near our own (see Sen. *Prov.* 1.6, Suet. *Tib.* 61.6, Dio 48.44.3, and Mart. 10.3.1 for *dicta* by slaves at convivia; cf. Sen. *Ira* 3.35.2, *Ep.* 47.3). If indeed abusive speech at convivia was quasi-institutionalized, its function may have been apotropaic, as Barton suggests (125–29, 142–43) — warding off from its targets divine or human envy, and perhaps expressly countering flattery.

[33] This passage is the more interesting in that Antyllus, the host, is juridically and socially a child according to Roman social categories, while his guests include adults upon whom he is passing judgment and bestowing rewards. For he cannot have been born before the mid-40s B.C. (Groebe *RE* s.v. Antonius 32; Pelling 1988 ad loc.). Having accompanied Antony to Egypt in the 30s (Plut. *Ant.* 57.3, Dio 51.6.1), he donned the *toga virilis* — normally assumed at age 15 or 16, and marking the transition to adulthood — only in 30 B.C., shortly before being captured and executed Octavian (Plut. *Ant.* 71.2–3, 81.1, 87.1; Suet. *Aug.* 17.5, Dio 51.15.5). While Plutarch offers no precise indication of Antyllus's age, nor of a particular date within the 30s for the events described, still Antyllus is repeatedly called a παῖς, and in §28.10–11 Philotas questions whether the vessels are actually in his power to give — presumably because of his youth. In Roman convivial practice, only adult males (i.e., those who had assumed the *toga virilis*) normally reclined, the posture marking their full participation as adults in the convivium; before this age they sat (Bradley 1998: 46). Could Antyllus have been hosting as a seated boy, while his adult male guests reclined? On the other hand, would these dinners in Alexandria with Greek guests necessarily have been held in a Roman convivial style?

legate of Syria and the latter city prefect, declaring them "exceptionally pleasant" and "friends of all hours" (*iucundissimi, omnium horarum amici*).³⁴ The emperor's characterization of his guests indicates that they well reciprocated by their convivial speech and behavior the emperor's initial offering of food and drink, and so confirmed an amicable social bond; as a result he bestowed upon them these still greater gifts.³⁵ But while Flaccus and Piso were distinguished aristocrats and therefore could be regarded a priori as suitable candidates for such posts, the same cannot be said for another fortunate guest discussed later in the same section. For Suetonius goes on to say (§42.2) that Tiberius once preferred a candidate of low birth for a quaestorship over candidates of higher birth, because he finished off an amphora of wine after Tiberius drank his health.³⁶ Now, these anecdotes, and the others that accompany them in §42 of the life of Tiberius, are presented as noteworthy instances of excess, illustrating this emperor's immoderation in food and drink, and the value he places on similar immoderation in others; thus they pave the way for the subsequent account (§§43–45) of

---

³⁴ Pomponius Flaccus: cos. ord. A.D. 17 (*PIR*² P 715, which however does not place him in Syria until A.D. 32). L. Calpurnius Piso Frugi: cos. 15 B.C. (*PIR*² C 289); d. A.D. 32. Pliny *Nat.* 14.145 likewise says that Piso was made *praefectus urbi* after a drinking bout with Tiberius (cf. Sen. *Ep.* 83.14 for Piso's drunkenness), though Tac. *Ann.* 6.11.3 (cf. 6.10.3) gives a date inconsistent with this account (unless emended).

³⁵ Although Suetonius does not indicate clearly, I assume here — perhaps circularly — that Tiberius was the host precisely because he bestowed these offices. For the host commonly provided, in addition to the food and drink, further gifts for his guests to take away (*apophoreta*), gifts procured and prepared for distribution in advance. These might be small or substantial, often graded like the food and wine according to the status of the recipients (see e.g., Suet. *Aug.* 75 and Mart. 14.1.5–6 [and passim] for differential distributions at public festivals; also Petr. *Sat.* 40.4, 56.8, 60.4 for the *apophoreta* at Trimalchio's convivium — in one case [§56.7–8] distributed by lot). Emperors might give very rich gifts indeed to aristocratic guests: Domitian, on Dio's account (67.9), terrified a group of senators and equestrians by staging a dinner party as a funeral banquet, but at the end he gave each guest a large silver grave stele — inscribed with the guest's name — and expensive slave boys. (On this passage, and on the generally close association of the convivium with death and funerary ritual, see Dunbabin 1986: 194–95 and passim.) Perhaps the public offices distributed by Tiberius here should not be categorized as *apophoreta*, since they seem to have been given ad hoc and not provided for in advance: but even so, the expectation that hosts would provide their guests with presents beyond food, drink, and entertainment might invite readers to infer that Tiberius was the host. Cf. Suet. *Cal.* 18.2, where Caligula awards a praetorship to a senator who eats with notable gusto at a public banquet.

³⁶ *Ignotissimum quaesturae candidatum nobilissimis anteposuit ob epotam in convivio propinante se vini amphoram*. For the *propinatio*, in which one reveler toasts another by taking a sip from his own cup and then passing it to the honoree to drain, cf. Juv. *Sat.* 5.127–30, Plaut. *Curc.* 359. In this case, then, Tiberius picks up the amphora itself, takes a sip, and passes it to the man in question. For other sorts of prizes given for heavy drinking, see Pliny *Nat.* 14.140.

Tiberius's even more excessive sexual behavior while in retirement at Capreae. But regardless of this implied excess and exceptionality, Suetonius's anecdotes here presuppose that the reader accepts that the emperor has such gifts at his disposal, and that at convivia guests may be further rewarded by their host for appropriate speech and behavior (it is with such hopes, presumably, that the provincial in Lugdunum offered 200,000 sesterces to dine with Caligula). The quality of excess, in Suetonius's account, is in the kind of behavior that is rewarded so handsomely, especially considering that Tiberius is publicly condemning such behavior at the very same time.[37]

Yet the balance between fellow feeling and antagonism in the convivium was a fine one, and the kinds of speech discussed so far by which guests could please their hosts might also give offense, eliciting reprisals and initiating a cycle of hostile reciprocation. Suetonius reports (*Tib.* 54) that Tiberius liked to pose questions to his dinner guests derived from his daily reading. A scholar (*grammaticus*) named Seleucus learned from the emperor's slaves what he had been reading, and so arrived at dinner well primed—presumably hoping to impress and please his host, and so gain further rewards. But he overreached: Tiberius found out, ejected Seleucus from his company, and later forced him to suicide. Likewise, complaisant, deferential speech, which we have seen could earn guests further rewards from their hosts, might infuriate them instead. Seneca, in *De Ira* 3.8.6, describes an agreeable client dining with Marcus Caelius Rufus; Caelius becomes so vexed at his guest's *adsentatio* (flattery, "saying yes") that he cries out, "contradict me, that there may be two of us" (*dic aliquid contra ut duo simus*). Nor was Caelius alone in his preference for pugnacious guests: other hosts too are said to be pleased by "free" convivial speech precisely because they then feel assured that they are not being flattered, for they associate flattery with complaisant speech. Thus Plutarch reports that Antony could not believe that guests who spoke boldly in the convivium might seek to flatter him in other settings; as a result he was regularly taken in by flattery (*Ant.* 24.7–12). Similarly, Horace in *Epistula* 1.18.15–20 describes a guest who makes a show of quarreling with his host to prove his candor and independence—yet he disagrees only on trifling matters, never on important ones. In these two cases, guests ostentatiously employ convivial "free" speech in order to leave the impression that, when they elsewhere express agreement, they are not being complaisant flatterers, but

---

[37] *Tib.* 42.1: *in ipsa publicorum morum correctione*; also, in the same section: *Sestio Gallo, libidinoso ac prodigo seni, . . . a se ante paucos dies apud senatum increpito, cenam ea lege condixit ne quid ex consuetudine immutaret aut demeret utque nudis puellis ministrantibus cenaretur.*

really do agree; thus they actually exploit the host's resistance to complaisant speech as part of a complex strategy to flatter.

But if complaisant, flattering speech could sometimes give offense rather than pleasure, the same is true of "free" or abusive convivial speech. The role of such speech in a cycle of hostile reciprocity is depicted by Horace in *Sermo* 2.8 when the guest Vibidius expressly declares that the company should seek vengeance by drinking to the point of "causing harm" (*"nos nisi damnose bibimus moriemur inulti" / et calices poscit maiores*, vv. 34–35) It is unclear precisely what the host Nasidienus has done to incite his guests to seek vengeance; perhaps his exposition of the novelty and exotic origins of the dishes (26–30) angers them, a phenomenon discussed in section 2 above. At any rate, Nasidienus blanches at Vibidius's declaration, fearing (according to the speaker Fundanius) either that the wine will dull his guests' palates—thereby negating an important aspect of the host's display, namely the novel flavors of the dishes (cf. 26–30)—or that, because of heavier drinking, the guests will "speak ill more freely" (*maledicunt liberius*, 37): in this case, the host evidently does not relish the prospect of the mocking, abusive, "free" speech associated with convivial wine drinking.[38] After the collapse of a dusty tapestry onto the food (54–59), Nasidienus seeks to salvage things with a new offering of food, as if starting the convivium over. But the earlier pattern is replicated: he again expatiates on the exotic origins of the food offered (85–93), which is again taken by the guests as initiating a cycle of hostile reciprocation requiring vengeance, which they exact by fleeing without tasting anything (*quem nos sic fugimus ulti . . .* , 93–95).[39] Other texts do not depict equally full cycles of hostile reciprocity, but there are many hints or declarations that, especially if a guest speaks "freely," his relationship with the host will turn into an antagonistic exchange of reprisals. Juvenal's speaker in *Satire* 5 reminds the unfortunate Trebius that he will be put unceremoniously out of doors if ever he dares to speak "as though he has three names"[40]—i.e., as though he is a free Roman citizen, which

---

[38] [*Vibidius*] *calices poscit maiores. vertere pallor / tum parochi faciem nil sic metuentis ut acris / potores, vel quod maledicunt liberius vel / fervida quod subtile exsurdant vina palatum* (Hor. *Serm.* 2.8.35–38).

[39] For a summary of the scholarly debate regarding the cause of the ill feeling represented in this poem, see Caston 1997: 233–34 and n. 2. I find her suggestion (245 n. 50) congenial that the "fall of the curtain," in a poem filled with comedic elements and whose narrator is a comic poet, "divides the poem and initiates a new drama . . . following Roman custom." From the point of view of convivial social dynamics, however, the new drama virtually replays the old. For guests avenging themselves upon an outrageous host, cf. Mart. 3.82.33.

[40] *Duceris planta velut ictus ab Hercule Cacus / et ponere foris, si quid temptaveris umquam / hiscere tamquam habeas tria nomina* (Juv. *Sat.* 5.125–27).

of course he is. This phrase conceals a pun on the unexpressed word *libertas*, which means "the condition of not being a slave," but also has a more restricted (but related) usage signifying "freedom of speech." The point is that if Trebius speaks in a way appropriate to a free citizen, i.e., "freely," he will give offense and incur retaliation. Plutarch too, in his treatise on pleasant convivial conversation (*Mor.* 629E–634F), specifically notes the perils of making jokes under the influence of wine, which are more likely to be ill calibrated and so cause anger (631C): indeed, he suggests in passing that angry outbursts in convivia are utterly common occurrences (631C, 634E).[41] Thus "free" speech/abuse, like praise/flattery, was a double-edged mode of speech in convivial settings: it was capable of pleasing the host and assembled company, and also capable of alienating them. Manifestly, it was a kind of virtuosity for a guest to select the right combination of strategies for a given group on a given night, and to shift strategies at appropriate moments, so as to maximize the gift-weight of his own performance and consequently to maximize the gifts that might accrue to him subsequently.

4. DINING WITH RULERS: THE CONSTRUCTION OF IMPERIAL AUTHORITY

In this socially delicate situation, where the protocols for proper speech and behavior were complex and frequently contradictory, and where the host's reception of any given speech or action on the part of a guest was highly contingent, the prospect of dining with the emperor, with his power massively to reward or penalize his guests at will, must have been simultaneously alluring and terrifying to Julio-Claudian aristocrats. I noted above some of the benefits that elites reaped upon pleasing the emperor at dinner, and also some risks they incurred; in this section I examine in greater detail the principles for the emperor's reception of convivial speech and action: that is, I aim to discover how the give-and-take of convivial interaction comes to generate amicable or hostile reciprocity between emperor and elites, and what these outcomes are taken as signifying about the legitimacy of the power the emperor wields. Thus I hope to show how writers of the Julio-Claudian

---

[41] Other passages in which wit or mockery produced by socially inferior guests causes them to fear or suffer reprisals at the hands of the socially superior host: Plut. *Pomp.* 33.5, *Ant.* 59.8, Sen. *Suas.* 7.13; see also section 4 below. Martial mentions guests who scatter abuse and insults at a dinner, supposing themselves pleasing on this count (as being masters of one convivial speech genre), but who in fact are widely disliked (6.44, 9.9(10), cf. 1.41). Sen. *Ira* 3.37.1 recommends that you avoid dining with members of "the crowd," because their wit in the convivium may sting you, inciting anger.

period use the convivium, with its complex but utterly familiar social roles and power relations, as a conceptual "handle" on the emperor's authority—a familiar framework in which to locate this evolving locus of power and so to enmesh it in a series of relationships that crystallize and expose salient aspects of that power. Specifically, placing the emperor in a convivial context reveals both some of the threats that his power poses to aristocrats who confront it, and also some of the resources available to these aristocrats to manipulate and exploit that power to their own advantage.

A pair of exemplary anecdotes related by Seneca in *De Beneficiis* (3.26–27) encapsulates a set of elite anxieties about dining and drinking in the shadow of the emperor's power. While this treatise dates perhaps to the middle of Nero's reign, the stories told here describe two aristocrats' encounters with this power in the reigns of Tiberius and Augustus, respectively. Yet Seneca begins by characterizing these anecdotes as "examples of our own day," indicating that they are directly relevant to the situation of his own readers. First, then, the Tiberian anecdote:

(3.26.1) nostri saeculi exempla non praeteribo. Sub Tiberio Caesare fuit accusandi frequens et paene publica rabies, quae omni civili bello gravius togatam civitatem confecit. excipiebatur ebriorum sermo, simplicitas iocantium. nihil erat tutum: omnis saeviendi placebat occasio, nec iam reorum expectabantur eventus, cum esset unus. cenabat Paulus praetorius in convivio quodam imaginem Tiberi Caesaris habens ectypa et eminente gemma. (§2) rem ineptissimam fecero si nunc verba quaesiero quemadmodum dicam illum matellam sumpsisse; quod factum simul et Maro ex notis illius temporis vestigatoribus notavit et servus eius quoi nectebantur insidiae. is subsidians ei ebrio et anulum extraxit et cum Maro convivas testaretur admotam esse imaginem obscenis et iam subscriptionem componeret, ostendit in manu sua servus anulum. si quis hunc servum vocat, et illum convivam vocabit.

I will not omit exempla from our own age. Under Tiberius Caesar there was a constant and nearly universal frenzy of accusations, which crushed the Roman citizenry more heavily than any civil war. The words of people who were intoxicated were seized upon, as was the guilelessness of people as they joked. Nothing was safe: any pretext for savagery was acceptable, nor were verdicts on defendents any longer awaited with expectation, since there was but one verdict. Paulus, an ex-praetor, was dining in a convivium while wearing [a signet ring with] an image of Tiberius Caesar carved in relief on the gemstone. I will be acting absurdly if I now to try to find euphemisms with which to express that he picked up a chamber pot; a deed noted both by Maro, who was one of the well-known informers of the time, and by a slave of the man for whom these snares were being woven. The slave sat down next to his drunken master and removed the ring; when Maro called his fellow diners to witness that the image had been brought in contact with something polluted, and was on the verge of drawing up an indictment, the slave exhibited the ring upon his own hand. If anyone calls this man a [mere] "slave," he will also call Maro a "dinner companion."

Seneca sets the stage by describing the reign of Tiberius as a period when anything could serve as a pretext for bringing an accusation of treason (*maiestas*), including the speech of people who were drunk, and the frankness of people as they joked. Drunken speech and jokes were, as we have seen, hallmarks of the convivium, and it is in this context that Paulus—an ex-praetor, hence a relatively high-ranking senator—is put at risk by his behavior while drunk, according to Seneca. For the implication here, presumably, is that Paulus's handling of a chamber pot while wearing a ring bearing the emperor's image is an inadvertance attributable to intoxication, and that he would not, if sober, have furnished such a pretext for accusation (entirely aside from the question whether such an action is invidious, even if done while sober, which Seneca may imply it is not: "nothing was safe, any pretext for savagery was acceptable").[42] The emperor himself is not present at this dinner, but the informer (*delator*) Maro provides him with invidious eyes and ears, interpreting the convivial goings-on to the emperor in the worst possible light and personally drawing up the accusation of treason.[43] Thus, on Seneca's account, a high-ranking aristocrat's life is brought into serious danger through actions that are perhaps unremarkable in a convivial context, namely drinking and handling a chamber pot. For thanks to an unforeseen encounter with the emperor's power as it is appropriated and extended by a *delator*, these unremarkable actions stand to be interpreted in bad part, initiating hostile reciprocation between Paulus and Tiberius in which Paulus's death is the inevitable conclusion.

[42] This passage seems to require that we regard the use of the chamber pot during the convivium as nothing extraordinary, the kind of thing that only a *delator* could regard as a basis for accusation (cf. Suet. *Tib.* 58). Martial 3.82.16–17 also portrays a member of the convivial gathering (the host Zoilus) relieving himself without leaving the triclinium: *et delicatae sciscitator urinae / domini bibentis ebrium regit penem*. Throughout this poem Martial portrays Zoilus's convivial conduct as outrageous, so presumably some feature of this vignette is notably offensive. Perhaps, however, Zoilus's offensive conduct consists not in relieving himself without leaving the room, but in having a slave whose appointed task is to stimulate and direct the flow of urine. For another instance of urination in the convivium, see Mart. 6.89; also Bradley 1998: 44.

[43] See Barton 1993: 88–89 for the link between *curiositas* and *invidia*, and for the portrayal of *delatores* (and other "spy" figures) as *curiosi*, hence envious. In this representation, the charge of *maiestas* emerges as a matter of the emperor's envy of individual aristocrats. In section 6 below, however, I suggest an altogether diffferent rationale for emperors to have aristocrats prosecuted on false charges.

The anecdote immediately following serves as a counterpoint, though it describes a similar situation (*Ben.* 3.27.1): "Under the deified Augustus, people's own words were not yet dangerous to them, but they were already troublesome. Rufus, a man of senatorial status, at a dinner party expressed the hope that Caesar would not return safe from the journey he was planning, and added that all the bulls and calves hoped the same. The sort of people were present who listen carefully to such words" (*sub divo Augusto nondum hominibus verba sua periculosa erant, iam molesta. Rufus, vir ordinis senatorii, inter cenam optaverat ne Caesar salvus rediret ex ea peregrinatione quam parabat, et adiecerat idem omnes et tauros et vitulos optare. fuerunt qui illa diligenter audirent*). The words spoken by Rufus here are again typical of the "free" and jesting speech associated with *convivia* and the wine served there: not only does he wish an ill journey upon the emperor, but declares that the bulls and calves — the victims of the eventual sacrifice in thanksgiving for the emperor's safe return — also hope against that return. (Seneca explicitly notes Rufus's intoxication in the next sentence, where he says Rufus was informed the next morning "what he said while drunk at dinner," *quae inter cenam ebrius dixisset*.) Again, Seneca points out the senatorial status of the speaker of the dangerous words; and again, although the emperor himself is absent, some *delatores* are present, those who would report these words to Augustus and draw up an accusation of treason. Once again, then, the emperor's power, or rather the particularly intrusive and insidious extension of it that the *delatores* construct, threatens grave danger against a high-ranking aristocrat because he has spoken in the "free," jesting manner that is often regarded as appropriate and even desirable in the convivial setting. At this point, however, the threatened aristocrat takes vigorous action on his own behalf. On the advice of his slave, he serves as his own *delator:* he approaches Augustus, reports his convivial utterances, declares that he was not of sound mind, and asks forgiveness (§2).[44] Augustus grants it, whereupon Rufus immediately requests a large sum of money in addition, as a visible token of this forgiveness: this too he receives (§3). Thus Rufus, confronted with the threat that the *delatores* would use his words to initiate hostile reciprocity between himself and Augustus, bypasses them, confronts the emperor directly, and confirms a pattern of amicable reciprocity instead. For upon apologizing for his words and wishing that they might recoil upon himself — speech that amounts to an amicable offering, a gift to cancel out any injury caused by his earlier

---

[44] *Servus . . . hortatur ut Caesarem occupet atque ipse se deferat. usus consilio descendenti Caesari occurrit et cum malam mentem habuisse se pridie iurasset, id ut in se et in filios suos recideret optavit et Caesarem ut ignosceret sibi rediretque in gratiam secum rogavit* (Sen. *Ben.* 3.27.2).

words—he receives a further gift in turn. It is crucial to the transaction here, and to the power relations exhibited through it, that Augustus adds this further gift, for it demonstrates beyond doubt Rufus's return to favor (*in gratiam*, §2), which consists precisely in the confirmation of an amicable pattern of gift giving and reciprocation. And so Seneca declares in his concluding judgment: "Caesar acted honorably in forgiving, and in adding generosity to his clemency" (*honeste fecit Caesar quod ignovit, quod liberalitatem clementiae adiecit*, §4).

Now, these anecdotes involving Paulus and Rufus are two in a series of exemplary accounts that collectively seek to demonstrate that slaves can bestow benefits (*beneficia*) upon their masters (*Ben.* 3.18ff.): Seneca indicates in these two anecdotes the magnitude of the service done by each aristocrat's slave by intervening in a probably life-saving way. In each, however, the critical social difficulties arise where the emperor's power (as extended by the *delatores*) collides with the expectation of carefree speech and behavior under the influence of wine in the convivium. Here, suggests Seneca, lurk potentially life-threatening snares for Roman aristocrats. The other anecdotes in this series describe aristocrats imperiled by the fall of their city after a seige (3.23.2–4) or by proscription in civil strife (§25), or seized as prisoners of war (§23.5, 24): in each case, either their life or their honor is saved by a slave. This series thereby, albeit incidentally, equates the perils to life and limb for aristocrats dining in an accustomed, socially acceptable manner under the principate with the perils of being on the losing side in a war, or even civil war (cf. §26.1, quoted above). Similar aristocratic anxieties about speaking, acting, and drinking at convivia over which the emperor's power looms are widely attested in early imperial literature, as I will show below. These two anecdotes further suggest, however, that this anxiety may be mitigated or exacerbated by the *way* in which the emperor exercises his power, for there is an implied contrast between Augustus and Tiberius. In Tiberius's case, Seneca implies, any false step by an aristocrat resulted in a terminal cycle of hostile reciprocity: no correction was possible, and there was no difference between the power the emperor exercised personally and his power as it was invidiously extended by the *delatores*. This pattern, as I will show, is elsewhere associated with the behavior of a tyrant, the illegitimate authority figure par excellence. For Augustus, meanwhile, such a correction was possible, and his willingness to maintain an amicable, mutually beneficial mode of gift-exchange is deemed praiseworthy, the mark of an authority legitimated by its exchange practices. Thus, for Seneca, the manner in which an emperor's power intervenes in the convivium—invidiously (as through *delatores*) or otherwise—is an index of his legitimacy.

Many of the points raised by Seneca in these two richly informative anecdotes can be corroborated and nuanced by other representations of Julio-Claudian emperors, or foreign kings, in Julio-Claudian or near-contemporary literary sources. The contrast Seneca develops between Augustus and Tiberius regarding their reception and reciprocation of convivial "free" speech and behavior is articulated with respect to a variety of other rulers as well. Alexander the Great, the most sympotic of rulers, is a particularly fertile locus for exploring the social dynamics of the convivium in the presence of regal power. The story of the king's murder of his companion Clitus, whether narrated in isolation or included in a full-scale life of the king, is deployed by Roman imperial authors as an exemplum for the potential perils of "free" convivial speech by courtiers in the face of ruling power, and for the illegitimate use of that power. The brief account given by Seneca (*Ira* 3.17.1) simply declares that Alexander murdered his friend at dinner for "flattering him insufficiently, and too slowly making the transition from a free (-speaking) Macedonian to Persian slavery" (*qui Clitum carissimum sibi . . . inter epulas transfodit manu quidem sua, parum adulantem et pigre ex Macedone ac libero in Persicam servitutem transeuntem*). Thus the ambit in speech of "Persian slavery," to which Clitus failed to reduce himself at this convivium and consequently was killed, is circumscribed by the term "flattery" (*adulatio*).[45] Seneca's disapproval of Alexander here is patent: he classifies this action as "bestiality" (*feritas*, §17.1) — placing it entirely outside the pale of human behavior — and later reiterates (§17.4) that by such behavior Alexander excluded himself from common humanity.[46] A much lengthier account of this deadly banquet is given in the history of Alexander by Quintus Curtius Rufus (8.1.22–2.12), who is generally held to have written this work during the reign of Tiberius and/or Claudius and therefore was Seneca's slightly older contemporary.[47] Curtius depicts Clitus and Alexander as squabbling

---

[45] The historians of Alexander all point to a tension between inherited Macedonian social practices, embraced by some of Alexander's soldiers and officers, and the various specific social practices of conquered peoples that Alexander consciously took up for himself and urged upon other Macedonians. For claims that Alexander specifically appropriated foreign habits of dining and drinking, see Curt. 6.2.1–3, Arrian 4.8.2; this idea is presumably at the root of Seneca's presentation here (likewise, at *Ben.* 2.12.2, *Persica servitus* is what Caligula seeks to impose on Rome in place of *mores liberae civitatis*). In Plutarch's version (*Alex.* 51.1–5), Clitus reproaches Alexander specifically for putting Persians in positions of power over Macedonians.

[46] *Tamen cum dissimillimus esset homini qui illa patiebatur* [sc. Telesphorus], *dissimilior erat qui faciebat* [sc. Alexander]. See also *Ira* 3.23.1, where Alexander's murder of Clitus makes him more destructive than the lion to which he threw Lysimachus (cf. §17.2), since Lysimachus at least survived. Cf. *Ep.* 83.19: [sc. Alexander] *intellecto facinore mori voluit, certe debuit*.

[47] While the grounds for dating this work are tenuous, a Julio-Claudian date is plausible

over the amount of credit owed to others for Alexander's victories. He states repeatedly that both were drunk (8.1.22, 28, 33, 41, 43), and insists that, until the very end, Alexander was remarkably restrained in the face of Clitus's rash, abusive speech (§§ 31–32, 38–40, 45). Nevertheless, he concludes, killing Clitus was outrageous: "the king usurped the abominable role of the executioner, avenging verbal immoderation, which could have been attributed to wine, with unholy slaughter" (*detestabile carnificis ministerium occupaverat rex, verborum licentiam quae vino poterat imputari nefanda caede ultus*, 8.2.2). That is, the king went astray precisely in not choosing simply to disregard Clitus's words in view of Clitus's drunken state. He chose instead to reciprocate in a hostile manner, and in so doing took on the role of the *carnifex*, the public slave who carries out executions—a travesty, even inversion, of a king's proper role.[48] Whatever the evidentiary value of these accounts for Alexander's life and the history of his campaigns, their relevance to the Julio-Claudian elites for whom Seneca and Curtius were writing is clear. In this episode, at least, Alexander is made into a negative exemplum for how a ruler should receive and reciprocate convivial "free" speech: in acting as he does, he reduces himself to slavishness and/or bestiality, the antithesis of kingly dignity. By the same token, the fate of Clitus stands as a warning of the perils of "free" convivial speech for aristocrats confronted with such a ruler.[49] For it is presumably with such kingly touchiness in mind that Pliny the Elder can write, describing the physiosocial effects of wine, "some people speak things that bring death, and they do not repress words that will return to them through their throat, when so many people have thus been killed, and truth is now widely imputed to wine" (*Nat.* 14.141),[50] and that, according to

---

and generally accepted. The author himself is often identified with the senator Curtius Rufus (cos. suff. 43) mentioned at Tac. *Ann.* 11.21 and Pliny *Ep.* 7.27, and/or with the rhetor of the same name mentioned in the index to Suetonius's *De Gram. et Rhet.* On these questions of identity and date, see Atkinson 1980: 19–57, Kaster 1995: 336–37.

[48] For the role of the *carnifex*, see e.g., Tac. *Ann.* 5.9, Suet. *Cl.* 34, Pliny *Ep.* 4.11; also Hitzig, *RE* 3.1599–1600.

[49] A similar example, given by Diodorus Siculus (20.63), involves Agathocles of Syracuse, a tyrant *ex hypothesi*. Agathocles is always accessible, expansive, and full of jokes and mockery at the public banquets he sponsors, and so by his own example encourages the citizenry to drink and speak in the same way at these events. He thereby discovers, on the *in vino veritas* principle, who opposes his rule (20.63.1). He subsequently invites some 500 of these malcontents to a separate banquet, where he has them slaughtered (§6).

[50] Pliny *Nat.* 14.141: *tunc . . . alii mortifera elocuntur rediturasque per iugulum voces non continent, quam multis ita interemptis, volgoque veritas iam attributa vino est.* The anecdote in Diodorus Siculus regarding the tyrant Agathocles (see the previous note) precisely exemplifies the claims Pliny makes here, including the explicit claim that unvarnished truth emerges through drunken utterances: τῆς ἀληθείας ἐκφερομένης ἀπαρακαλύπτως διὰ τὸν οἶνον (20.63.1).

Seneca, people who fear their own recklessness and scurrility when drunk order their slaves to carry them out of the convivium (*Ira* 3.13.5).[51] Elsewhere Seneca declares that under the reign of a tyrant "pleasures themselves must be feared," for example, drunks at convivia must watch their tongues lest they be subject to prosecution (*Clem.* 1.26.2).

If it is an abuse, or illegitimate use, of a ruler's power to reciprocate with hostility an aristocrat's inadvertent or even intentionally insulting speech or behavior at a convivium, it is still worse for a ruler to do an injury to his aristocratic guest unprovoked, and worst of all to reciprocate a benefaction with an injury. Again, Seneca provides a rich store of exemplary anecdotes describing such situations. As an instance of the former case, Seneca describes a convivium (*Const.* 18.2) in which the emperor Caligula, who had a bent for insulting people, decried in a loud voice (i.e., such that many could hear) to a fellow diner named Valerius Asiaticus the poor sexual performance of Valerius's wife. Seneca laments that Valerius, as the emperor's friend, as a husband, and as ex-consul, should have to hear such things, and that the emperor should both have committed adultery and announced the fact, along with his dissatisfaction with the woman, to her husband. Now, Seneca does not indicate which, if either, of these men was host. If the emperor was a guest, his words might be regarded as an unsuccessful bon mot; we have seen above how guests who deployed abusive speech in an effort to be pleasing could misfire. The tone of the passage, however, implies a gratuitous insult, which better accords with Caligula being the host and presenting to his socially inferior guest(s) a humiliating status quo—the behavior stereotypically attributed to the patron/host when giving dinner to his clients/guests. But just as those hosts could destroy the binding function of their own offering of food, etc., by the injury they do in humiliating their guests (i.e., they mishandle their exchange relations, and so lose the accompanying economic and social advantages), so here with Caligula and Valerius. For Seneca here describes Valerius as "a fierce man, one scarcely likely to endure with equanimity the insults of another" (*ferocem virum et vix aequo animo alienas contumelias laturum*), inviting the reader to expect hostile reciprocation. Although Seneca does not mention that Valerius for this reason allegedly participated in the plot to kill Caligula, he perhaps assumes that his reader knows this:[52] for he next (§18.3) describes the insulting

---

[51] *Ira* 3.13.5: *qui vinum male ferunt et ebrietatis suae temeritatem ac petulantiam metuunt, mandant suis ut e convivio auferantur*. Various versions of the Clitus story describe attempts to defuse the confrontation by removing Clitus from the banquet: e.g., Curt. 8.1.38, Plut. *Alex.* 51.8.

[52] Valerius Asiaticus: *PIR*[1] V 25. Cos. ord. A.D. 46; cos. suff. unknown. For his actions following the assassination of Caligula, see Tac. *Ann.* 11.1, Jos. *Ant.* 19.102, Dio 59.30:

watchwords the emperor gave Cassius Chaerea, which led Chaerea to deal the emperor's death blow; and Seneca places the anecdotes about Valerius and Chaerea together under the rubric of actions by Caligula that brought about his death (*ea referam quae illum exitio dederunt*, §18.1). Thus, on Seneca's account, Caligula's insult to his dinner guest—his incorrect estimate of the level of the social status quo that Valerius would assent to have displayed to others—initiates hostile reciprocation that leads to Caligula's own death: an exemplary demonstration of the consequences for an emperor of mishandling his exchange relationships with aristocrats.

Seneca gruesomely explores the more extreme case noted above—namely, a ruler reciprocating a clear benefaction with an injury—in *De Ira* 3.14–15, the dense and suggestive passage with which I began this book (see the Introduction). Here the Persian courtier Praexaspes at a dinner party urges a fellow diner, the king Cambyses, not to drink so heavily. Thus he cleaves to the principle that Seneca enunciates elsewhere (*Ben.* 6.33.1), that one can begin to repay major gifts from one's ruler by giving him good advice.[53] In this case, however, the king takes offense, and angrily proves the steadiness of his hand by shooting an arrow through the heart of Praexaspes' son. Cambyses, then, has misrecognized a benefaction, in the form of good advice, as an injury and then reciprocated it with an injury rather than with a benefaction. In so doing, he initiates a bloody cycle of hostile reciprocation, showing himself suited to suffer in turn precisely what he has inflicted: "O bloodthirsty king! Worthy to have the bows of all of his friends turned against him! (*o regem cruentum! o dignum in quem omnium suorum arcus verterentur!* §4) If the appropriate reciprocation for the ruler's offerings is that he himself be killed, it is because he has delegitimated himself by disastrously mishandling this exchange situation, alienating rather than binding and subordinating his aristocratic dinner companions.

Yet it may not be possible (at least immediately) to reciprocate such a ruler as he deserves, and therefore a different exchange strategy must be embraced, as the subsequent anecdote reveals (*Ira* 3.15). Here Harpagus, another Persian courtier, is remunerated for his good advice to the king by an invitation to a dinner in which he is fed his children's

---

he is reported to have quieted a group of tumultuous soldiers, angrily demanding to know who had killed the emperor, by declaring "would that I had killed him."

[53] Seneca explicitly declares in §14.6 that Praexaspes' words constituted good advice: *accessit itaque ad numerum eorum qui magnis cladibus ostenderunt quanti constarent regum amicis bona consilia*. See ch. 2.7 and n. 87 above for the ideal of the *amicus minor* who gives his superior friend good advice.

flesh. At this point, presumably, this king (like Cambyses in the previous account) has made himself a worthy target for further hostile reciprocation. Here, however, upon recognizing the nature of the food and then being asked by the king how he enjoyed his meal, Harpagus replies, "at the king's table, every meal is pleasant" (*apud regem omnis cena iucunda est*, §1). With this reply, says Seneca, he avoids still further retaliation by the ruler, namely being invited to dine on the leftovers (*quid hac adulatione profecit? ne ad reliquias invitaretur*). A harsh reply, Seneca implies, would perpetuate the cycle of hostile reciprocity, which this courtier would not be able to sustain; therefore he replies in a manner that presents the injury he has just received as a benefit, and so takes upon himself the task of restoring positive reciprocity between himself and the king. That is, he assents to the wretched social status quo that the ruler's action puts on display. But as the anecdote discussed above regarding Augustus and Rufus suggests (and other passages below corroborate), the task of restoring amicable reciprocity, and so of effacing the humiliating display of power differentials, is properly the ruler's, if he is ruling appropriately. These Persian kings are poor gift-transactors, as Seneca presents them, being unable to distinguish benefits from injuries and unaware or neglectful of their proper role in their exchange relationships with aristocrats. When their incompetence in transacting exchanges results in bloodshed, Seneca can call them *carnifices* (*Ira* 3.15.3) — the same label elsewhere applied to Alexander after the Clitus episode (Curt. 8.2.2) — indicating that through their actions they have reduced themselves to the status of the public slave who carries out executions. As *carnifices*, they are worthy to be killed (§14.4) or, lacking other alternatives, escaped through suicide (§15.3–4).

Such behavior is not limited to Persian kings. At *De Ira* 2.33.3–6 Seneca offers a similar analysis of an exchange between Caligula and an equestrian named Pastor. Caligula had imprisoned the latter's son, says Seneca, on account of his dress and hairstyle.[54] His father begged the emperor for his son's release, whereupon Caligula immediately ordered the young man executed. Then Caligula invited Pastor to dinner. Pastor arrived with "no reproach in his face" (*vultu nihil exprobrante*); he donned convivial garb; he repeatedly drank large cups as the emperor toasted him. Caligula stationed someone to observe whether he gave any hint of grief or displeasure; he gave none: indeed, says Seneca, he dined "as though he had succeeded in securing his son's release" (*cenavit tamquam pro filio exorasset*). Why did Pastor behave this way?

---

[54] Wardle 1994: 272 compares this passage with Suet. *Cal.* 35.2, regarding Caligula's cruelty to men who had full heads of hair. For Caligula's own baldness, see Sen. *Const.* 18.1 and Suet. *Cal.* 50.1 (with Wardle ad loc).

Because, says Seneca, he had another son, whom Caligula was sure to execute if any displeasure was shown. In this account, Pastor's request for a gift from the emperor, the life of his son, is reciprocated by an outrageous injury, and followed immediately by an utterly unwanted gift, a dinner invitation, which in fact constitutes a further injury since it is completely inappropriate to the guest's circumstances.[55] The guest is then observed, a phenomenon frequently attested in descriptions of convivia, to determine if his behavior is satisfactory—though here the guest's aim in seeking to please his host is not to gain an invitation for tomorrow, to say nothing of any greater gift, but rather to avoid losing his other son. Like the Persian courtiers, Pastor here must take upon himself the task of breaking the cycle of hostile reciprocity, for he (like they) cannot sustain further injury. While Pastor's experience illustrates the general claim that a courtier can only survive to old age "by accepting injuries and giving thanks for them" (*iniurias accipiendo et gratias agendo*, 2.33.2), it remains the case that the ruler who conducts his exchange relations in this way exposes himself first to aristocratic censure, and eventually to assassination. Seneca concludes this account by calling Caligula a *carnifex* (2.33.6), which we now recognize as a regular label for rulers who lose their legitimacy (in aristocratic eyes) by engaging in violent hostile reciprocity with their aristocratic subjects.

[55] Mourning and dining are generally portrayed as incompatible. The emotional distress of a grieving father forced to attend a convivium is portrayed by the declaimers in Sen. *Cont.* 4.1. The lemma of this declamation is as follows: *amissis quidam tribus liberis cum adsideret sepulchro, a luxurioso adulescente in vicinos hortos abductus est et detonsus coactus convivio veste mutata interesse. dimissus iniuriarum agit*. *Iniuria*, the rubric under which this prosecution is brought, is the very category to which the younger Seneca assigns Pastor's experience of Caligula: for Seneca introduces this anecdote as exemplary of the general assertion *saepe adeo iniuriam vindicare non expedit ut ne fateri quidem expediat* (*Ira* 2.33.2). In *Cont.* 4.1, one of the handful of *sententiae* preserved on the father's side is this: *cum miserrimum sit flere, quam infelix sum cui ne hoc quidem licet!* Similarly the younger Seneca declares on Pastor's behalf (*Ira* 2.33.6): *dignus fuit cui permitteretur a convivio ad ossa fili legenda discedere; ne hoc quidem permisit benignus interim et comis adulescens*. See also the *Senatus Consultum de Pisone Patre* ll. 66–68, where one of several pieces of evidence adduced to show that Piso rejoiced in Germanicus's death is this: *frequenterque convivia habuisse eum his ipsis diebus quibus de morte Germanici Caesaris ei nuntiatum erat* (cf. Tac. *Ann.* 3.9.3); and especially Sen. *Cont.* 4 pr. 5, where Augustus is said to have complained in a letter to Asinius Pollio that one of his close friends held a *plenum convivium* (to which Augustus was presumably invited) shortly after Augustus had learned that his (grand)son Gaius had died in Syria. Pollio writes back, *eo die cenavi quo Herium filium amisi*. In light of the declamation immediately following (*Cont.* 4.1, just described) and the Pastor story, one wonders under what circumstances Pollio dined out that evening: could his point be that it was at Augustus's invitation, which he did not feel free to decline? Cf. Plut. *Mor.* 124A (invitations by the powerful are very difficult to decline, almost "compulsory" [ἀνάγκαι]); Marc. Aur. *Med.* 1.16.2 (as emperor, you should not force your friends to come to dinner); also Tac. *Ann.* 11.2.2, Plut. *Mor.* 632F.

This collection of negative exempla shows a variety of ways in which convivial exchanges between aristocrat and ruler can go wrong—particularly on account of the aristocrat's speech—causing him harm and calling the ruler's legitimacy into question. Yet anecdotes also survive from the Julio-Claudian period showing a different pattern of exchange: anecdotes in which admittedly offensive speech by aristocrats in convivial settings, usually involving wine, is regarded by the ruler as so much hot air and consequently not taken as an affront, hence not triggering retaliation. Augustus's exchange with Rufus, as described by Seneca (*Ben.* 3.27), exemplifies this view of drunken convivial speech, and Quintus Curtius also recommends it (8.2.2) as the view Alexander should have taken regarding Clitus. A recurrent exemplum of this sort involves king Pyrrhus of Epirus and a group of youths from Tarentum. The earliest surviving version of this story dates from the Julio-Claudian period and is given by Valerius Maximus (5.1 ext. 3). I quote his account in full:

> aeque mitis animus Pyrrhi regis. audierat quodam in convivio Tarentinorum parum honoratum de se sermonem habitum. accersitos qui ei interfuerant percunctabatur an ea quae ad aures ipsius pervenerant dixissent. tum ex his unus "nisi," inquit, "vinum nos defecisset, ista quae tibi relata sunt prae his quae de te locuturi eramus lusus ac iocus fuisset." tam urbana crapulae excusatio tamque simplex veritatis confessio iram regis convertit in risum. qua quidem clementia et moderatione adsecutus est ut et sobrii sibi Tarentini gratias agerent et ebrii bene precarentur.

> Equally gentle was the spirit of king Pyrrhus. He had heard that, in a certain convivium of Tarentines, some less-than-honorific words were spoken about him. Summoning those who had been present at it, he inquired whether they had said the things that had come to his ears. One of them then said "yes, and had the wine not given out on us, what was related to you would have seemed as play and joking in comparison to what we were going to say next about you." So urbane was this plea of drunkenness, and so candid was the confession of truth, that they turned the king's anger to laughter. With this clemency and moderation he brought it about that Tarentines who were sober gave him thanks, and those who were drunk wished him well.

On this account, a joke defuses the confrontation (likewise in Quintilian's version, *Inst.* 6.3.10) by turning the king's anger into laughter. That is, the potential cycle of retribution initiated by the disrespectful convivial speech that displeased the king is interrupted by a new speech offering that does please him, and that he accepts as a replacement for the offensive speech. Just as Rufus's apology to Augustus displaces his earlier words and enables a cycle of amicable reciprocation to be preserved, so here the joke, in turn reciprocated by the king's clemency, leads to further amicable speech offerings on the part of the Tarentines—now *including* those who are drunk at dinner parties, the very ones who had previously spoken ill of him. Crucially, however, this joke saves the situation only because Pyrrhus accepts its premise: that abusive speech directed at him by drunken *convivae* is nothing more than a situational desideratum, and precisely does *not* communicate the "true" views of the drinkers, or at any rate views that will be translated into action. The partiers and the king agree, in short, that *veritas* emphatically does not reside *in vino*. Valerius approvingly cites Pyrrhus's "gentle spirit," "clemency," "moderation," and later in this section, the "depth of his human feeling" (*mitis animus, clementia, moderatio, altitudo humanitatis*), and implicit approval is present too in other versions of the story.[56] But Pyrrhus is not merely praiseworthy; he is also effective: for on this account he strengthens his authority by gaining the good will of (and presumably subordinating in gift-debt) all Tarentines sober and drunk. Below (section 5) I discuss in greater detail the idea that *clementia* is itself a gift given by rulers to their subjects, a gift that not only restores interrupted cycles of amicable reciprocation, but also imposes further gift-debts and so further legitimates the ruler.[57]

---

[56] See Dio 10.40.47 (Zon. 8.6.5–7), Plut. *Pyrrhus* 8.12; cf. *Mor.* 184D. Pliny praises Trajan for taking this same view of convivial speech: *non enim . . . spectator adnotatorque convivis tuis immines* (*Paneg.* 49.6). According to Plutarch (*Mor.* 176A–B), Dionysius I of Syracuse had a more nuanced view of the truth-value of convivial speech. Hearing of slanderous speech spoken about him by two men at a symposium, he invited both to dinner. Observing that one drank freely and the other sparingly, he put only the latter to death, regarding only him as hostile by deliberate choice (δύσνουν καὶ πολέμιον ἐκ προαιρέσεως) (for similar logic see *Mor.* 631D).

[57] Immediately preceding the exemplum of Pyrrhus in Valerius, and functioning similarly, is an account of how Pisistratus behaved when confronted by free convivial speech (5.1 ext. 2). Pisistratus, a relatively gentle tyrant, is another foreign ruler upon whom Julio-Claudian anxieties concerning the junction of ruling power and convivial speech are projected. In Valerius's account, Pisistratus is verbally assaulted and spat upon in a convivium by a drunken friend named Thrasippus. Yet Pisistratus so restrains his anger, says Valerius, "that you would think it was a courtier who was being told off by a tyrant" (*ut putares satellitem a tyranno male audire*)—rather than the other way round. The next day Thrasippus is prepared to punish himself by committing suicide, but Pisistratus persuades him to abandon this plan by restoring him to the favor in which he was previously held (*in eodem gradu amicitiae*). The sequence of events here—offense given, repentance by the offender (i.e., replacement of the offensive conduct with a more acceptable offering), and restoration of the previous relationship—is structurally very close to the transactions involving Pyrrhus, and also those involving Rufus and Augustus: here too the ruler has chosen to maintain a pattern of amicable reciprocity between himself and his aristocratic courtier, when he might have chosen otherwise, and here too the ruler earns praise for his actions (*si nihil aliud dignum honore memoriae gessisset, has tamen factis abunde se posteritati commendasset*). Cf. Sen. *Ira* 3.11.3–4.

I conclude this section by returning to the Julio-Claudian emperors themselves, with three more examples of how they receive and reciprocate potentially offensive aristocratic speech and action in convivial contexts. The exemplary accounts from Seneca (*Ben.* 3.26–27) involving Augustus and Tiberius, with which I opened this section, both feature *delatores* as crucial mediators between the free-speaking aristocrat and the emperor: for though the latter is not present at these convivia, the informers bring or threaten to bring the goings-on there before his eyes, and in the worst possible light. Tacitus is much concerned with the prosecutions for *maiestas* in the Julio-Claudian period, and a series of passages early in book 6 of the *Annales* helps to clarify the workings of informers at dinner parties, to which the Senecan accounts refer. In *Annales* 6.5, Tacitus relates that Cotta Messalinus was prosecuted for *maiestas* (A.D. 32) on account of making derisive jokes directed against Caligula, Livia, and Tiberius. The joke at Livia's expense was delivered at a priestly feast celebrating her birthday, which Cotta declared a funeral banquet (*cena novendialis*) — a somewhat obscure joke perhaps turning on her failure to be deified (see Koestermann 1963 ad loc.). In the midst of the prosecution, Cotta appealed to Tiberius himself, who sent a letter from Capreae "in which, after recalling in the manner of a legal defense the beginnings of the friendship between himself and Cotta and after mentioning Cotta's frequent services, he demanded that neither words whose meanings had been distorted for the worse, nor the frankness of tales told at convivia, be turned into causes for accusation" (*litterae . . . quibus in modum defensionis, repetito inter se atque Cottam amicitiae principio crebrisque eius officiis commemoratis, ne verba prave detorta neu convivalium fabularum simplicitas in crimen duceretur postulavit*). That is, by describing their friendship and the frequent gift-exchanges that sustained it, Tiberius advised the senate to accept the "hot air" view of Cotta's convivial speech and other jokes: he refused to allow Cotta's words to overturn the longstanding amicable reciprocity of their relationship, and reinforced the amicable pattern by intervening here and thus saving Cotta's life and/or property. Shortly thereafter, however (*Ann.* 6.7.2), Tacitus reports that Tiberius himself urged a *delator* to bring an accusation before the senate against two men who had been friends of Sejanus, even though (Tacitus avers) they did not abuse this connection. Tacitus then digresses briefly by lamenting in general terms the blight of delation under Tiberius (6.7.3), noting inter alia that "people speaking in the forum or in the convivium on any matter at all were accused" (*in foro in convivio quaqua de re locuti incusabantur*). Thus Tacitus portrays a regime in which the absent emperor allowed and encouraged *delatores* to extend and exercise his power in harmful ways. Some of those who were swept up in this net were released for one reason or another (for example, after a reckoning was made of the history and balance of the exchange between Tiberius and the accused). But Tacitus focuses upon, and laments, the capriciousness of this process from the aristocrat's point of view: in one case Tiberius objects to prosecuting someone on the basis of his convivial speech, while he elsewhere encourages prosecutions on this basis; friendship with Sejanus is at one time regarded as a benefit to the emperor, but as an injury at another.[58] Reading Tacitus's portrait of delation here through the filter of exchange, it seems that delation is a rhetorical strategy whereby almost any utterance or action by an aristocrat can be argued to be an offense or injury against the emperor—often regardless both of intent and of the prior exchange history between the two—an injury that invites retaliation and stands to throw almost any exchange relationship into a cycle of hostile reciprocity. So while *delatores* provide the emperor with invidious eyes and ears, the emperor, for his part, may or may not choose or be able to read through this *invidia* in order to maintain or restore amicable reciprocity in particular cases.[59]

The passages discussed so far might seem collectively to suggest that nothing an aristocrat says or does in a convivium warrants retaliation; that no transgression of speech or action, perceived or real, is legitimately punishable by the emperor. Yet a couple of widely diffused and often repeated anecdotes suggest that castigation by the emperor is appropriate in some circumstances, and indeed may help to legitimate his rule if properly modulated. One such anecdote places Augustus at a convivium hosted by Vedius Pollio, an equestrian—one of very few detailed accounts we have of a convivium in which a man of higher status is the guest, rather than the host, of someone of lower status.[60] I quote here the story as given by Seneca (*Ira* 3.40):

---

[58] On the changed attitude toward connections with Sejanus, see also Dio 58.12.3, 19.3–5.

[59] Likewise, at *Ann*. 14.48 Tacitus suggests that the delation of the praetor Antistius, for circulating insulting poems about Nero at a convivium, was a setup to allow Nero to deliver him from the senate's death sentence by use of his tribunician veto, to Nero's own greater glory. Here, the emperor's clemency is portrayed as a gift that imposes a gift-debt on the condemned, and wins praise from all and sundry. But Thrasea seeks to steal Nero's thunder by arguing that Antistius should only be exiled, making him an *exemplum publicae clementiae*, rather than an exemplum of Nero's clemency. Lendon 1997: 142–45 offers a riveting analysis of the hostile exchange relationship between Thrasea and Nero.

[60] See the discussion above (section 2) of the social dynamics of this situation, for which the evidence is sparse. In Hor. *Serm*. 2.8, where Maecenas is said to be present and presumably outranks the host Nasidienus, he is a *muta persona* playing no role in the give-and-take of this convivium: indeed he is never even mentioned after the initial gestures of deference to him (vv. 16–17). Emperors are perhaps more likely to dine out when traveling: the events involving Augustus and Pollio may have occurred at Pollio's estate at Pausilypon in Campania, which Pliny (*Nat*. 9.167) expressly says had fishponds (thus Syme 1961: 23).

(§2) fregerat unus ex servis eius crustallinum; rapi eum Vedius iussit ne vulgari quidem more periturum: murenis obici iubebatur, quas ingentis in piscina continebat. quis non hoc illum putaret luxuriae causa facere? saevitia erat. (§3) evasit e manibus puer et confugit ad Caesaris pedes, nihil aliud petiturus quam ut aliter periret, ne esca fieret. motus est novitate crudelitatis Caesar et illum quidem mitti, crustallina autem omnia coram se frangi iussit complerique piscinam. fuit Caesari sic castigandus amicus; bene usus est viribus suis.

One of his slaves had broken a crystal goblet; Vedius ordered that he be snatched away to perish in no common manner: he ordered that he be thrown to the lampreys, the giant ones he kept in his fishpond. Who would not think that he did this for the sake of extravagant display? It was savagery. The boy escaped from his hands and fled to the feet of Caesar, intending to ask nothing other than to die in some other way, and not be fish bait. Caesar was shocked by this innovation in bloodthirstiness and ordered that the slave, for his part, be released, but that all the crystal goblets be broken as he watched and that the fishpond be filled in. This was the proper way for Caesar to rebuke his friend; well did he employ his power.

Accepting Seneca's suggestion that Pollio acted in part *luxuriae causa*—i.e., he was engaging in conspicuous consumption—we can see his extraordinary behavior as an over-the-top attempt at the kind of display by which hosts often sought to impress their guests. This instance is particularly extreme, perhaps, because it is linked to the unsurpassed status of the guest of honor: for in such a case, as discussed above (section 2), the normal obligation incurred between guest and host is reversed; Augustus simply by attending would be regarded as giving a greater gift to Pollio than Pollio would give through providing food, drink, entertainment, and the like. In this situation an otherwise unremarkable accident, and the bad impression it might leave, could seem to Pollio far more humiliating and damaging than ordinarily.[61] Now, to impose corporal punishment upon a slave for a transgression is no surprise, nor perhaps is the imposition of such punishment for the sake of display.[62] What is spectacular here is (1) that a slave is actually being put

---

[61] [Quint.] *Decl. Min.* 301, discussed in section 2 above, also suggests how a socially inferior host might overreach in seeking to avoid humiliation before a socially superior guest: the poor man in this declamation excuses his false assertion that the serving girl was a slave (in fact she was his daughter) by saying that he was embarrassed to admit before his guest that he had no slave (§14: *erubui videri sine ancilla; hoc mali habet ambitus*).

[62] The threat of corporal punishment that hung always over slaves' heads was regarded by Roman aristocrats as the hallmark of the slave's condition: on these matters see ch. 4.2–4 below. Suet. *Cal.* 32.2 describes another spectacularly cruel punishment of a minor transgression by a slave at a convivium; display is a major component of this punishment. Cf. Sen. *Cont.* 9.2.4 for the claim that, if a slave transgresses at a convivium, he would be

to death for nothing more than breaking a cup—perhaps "savagery" and "bloodthirstiness" (*saevitia, crudelitas*) as Seneca avers, but also an acknowledgement of the exceptionally high stakes of the current convivium, and/or an implicit claim that the goblet was of immense value;[63] (2) Pollio's willingness to kill so valuable a slave: for only the most sexually attractive adolescent boys were put into service pouring wine, and such slaves cost a great deal;[64] (3) the mode of punishment, which is presented here as no ordinary bloodthirstiness, but an innovative form of it (*novitas crudelitatis*): for not only is the slave to be eaten alive by lampreys, but this will happen before the very eyes of the guests, assuming that the *piscina* is located near the couches.[65] Moreover, the presence of lampreys in the *piscina* suggests that they are themselves on the menu, so there is the unappetizing possibility that the guests will shortly be dining upon the very fish that have just consumed the slave.[66] This is

---

taken out of the dining room for punishment. See also Petr. *Sat.* 34.2–3, Sen. *Ira* 3.35.2, *Ep.* 47.3; D'Arms 1991: 175.

[63] Seneca presents the punishment as unduly harsh in §40.4: *si calix tuus fractus est, viscera hominis distrahentur?* But on the high value of crystal and its vulnerability to breakage, see Mart. 12.74, 14.94, 14.111, 9.73 (at 12.74.7–8 Martial contrasts crystal goblets with cheap cups that slaves can handle without fear of dropping one). Breaking a glass in the convivium may also have been regarded as an ill omen or bad luck; see Petr. *Sat.* 51 and Smith 1982 ad loc. If so, a dropped cup (*phiale*) was a fitting signal at which the conspirators rose from their dining couches to assassinate Sertorius (Plut. *Sert.* 26.10).

[64] For the sexual desirability of cupbearers (the Ganymede figure), see e.g., Sen. *Ep.* 47.7; Mart. 9.25, 10.98, 11.70.5–6; Juv. *Sat.* 5.56–63; Suet. *Caes.* 49; and D'Arms 1991: 175–76. Martial twice gives HS 100,000 as the price for such a slave (11.70, 1.58; cf. 3.62.1). This price is very high compared with other prices for slaves attested in literary and documentary sources: see Duncan-Jones 1982: 348–50. But even if Martial is giving an exaggeratedly high figure, he presupposes that his audience recognizes that these are among the most expensive of slaves (likewise Juv. *Sat.* 5.56, 60).

[65] For the novelty, see also §40.4: *e convivio rapi homines imperas et novi generis poenis lancinari?* On the other hand, Sen. *Clem.* 1.18.2 says that this was Pollio's customary way of punishing slaves; likewise Dio 54.23.2 and Pliny *Nat.* 9.77. Pliny further remarks that the point of this mode of execution was to make the victim's dismemberment as easy for spectators to see as possible (*quia in alio genere totum pariter hominem distrahi spectare non poterat*). For keeping live fish in a pool in the triclinium until the moment comes to eat them, see Sen. *Nat.* 3.18.3–5. Higginbotham 1997: 31–33, 241 n. 91 discusses the conjunction of dining facilities and fishponds at a number of sites; the physical remains at Pollio's estate are consistent with the literary accounts (191–94).

[66] Sen. *Clem.* 1.18.2 points to this possibility: *o hominem* [sc. Pollio] *mille mortibus dignum, sive devorandos servos obiciebat muraenis quas esurus erat, sive in hoc tantum illas alebat ut sic aleret*. For lampreys as delicacies, see Hor. *Serm* 2.8.42, Juv. *Sat.* 5.99–102, with Pliny *Nat.* 9.76 (a description of how lampreys change color as they die, suggesting the knowledge of the epicure: cf. Sen. *Nat.* 3.18); see also Higginbotham 1997: 43–46 on the commercial importance of these fish in antiquity. For the ironic inversion whereby men, as they eat fish, contemplate man-eating fish, consider that diners in the triclinium at Sperlonga observed a sculptural group representing Scylla—rising from the

all too much for Augustus, who orders the slave released, the remaining goblets smashed, and the *piscina* destroyed.[67] Note, however, that this punishment is precisely tailored to the offense: no arbitrary corporal punishment for the malefactor, but the elimination of exactly and only those objects and circumstances that directly contributed to this incident. Seneca approves of Augustus's conduct, declaring that he applied his power appropriately, and that *this* is the way for Caesar to rebuke a friend (and not, implicitly, by the bloody punishments threatened or employed by tyrannical rulers against their courtiers in the anecdotes discussed above). While we must imagine that Pollio was utterly humiliated, it remains true that Augustus had also done him the great honor of coming to dinner in the first place; and the fact that Seneca pointedly refers to Pollio as Augustus's *amicus* (likewise Dio 54.23 and Pliny *Nat.* 9.77) suggests that no destructive cycle of hostile reciprocity ensued. Indeed, Vedius later made Augustus heir to a substantial portion of his estate (Dio 54.23.5–6)—strong evidence that reasonably warm relations endured, since testamentary dispositions often acknowledged and reciprocated gift-debts (see section 5 below). Thus Augustus is praised for his virtuoso handling of this hostile exchange with Vedius: he punished in precisely the right degree someone who deserved punishment, thus making the mutual damage self-limiting and facilitating a quick return to amicable reciprocity.

A final instance of such virtuosity involves the emperor Claudius, in an anecdote found in three versions from the early second century (Tac. *Hist.* 1.48, Plut. *Galba* 12, Suet. *Cl.* 32). Dining as the emperor's guest, Titus Vinius, a senator of praetorian rank,[68] stole a gold drinking vessel (silver in Plutarch). Inviting him back the next evening, Claudius had him served, alone of all the guests, on earthenware. This singling-out of Vinius in so visible a way constitutes the emperor's acknowledgement and reciprocation of the theft. Now, theft, like abusive speech, could be regarded as amusing and desirable convivial behavior: Catullus attributes to the napkin thief Asinius Marrucinus the view that his actions are witty and piquant, though Catullus himself insists they are quite the

---

piscina with two fish tails—devouring Odysseus's men. The Sperlonga sculptures date to the reign of Tiberius, approximately. On the Scylla group see Säflund 1972: 46–48; on its disposition in relation to the couches see pp. 79, 92. I thank Ann Kuttner for drawing my attention to this sculptural group.

[67] Breaking these valuable goblets constitutes punitive damages, since their loss presumably causes Pollio emotional as well as financial pain (see Dio 54.23.3; also Petr. *Sat.* 64.10–13, where Trimalchio struggles to conceal his distress when his crystal is broken). But Dio sees this as a move to protect the slave as well: for he says that Pollio could not subsequently punish the slave for a deed that Augustus too had done (54.23.4).

[68] T. Vinius: *PIR*[1] V 450. Cos. ord. A.D. 69; killed along with Galba that same year.

opposite.⁶⁹ Indeed, Catullus's stance here is also that of Martial as he condemns those diners who scatter insults at all and sundry and think themselves pleasing on that count (see section 3 above). Claudius's witty humiliation of Vinius, therefore, plays the same role in the gift economy of the convivium as Catullus's poetic reply to Asinius, and Martial's replies to convivial "free"-speakers: each constitutes hostile, but relatively lighthearted, reciprocation for an offensive action that the perpetrator thought (mistakenly) other diners would find pleasing and appropriate. Suetonius simply relates Claudius's action without providing any ethical evaluation of it. Plutarch, however, says that Vinius's theft inspired laughter rather than anger on account of the "rather comical moderation" of the emperor — a formulation that can only constitute praise, implying that the punishment was not excessive relative to the crime. Tacitus, on the other hand, says that Vinius was thereby "spattered with slavish disgrace";⁷⁰ yet his account also indicates that Vinius's career had advanced well under Claudius (a praetorship and military prefecture), suggesting an entirely civil relationship of amicable reciprocity between them. Moreover, following the cup anecdote Tacitus remarks that Vinius went on to be proconsul of Gallia Narbonensis: whether under Claudius or Nero is unclear, but if the former, then the "slavish disgrace" he suffered in the course of this hostile exchange with the emperor manifestly did not spin into a retaliatory cycle that ended Vinius's public career, much less his life; on the contrary, amicable reciprocity must soon have been restored. Like Augustus, then, Claudius here wins positive exemplary status for himself by chastising a convivial transgression in just the right degree, so that no destructive cycle of hostile reciprocity perpetuates itself; the accounts of these two exercises of imperial power in turn look askance at the heavyhanded, destructive, negative exempla involving figures like Tiberius, Caligula, and the Persian kings.

Here I end my investigation of the emperor as a participant in convivia. In the next two sections I seek to extend some of the results gained here, and to show that the exchange methodology I have elaborated can helpfully illuminate the sociopolitical consequences of other

---

⁶⁹ Cat. 12.1–5: *manu sinistra / non belle uteris in ioco atque vino: / tollis lintea neglegentiorum. / hoc salsum esse putas? fugit te, inepte: / quamvis sordida res et invenusta est.* For another poetic condemnation of a napkin-thief, see Mart. 8.59; for efforts by hosts to prevent cup-theft, cf. Juv. *Sat.* 5.39–41. For the extreme humiliation suffered by someone falsely accused of stealing a golden cup from the king's board, see Curt. 9.7.24–26.

⁷⁰ Plut. *Galba* 12.3: τοῦτο μὲν οὖν διὰ τὴν Καίσαρος μετριότητα κωμικωτέραν γενομένην γέλωτος, οὐκ ὀργῆς ἄξιον ἔδοξεν (I take τοῦτο to refer to Vinius's theft rather than Claudius's retaliation). Tac. *Hist.* 1.48: *servili deinceps probro respersus est.*

transactions of goods and services between emperor and aristocracy. However, two brief conclusions may be drawn from this discussion of convivia that are applicable to the discussions to follow. First, whereas a focus on "patronage" tends to emphasize the enduring power relations between superiors and inferiors, and while it is true that the history of prior exchanges in a relationship between two individuals strongly affects the evaluation of any given exchange, my analysis so far suggests that such power relations are perhaps more contingent than the "patronage" model would suggest. For in the convivium, at least, the power relations between host and guest are constantly being asserted, tested, and defended in the course of the exchange of goods and services, especially speech. The construction of authority through convivial exchange emerges as a dialogical process, whose stakes are all the higher when the emperor is a participant and it is his authority that is continuously under negotiation. The second conclusion, a corollary of the first, is that the character of the relationship between emperor and elite is also constantly under negotiation. MacMullen 1986: 515–19 discusses the "help your friends and harm your enemies" social dynamic that is well attested for the late republic and early empire, rightly bringing out the importance of both amicable and hostile reciprocity. But my discussion of convivial interactions suggests that the categories of those you help and those you harm are not necessarily static. Any personal relationship, including those involving the emperor, may go through both amicable and hostile phases, and may alternate between these repeatedly, since any given offering may be intended as either amicable or hostile, and may be received either as intended or otherwise. Convivia may however exaggerate the fluidity of the categories of friend and foe by introducing the factor of wine, which apparently has a unique capacity to render speech especially pleasing or displeasing. These conclusions, though derived from an analysis of just one arena of social exchange, should be borne in mind for the more general discussion to follow. For I will argue that "contingency" and "constant negotiation" are characteristic of exchange broadly between emperor and aristocracy, and indeed are fundamental to the articulation and construction of the emperor's authority in the Julio-Claudian period.

5. Imperial Authority and Gift Giving

It is well known, and massively documented, that the emperor had at his disposal an enormous quantity of goods and services, of every variety and size, to bestow on people of all ranks and stations, in every part of the Roman world, and that these goods and services were constantly and continuously being disbursed either by him or in his name. A full list of attested dispensations, if such a list could even be compiled, would run to many pages, and is neither possible nor necessary to produce here, especially since several thorough overviews of imperial giving already exist.[71] As noted in section 1 above, however, an objection has been raised regarding the social efficacy of the emperor's giving: Veyne and others have suggested that much, if not all, of such giving should be seen as the operation of a (in Weberian terms) rational-legal bureaucracy discharging normal, necessary governmental functions: that the emperor is not a gift-transactor but an *euergetes*, a sponsor of essentially public services whose beneficiaries feel no obligation or gratitude, nor incur gift-debt. For the most part Veyne is speaking of distributions aimed at large numbers of people: donatives to soldiers, grain to the urban plebs, public works (1990: 390–92, 361–66) — cases in which, indeed, it would be hard to maintain that there is a *personal* relationship forged between emperor and each of the numerous beneficiaries of such distributions. Yet he also maintains this view for ad hoc imperial grants to specific individuals, such as grants of citizenship, entry into the equestrian order (348), and even grants of senatorial census (356).[72] Here I seek in part to test Veyne's contention, especially the latter portion: to consider whether the emperor's ad hoc distributions to individual aristocrats are better regarded as gift giving, with the concomitant social obligations, or as euergetism which entails no such obligations. To this end, I examine texts dating from or referring to the Julio-Claudian period in which claims of personal subordination to the emperor are directly linked with statements that one has received goods and services from him. More broadly, I aim here to document the range of views of their relationship with the emperor that contemporary aristocrats articulate, in light of what they receive from him. I will argue that the social dynamics described above for the giving and receiving of food, speech, etc. in convivial contexts are also operative in other arenas of exchange between ruler and subject (especially aristocratic

---

[71] E.g., Millar 1977 passim (but see especially chs. 4, 6, 8), Saller 1982: 41–69, Veyne 1990: 292–482.

[72] Veyne 1990: 341–51 (esp. 349); also 16 on the absence of reciprocity in euergetism. MacMullen 1986: 520 states essentially the same position even more strongly (though without endorsing or rejecting it): "[T]oward him [sc. the emperor], the recipient could never feel an obligation, no more than to 'The Government' in the abstract — no more than to the weather." MacMullen may here be paraphrasing Seneca, who at *Ben.* 6.13.3–14.2 and 6.19.2–5 briefly discusses the obligations incurred by a member of a collectivity which receives a collective gift (e.g., if one is a Gaul, and Caesar gives the Gauls citizenship, what is one's obligation to Caesar), and then passes on (6.20–23) to a discussion of what one owes to the sun and moon, which may also be regarded as benefactors of a collectivity, since they shine upon humankind as a whole.

subjects); in particular they apply to those exchanges in which the emperor gives *clementia*. Thus I seek to broaden the results obtained above, and so to articulate better the social consequences of exchange in elite Roman society.

In a number of texts, the ability to give and the potential to rule (i.e., to make oneself preeminent and subordinate others) are closely linked. I begin with a pair of texts describing events that fall just outside the bounds of the Julio-Claudian period, specifically the rise of Julius Caesar and the rise of Otho. According to Plutarch (*Caes.* 5.8–9), Julius Caesar's enormous cash outlays early in his career on such things as public banquets, gladiatorial displays, and repairing the Appian way could in retrospect seem otherwise than they appeared at the time: for while he "appeared to purchase short-lived, ephemeral fame at great expense, in fact he bought the greatest things very cheap," because he "thereby disposed the people to seek novel offices and honors for him, by which they might recompense him."[73] The "greatest things," then, are these novel offices and honors, which are implied to be either identical with or a necessary precondition for his acquisition of supreme power. At the other end of our period, Suetonius reports (*Otho* 4) that when Otho, having assisted Galba's revolt against Nero, was told by an astrologer that he would shortly become emperor himself, he began to prepare a bid for power: whenever he hosted the *princeps* for dinner, he gave a gold coin to each member of the latter's guard; he also sought to win over other soldiers in other ways, for example settling a land dispute between a soldier and his neighbor by buying up the land in question and bestowing it upon the soldier. Eventually, says Suetonius, "there was scarcely anyone who did not feel and assert that Otho alone was worthy to succeed to imperial power" (. . . *ut iam vix ullus esset qui non et sentiret et praedicaret solum successione imperii dignum*).[74] In both of these passages, the gift giving of the would-be ruler is said to win over a crucial group of supporters (the people in Caesar's case, the soldiers in Otho's), who consequently regard him as socially preeminent and look to reify that preeminence by installing him in an appropriately lofty office. The expenditures described in these passages therefore func-

---

[73] Plut. *Caes.* 5.8–9: δοκῶν μὲν ἐφήμερον καὶ βραχεῖαν ἀντικαταλλάττεσθαι μεγάλων ἀναλωμάτων δόξαν, ὠνούμενος δὲ ταῖς ἀληθείαις τὰ μέγιστα μικρῶν. . . . οὕτω διέθηκε τὸν δῆμον, ὡς καινὰς μὲν ἀρχάς, καινὰς δὲ τιμὰς ζητεῖν ἕκαστον αἷς αὐτὸν ἀμείψαιντο. On Caesar's giving early in his career, see Sal. *Cat.* 54, Suet. *Iul.* 26–28. Interestingly, Caesar himself recognizes that others have acquired power through these same sorts of techniques: *B.G.* 1.18.3–5.

[74] For an instance in which Caesar, like Otho here, legitimates his authority through his handling of a soldier's land dispute, see sec. 6 below. For the idea that large-scale giving leads to absolute power, cf. Sal. *ad Caes.* 2.6.4–5 (speaking of M. Drusus): *metu ne per tantam gratiam solus rerum poteretur*.

tion in the same way that invitations to dinner ideally function, as discussed in section 2 above. Just as the provision of food, drink, etc., generally aims to gain the good will of the guests, and to obligate them to their host as the subordinate partners in a hierarchical relationship, so Caesar and Otho are presented as giving in the expectation that their offerings will be reciprocated by grateful, enthusiastic support for their ambitious aims; these expections are ultimately fulfilled. Thus their distributions appear to function socially as gift-transactions rather than as *euergesiai*—and these are distributions not to individuals but to collectivities.

If dynasts could rise to power at least in part through their giving, their ability to maintain and legitimate their power depended on continued liberality and generosity, especially directed toward the aristocracy. Numerous passages in texts dating from or referring to the Julio-Claudian period imply or assert that the allegiance and good will of Roman aristocrats (and other Romans) is won over or retained, in general or in specific cases, by imperial giving.[75] Here I focus on one particular Julio-Claudian text, namely the Roman history of Velleius Paterculus (written in the late 20s A.D., midway through Tiberius's reign), in which the connection between giving and legitimate authority is asserted repeatedly. In this text, questions of aristocratic gratitude or ingratitude toward the Caesars are among the author's central preoccupations. Velleius initially sets out the connection between giving, gratitude, and the establishment of social hierarchies in his description of the assassination of Julius Caesar (2.56–57):

(§56.3) Neque illi tanto viro et tam clementer omnibus victoriis suis uso plus quinque mensium principalis quies contigit. quippe cum mense Octobri in urbem revertisset, idibus Martiis, coniurationis auctoribus Bruto et Cassio, quorum alterum promittendo consulatum non obligaverat, contra differendo Cassium offenderat, adiectis etiam consiliariis caedis familiarissimis omnium et fortuna partium eius in summum evectis fastigium, D. Bruto et C. Trebonio aliisque clari nominis viris, interemptus est. . . . (§57.1) laudandum experientia consilium est Pansae atque Hirtii, qui semper praedixerant Caesari ut principatum armis quaesitum armis teneret; ille, dictitans mori se quam timere malle, dum clementiam quam praestiterat expectat, incautus ab ingratis occupatus est.

---

[75] See, e.g., Sen. *Polyb.* 12.3; *Ben.* 1.5.1–2, 2.27.4–28.4, 5.4.3; *Ira* 3.31.2–3; Curt. 6.10.36, cf. 6.6.11, 7.5.38; Dio 52.34.11, 53.4.1, 55.19.5, 60.11.7; similarly Tac. *Hist.* 3.37. On gratitude to the emperor more broadly, see Lendon 1997: 154–60. For other ancient articulations of the idea that kingly/imperial authority is based on giving, see Kloft 1970: 134–40, 157. Conversely *avaritia*, which alienates people, is characteristic of tyrants: Kloft 153–55, Tabacco 1985: 116–18.

Nor was that great man, who put all his victories to such clement use, allotted more than five months of princely peace. For while he had returned to the city in the month of October, on the Ides of March he was assassinated, the authors of the conspiracy being Brutus and Cassius, of whom the former he had failed to obligate by promising the consulship, while he had offended Cassius by putting him off; and with other counsellors of slaughter also as accessories who were the most intimate of all with him and had been lifted to the highest summit by the good fortune of his faction, namely Decimus Brutus and Gaius Trebonius and other men of famous name. . . . In retrospect, the advice of Hirtius and Pansa was praiseworthy, who always recommended to Caesar that he hold by arms his leading position which had been acquired by arms; but Caesar, who kept saying that he preferred to die than to fear, was taken off-guard by ungrateful men while he awaited the clemency he had bestowed.

The exchange language in this passage is explicit. Caesar had promised Marcus Brutus a consulship, but this promise failed to obligate him, i.e., to bind him and make him perceive himself as a gift-debtor—though Velleius, an external observer to the transactions between Caesar and Brutus, plainly implies that the latter should have felt himself obligated. According to Velleius other conspirators too, notably Decimus Brutus and Trebonius, owed their high status to the success of Caesar's enterprise, which they had supported hitherto. And because the conspirators owed their position to Caesar, they richly warrant the label "ingrates" (*ingrati*), which they receive in §57.1. However, the claim there that Caesar "was awaiting the *clementia* he had previously given" may again allude particularly to Marcus Brutus, whom Caesar had spared and forgiven after the defeat of the Pompeian forces at Pharsalus: for at 52.5 Velleius writes, "by the immortal gods, what a reward for his good will toward Brutus did this ever-so-merciful man later receive! (*pro dii immortales, quod huius voluntatis erga Brutum suae postea vir tam mitis pretium tulit!*) — implying that it was Caesar's clemency, his gift of life itself (rather than, or in addition to, the promised consulship), that Brutus reciprocated with murder. Thus Velleius presents both *clementia* and offices as gift-offerings by Caesar that Caesar believes, and Velleius himself affirms, should have bound the recipients into subordinate relationships to Caesar, and which should have precluded them (if they were duly grateful) from attacking him as they ultimately did.[76]

[76] See also App. *B.C.* 2.146; on M. Brutus as an ingrate see Rawson 1991: 490. Caesar's expectation of grateful reciprocation, attributed to him by Velleius, again suggests that the "gift-transactor" is a more appropriate model for his actions than the "euergetes" described by Veyne. Indeed, MacMullen 1986: 521 points to evidence that Caesar kept records of people to whom he granted citizenship (Cic. *Att.* 13.36.1), and an imperial secretariate *a commentariis beneficiorum* is epigraphically attested (e.g., *CIL* 6.1884,

In the death notices for several of these conspirators, Velleius reiterates their ingratitude to Caesar. He reports that Decimus Brutus, having been deserted by his army and plotted against by Plancus, was eventually killed (63.3, 64.1). Thus, says Velleius, "he paid the most appropriate penalty to Gaius Caesar, a man who deserved the very best from him: he was his killer, even though he had been the first of all his friends, and he shifted the envy for the good fortune from which he had profited onto the author of that good fortune, and he considered it fair to keep what he had received from Caesar, and for Caesar, who had given it, to perish" (*iustissimas . . . optime de se merito viro C. Caesari poenas dedit, cuius cum primus omnium amicorum fuisset, interfector fuit et fortunae, ex qua fructum tulerat, invidiam in auctorem relegabat, censebatque aequum quae acceperat a Caesare retinere, Caesarem, qui illa dederat, perire*, §64.1–2). Brutus's death can be called a "most appropriate penalty" for his actions on the Ides of March because he was betrayed by his own supporters, just as he himself had earlier betrayed Caesar, his friend (*primus omnium amicorum*) and benefactor, whose gifts on this account he had reciprocated with murder. Likewise for Trebonius: "Now in Asia, Dolabella had taken Gaius Trebonius the ex-consul, whom he succeeded [sc. as proconsul], by surprise at Smyrna and killed him, a man most ungrateful in regard to Caesar's deserts, and a participant in the murder of him by whom he himself had been promoted to the lofty position of consul" (*iam et Dolabella in Asia C. Trebonium consularem cui succedebat fraude deceptum Zmyrnae occiderat, virum adversus merita Caesaris ingratissimum participemque caedis eius a quo ipse in consulare provectus fastigium fuerat*, §69.1). While Velleius does not explicitly compare Trebonius's death to Caesar's, it may nevertheless be implied that Trebonius's death by deceit, after holding a proconsular post for which he qualified only because Caesar had appointed him consul, is again appropriately parallel to Caesar's death: he, like Caesar, reaped first the sweet fruit, and then upon betrayal the bitter fruit, of his high position (which was itself a gift from Caesar).[77]

Nor is it just the tyrannicides who are ungrateful: the failure by any party to fall eagerly in line with the aims and interests of the Caesars can be portrayed as ingratitude on the ground that nobody who is in a position to resist can have arrived in that position except by receiving numerous gifts from the emperor. The senate as a whole showed its

---

8626, 8627), which may imply that emperors in general kept detailed records of *beneficia* disbursed.

[77] Cf. App. *B.C.* 2.146 for this same view: the conspirators are implicitly ingrates, since all except Decimus Brutus had actually been Caesar's prisoners at some point (whereupon they were released, their property restored, their careers preserved, etc.).

ingratitude to the youthful Octavian when, after he alone in late 44 B.C. shook it from its *torpor* under the oppression of Antony by winning over two legions and raising the seige at Mutina (§61), it sent legates to address Octavian's army without him being present (62.5). The soldiers, however, were not as ungrateful as the senate, Velleius says (*non fuit tam ingratus exercitus quam fuerat senatus*): they refused to take orders from anyone but Octavian. Likewise, Antony's son Iullus Antonius is described as "a singular example of Caesar's clemency" (*singulare exemplum clementiae Caesaris*), since Augustus not only did not put him to death after his father's defeat, but even bestowed upon him a priesthood, the consulship and other high offices, and marriage to his sister Octavia's daughter, the elder Marcella (§100.4). Yet for all that he reputedly committed adultery with Julia, and so was a "violator of Augustus's household" (*violator eius domus*, §100.4). While Velleius does not expressly label Iullus an ingrate on this count, the pattern of action elsewhere characterized as ungrateful—reciprocating amicable gifts, such as life itself and high office, with some sort of offense—is plainly operative here. Finally, at 2.129.2 Velleius describes someone whose name has fallen out of the text (perhaps Archelaus or Libo Drusus) as an ingrate and a plotter of revolution, whose schemes Tiberius suppressed. Although this passage does not catalogue Tiberius's prior benefactions to the plotter (unless this information too has been lost in the lacuna), we can infer their existence as part of the logic by which any and all resistance to the Caesars is denounced as ingratitude.[78]

Velleius's contention that elites who resist the Caesars are ingrates, since they owe everything to them, closely resembles the claims put forward by the Julio-Claudian emperors themselves to a share in any testamentary bequests left by members of specified groups of people. Caligula is reported to have rescinded, retroactively to the start of Tiberius's reign, the wills of all senior centurions (*primipili*) who did not name Tiberius or himself as an heir, on the ground that any such will was "ungrateful" (Suet. *Cal.* 38.2; cf. Dio 59.15.1–2). Similarly, Nero is said to have seized an increased share of the bequests of freedmen who

---

[78] Vell. Pat. 2.129.2: *quam celeriter ingratum *** et nova molientem oppressit!* On the location of the lacuna, and the names that are candidates to fill it, see Watt's (1988) apparatus and Woodman's (1977) note ad loc. The ingratitude of Libo Drusus, Silius, and Piso is implied at 2.130.3, where Velleius describes their treasonable reciprocation for Tiberius's benefactions: *quid hic meruit primum ut scelerata Drusus Libo iniret consilia, deinde ut Silium Pisonemque tam <infestos haberet, quorum> alterius dignitatem constituit, auxit alterius?* (suppl. Burman). Cf. Dio 53.4.1–2 for the claim (placed in the mouth of Augustus, addressing the senate) that those who are bound to him by an exchange of benefactions will therefore not desire revolution. The idea that plotters are ingrates by definition is abundantly attested after the Julio-Claudian period as well; Lendon 1997: 155–58 adduces some examples, including Suet. *Vesp.* 14 and Dio 66(65L).16.3–4.

bore the name of any family to which Nero was related; he also made the wills of those who were ungrateful devolve entirely to the fiscus (Suet. *Nero* 32.2). The ethical basis for these confiscations, presumably, is that imperial freedmen and centurions could be regarded as owing their position, and at least some part of their wealth, directly to the emperor, hence could be thought to owe a sizeable gift-debt that should be acknowledged and reciprocated in their wills. These emperors' expectation regarding the wills of these particular groups of subordinates, then, is precisely Velleius's expectation regarding the behavior of each member of the aristocracy: the underlying ideological structure of gift-debt, social subordination, and expressions of gratitude is the same in each case.[79]

Besides those aristocrats who, by resisting the Caesars, bit the hands that fed them and so showed themselves ingrates, Velleius describes others who were notable for conducting their exchange relations otherwise. An odd case is Asinius Pollio, who on Velleius's account refused to accompany Octavian on the climactic campaign against Antony, declaring (2.86.3) that he had exchanged too many gifts with Antony to permit him to take up arms against him; consequently he would sit out the war and himself become "booty for the victor" (*"mea," inquit, "in Antonium maiora merita sunt, illius in me beneficia notiora; itaque discrimini vestro me subtraham et ero praeda victoris"*). For the conclusion to follow from the premises, we must interpret Pollio as meaning that his exchange of services with Antony forged a personal bond so strong that he could not take up arms against him (and not that the exchange acquitted both parties of any mutual obligation, for then the conclusion does not follow).[80] At any rate, Pollio is no ingrate to Antony. A more transparently positive example of gratitude is Messalla Corvinus, whom Velleius asserts (2.71.1) was second only to Brutus and Cassius in au-

[79] The imperial annulment of wills as *testamenta ingrata* has been thoroughly discussed by Gaudemet 1953 and Rogers 1947. Gaudemet (131–37) connects the confiscation of *testamenta ingrata* with the older *querela inofficiosi testamenti*, whereby parents could challenge the wills of children as being ungrateful; he argues that the construction of the emperor as *pater patriae* authorized him to make a similar claim on the wills of all citizens. This argument is ingenious. It is well attested, however, for both the republic and empire, that benefactions were commonly acknowledged and reciprocated by testament, including benefactions from people who were not members of the testator's own family, and (I presume) could never plausibly have claimed to be. (For the republic see e.g., David 1992: 137–45; for the empire, Saller 1982: 124–25, Sen. *Ben.* 4.11.3–6, 22.1–2; see also Val. Max. 7.8.5–9). Therefore I am inclined to see the emperor's rescinding of ungrateful wills not in terms of specifically familial social dynamics, but in terms of gift-exchange more broadly. Champlin 1991: 5–28 does not mention gratitude as a motive of testators (though cf. 150–53).

[80] My interpretation of this *dictum* of Pollio accords with Woodman's (1983 ad loc.), who discusses the opposing view of A.B. Bosworth in *Historia* 21 (1972) 447–48.

thority among the republicans; he refused after the republican defeat at Philippi to become leader of this faction, preferring to be saved by Octavian's benefaction than to attempt arms further; Velleius concludes that "there was no greater example of a grateful and pious man than Corvinus was in regard to Caesar." Velleius does not specify by what means Corvinus demonstrated his gratitude and piety, though he later names him, along with Octavian, as consul of 31 B.C., from which one can infer that they continued to engage in amicable exchange: Octavian saw fit to grant and share with him this prestigeous magistracy.[81]

Most conspicuous as examples of elite gratitude toward the Caesars, however, are members of Velleius's own family, himself included. While he never explicitly labels himself or his relatives as *grati*, he carefully documents his family's services to the Iulii and Claudii Nerones over three generations and makes equally clear the rewards they receive for their services: a multigenerational account of amicable reciprocity is charted in detail. We are told that Velleius's father's brother served as an assistant prosecutor (*subscriptor*) to Agrippa in a prosecution of Cassius in 43 B.C. (2.69.5); his grandfather committed suicide in 40 B.C. when because of his age he could not accompany Tiberius Nero (the emperor's father) to Campania, with whom he had a noteworthy friendship (*singularis amicitia*) and of whom he was an partisan (*adiutor partium*, §76.1). Velleius himself was cavalry commander (*praefectus equitum*) under Tiberius in Germany in A.D. 4, as apparently was his father before him (104.3). He was elected quaestor in A.D. 6, whereafter he went off to Illyria as an imperial legate (*legatus Augusti*) under Tiberius's command (111.3). His brother distinguished himself in the Dalmatian wars of A.D. 8–9, gaining the praise of both Tiberius and Augustus; he also received further honors and gifts, as did Velleius himself, in Tiberius's subsequent triumph (115.1, 121.3). Finally, in A.D. 14 both Velleius and his brother were elected to praetorships as candidates specially selected by Augustus (*candidati Caesaris*, 124.4).[82] The advan-

---

[81] App. *B.C.* 5.113 provides a significantly different account. He says that, after the deaths of Brutus and Cassius, Corvinus delivered a fleet he commanded to Antony, and only later went over to Octavian. Appian also reports here that after Sextus Pompeius defeated Octavian's fleet off Tauromenium, Octavian's personal safety and indeed the fate of his cause hung for a time entirely upon the loyalty and vigorous action of Corvinus. He suggests that Corvinus's behavior here was notable given that he had actually been proscribed by the triumvirs and might then have avenged himself. So while Velleius makes him an *exemplum hominis grati ac pii*, Appian makes him a ζήλωμα τῆς Ῥωμαίων ἀρετῆς; for Velleius it is Octavian who strikingly rectified an exchange relationship that had been in a hostile phase, while for Appian it is Corvinus whose role in reconfirming a pattern of amicable exchange is more striking and exemplary.

[82] For a detailed discussion of Velleius's family, along with its connections to the Claudii Nerones and the Vinicii, see Sumner 1970: 262–79. See also Kuntze 1985: 254–59, who

tages for an aristocratic family of maintaining amicable reciprocity with members of the imperial household—providing services, displaying gratitude, and receiving benefactions such as military commands and public offices—can hardly be clearer than in the examples of Velleius and his family, who stand in implied but plain opposition to the ungrateful elite plotters who sporadically appear in Velleius's text. For this text presents the view that the imperial household's giving rightly compels gratitude on the part of the recipients, creating hierarchical relationships and demanding amicable reciprocity. On this account, the regime's legitimacy at least in part resides in and is constituted by its giving. Those whose relationship to the Caesars is based on such exchange, such as the Velleii, not only gain materially and socially, but also may claim moral virtue. Those who do not relate to the Caesars on these terms—who deny their subordination and/or reciprocate benefits with injuries—are ingrates, ipso facto morally vicious. Indeed, Velleius's history itself, with its panegyrical portrayal of Tiberius and its catalogue of the history of the amicable exchange relationship between the Julio-Claudians and the Velleii, can be seen as a gift offering in the context of that relationship.[83] Perhaps this work itself helped to perpetuate these amicable relations, for they appear to have continued for another generation: Velleius's sons both reached the consulship under Nero in the early 60s A.D. (Sumner 1970: 297).

I next apply the principles of gift-exchange to a particular kind of offering given by the emperor to aristocrats, namely "clemency," forgiveness for some sort of transgression. Seen as a gift, clemency is striking inasmuch as it can only be given by the superior party to the subordinate one, in response to a hostile offering by the latter, or following a sequence of hostile exchanges. The term *clementia* itself, along with the other terms that mark this kind of offering (e.g., *lenitas, venia, misericordia*, and forms of *ignoscere*, all of which I will translate generically as "clemency"), generally carry positive connotations; thus they are used to indicate amicable offerings that terminate hostile reciprocity, with a view to winning the recipients' good will, subordinating them, and inviting amicable offerings in return. This is perhaps the ideal functioning of clemency: we have already seen several such cases, in which rulers forgive aristocrats who speak ill of them in convivia and so

---

observes that Velleius's portrayal of his own and his family's rise, through their loyalty and competence, coheres with late republican portrayals of *novi homines* whose claims to social distinction rest on deeds rather than birth, and also with his presentation of Sejanus and other *novi homines* at 2.127–28 (262–67)—though she denies (269–70) that there is any systematic denigration of *nobiles* in relation to *novi homines* in Velleius' work.

[83] On the panegyrical elements in Velleius's Tiberian narrative, see Woodman 1975: 287–96.

(re)confirm amicable relations between themselves and the offenders.[84] In some cases, however, clemency functions rather as a hostile offering, creating no good will but merely shifting the field of antagonistic exchange between the transactors. This bifurcation in the functioning of clemency recalls the capacity of verbal sallies in convivial settings to be either hostile or amicable; indeed, it is a characteristic capacity of the gift (see section 1 above).[85]

The functioning of clemency as a gift is nowhere more fully articulated than in Caesar's famous letter to Oppius and Balbus (Cic. *Att.* 9.7C), written very early in the civil war (early March, 49 B.C.), shortly after he captured Corfinium. Here Caesar explains his rationale for sparing and releasing the defenders of the city, after their capitulation (§1):

> temptemus hoc modo si possumus omnium voluntates recuperare et diuturna victoria uti, quoniam reliqui crudelitate odium effugere non potuerunt neque victoriam diutius tenere praeter unum L. Sullam, quem imitaturus non sum. haec nova sit ratio vincendi, ut misericordia et liberalitate nos muniamus.

> Let us test in this manner whether we can regain everyone's good will and enjoy a lasting victory, since the others, thanks to their bloodthirstiness, could not escape hatred, nor were they able to maintain their victory for any length of time, with the single exception of Lucius Sulla, whom I will not imitate. Let this be a new means of conquering, that we fortify ourselves with our clemency and liberality.

As Caesar presents it, his clemency and liberality are symbolic violence: they constitute a way of "fortifying" himself against his enemies and are a "new means of conquering," with the aim of securing a "lasting victory." Normally, victory is gained and fortifications constructed through the deployment of military force. But Caesar hopes that his clemency (*misericordia*) will achieve these same ends more effectively than military force: that is, while it stands in for and displaces force, it not merely replicates but actually enhances its effects.[86] Equally significant is

---

[84] E.g., *Ben.* 3.27.4, where Augustus forgives Rufus his verbal transgression and adds further gifts, solidifying their amicable relationship; likewise Val. Max. 5.1 ext. 3, where Pyrrhus forgives the drunken speech of the Tarentine youths, thereby winning over the entire citizenry.

[85] On the semantics of *clementia* and related words, see Hellegouarc'h 1963: 261–63, Weinstock 1971: 233–43, and Moore 1989: 83–85. The bibliography on the clemency of Iulius Caesar and/or subsequent emperors is large, and I have been able to examine only a small portion. To my knowledge, however, only Wistrand 1979: 47–48 has observed the exchange dynamic that is present in the granting of clemency, the dynamic which I discuss here at some length.

[86] Caesar's image of the "fortified" leader evokes the stereoype of the Graeco-Roman

Caesar's reasoning for why this policy should advance his ends more effectively than being bloodthirsty. Unlike cruelty, he suggests, clemency has the capacity to win people's good will (*voluntates recuperare*). However, it also imposes a gift-debt upon its recipients, as he goes on to explain in the next section: for regarding the adjutants of Pompey whom he captured and then released, he says, "if they wish to show their gratitude, they ought to urge Pompey to prefer friendship with me over friendship with those who have always been utterly hostile to both him and me" (*si volent grati esse, debebunt Pompeium hortari ut malit mihi esse amicus quam iis qui et illi et mihi semper fuerunt inimicissimi*, §2). Thus Caesar expects the recipients of his clemency to manifest their gratitude by advocating Caesar's interests (which he claims are also Pompey's interests) to Pompey himself.[87]

But if *misericordia* has displaced cruelty, could it be displaced by it in turn? At least some of Caesar's contemporaries suggest this possibility: Caelius, for one, warns Cicero that Caesar's restraint (*temperantia*) may not continue, since he is growing angry (Cic. *Fam.* 8.15.1). Nor is Caesar's clemency universally represented as an ethically positive alternative to cruelty, which is ethically negative—the division that Caesar presents in the passage quoted above. For even as Cicero observes the effectiveness of Caesar's *clementia* in gaining good will, he nevertheless describes it as "treacherous" (*insidiosa*, literally "full of traps/ambushes"),[88] where the negative connotations of the adjective overwhelm the generally positive connotations of the noun. Moreover, since the noun *insidiae* often occurs in military contexts, referring to soldiers lying in am-

---

"tyrant," from which he seeks to differentiate himself: see Treu 1948: 209–15 (and passim for a detailed discussion of the whole letter). For further discussion of tyrant imagery in Julio-Claudian texts, especially in Sen. *Clem.* 1.12–13, see ch. 4.3 and n. 52 below. For tyrants occupying fortified citadels, see e.g., Sen. *Cont.* 2.5.20; Sen. *Clem.* 19.6; Suet. *Tib.* 40; Tabacco 1985: 42–45.

[87] On the utility of clemency as a way of gaining good will, see Cic. *Att.* 10.4.8, where Cicero reports Curio's assessment of Caesar's character and intentions: *ipsum autem non voluntate aut natura non esse crudelem sed quod popularem putaret esse clementiam; quodsi populi studium amisisset, crudelem fore.* Cf. *Att.* 8.9a.1, 8.13, 8.16.2 for Cicero reporting that Caesar's clemency is actually winning people over, gaining him support in the countryside. Indeed, in *B.C.* 1.22–23 Caesar presents himself as attending scrupulously to his exchange relations through his use of elemency. In §22 he spares the life of Lentulus Spinther, listing the services he had received from him; by presenting himself in this case as a careful and fair judge of his gift-obligations he adds credibility to his complaint in §23 that the senators who had taken refuge in Corfinium were ungrateful to him for the great benefits he had bestowed upon them (<*queritur*> *quod sibi a parte eorum gratia relata non sit pro suis in eos maximis beneficiis, dimittit omnes incolumes*).

[88] Cic. *Att.* 8.16.2: *huius* [sc. Caesar] *insidiosa clementia delectantur, illius* [sc. Pompey] *iracundiam formidant.*

bush, and since military matters are among the subjects of this letter, it seems likely that *insidiosa* here could be felt as carrying its military associations in particular. If so, Cicero too suggests that Caesar's clemency is symbolic violence: but in this characterization it is axiologically identical to the violence it displaces, rather than axiologically opposite, as Caesar presents it. An ambush is still an ambush. In Cicero's presentation, then, Caesar's clemency does not terminate hostile reciprocity, but perpetuates it through nonviolent means.[89]

These civil war-era articulations of the social aims and consequences of Caesarian clemency—the view that it displaces violence, and the implication that it operates socially as a gift—appear to be foundational for the ideology of imperial clemency throughout the Julio-Claudian era. For in other texts dating from or referring to this period, the emperor's clemency is described as operating either as an amicable gift that gains the recipient's good will, terminates a hostile exchange, and reestablishes a warm social bond, or as a hostile gift that merely shifts the ground on which antagonistic exchange takes place. I first discuss some texts that emphasize the socially cohesive function of the gift of clemency. One valuable passage is from Seneca's *De Clementia* (1.9), a treatise addressing precisely this topic. Here Seneca describes how Augustus acted upon detecting a plot by Cornelius Cinna, a grandson of Pompey, who sought to assassinate him. When first apprised of the plot, Augustus decides to "avenge himself" upon Cinna (*constituit se ab eo vindicare,* §3). Subsequently he spends a sleepless night, evaluating in part whether his own life is worth the cost of this plotter's life and all the others who have targeted him hitherto (§5). His wife Livia then speaks up, suggesting that since severity against previous plotters did not dissuade others from making similar attempts, perhaps Augustus should in this case take the opposite tack and try *clementia* (§6). And so he does: summoning Cinna, he enumerates his own benefactions to him, including saving his life though he was a "born enemy,"[90] granting him his ancestral property, and giving him a priesthood (§8): thus, implies Augustus, Cinna is an ingrate for plotting against him (*cum sic de te meruerim, occidere me constituisti*). Nevertheless, Augustus declares he will again grant Cinna his life: he says, "Cinna, I give you your life a second

---

[89] On the threat/fear that Caesar's clemency may revert to cruelty, see e.g., Cic. *Att.* 8.9a.2 (*metuo ne omnis haec clementia ad unam illam crudelitatem conligatur*); 9.16.2; 10.4.8. In contrast to *insidiosa clementia*, Cicero later speaks publicly of Caesar's clemency as ethically positive, e.g., *Lig.* 6, 30.

[90] *Clem.* 1.9.8: *ego te, Cinna, cum in hostium castris invenissem, non factum tantum mihi inimicum sed natum, servavi*. He is a "born enemy," presumably, in view of the fourteen years of military rivalry (49–36 B.C.) between the Pompeii and the Iulii, extending over two generations of both families.

time—the first time you were my enemy, now you are a plotter and parricide. From this day forth, let there be friendship between us; let us contest whether it is with better faith that I granted you your life, or that you owe it to me" (*"vitam," inquit, "tibi, Cinna, iterum do, prius hosti, nunc insidiatori ac parricidae. ex hodierno die inter nos amicitia incipiat; contendamus utrum ego meliore fide tibi vitam dederim an tu debeas,"* §11). Augustus's words here explicitly mark his clemency as a gift (*vitam . . . iterum do*), whose aim is to rectify an exchange relationship that threatens to devolve into terminal hostility (plotting reciprocated by execution). Rather than competing for power and standing through violence, Augustus suggests that they compete instead (*contendamus . . .*) in the realm of amicable reciprocation. In this realm, Cinna is already behind: he "owes" (*. . . an tu debeas*). This rectification is successful, for Seneca says that amicable reciprocity obtained thereafter: he notes, on the one hand, that Augustus later bestowed the consulship upon Cinna, and on the other, that Cinna was "most friendly and trustworthy" (*amicissimum fidelissimumque*) and even made Augustus his sole heir—the will, as noted above, being a place where gift-debts were commonly acknowledged and reciprocated. Moreover, says Seneca, Augustus was never again targeted by plotters (§12).[91]

Whether Augustus actually used the arguments and strategies that Seneca here attributes to him, we cannot know. But Seneca relates this anecdote in the context of a work addressed to the emperor Nero, the last of the Julio-Claudian line, shortly after his accession in A.D. 54. In general, as its title (*De Clementia*) suggests, this work urges Nero to adopt clemency rather than severity as a practice for himself, and the example of Augustus is one argument in this exhortation. The account of Augustus and Cinna shows how a Julio-Claudian aristocrat, namely Seneca, could imagine imperial clemency functioning: as a potent gift specially tailored to rectify hostile exchanges, to (re)impose gift-debt (ideally accompanied by gratitude and goodwill) upon its recipients, and thus to subordinate them. As Seneca asserts at §21.1, "no one has ever saved a life who was not greater than the person he saved" (*servavit quidem nemo nisi maior eo quem servabat*). Moreover, Seneca presents this view of the functioning of clemency to the reigning emperor, implying that it will be as powerful a tool in his own arsenal of authority-enhancing strategies as it was for his predecessor Augustus. Seneca spells out these conclusions for Nero at *Clem*. 1.10.2–3: "This

---

[91] My observations on this passage (*Clem*. 1.9) are indebted to the excellent analysis of Warren 1996: 11–13. His discussion of Seneca's representations of cruelty and clemency by rulers in Sen. *Clem*. and *Ben*. shows that clemency is portrayed not just as a means of breaking cycles of violence, but of displacing them, of moving agonistic conflict into other realms (see also his p. 3).

clemency brought Augustus through to safety and security; it rendered him popular and pleasing to others . . . today too, it furnishes him a reputation that is scarcely in the power of living emperors. . . . we assert that Augustus was a good emperor, and that the name of 'parent' befits him, for no other reason than that he did not avenge even insults with cruelty" (*haec eum* [sc. Augustus] *clementia ad salutem securitatemque perduxit; haec gratum ac favorabilem reddidit . . . haec hodieque praestat illi famam quae vix vivis principibus servit. . . . bonum fuisse principem Augustum, bene illi parentis nomen convenisse fatemur ob nullam aliam causam quam quod contumelias quoque suas . . . nulla crudelitate exsequebatur*, etc.). Nero, then, can win acclaim in posterity (as Augustus does), as well as in his own age, by following Augustus's example of maintaining and legitimating his authority through clemency, rather than through the putative alternative of severity—by seeking always to rectify hostile exchange relationships, not to reciprocate hostile offerings in kind.[92]

Another Senecan text emphasizing the socially cohesive force of the gift of clemency is found at *De Beneficiis* 2.25.1. Here Seneca describes the interchange between Augustus and Gaius Furnius, who sought from the *princeps* the pardon of his father, a partisan of Antony. Upon gaining his petition, Seneca says, Furnius declared to Augustus that he could never reciprocate this gift; that he would necessarily live and die as an ingrate (*effecisti ut et viverem et morerer ingratus*). Paradoxically, Seneca says, this declaration showed his gratitude—for what better reveals a grateful mind than to declare that one can never adequately reciprocate?[93]—and so in turn obligated Augustus, disposing him to grant further requests to Furnius as well (*nullo magis Caesarem Augustum demeruit et ad alia impetranda facilem sibi reddidit*). Here, according to Seneca, the clemency that Augustus granted to Furnius's father sets an amicable exchange into motion: Furnius expresses his gratitude in the paradoxical way just noted, inciting Augustus in turn to

---

[92] Dio provides an account of the Cinna episode (55.14–22) that, though longer than the Senecan version, is perhaps less rich since it is not presented directly to a reigning emperor as a model for him to emulate. In Dio's version, however, Livia delivers a lengthy speech elaborating some themes that are merely adumbrated by Seneca. In particular, Dio's Livia emphasizes not only the capacity of clemency to gain the good will of those who receive it (whereupon they desire to reciprocate amicably, and also hope to receive further benefits: e.g., 55.21.3), but also its exemplary quality, its power over the minds of others who witness these transactions (55.16.5, cf. 19.5). Conversely, violence and harshness alienate people and make them hate their ruler: 16.6, 21.2 (cf. Sen. *Ben.* 7.19, *Clem.* 1.12.3–4, 13.1–2; also Treu 1948: 209–15 on the image of the cruel tyrant who walls himself off with bodyguards).

[93] *Ben.* 2.25.1: *quid est tam grati animi quam nullo modo sibi satis facere, quam ne ad spem quidem exaequandi umquam beneficiis accedere?*

bestow still more gifts upon him. Now, the exchange described in this passage must have occurred not long after Antony's defeat in 31 B.C., and Furnius (PIR^2 F 591) is known subsequently to have served both as a *legatus Augusti* in Spain and as consul in 17 B.C. Perhaps Seneca merely hints at the gifts forthcoming from Augustus because he relies on his audience to know at least of Furnius's consulship, and to recognize it as a gift of the emperor. In any case, this passage describes the ideal operation of imperial clemency: it obligates the recipient, wins his good will, and sets in motion a sequence of friendly offerings and counter-offerings.

But if clemency ideally has the social efficacy portrayed in these Senecan passages, then it frequently fails to attain this ideal. For sometimes a sequence of amicable exchanges inaugurated by clemency reverts to the hostility or violence from which it emerged, and sometimes clemency fails to inaugurate amicable exchange at all, but merely transfers a hostile exchange onto a new field of competition. We have already seen an instance of the first kind of failure: according to Velleius, Caesar spared Marcus Brutus, who had fought against him in the battle of Pharsalus (2.52.5), and awaited a return in due course for this and other offerings (such as the promised consulship, §57.1), only to be assassinated by Brutus himself and others (§§56.3, 57.1). On this account, Caesar's attempt to establish amicable reciprocity ultimately failed, exposing the beneficiaries as ingrates: for the violence that Brutus and other Pompeians had directed against Caesar during the civil war, which Caesar subsequently displaced by his clemency, was finally resumed. Yet the actions of Brutus admit of at least one alternative analysis, which Seneca offers in *De Beneficiis* 2.20. He begins, "It is often debated regarding Marcus Brutus whether he ought to have accepted his life from the deified Iulius, when he believed that he should be killed" (*disputari de M. Bruto solet an debuerit accipere a divo Iulio vitam cum occidendum eum iudicaret*, §1 — apparently a school exercise in deliberative rhetoric). On this matter, Seneca declares that Brutus rightly accepted Caesar's gift of life and pardon after Pharsalus, but was not therefore obliged to regard him as a father-figure (*vitam accipere debuit, ob hoc tamen <non> habere illum parentis loco*, §3)[94] — for it

---

[94] The idea that one's savior is to be regarded *loco parentis* has broader currency: Cic. *Planc.* 72 and Polyb. 6.39.6–7 imply that the recipient of the *corona civica*, a military decoration awarded for saving a fellow citizen's life in battle, was thereafter to be treated as a parent by the man he saved (see Maxfield 1981: 70–72.) This association of ideas gives special point to the words Seneca ascribes to Augustus at *Clem.* 1.9.11, discussed above. Having once preserved the plotter Cinna's life, Augustus now calls him *insidiator ac parricida*. The term "parricide" can designate murder generally, and is not restricted to the murder of one's father or a near relative. But in this case, since the criterion of life

was only by doing injuries that Caesar came into a position to confer benefits upon Brutus in the first place (*quia in ius dandi beneficii iniuria venerat:* namely, by initiating the civil war?). Seneca concludes that "failing to kill" is not the same as "saving," and hence that Caesar granted Brutus not a benefit, but merely *missio*, discharge from military service (*non enim servavit is qui non interfecit, nec beneficium dedit sed missionem*). On this account, Brutus incurred no obligation to Caesar and therefore was guilty of no ingratitude in killing him.[95] Yet precisely by arguing that Brutus should be acquitted of ingratitude, this passage confirms the strength of the expectation, articulated clearly by Velleius, that imperial clemency will indeed obligate and subordinate its beneficiary: its failure to do so, not its success, requires comment and explanation.

Finally, I adduce one instance of clemency itself being portrayed as a hostile offering, one which is even more hostile than the violence it replaces. The passage in question is from Lucan, and provides an interpretation of Caesar's actions at Corfinium that is entirely at odds with Caesar's own presentation of his behavior there, quoted above (apud Cic. *Att.* 9.7C). At 2.507, the gates of the city are opened and Domitius, the commander of the Pompeian defenders, is brought before Caesar:

> ecce, nefas belli! reseratis agmina portis
> captivum traxere ducem, civisque superbi
> constitit ante pedes. voltu tamen alta minaci
> nobilitas recta ferrum cervice poposcit.
> scit Caesar poenamque peti veniamque timeri.
> "vive, licet nolis, et nostro munere," dixit,

---

saving has been explicitly invoked, we are entitled to take *parricida* here in the narrower, more pointed sense of "murderer of one's own father." For the figuration of the emperor as "father," see chapter 4.3–4 below.

[95] For *missio* as release from military service, see *OLD s.v.* 2a-b. Contra Seneca's claim that *missio* does not constitute a *beneficium*, Caesar, who uses the word *missio* to describe his release of the Pompeian troops after Ilerda (*B.C.* 1.86.1), insists that he succeeded in binding them to himself; his proof is that they subsequently came to him, not to their Pompeian commanders, when they had disputes to settle (87.2). But Seneca is not entirely consistent himself, first implying that Caesar did give a benefit, though Brutus was not obligated by it, and then denying that Caesar gave a benefit at all. In either case, however, Brutus is regarded as incurring no obligation. At *Ben.* 6.4 Seneca asserts that receiving an injury from someone can wipe out an obligation previously incurred by accepting a benefaction from him; here at 2.20 the same principle is manifest, but with the order of events reversed: the injury initially done by Caesar cancels in advance the obligation that would ordinarily accompany his subsequent benefit (if it was a benefit at all). For similar deliberation about whether an obligation has been incurred, see *Ben.* 2.12 (§1: *C. Caesar dedit vitam Pompeio Penno, si dat qui non aufert*), and *Ben.* 2.7–8; 2.18.7–19.2; 6.27.4; on reckoning the balance of injuries and benefits see *Ep.* 81.3–8, 15–18.

"cerne diem. victis iam spes bona partibus esto
exemplumque mei. vel, si libet, arma retempta,
et nihil hac venia, si viceris, ipse paciscor."

(2. 507–15)

Lo, the moral outrage of war! Having unbolted the gates, the troops hauled out their leader as a captive, and he took a stand before the feet of his arrogant fellow citizen. Nevertheless, his lofty nobility with its threatening visage demanded the sword with neck erect. Caesar knew that punishment was being demanded and clemency was feared. He said, "Live, even if you do not wish it, and by my gift look upon the light of day. Be a token of good hope to the defeated faction, and an exemplum of me. If you wish, you can even venture to take up arms again, and if you win, I make no demands for myself on the on the strength of my clemency here."

Caesar explicitly presents his clemency toward Domitius, his *venia* (515), as a gift (*munus*): "Live, and by my gift look upon the light" (512–13). He even describes the reciprocation that he expects, namely that Domitius will be an exemplum of this *venia*, a "token of good hope" (*spes bona*) for his opponents—though this reciprocation requires no good will on Domitius's part, nor that he consciously act on Caesar's behalf: simply by living and being before the eyes of others, even if he continues in armed resistance to Caesar, he benefits Caesar in return.[96] However, precisely by conceding this point—"you can even take up arms again, if you wish" (514)—Caesar hints at an alternative form of reciprocation, one more actively amicable: that Domitius might, on the contrary, withdraw from the war and so cease to serve the Pompeian cause; that is, Caesar's gift might at least manage to detach Domitius from the Pompeians, if not to bind him to Caesar as an active supporter.[97] Just a few lines later, Domitius does mention the possibility of withdrawal, albeit with contempt: "Will you return to Rome and the refuge of peace, ignoble one?" (*Romamne petes pacisque recessus / de-*

---

[96] Sen. *Clem.* 1.21.2 closely resembles the passage of Lucan quoted here: *perdidit enim vitam qui debet, et quisquis ex alto ad inimici pedes abiectus alienam de capite regnoque sententiam expectavit, in servatoris sui gloriam vivit plusque eius nomini confert incolumis quam si ex oculis ablatus esset*; also §21.4.

[97] This separation from the Pompeian cause is precisely the outcome for the Pompeian troops who surrender at Ilerda, according to Lucan (and also Caesar: see note 95 above). Lucan's Caesar releases these troops unharmed (4.363–64, 381–85) and they are said to have "received peace as a gift" (*donata pace*, 385). They therefore regret having taken up arms against him (*paenituit*, 387), and while they are not now partisans of Caesar, they are explicitly detached from Pompey: *sollicitus . . . abest favor: ille salutis / est auctor, dux ille fuit* (399–400)—that is, if either side seeks their help, they can invoke the services done them, and the obligations they consequently incurred, to the leader of the other side as a reason for staying out.

gener? 522–23). The strength of the expectation that he will reciprocate amicably — in this case, by ceasing to oppose Caesar — is clear, even if the possibility is not seriously entertained. Thus, in the background of this passage is the assumption that Caesar's clemency has considerable power to separate his defeated opponents from the Pompeian community and win them over to himself, because it imposes an obligation and inspires gratitude just like any gift.

But Domitius does not withdraw from the war; he returns to battle as a Pompeian. On what grounds? The narrator provides an interpretive framework at 2.517–21: "alas, how much better could Fortune have spared Domitius's Roman shame, precisely by carrying out the slaughter: the worst of punishments for a citizen is to be forgiven for following the troops of the fatherland, the leadership of Pompey, and the entire senate" (*heu quanto melius vel caede peracta / parcere Romano potuit Fortuna pudori! / poenarum extremum civi, quod castra secutus / sit patriae Magnumque ducem totumque senatum, / ignosci*). The problem with Caesar's clemency here, as Lucan presents it, is that a Roman citizen is pardoned for his staunch support of the interests of the Roman state — the state here represented in the phrases "troops of the fatherland" and "the entire senate," with "Pompey the leader" sandwiched in between to guarantee (for now) his association with this cause. Normally, such support would be expected to win one acclaim for one's *pietas* and *virtus*, as I argue in chapter 1.2 (and passim) above. Now, I further argued (ch. 1.3) that Lucan generally ascribes to the Pompeians an "assimilating" view of the conflict — that the Caesarians remain, despite their insurrection, members of the same community of moral obligation as the Pompeians. Thus at 2.508, Caesar is called Domitius's "arrogant fellow citizen" (*civisque superbi*), which I take to be Domitius's own point of view: he focalizes the narrative here; the implied ethical evaluations are his own. This, the assimilating perspective shared by Domitius and the narrator, is the perspective from which the subsequent lament (517–21) makes sense. From this perspective, the "shame" of Domitius as a Roman derives from the very fact of being pardoned, for pardon implies that Domitius transgressed against the *res publica* — that he engaged in hostile exchange with it, like a criminal or foreign enemy[98] — when in fact he was supporting its interests and fol-

---

[98] Most likely the latter, since — in Lucan at any rate — Caesar and his troops generally take the "alienating" view that their opponents, the Pompeians, are a foreign enemy (as argued in ch. 1.4 above). Before the civil war, the vocabulary of clemency (*clementia, mansuetudo, misericordia* etc.) was indeed commonly used to characterize the actions of the Roman state vis-à-vis its conquered foreign enemies: see e.g., Hellegouarc'h 1963: 262, Weinstock 1971: 234–35. However, it also occurred in legal contexts, to characterize possible courses of action by juries in regard to defendants (Weinstock 234 n. 8 points to

lowing legitimate authority. Indeed, such pardon constitutes the "worst of punishments for a citizen" (519) because, by presenting him as having opposed the state's interests, it alienates this citizen (*civis*) from the very community that gives meaning to this term. Execution is preferable because it poses no such threat to the citizen-soldier's solidarity with his community.[99] In fact, Domitius has been engaged in hostile exchange only with Caesar, who by his clemency (*venia*) aims to terminate that exchange; yet this termination, in Domitius's view, would necessarily detach him from the civic community: the social bonds that Caesar's clemency aims to forge are irreconcilable with Domitius's self-identification as a properly socialized Roman citizen. Faced with this unpalatable option, Domitius elects instead to regard Caesar's *venia* as a hostile offering, worse even than the continuation of violence. Domitius returns immediately to war, looking not for victory but rather to die as soon as possible (*iam dudum moriture . . . omnes lucis rumpe moras*, 524–25). For as long as he lives, he serves willy-nilly as Caesar's *exemplum* (514); only by dying can he "escape Caesar's gift" (*Caesaris effuge munus*, 525) and thus make suitably hostile reciprocation for the *venia* he received. When he finally dies (according to Lucan) in battle at Pharsalus, he "rejoices that he has escaped being forgiven a second time" (*venia gaudet caruisse secunda*, 7.604).

I have not been able here to survey all occurrences of *clementia* and related terms in Julio-Claudian literature. But my readings of these particular passages provide, I hope, some basis for my contention that imperial clemency in this period could be regarded as a gift, whether hostile or amicable, that involves all the social consequences that normally accompany gift-exchange in either of these modes. Other imperial offerings also appear to have this effect: I have adduced a number of pas-

---

e.g., Cic. *Sulla* 87–88, *Clu.* 105–106). Plut. *Cato Minor* 64.7–9 ascribes to Cato this same rationale for refusing to ask Caesar for clemency: clemency is to given only to criminals and foreign enemies, neither of which he considers himself. At 66.2, however, he gives a different reason: he asserts that Caesar has wrongly appropriated despotic power precisely through his granting of clemency, and Cato refuses to be grateful to him for this.

[99] Fantham 1992 ad loc. aptly compares 9.1059–62, where the ideas, language, and situation are similar: Lucan rejoices that *Fortuna* spared *Romanus pudor* by arranging for Pompey to die before Caesar could pardon him (though at 8.627–29 Pompey seems to regard it as shameful to be slain by Achillas, but less shameful if the deed is attributable to Caesar; cf. 8.679). This passage admits of the same interpretation I provide for 2.517–21. I work here with Kaster's (1997: 4) definitions of *pudor* as (1) "a displeasure with oneself caused by a vulnerability to just criticism of a socially diminishing sort," and (2) "an admirable sensitivity to such displeasure," (2) being the sense required in this case. The socially diminishing criticism to which Romans are putatively subject in these passages is that the state's staunchest advocates, by receiving pardon for their advocacy, are thereby cast as its enemies or as criminals.

sages, particularly from Velleius Paterculus, suggesting that at least some Julio-Claudian aristocrats expected themselves and their peers to manifest gratitude and deference upon receiving a wide variety of goods and services from the emperor. The Roman aristocracy—especially the senatorial-equestrian aristocracy based in Rome, which included the emperor himself—was certainly a sufficiently small community (only a few thousand individuals) that most of its members knew one another personally. I suggest that within this community there was *always* the expectation that goods or services bestowed by the emperor would be received as personal gifts, which would normally impose a debt of gratitude upon the recipient, earn his good will, and socially subordinate him. Particular offerings in particular circumstances could be argued not to be gifts, or not to subordinate the recipient, but such arguments had to be made ad hoc. Veyne's view that most if not all imperial distributions constitute "euergetism," acts by the state that impose no obligation upon recipients, I believe cannot hold, at least not for the emperor's relations with individual aristocrats: my analysis here suggests that the emperor's giving to individuals of this status is best understood as gift giving. Veyne's case is inherently more plausible in regard to imperial distributions to collectivities, where a personal relationship between the emperor and each of thousands of individual recipients is out of the question. Yet in the examples of such giving by Caesar and Otho, with which I opened this section, our sources indicate that the recipients were collectively grateful and reciprocated concretely. Further study of recipients' attitudes in these cases is needed, but even here Veyne's contention is not unproblematic.

6. The Emperor as Gift-Debtor

In the previous two sections I examined how distributions of gifts, broadly defined, by Julio-Claudian emperors were seen as establishing, sustaining, or undermining their authority and legitimacy as rulers. Invitations to dinner and other offerings made in the context of the convivium (section 4), and a wider range of offerings, particularly clemency (section 5), are presented as eliciting gratitude and creating a social hierarchy, or significantly failing to do so. In this section I propose to examine the other side of the coin: the emperor's reception of gifts, and the consequences of such gifts for his authority and legitimacy in light of the social dynamics of gift-exchange as articulated above. Among the studies of imperial patronage, the sociopolitical significance of this reverse flow of goods and services has been relatively neglected: portions of Millar's discussion of the sources of imperial wealth (1977: 133–201, esp. 139–44), along with a short but very useful analysis of aspects of this question by Lendon, are the only detailed discussions I have encountered. Lendon's contribution (1997: 120–29), an examination of the social stakes for the emperor of being honored by others ("honor" being the conceptual kernel around which Lendon constructs his analysis here and throughout his book), argues that the emperor was concerned like all Roman aristocrats to augment and protect his honor, and therefore comported himself in accordance with the rules of the honor-game as it was played by aristocrats generally. For in addition to bestowing honors upon others, he also sought, and stood to benefit from, honors given by the urban plebs, the soldiers, the senate, cities and towns, and so on, while his position was potentially undermined if he was dishonored by the same. Indeed, Lendon says (126), "[t]he emperors could also be counted upon to pay back favours done them. When they failed to do so, they felt the lash of aristocratic censure" — favors, on his account, being quanta of honor which must be allocated appropriately (i.e., in accordance with due reciprocity) if the emperor is to be regarded as acting properly. I agree that the emperor was put under scrutiny and hence at risk by his conduct upon receiving offerings made to him, and was to a high degree constrained by the expectations of others about what kind of conduct was appropriate to the most honorific person in society. In this section, I aim to broaden and nuance Lendon's conclusions by applying the analytical framework developed so far in this chapter to the inflow of material goods (and some services) to the emperor in the Julio-Claudian period, along with the emperor's handling of the exchange relationships constantly being established, reestablished, and reconfigured by these inflows. I will argue that, generally speaking, the Julio-Claudian emperors are portrayed as seeking to avoid accepting significant gifts, at least from individuals: they do not willingly allow persons they have subordinated in gift-debt to claw their way out, much less do they wish to be subordinated (or be perceived to be subordinated) in gift-debt themselves. The imperative to maintain gift-dominance drove the emperor to avoid receiving gifts that did not admit of immediate and greater reciprocation just as surely as it drove him to give such gifts.

I begin with aristocratic views of the reception of gifts, views attested in passages scattered through the literature of the late republic and empire. In general, these passages claim or imply that high-ranking aristocrats seek to avoid incurring gift-debt, or if they do incur it, they at any rate seek to conceal this condition from others. A famous and much-quoted passage from Cicero (*Off.* 2.69) describes this impulse: "Those who consider themselves wealthy, honorable, and fortunate do not wish even to be bound by a benefit; rather, they reckon that they have given a benefit when they have accepted something, however great it may be, and even suspect that something is demanded or awaited from them, but think it the equivalent of death to have availed themselves of patronage, or to be called clients" (*qui se locupletes honoratos beatos putant, ii ne obligari quidem beneficio volunt; quin etiam beneficium dedisse arbitrantur cum ipsi quamvis magnum aliquod acceperint, atque etiam a se postulari aut exspectari aliquid suspicantur, patrocinio vero se usos aut clientes appellari mortis instar putant*). This passage was mentioned briefly above (section 2), where I argued that aristocrats may regard themselves as doing a greater benefit than they receive when they accept a dinner invitation from someone of much lower social status. Cicero's claim in this passage, however, obviously applies to *any* benefit received, which some aristocrats will regard as a benefit given (presumably because they have stooped to accept it, and so have entered into an exchange relationship with the other, far inferior, party). Indeed, they consider accepting patronage (*patrocinium*) from another or being called a client as "the equivalent of death."[100]

This same fear is implied or expressed in several Julio-Claudian texts as well. Beginning in *De Beneficiis* 5.2.1, Seneca seeks to refute an assertion that, he says, his (aptly named) addressee Liberalis regards as a "noble sentiment" (*velut magnifice dictum*): namely, that it is shameful to be outdone in giving gifts (*turpe esse beneficiis vinci*). Against this view he argues, inter alia, that if this were true one would have to decline all gifts from extremely powerful men, namely *principes* and kings, who are in a position to give much, but to whom one cannot reciprocate in kind or quantity.[101] Seneca thus implies that his addressee's anxieties (and, by extension, those of his audience generally) are status related: Liberalis and his ilk believe that to be outdone in benefits, to give less than one receives, is to be subordinated. Yet this, Seneca implies, is manifestly Liberalis's (and everyone else's) position in relation to the emperor: Does he consider it shameful to have received imperial benefactions? The implied answer is no, presumably because the emperor, unlike other aristocrats, is regarded as superior beyond competition in the ordinary course of events; one simply accepts imperial benefactions as honors and is duly grateful for them (though see

---

[100] On this attitude among late republican senators see also Dio 46.34.1–2; in general on unwanted obligation/subordination that can come with receiving a gift, see Barton 1993: 118–19 and, for this problem in other cultures, Miller 1993: 15–52 ("requiting the unwanted gift").

[101] *Ben.* 5.4.2: *nam si turpe est beneficiis vinci, non oportet a praepotentibus viris accipere beneficium, quibus gratiam referre non possis, a principibus dico, a regibus, quos eo loco fortuna posuit ex quo largiri multa possent, pauca admodum et imparia datis recepturi.*

below on emperors subordinated in gift-debt). Elsewhere Seneca describes some of the strategies by which those who share Liberalis's anxiety avoid gift-debt, or at least avoid being known as gift-debtors. At *De Beneficiis* 2.23 he says that some people only accept gifts in secret, avoiding any witnesses to the benefit received (§1); or they thank their benefactor furtively by taking them aside and whispering in their ear (§2): such people are ingrates (*ingratus est qui remotis arbitris agit gratias*), which is worse than being known as a client, the thing they mistakenly fear most (. . . *et dum opinionem clientium timent, graviorem subeunt ingratorum*, §3). Such people may also accept fastidiously, as if doing a favor by deigning to accept: they say, "I certainly have no need of it, but since you wish it so much, I will put myself at your disposal" (*non quidem mi opus est, sed quia tam valde vis, faciam tibi mei postestatem*, 2.24.3)—precisely the attitude that Cicero describes in the passage just quoted. As we saw in chapter 2.4 above, in Seneca's Stoic ethical framework gratitude is a mental disposition involving only a warm feeling toward one's benefactor, the *wish* to reciprocate, and is not correlated with making a concrete, visible return; ingratitude is the opposite disposition. Those who hate receiving gifts, then, are by definition ingrates, the most extreme case of which Seneca invokes briefly in *Ep.* 81.31–32: people who consider it so shameful (*turpe*) not to make a return that they actually wish their benefactor dead.[102]

Valerius Maximus also addresses this aristocratic anxiety in several exempla that appear in book 5.2, under the rubric "On Grateful People" (*De Gratis*). In this section Valerius is concerned in part with visible expressions of gratitude by aristocrats, especially when directed toward their social equals or inferiors. At 5.2.7, the gratitude of the lofty Metellus Pius toward the (somewhat) more humble Quintus Calidius is described approvingly. Valerius explains that Calidius, a tribune of the plebs in 98 B.C., sponsored the law by which Pius's father Metellus Numidicus, the distinguished ex-consul, censor, and *triumphator*, was recalled from exile. Pius displayed his gratitude in a striking manner: "He constantly called Calidius the patron of his household and family. Nor

---

[102] A slightly different manifestation of the same aristocratic impulse, which Seneca discusses at *Ben.* 2.17.6, is the person who, having given a benefit, resists accepting a return. In §5 Seneca says that this person seeks to make his gift seem as large as possible by making reciprocation impossible—the consequence of which is that he forces his gift-debtor to be an ingrate. He does not explicitly attribute a motive to the person who so behaves, but in §7 he compares this man to a *fenerator* who refuses to accept repayment. In the latter case we infer that the creditor wishes to continue to accumulate interest on his loan, so avoids accepting repayment. Similarly, then, we may infer that the gift-creditor seeks to keep others indebted and hence socially subordinated. Cf. *Ben.* 4.40.2; Saller 1982: 127–28.

did he thereby subtract anything from the preeminence that beyond doubt he enjoyed: because it was with a grateful spirit, not an abject one, that he lowered his lofty dignity before the extraordinarily meritorious action of a man far inferior to him" (*quin etiam patronum eum domus et familiae suae semper dictitavit. nec hac re de principatu, quem procul dubio obtinebat, quicquam decerpsit, quia non humili sed grato animo longe inferioris hominis maximo merito eximiam summittebat dignitatem*). Valerius's pointed insistance that a "grateful spirit" (*gratus animus*) is distinct from an "abject" one (*humilis animus*), and therefore that Pius's actions subtracted nothing from his high rank, implicitly addresses the expectation that to express gratitude — to acknowledge that one has received a significant gift — is precisely to acknowledge oneself socially subordinated. Indeed, to express gratitude by calling one's benefactor a *patronus* can hardly fail to reinforce the suggestion, already implicit in the mere expression of gratitude, that the benefactor is socially superior.[103] Moreover, in a similar exemplum earlier in this section (Val. Max. 5.2.5), the senator Quintus Terentius Culleo, freed by Scipio Africanus from Carthaginian captivity, expresses his gratitude by donning the *pilleus* as though a freedman and marching in Africanus's triumphal procession. While this display of gratitude involves no striking social inversion (as in the case of Metellus Pius and Calidius), since Africanus is himself a high-ranking aristocrat, nevertheless it is a spectacular symbol of self-abasement for a senator to appear in public in the characteristic garb of the freedman — granted that this symbolic display has particular point here, since Culleo, as a prisoner of war, was therefore a slave in Carthaginian society, and so was in fact restored to freedom by Scipio. Thus, despite Valerius's explicit assertion that expressing gratitude does not entail social subordination, nevertheless the symbols by which the *gratus animus* is exhibited in these passages are precisely the symbols of real social subordination. Furthermore, the very fact that both Valerius and Seneca engage in polemics on this matter suggests

---

[103] Even if one chooses to translate *patronus* here in a loose, general way, e.g., "protector" (Brunt 1988: 405, who incorrectly cites this passage as Cic. *Planc*. 69), it still implies a social hierarchy: *patronus* is often explicitly correlated with *cliens* or *libertus* (e.g., TLL s.v. *patronus*, 782.21–42), and maintains its implications of superior status and power even when not explicitly correlated with one of these terms. Brunt goes on to say, "For instance Cicero's appearance in 63 as counsel for Piso, the consul of 67, in a *repetundae* trial did not make Piso his *cliens*" (405). Perhaps not, but it does significantly impact the balance of the exchange relationship between Cicero and Piso, and may well make the latter the former's gift-debtor, a condition inseparable from issues of status and standing: see David 1992: 167–68, and n. 21 above. On the honor consequences of all such displays of deference among aristocrats, including those by superiors to inferiors, see Lendon 1997: 59–60.

that they imagine that their intended audience of elite Romans is likely to hold the opposite view.

Given this well-attested conceptual linkage whereby acknowledging the receipt of a gift, and expressing gratitude, is tantamount to announcing one's own social subordination to one's benefactor, we may wonder whether emperors, the highest-ranking aristocrats of all, could be expected to accept a gift of any significant size, or at any rate to acknowledge its receipt, and so to present themselves as gift-debtors (or perhaps no longer gift-creditors) in relation to the giver. Indeed, literary texts portray Julio-Claudian emperors as holding the same (negative) view of incurring gift-debt, or being known as gift-debtors, that aristocrats in general are represented as holding in the texts cited above. Thus Tacitus reports (*Ann.* 4.18) that Gaius Silius incurred the enmity of Tiberius in part because he boasted that, when some legions had mutinied upon Tiberius's accession, he had kept the troops under his own command quiet; had they too revolted, Tiberius would have fallen (§§1–2). Tiberius's thoughts in response to this boast are given by Tacitus as follows (§3): "Caesar considered his position demolished by these claims, and regarded himself as unequal to so great a service. For benefits give joy only so long as they seem able to be repaid; when they far outstrip that ability, hatred is returned in place of gratitude" (*destrui per haec fortunam suam Caesar imparemque tanto merito rebatur. nam beneficia eo usque laeta sunt dum videntur exsolvi posse: ubi multum antevenere, pro gratia odium redditur*). As noted above (n. 2), it is precisely when gifts far exceed the recipient's ability to reciprocate that his gift-debt becomes chronic, and he is rendered a client, the intolerable condition for a high-ranking aristocrat. Any putative gratitude by Tiberius for Silius's services, once the latter has publicly portrayed the former as his gift-debtor, becomes hatred, since the effect of Silius's statements is to undermine the emperor's dominant social position. For this and other reasons, says Tacitus, Silius is prosecuted for *maiestas* and commits suicide (19.4).[104] Dio (59.23.2–4) represents Caligula as similarly anxious about the power relations implied in the honors voted him by the senate. Dio says that this emperor was irritated both by small honors, feeling that these constituted a slight, and by large ones, since they seemed to preclude further honors: for he did not wish it to appear that anything that brought him honor was in the senators'

---

[104] Seneca *Ep.* 19.11 attributes the same touchiness about substantial gift-debt to gift-recipients generally: he notes that one may mistakenly believe that one wins over another's mind by giving gifts, when one may in fact be incurring hatred (*nullum habet maius malum occupatus homo . . . quam . . . quod beneficia sua efficacia iudicat ad conciliandos animos, cum quidam quo plus debent magis oderint: leve aes alienum debitorem facit, grave inimicum*). See also *Ep.* 81.32.

power to grant, since this would imply that they were greater than he, and could gratify him as though he were their inferior.[105] These passages, then, directly portray these emperors as seeking to avoid being perceived as gift-debtors for fear of undermining their position of social dominance. While Tacitus and Dio were of course not contemporaries of Tiberius and Caligula respectively, and obviously were not privy to the inmost thoughts and fears of these emperors, it is nevertheless significant that they could put such thoughts into their subjects' minds: for these authors, being Roman aristocrats themselves, presented it to their readers as plausible that these emperors could anxiously seek to avoid incurring gift-debt for fear of being socially subordinated. These authors assume, in other words, that these emperors thought and acted in a typically aristocratic fashion.

It is possible to check these representations, to some extent, by examining some of the transactions by which goods and services flowed to the emperor in the Julio-Claudian period, and considering whether any of these transactions could be regarded as imposing a gift-debt upon him. One major, regular source of funds of which the emperor disposed was money and property left to him by testament, or which fell to him by reason of an invalid will or absence of heirs. Also, starting perhaps in the reign of Tiberius, the emperor received into his *fiscus* at least some portion of the *bona damnatorum*, the goods of men who were convicted of certain serious crimes—especially, but not exclusively, crimes against the state such as *maiestas* or *repetundae* (Millar 1977: 170–71).[106] None of these sources of money could have been regarded as gifts for which the emperor incurred an obligation: as noted above, wills that were not "ungrateful" were thought to reciprocate outstanding gift-debts, and to seek to square accounts (to the extent possible) in a final reckoning, but manifestly could not impose a gift-debt in return. Likewise the *bona damnatorum*, wealth confiscated ostensibly as pun-

---

[105] Dio 59.23.3: οὐδὲ γὰρ οὐδὲ ἐβούλετο δοκεῖν τι τῶν τιμήν τινα αὐτῷ φερόντων ἐπ᾽ αὐτοῖς ὡς καὶ κρείττοσιν αὐτοῦ οὖσι καὶ χαρίζεσθαί οἱ ὡς καὶ ἥττονί σφῶν τι δυναμένοις εἶναι.

[106] In using formulations such as "the emperor's money," I mean money that our sources present as coming under his authority and being at his disposal, money of which he is the transactor, with all the social consequences that various forms of transaction entail. I purposely gloss over, and cannot discuss here, the fiendishly complicated questions about the nature and number of coffers in which monies disposed of by the senate or emperor or magistrates resided, and about the disposition of particular monies at particular times. It seems fairly safe, at any rate, to say that when the word *fiscus* appears in the Julio-Claudian period, it indicates funds administered directly by the emperor himself. The landmark discussions of these questions in the modern era are Brunt 1966 (with further comments at Brunt 1984) and Millar 1977: 153–201, 623–25. See also Eck et al. 1996: 179–80 on the new information conveyed by the *Senatus Consultum de Pisone Patre*.

ishment for criminal activity, were therefore not gifts (more on this matter shortly). Less regular, but occasionally significant, sources of money for the emperor included *manubiae*, the spoils of war, from which (for example) Augustus in 29 B.C. made distributions of money to the plebs and veterans, constructed public buildings, and placed dedications in temples (*R.G.* 15.1, 3; 21.2; cf. Millar 191–92); also Caligula raised money by liquidating imperial property, such as gladiators and furniture, at auction (cf. Millar 147–48). In the latter case, discussed at length below, money flowed in as a result of commodity-exchange transactions; there is little in these transactions that could have been regarded as gift-exchange.

Yet the emperor did without doubt receive money, goods, and services every day from people who approached him on the street, at his morning *salutatio*, or elsewhere. Attested gifts of this sort include valuables or curiosities given by visiting foreign dignitaries, freaks or rarities that found their way to him from all parts of the empire and beyond, and even such pedestrian items as short poems or small sums of money. In many and perhaps most of these cases, the emperor seems to have reciprocated immediately with a substantial monetary gift, and so not only did not incur a gift-debt, but sent the giver financially enriched and therefore gift-indebted himself. A well-documented example of this kind of transaction is the *strena*, the offering of money to the emperor on the Kalends of January—a custom attested from Augustus to Caligula, but discontinued by Claudius and apparently never resumed thereafter. Dio reports (54.35.1) that Augustus reciprocated these new year's gifts at least twofold, to senators as well as to everyone else,[107] while Suetonius (*Aug.* 57.1) says that these offerings were made to him even in his absence and were used to buy magnificent statues of the gods, which were distributed throughout the neighborhoods of the city (*vici*)—a somewhat different mode of reciprocation. Tiberius for his part is said to have given back on the spot four times the amount of money offered him, if he was approached in person. Eventually, however, being vexed throughout January by those who had not been able to approach him on the Kalends, and also dismayed at the expense incurred, he limited these transactions to New Year's Day only, and sought to be out of town that day (Suet. *Tib.* 34.2, Dio 57.8.6, cf. 57.17.1). Such transactions, then, depleted the *fiscus* rather than filling it: but in this way the emperor avoided incurring gift-debt, even as he accepted gifts. By both receiving a gift and reciprocating in greater part at the same instant, he

---

[107] The point of this observation, presumably, is that senators would offer larger sums than most people, yet that even these offerings were returned twofold (or more), just as smaller offerings were.

indebted others in turn, or increased their existing gift-debt, and so avoided having their offerings debited to himself.[108] My interpretation of the emperor's handling of these *strena*-transactions, then, tends to corroborate the literary sources that portray him as striving to avoid receiving significant gifts, and thereby avoiding any erosion of his dominant social position that accepting such gifts could potentially entail.

Other objects and services offered to the emperor have similar, but often more complex, social consequences. Macrobius (*Sat.* 2.4.29–30) describes several transactions in which Augustus was given, or "bought," talking birds, which had been trained to say things that would please him, in exchange for munificent sums of money. Tacitus reports (*Ann.* 15.54.4) that Milichus, a freedman of one of the Pisonian conspirators, exposed the plot to Nero in hopes of receiving a large reward; this he eventually was granted in the form of money and the honorific cognomen *soter*, "savior" (15.71.1). These two transactions work rather like the *strena*-transactions just discussed, though they reveal more clearly that the expectation of significant material enrichment or status enhancement is a major motivation for giving gifts to the emperor, at least for non-elites. Yet these hopes could be disappointed: Macrobius (*Sat.* 2.4.26) tells of a soldier who captured an owl that was disturbing Augustus's sleep, expecting a "great reward" (*ingens praemium*). Displeased by the amount of money that he actually received, he revoked his service, releasing the owl. When an emperor's reciprocation for some offering was perceived as inadequately munificent, it could be taken as an insult or dishonor, triggering hostile exchange. Thus, according to Tacitus (*Ann.* 15.51.2), Volusius Proculus entered the Pisonian conspiracy because he considered that Nero had not adequately rewarded him for his assistance in killing the emperor's mother Agrippina. Earlier, Tacitus describes a similar hostile exchange (*Ann.* 4.29.3): Vibius Serenus, who had worked for the condemnation of the plotter Libo Drusus in A.D. 16, complained in a letter to the emperor Tiberius that he had received no return for his services (*exprobraverat suum tantum studium sine fructu fuisse*), and he added other defiant statements. Tiberius reciprocated by having charges brought against him eight years

---

[108] In general, a ruler's ad hoc gifts to subjects were expected to be munificent, suiting the dignity of the giver. See, e.g., Sen. *Ben.* 2.16, where Alexander gives someone a city; the discomfited recipient, objecting that such a gift ill suits his fortune, is told *non quaero quid te accipere deceat, sed quid me dare* (an attitude that Seneca condemns); similarly, *Ben.* 2.17.1, Plut. *Lucul.* 41.2. On Galba's stinginess in such situations, which caused him to be mocked (i.e., he failed to give munificently, as was considered proper to the emperor's station), see Suet. *Galba* 12.3, with Millar 1977: 142–43.

later, and succeeded in having him exiled (*Caesar octo post annos rettulit, medium tempus varie arguens;* cf. 4.13.2).[109]

Emperors appear reluctant to accept major gifts, or at any rate to acknowledge them, even in circumstances of dire financial need. Two examples of Augustus's behavior illustrate this impulse. Dio (55.12.4) reports that, after a fire on the Palatine in A.D. 4, Augustus accepted contributions of at most one *denarius* per individual and one *aureus* per city, though many people offered large sums; Suetonius (*Aug.* 57.2) gives a similar account. Likewise, when setting up the military treasury (*aerarium militare*) in A.D. 6, Augustus contributed a very large initial amount himself (170,000,000 sesterces, *R.G.* 17), and added further annual subventions (Dio 55.25.3); he also accepted contributions from client kings and cities, but accepted no contributions from individuals, though many offered (ibid). In each case, considerations of gift-debt suggest a rationale for Augustus's action. Even though a fire in an aristocrat's house was precisely the sort of disaster that could provide the opportunity for his clients to reciprocate in an extraordinary way the gifts and services they themselves had long received, or for other aristocrats to impose a gift-debt with a munificent donation (cf. Juv. *Sat.* 3.212–22, Mart. 3.52), Augustus might have hesitated to allow any individual, especially among high-ranking aristocrats who stood as potential rivals, to make a major contribution lest the donor present himself publicly (as Silius did, according to Tacitus) as having saved the emperor from being overwhelmed by disaster.[110] By the same token, if the refusal to accept any reciprocation under any circumstances—espe-

---

[109] There is further complexity to the exchange between Vibius and Tiberius. As Eck et al. observe (1996: 101–103), the prosecutors of Libo Drusus were given a share of the *bona damnatorum*, and those who were senators received praetorships *extra ordinem* (perhaps this status enhancement was unavailable to Vibius, however, since he must already have been a praetor; hence his complaint). He may also have sought to mend fences in the years between his risky letter and his exile: for as proconsul in Baetica in A.D. 21 or 22, he placed his name particularly prominently atop copy A of the *Senatus Consultum de Pisone Patre*—perhaps trying to show himself as a particularly diligent and active executor of his charge to erect these monuments.

[110] Thus at Tac. *Ann.* 4.64 and 6.45, Tiberius is said to have used his own money to make good the losses of individual property owners after fires on the Caelian and Aventine, respectively. In each case, Tacitus expressly notes that the emperor was widely praised (but cf. Suet. *Tib.* 48). Similarly, Tac. *Ann.* 15.43.2 notes Nero's subventions to individuals after the great fire; at 44.2 he says that these contributions, among other measures, failed to quell Nero's *infamia*, the report that he had started the fire—implying that such contributions would normally be expected to generate positive *fama* for the donor. In Augustus's case, then, any major contributor to the restoration of the Palatine might also have received positive public acknowledgement. See Veyne 1990: 361–66 for the emperor as *euergetes*, monopolizing the construction of public buildings in the city of Rome, as well as directly or indirectly sponsoring construction elsewhere in the empire.

cially these circumstances, which are clearly appropriate for reciprocation from one's gift-debtors — was a mark of arrogance and overly scrupulous reckoning of accounts, then Augustus could hardly have refused all reciprocation.[111] Allowing everyone to make very small contributions was perhaps, from his point of view, a reasonable middle path. Patronage of veterans was an even more sensitive area: only the emperor was to be seen as a patron to soldiers, and Tacitus and Dio, at least, attribute to Tiberius the anxiety that others might usurp this exclusively imperial prerogative.[112] Such considerations might justify Augustus' decision to accept no individual contributions to the *aerarium militare* except his own, and to fund this treasury for the long run by levying an inheritance tax, the *vicesima hereditatium*. From the evidence discussed here and over the last several pages, then, the emperor emerges as one who, in his own view and in that of others, should systematically dispense gifts significantly larger than those he receives.[113] If he does not or cannot, his authority is at risk: he is exposed at least to aristocratic censure, and at worst to aristocratic plotting.

Caligula's efforts to raise money admit of a similar analysis. Having quickly consumed the large surplus bequeathed him by Tiberius, and consequently in dire financial straits, he began to look for new sources of revenue. According to Suetonius (*Cal.* 38.1) he settled upon a combination of false accusations, auctions, and taxes; he also employed a miscellaneous group of ad hoc techniques (41–42). However, few or none of these techniques, as described by Suetonius, involved accepting gifts from wealthy individuals: indeed, they can be seen as expedient frameworks chosen precisely to facilitate the exaction of wealth from these individuals *without* the emperor incurring gift-debt. First I exam-

---

[111] Seneca (*Ben.* 2.17.6) calls people who refuse to accept reciprocation *superbi et imputatores*; cf. n. 102 above.

[112] Tac. *Ann.* 1.69 describes Tiberius's suspicions about the gifts Agrippina gave her husband's soldiers; similarly *Ann.* 6.3; Dio 58.18.3–4, 59.22.5; Suet. *Otho* 4.2, *Dom.* 10.3. Also, in the *Senatus Consultum de Pisone Patre* (ll. 52–57) Piso is said to have undermined military discipline by giving to the soldiers donatives in his own name (but drawn on the imperial *fiscus*), rejoicing that some soldiers were thereafter called *Pisoniani* in contrast to others called *Caesariani*; the threat this posed to the emperor is manifest (but cf. Eck et al. 1990: 175–77 for a different interpretation). For discussions of the imperial monopoly on patronage of soldiers, including some of these passages, see Campbell 1984: 157–59, 172; Lendon 1997: 260–62.

[113] Plutarch neatly confirms this view in the opening of his *Regum et Imperatorum apophthegmata*, addressed to Trajan, where he claims that exactly this pattern of exchange is characteristically "kingly" (Plut. *Mor.* 172 B: Ἀρτοξέρξης ὁ Περσῶν βασιλεύς, ὦ μέγιστε αὐτόκρατορ Τραϊανὲ Καῖσαρ, οὐχ ἧττον οἰόμενος βασιλικὸν καὶ φιλάνθρωπον εἶναι τοῦ μεγάλα διδόναι τὸ μικρὰ λαμβάνειν εὐμενῶς καὶ προθύμως). This essay itself is such a small gift (172C), though Plutarch does not specify what greater gift he hopes it will elicit in return.

ine the auctions. According to Dio (59.14.1–4), Caligula auctioned off gladiators who had survived shows previously given; he encouraged the wealthy to put on extravagant shows, and even forced people to give shows, in order to create demand and elevate the prices for these gladiators. He also made sure that they fetched the highest possible prices by raising the bids himself. Suetonius (*Cal.* 38.4) adds the story that, at one such auction, a drowsy senator's nodding head furnished Caligula the excuse to sell the man, oblivious as he dozed, thirteen gladiators for nine million sesterces; he also reports (§39.2) that Caligula, when auctioning off a variety of imperial treasures in Gaul, chided the bidders for their lack of shame at being wealthier than the emperor (*avaritiae singulos increpans et quod non puderet eos locupletiores esse quam se*). According to Dio and Suetonius, then, these were plainly no ordinary auctions: the emperor's words and deeds show that these auctions were a facade enabling him to plunder wealthy aristocrats. Yet this facade, and the way it enabled these exactions, was central to the success of the whole enterprise. For auctions are by definition a mode of price setting, hence a mode of commodity-exchange, which creates a relationship between the objects exchanged but not between the transactors. These transactions created no gift-debts for the emperor because they were not gift-exchange transactions. The aims and actions of the bidders under these circumstances, as described by Suetonius and Dio, are even more revealing. Suetonius says (*Cal.* 38.4) that some bidders, forced to buy at gigantic prices and thus stripped of their wealth, cut their veins—presumably to avoid the disgraceful poverty in which they would consequently be living.[114] Perhaps we are to understand that these bidders were taken by surprise, unaware that they would not be at liberty to stop bidding. Dio, meanwhile, attributes to the bidders a variety of motives: he writes (59.14.4), "People bought [the gladiators] for great sums of money, some actually wanting them, others reckoning they would gratify the emperor, and the majority, as many as had a reputation for substantial wealth, wishing to spend down some of their resources with the auction as an excuse, so that by becoming poorer they might save their lives."[115] Those purchasing because they wanted the gladiators are implied to have been willing to pay the price; for these

---

[114] Suet. *Cal.* 38.4: . . . *ut quidam immenso coacti quaedam emere ac bonis exuti venas sibi inciderent.* For suicide to preserve honor, cf. Sen. *Helv.* 10.9–10: the gourmand Apicius, discovering he has consumed his patrimony and is reduced to a mere ten million sesterces, ends his life by poison. Also Cic. *Q. Fr.* 1.4.4, Pliny *Ep.* 3.9.5, Tac. *Hist.* 4.11, Suet. *Tib.* 61.4, Dio 58.15.2.

[115] Dio 59.14.4: . . . ὥσθ' οἱ μὲν καὶ δεόμενοι τῶν ἀνθρώπων, οἱ δὲ χαριεῖσθαι αὐτῷ νομίζοντες, καὶ οἵ γε πλείους, ὅσοι ἐν δόξῃ περιουσίας ἦσαν, ἀναλῶσαί τι τῶν ὑπαρχόντων ἐπὶ τῇ προφάσει ταύτῃ, ὅπως πενέστεροι γενόμενοι περισωθῶσιν, ἐθέλοντες, μεγάλων αὐτοὺς χρημάτων ἠγόρασαν. Thus Dio's bidders prefer impoverishment over death, while Suetonius's bidders prefer death over impoverishment.

the auction was perhaps something approaching a fair commodity-exchange. Those who wished to gratify the emperor by placing high bids, however, are implied to regard this transaction as having a gift-exchange component, despite the commodity-exchange framework of the auction: they presumably hope to receive a larger reward later—the standard pattern for imperial reciprocation of gifts, discussed above.[116] Finally, those who used the auction as an opportunity to shed wealth lest they lose their lives presumably regarded the auction as simply a safer means of exaction than the alternative of prosecution, condemnation, and confiscation, which they wished to forestall.[117]

Prosecuting wealthy men on false charges, and confiscating their wealth upon condemnation or suicide, is yet another strategy by which emperors could exact aristocratic wealth without being reduced to accepting, or appearing to accept, significant gifts. This motive for prosecution is frequently attributed to Julio-Claudian emperors in our literary sources. The youthful Octavian is said to have proscribed certain men because he craved their Corinthian bronzes (Suet. *Aug.* 70.2). While Dio declares that Tiberius never killed anyone for his money or confiscated anyone's wealth (57.10.5), Tacitus reports that under Tiberius a Sextus Marius was thrown from the Tarpeian rock after conviction for unchastity (*incestum*), though the fact that Tiberius subsequently seized Marius's gold and silver mines for himself proved that it was really his wealth that brought him down (*Ann.* 6.19.1). Caligula is frequently said to have secured convictions on false charges in order to confiscate wealth (e.g., Suet. *Cal.* 38.3, Dio 59.10.7–8, 18.1); in one instance (Dio 59.18.5), when the victim turned out to be poor, Caligula exclaimed, "he deceived me and died needlessly, for he could have lived." Similar accounts circulate about Nero as well (Suet. *Nero* 32.1, Dio 63(62L).17.2). Since by the reign of Tiberius, probably, at least a portion of any *bona damnatorum* was allotted to the emperor, emperors had an incentive to bring such charges: wealth transferred under this rubric was technically forfeit as a legal penalty, hence could not be mis-

---

[116] See also Dio 59.8.3, 59.11.4 for instances of aristocrats saying things that they calculate will please the emperor, in hopes of receiving a great reward. In the first instance the effort fails spectacularly (similarly, Suet. *Cal.* 27.2); in the second it succeeds.

[117] Another of Caligula's attested money-raising schemes, structurally similar to the auctions, is the prostitution of Roman matrons and freeborn youths in the palace itself (Suet. *Cal.* 41.1, Dio 59.28.8–9). Again, significant amounts of money are exacted from purchasers under a commodity-exchange framework, so that the emperor receives no gifts. Dio however, focusing upon the motivations of the customers, describes their participation as follows (59.28.9): τοὺς μὲν ἐθελοντὰς τοὺς δὲ καὶ ἄκοντας ὅπως μὴ καὶ δυσχεραίνειν τι νομισθῶσι—the former apparently regarding the exchange as a fair price-setting process, while the latter, concerned about their relationship with the emperor as forged through or conditioned by their participation in this exchange, see it as having a gift-exchange component. See McGinn 1989: 83–85 and n. 39 for discussion.

taken for a gift.[118] For if an emperor simply threatened or demanded of aristocrats to yield up their wealth without providing any extraneous reason why that wealth should be forfeit, the resulting transfers could not reliably be distinguished by external observers from the willing and spontaneous offering and acceptance of a gift (cf. Millar 1977: 143), especially if the plundered aristocrats, who might seek to make the best of the situation, asserted that they had given willingly and spontaneously (see below). Now, it is obvious that emperors who exacted wealth through false prosecutions incurred ill will for doing so, and are pilloried after their deaths in the literary sources; such behavior is also likely to have spurred aristocratic plotting against them while they lived. That is, this behavior could be thought to have undermined their authority and legitimacy as rulers just as surely, if not more so, than accepting gifts (or apparent gifts) of money would have done. Nevertheless, the exaction of wealth through false prosecution was *some* sort of systematic strategy; it is too ubiquitous a phenomenon in the early empire to be dismissed simply as evidence of the sadism or paranoia of individual rulers—entirely apart from the fact that claims of paranoia or sadism cannot be verified, since these emperors cannot now be put on the couch.[119] My explanation of this strategy provides a less colorful but more culturally grounded reason for this behavior by emperors— even if, in the view of some contemporary and later Romans, as well as many modern readers, such a strategy actually did more damage to their position than it forestalled.

So far, I have spoken of the emperor's strategies for exacting aristocratic wealth without incurring gift-debt, and for receiving and reciprocating the sorts of gifts that he could expect to receive on a regular basis. But this is not to say that emperors never incurred gift-debt, never received gifts they could not or did not reciprocate immediately and in greater share. No individual can have been so fully in control of his resources and personal relationships as to avoid all such gifts, even if his day-to-day strategies of social interaction and exchange aimed to ward off foreseeable sources of indebtedness. Thus Tiberius could be thought to owe his very position as emperor to Silius's suppression of disquiet among his soldiers, or Caligula to the assistance of Macro (Dio

---

[118] In several passages where people are said to have been killed for their wealth, no criminal proceedings are mentioned or implied (e.g., Dio 59.22.3–4, 25.1, 62.14.3, 63(62L).11.1–12.1, Suet. *Cal.* 41.2): I assume that the rubric under which confiscation occurs in these cases is still that of *bona damnatorum*, and that the failure to mention the (presumably false) charges in these passages does not mean that none were proffered. See also Millar 1977: 166–69, Lendon 1997: 111–12 and nn. 20–21.

[119] For a brief psychology of "mad Caesars," and on their relations with senators, with parallels to the Soviet state and its show trials, see Veyne 1990: 409–14.

59.10.6), or even Octavian to Menas's desertion of Sextus Pompeius (section 2 above). There are also accounts of emperors, to their own surprise, being suddenly and publicly exposed as long-term gift-debtors, and consequently compelled to reciprocate in extraordinary ways. Seneca (*Ben.* 5.24) relates an anecdote in which Julius Caesar presides at a judicial inquiry regarding a land dispute between one of his veterans and the veteran's neighbors. He is reminded by this veteran of a time on campaign in Spain when Caesar had injured his ankle and was unable to walk; a soldier had given him a cloak to lie on and brought him water in a helmet. The veteran persuades Caesar that he is that very soldier, though unrecognizable because of the wounds he subsequently suffered in battle (*postea ad Mundam in acie oculus mihi effossus est et in capite lecta ossa*, §3). Caesar decides the case by bestowing the disputed land upon his veteran as a gift (. . . *et agellos . . . militi suo donavit*). Seneca frames this account with assertions that one may appropriately prompt the recipients of one's benefactions for reciprocation, especially when the recipient is immersed in public duties and may simply have forgotten (*Ben.* 5.23, 5.25.1).[120] Thus he presents the veteran as exemplifying the right way to ask that a benefit be returned, and Caesar as duly grateful, for he reciprocated appropriately once reminded of his debt. A similar anecdote regarding Augustus is given by Macrobius (*Sat.* 2.4.27):

> veteranus cum die sibi dicto periclitaretur, accessit in publico ad Caesarem rogavitque ut sibi adesset. ille advocatum quem ex comitatu suo elegerat sine mora dedit commendavitque ei litigatorem. exclamavit ingenti voce veteranus: "at non ego, Caesar, periclitante te Actiaco bello, vicarium quaesivi, sed pro te ipse pugnavi," detexitque impressas cicatrices. erubuit Caesar venitque in advocationem, ut qui vereretur non superbus tantum, sed etiam ingratus videri.

> When a veteran was standing trial on his appointed day, he approached Augustus in public and asked that he appear as his advocate. Augustus promptly gave a counselor whom he had selected from his retinue and commended the litigant to him. The veteran cried out with a loud voice, "yet I did not look for someone to take my place, Caesar, when you were in jeopardy in the battle of Actium, but I fought for you myself," and he exposed his scars.

---

[120] Elsewhere Seneca describes forgetfulness as the worst kind of ingratitude (*Ben.* 3.1.3–2.3), but at 5.22 he modifies this strong claim by placing some people (like Caesar) in an intermediate category between *grati* and *ingrati*. These people can be restored to the former category, and saved from the latter, by a gentle reminder; if they apologize and reciprocate immediately, they show themselves not to be hardened ingrates (5.22.1–2, 23). See also *Ben.* 7.23.3–25.2.

Augustus blushed and took up the duties of advocacy, inasmuch as he feared seeming to be not just arrogant, but also an ingrate.

Here the emperor unexpectedly finds himself tarred as a gift-debtor in a public setting, the visibility and public exposure of which Macrobius emphasizes with phrases such as "in public" and "with a loud voice": the reader is to infer that large numbers of people are observing this exchange. Accordingly, Augustus is depicted as being concerned mainly about how his actions will be interpreted by the onlookers if he does not immediately reciprocate in an extraordinary manner; he is compelled to take action lest he be regarded as arrogant and ungrateful.[121] Now, one may query the arithmetic of exchange in these two anecdotes involving veterans: modern as well as ancient readers of these accounts might suppose that Caesar and Augustus had already reciprocated these soldiers' military service on their behalf though salary, donatives, gifts of land, and military decorations as appropriate. Do we not infer that the land that Caesar's veteran already possesses, in Seneca's anecdote, was Caesar's gift upon discharge? Does a soldier's regular compensation, by tacit agreement and longstanding practice, fully reciprocate the standard risks, injuries, and hardships of military service—the loss of the soldier's eye and his head wound, for example? If so, does this soldier nevertheless have a further claim by virtue of the special service he did Caesar when the latter was injured? Conversely, does Augustus's veteran, who seems merely to have fought valorously (attested by the display of scars) but not provided any extraordinary service, have any further claim?[122] But such arguments are of no account in the highly public situations that these anecdotes describe. Caesar and Augustus could only lose face and look stingy if they quibbled about the relative balance of exchange: in this situation the only response appropriate to society's supreme gift-givers, whose authority indeed resided heavily upon their domination of virtually all their exchange relationships, was to give further.

A final example, demonstrating an inappropriate way for an emperor to handle such a situation, is also given by Seneca, as the negative exemplum balancing the positive one provided by Caesar. In *De Beneficiis* 5.25.2 he reports that, when someone approached Tiberius and began

---

[121] Dio's account of this event (55.4.2) is similar to Macrobius's, except that Dio gives no suggestion of a large audience of spectators, implied by Macrobius's *in publico* and *ingenti voce*. Thus his account lacks the overt suggestion that Augustus, if he does not yield, stands to lose face publicly.

[122] Exactly this sort of reckoning of the balance of exchange is attested in two Senecan declamations involving an *actio ingrati*, and is at the core of the *divisiones* that Seneca records for these cases: see *Cont.* 2.5.10–13, 9.1.9–11; similarly, [Quint.] *Decl. Min.* 333, 368.

THE EMPEROR'S AUTHORITY   209

to say "Remember . . . ," Tiberius interrupted with the declaration "I do not remember what I was" (*non memini quid fuerim*). Seneca denounces this response, declaring that the emperor preferred forgetfulness to the remembrance of old intimacy (*optanda erat oblivio*), and regarded only his current fortune. Caesar, by contrast, merely had a disordered memory (. . . *cuius memoriam multitudo rerum confuderat*, §25.1): Caesar could be (and was) saved from ingratitude, while Tiberius could not. Tiberius's action does eliminate the risk that he will suddenly be exposed as a gift-debtor, as were Caesar in the previous section (*Ben.* 5.24) and Augustus in the anecdote from Macrobius. But Seneca is arguing for a modified conception of the relationship between imperial authority and gift-debt: he suggests that it is properly imperial behavior to acknowledge and appropriately reciprocate one's gift-debts, not simply to avoid incurring them, or to avoid the public appearance of having incurred them.

There are a few hints that emperors may occasionally have exacted money from wealthy elites without the use of some kind of framing device (e.g., auctions, criminal charges) aimed to prevent the transfer of wealth from being debited to them as a gift. Dio says (59.21.4), for example, that when Caligula was in Gaul raising money by any means possible, individuals and cities brought him great gifts "willingly, of course" — the irony here suggesting that the donors were not willing, but that they claimed to be willing, perhaps to make the best of the situation by seeking to create the impression that the emperor was now their gift-debtor. Dio gives virtually the same account of Nero's money-gathering after the great fire of 64, asserting that money was taken from individuals and cities, some seized by force, and some supposedly given willingly.[123] Caligula, moreover, is said to have resurrected the tradition of accepting the *strena*, virtually discontinued by Tiberius, as a mode of raising money. We have seen that these New Year's gifts, as transacted by Augustus and Tiberius, were a net expense to the fiscus rather than a gain; thus it seems that Caligula must not have reciprocated these gifts when he received them.[124] None of these passages, however, presents enough detail about the exchanges in question to ground any reasona-

---

[123] Caligula in Gaul: τοῦτο μὲν γὰρ τούς τι ἔχοντας ἐπὶ πάσῃ προφάσει ἐσύλα, τοῦτο δὲ καὶ δῶρα οἵ τε ἰδιῶται καὶ αἱ πόλεις ἑκοῦσαι δῆθεν μεγάλα αὐτῷ ἦγον (Dio 59.21.4). Nero after the fire: χρήματα δὲ ὁ Νέρων παμπληθῆ καὶ παρὰ τῶν ἰδιωτῶν καὶ παρὰ τῶν δήμων, τὰ μὲν βίᾳ ἐπὶ τῇ προφάσει τοῦ ἐμπρησμοῦ, τὰ δὲ καὶ παρ' ἑκόντων δῆθεν ἠργυρολόγησεν (Dio 62.18.5). Similarly, Suet. *Nero* 38.3: *conlationibusque non receptis modo verum et efflagitatis provincias privatorumque census prope exhausit*. Cf. Tac. *Ann.* 15.45.

[124] Suet. *Cal.* 42, where he is described as standing in the vestibule of a temple to catch coins hurled at him; cf. Dio 59.24.4–5, where the senators present their New Year's offerings in front of his empty chair. See Wardle 1994 ad loc.

210   CHAPTER 3

bly defensible conclusions regarding their social dynamics and consequences. Only in one situation, in the Julio-Claudian period, are emperors portrayed as regularly accepting substantial, unreciprocated gifts: namely, when they receive "crown gold" from cities and other collectivities on the occasion of their accession or a military victory.[125] The emperor usually but not always accepted these crowns when offered, apparently without immediate reciprocation, and so perhaps showed himself more willing to engage in gift-exchange on relatively equal terms with cities than with individuals. Yet munificent cities did not pose the same risk to the emperor that munificent individuals posed: for while cities could and did exchange goods and services with individuals, including the emperor, they could not, as individuals could, threaten the emperor's position by liberating themselves from gift-debt or even imposing a gift-debt upon him in return: a city could not, through its exchange relations, threaten to depose the emperor and take his place.[126]

7. Conclusion

If the material presented in this chapter provides a basis for generalization, I would emphasize three features of the relationship between an emperor's giving and his legitimacy. First, a point about the nature of exchange itself. One might expect prima facie, and indeed it is true in general, that amicable reciprocity enhances social cohesion and legitmates ruling authority, while hostile reciprocity contributes to social disorganization and the delegitimation of a ruler. But these correlations by no means hold uniformly. In some cases, hostile offerings by subject

---

[125] See Millar 1977: 140–42 for the financial importance of these gold crowns, or cash as a substitute for them, to the imperial *fiscus*. See also e.g., Aug. *R.G.* 21.3, Dio 51.21.4, Pliny *Nat.* 33.54. Klauser 1944 provides a detailed history of the giving of gold crowns, from the ancient near east to late antiquity (pp. 138–43 for the Roman material).

[126] Recall, for example, that Augustus accepted contributions to the *aerarium militare* from client kings and cities, but not individuals (*R.G.* 17)—though he accepted only small contributions even from cities when rebuilding his house after the fire of A.D. 4 (Dio 55.12.4). Millar 1977: 142 argues for an "element of obligation" in the giving of crowns—as though it were de facto a sort of tax (also Klauser 1944: 139)—but notes too the importance of the formal presentation of the crown with accompanying speech, thus causing this transaction to maintain the character of a gift. Lendon 1997: 74–89 shows that the conceptualization of the honor of cities was similar to that of individuals, capable of augmentation and diminution in similar ways. For exchanges between Julio-Claudian emperors and cities, Lendon cites e.g., Suet. *Nero* 22.3 (honors given to Greek cities who sent Nero *coronae citharoedorum*), and Dio Chr. *Or.* 34.7–8 on Tarsus's sufferings on behalf of Octavian and Antony, and its subsequent rewards. Also, four million sesterces moved from Lugdunum to Rome and then back again within a couple of years, in each case as a subvention to alleviate a disaster. Lendon 124–27, 136–39 provides further examples of exchange between emperors and cities, most of them post-Julio-Claudian.

aristocrats may lead finally to enhanced social cohesion once the ruler reciprocates with clemency, as with Cinna's plot against Augustus and the offensive convivial speech of the young Tarentines regarding Pyrrhus; likewise, Augustus's humiliation of Vedius Pollio, and Claudius's humiliation of Vinius, are both presented as right and appropriate behavior, and so tend to confirm the emperor as an authority figure whose power over others is legitimate. On the other hand, amicable reciprocity can be highly competitive, and may involve increasing antagonism between the transactors. The efforts of high-ranking aristocrats in general and the emperor in particular to avoid incurring gift-debt, described in section 6, imply such competition (to be outdone is "the equivalent of death" or "incurs hatred"), as do those presentations of amicable reciprocity as a bare displacement of violence, a mode of fighting by non-bloody means.[127]

Second, according to the analyses of this chapter, the emperor's ability to establish and maintain legitimate authority through giving and receiving has two different components: account must be taken both of the history of his exchange relationship with the other party, and also of his conduct in the particular exchange being transacted at the moment. Not only does the emperor seek to maintain a long-term superiority over all his exchange partners in terms of the quality and quantity of gifts given, but he also seeks to act in an appropriately imperial way (which usually means to give more than he receives) in each individual exchange situation. Thus Caligula may have hosted Valerius Asiaticus (section 4 above) graciously at many convivia and helped to advance his career: but his behavior in just one convivium, according to Seneca, destroys everything. Similarly, as discussed in section 6, when Julius Caesar and Augustus were publicly put on the spot by their own veterans, the history of the relationship faded into insignificance, and the ruler's authority suddenly hung entirely upon his handling of this particular transaction. Discussions of the emperor's authority in terms of "patronage" tend to focus on the enduring hierarchical relationship between emperor and subject—i.e., the first of these two components—while not emphasizing the dialogical construction of that authority through the contingencies of individual transactions. One exception, however, is Wallace-Hadrill (1989b: 83), who rightly points to the latter component when he describes patronage as a "jittery system like the stockmarket" in which "your standing depends on appearances, what

---

[127] On the capacity of amicable reciprocity to produce social disorganization, and of hostile reciprocity to enhance social cohesion, see Lacourse 1987. See also Codere 1950: 118–29 for a striking case of competitive, antagonistic gift giving as a transparent displacement of violence: namely, the potlatching of the Kwakiutl, which historically did apparently displace armed conflict, and duly attracted all the metaphors of warfare ("fighting with property").

people are seen to think of you; it is never put to the polls, and yet you are on trial every minute." I have sought in this chapter to bring forward this second component, where legitimate authority is constructed or deconstructed in each individual exchange, while in no way denying the importance of the first component. A striking juncture of these two components, in fact, occurs when the ruler is praised for disregarding and considering harmless the insulting words spoken by a drunken diner at a convivium (section 4). In this situation, as we have seen, the ruler is supposed to efface the current hostile offering by the subordinate and substitute in its place the history of amicable exchange between the two—as Augustus does in the case of Rufus, or Tiberius in the case of Cotta, or as Alexander should have done in the case of Clitus. Yet the ruler who acts in this way wins praise in our sources for his handling of *this very situation:* that is, he successfully exploits the contingencies of the current exchange situation, and so helps to confirm his legitimacy, by the very fact of denying that his legitimacy is at all at stake in this situation, and by his insistence that there is only history and no current contingencies. Both the immediate and the historic exchange situations, then, are indispensible criteria for rendering an account of the authority confirmed or undermined, the power gained or lost, in the transaction of exchanges between emperor and aristocracy.

Finally, in virtually every giving situation discussed in this chapter, from the convivium to clemency to the many kinds of offerings received (or rejected) by the emperor, the question of reciprocity—whether it is owed, what form it takes, when and where it occurs, how it is reckoned against one or more prior offerings—is of primary importance. This is true particularly for transactions that occur between emperor and individual aristocrats (the exchange situation best documented in our sources), but also apparently for those between emperor and individual nonaristocrats (e.g., the veterans who expose Julius Caesar and Augustus as being obligated), and even, perhaps, for those between emperor and corporate entities, such as the people or the soldiers in general. Because issues of reciprocity loom so large in all these situations, I conclude that "gift-exchange" is a more appropriate model for understanding the sociopolitical consequences of exchange with the emperor than is Veyne's "euergetism": for many of the exchange situations discussed in this chapter would simply be incomprehensible if we deny that there is norm of reciprocity, and that reciprocity both entails and presupposes personal bonds and social hierarchies. This norm and its social consequences are fundamental aspects of social relations in Roman society, and consequently provide fundamental categories by and through which Romans of the Julio-Claudian period could construe and construct the autocrat, the most important gift-transactor of all.

Chapter Four

MODELING THE EMPEROR: THE MASTER-SLAVE RELATIONSHIP AND ITS ALTERNATIVES

I. Overview

THIS CHAPTER is largely a study of metaphor, but from the point of view of its sociopolitical engagement. There are two social relationships in Roman society, those of master to slave and father to child (usually son), that are used pervasively in the Julio-Claudian period as metaphors for the relationship of the emperor to his subjects, particularly his aristocratic ones. The metaphorical nature of these usages is assured by the fact that these subjects are generally neither the emperor's chattel slaves nor his children, biological or adopted. These metaphors, however, carry important social implications: for, as I will argue, to apply the language and imagery of either of these two relationships to the relationship of emperor to subject is to project upon the latter relationship not only the power structure of the master-slave or father-son relationships, but also their ethical structure. That is, these metaphors suggest that the emperor is exploitative and oppressive, or benevolent and nurturing; to present the emperor's authority in the language and imagery of either of these relationships is to take a position regarding whether his authority is legitimate or illegitimate, to be accepted or rejected. This is the dimension of these metaphors that I examine in this chapter. I develop a sociology of both the master-slave and father-son relationships, so as to recover the specific social and ethical implications of particular terms and images; I also discuss a theory of metaphor that accounts for distinctive features of the projection of these terms and images from one domain of experience into another. I then trace in detail the competing deployments of these metaphors in Julio-Claudian literature and society to construct ethically contrasting images of the new order and the emperor's place in it. Finally, I consider yet another metaphorical usage of the master-slave relationship: the Stoic usage, well attested in Seneca, whereby a person's relationship to *fortuna* and to externals is constructed as one of "slavery," "freedom," or "mastery." This usage too, I argue, has important sociopolitical implications for Seneca's intended readership of Julio-Claudian elites.

2. Freedom and Slavery: A Social Metaphor in Political Discourse

I begin with the master-slave relationship. My argument that this relationship can serve as a metaphor that systematically structures relationships among aristocratic Romans—particularly between the emperor and other aristocrats—is best approached through a series of examples, which I present here without further ado. The first is a sentence from the beginning of Augustus's *Res Gestae*, ("Things Accomplished"), which this emperor wrote in the later years of his life. This text was inscribed on bronze columns that were erected in front of his mausoleum and was reproduced in various media in cities throughout the empire, so as to gain a wide readership among contemporaries and posterity. The aged *princeps* here describes his youthful actions following Caesar's assassination as follows: "When I was eighteen years of age, I raised an army on my own initiative and at my own expense, with which I claimed the republic as free, which had been oppressed by the despotism of a faction" (*annos undeviginti natus exercitum privato consilio et privata impensa comparavi, per quem rem publicam a dominatione factionis oppressam in libertatem vindicavi*). The "faction" referred to here is accepted to be that of Antony, whom Octavian forced to withdraw from Rome in late 44 B.C.;[1] by referring to Antony's preeminence as a *dominatio*, he metaphorically represents Antony as a *dominus*—the common term for a master with respect to his slaves.[2] This social metaphor is extended and strengthened by Augustus's portrayal of his own actions on behalf of the state. For the phrase *vindicare in libertatem* describes a juridical procedure whereby a person called (for these purposes) an *assertor* or *vindex libertatis*, asserts in the presence of a magistrate, a slave, and the slave's master, that the slave is in fact a free person who is being illegally held in a servile condition. If the evidence is persuasive (or more so than the master's presumed counterevidence), the magistrate adjudges the slave free. This procedure was commonly used in a symbolic mode, at the master's instigation, as a way of manumitting slaves whose status was not actually in doubt (the *manumissio vindicta*).[3] Augustus's usage here, however, implies that the

---

[1] So Wirszubski 1950: 100–101, Brunt and Moore 1967: 38–39. The honorific senatorial decrees that Augustus goes on to say he was voted (*eo nomine senatus decretis honorificis in ordinem suum me adlegit C. Pansa et A. Hirtio consulibus*) are presumably those described by Cicero, e.g., *Phil.* 3.3–5, 37–38.

[2] The semantics of *dominus* are discussed below in this section, and further in section 4.

[3] For *vindicatio* see Watson 1967: 218–25; for the *manumissio vindicta* and its relationship to *vindicatio* see ibid. 190–94 and Treggiari 1969: 21–25.

Roman state was indeed being held illegally as a "slave" to its "masters," and that Augustus, by serving as *vindex libertatis*, restored it to its properly "free" condition.[4]

The second example is a famous coin commemorating Marcus Brutus's role in Caesar's assassination. The coin's obverse shows Brutus's head, while the reverse shows a pair of daggers flanking a *pilleus*, the high-crowned felt cap donned on certain occasions by ex-slaves as a mark of their manumission; it also bears the legend "EID MAR," the date of the assassination.[5] Manifestly, Brutus is here presenting Caesar's death as liberation from slavery—presumably not only for Brutus himself and his fellow conspirators, but for the state as a whole. I assume that Caesar himself is to be understood as the master. The parallel cannot be pressed, since upon a master's death his slaves, like the rest of his property, normally passed into the possession of his heirs, unless (as commonly occurred) the master stipulated in his will that particular slaves should be freed. Brutus, however, is representing Caesar's death as instantaneously, and without regard for any will, restoring to liberty the state previously enslaved to Caesar; a political change is structured and expressed in terms of a transition in social status.

The third example is a declamation, *Suasoria* 6, recorded by the Elder Seneca, who assembled his collection of various treatments of declamatory themes in the mid to late 30s A.D.; most of the declaimers he discusses were active in the reigns of Augustus and Tiberius. The theme of this declamation is "Cicero deliberates whether to beg Antony's pardon," and its imagined time is autumn of the year 43 B.C., after Cicero has delivered his Philippics against Antony and has subsequently been proscribed. The declaimer's task is to urge Cicero to try to reconcile with Antony and so save his own life, or to urge him to stand by his condemnations and insults, regardless of the consequences. Most of the declaimers take the latter course, arguing that Cicero will thereby retain

---

[4] The expressions *vindex libertatis* or *vindicare in libertatem*, characterizing political actions taken by aristocrats against other aristocrats, occurs frequently in late republican prose. Wirszubski 1950: 103 collects six representative instances, holding that this was, in Augustus's day, "an outworn phrase" (98) that "retained little of its original positive meaning" (104). Yet these expressions also occur in late republican and Augustan texts to indicate the release of someone held as a slave: e.g., Livy 2.5.8–10, 3.45.11, 3.46.7; Cic. *Att.* 7.2.8 (also other citations in *OLD* s.v. *vindico* 3a). Since these expressions were thus current in their primary domain of reference, I see no reason to doubt that their application to political relations among elites was in fact understood as a metaphor implying that the state was "enslaved" to a "master," and that "freedom" is now at hand. More on this below.

[5] Crawford 1974 no. 508/3, with discussion on p. 741; this coin was famous even in antiquity (Dio 47.25.3). See section 4 below for further discussion of the tyrannicides' self-presentation as "liberators."

his "freedom," even if he must die; they suggest that if he does beg Antony's pardon he will become a "slave" and Antony will be his "master." One declaimer, however, contends that Cicero should indeed beg Antony's pardon, since he is already an "experienced slave" of Pompey and Caesar, and that he "has a worn neck"—an allusion to wearing a yoke, a common image of subjugation and slavery. Thus the various treatments of this theme, as Seneca records them, are saturated with language and imagery deriving from the social institution of slavery: these are the terms in which a number of possible relationships between these two Roman aristocrats are figured.[6]

The fourth example, a passage from the younger Seneca's *De Ira*, was written perhaps in the late years of Claudius's reign (Griffin 1976: 396). In this passage Seneca evaluates the condition of aristocrats who attend upon a tyrannical ruler—aristocrats such as the unfortunate Persians Harpagus and Praexaspes, whose children died at the hands of their kings. He writes,

> non consolabimur tam triste ergastulum, non adhortabimur ferre imperia carnificum: ostendemus in omni servitute apertam libertati viam. . . . dicam et illi qui in regem incidit sagittis pectora amicorum petentem et illi cuius dominus liberorum visceribus patres saturat: "quid gemis, demens? quid expectas ut te aut hostis aliquis per exitium gentis tuae vindicet aut rex a longinquo potens advolet?" (Sen. *Ira* 3.15.3–4)

> We will not console so dismal a sweatshop of slaves; we will not urge them to endure the commands of executioners: we will show that in every slavery there is an open path to liberty. . . . I will say both to him who has come under a king who shoots arrows at the breasts of his friends, and to him whose master sates fathers with the entrails of their children: "Why do you groan, madman? Why do you wait for some enemy to claim you as free through the destruction of your people, or for a powerful king to rush in from far away?"

Though such men, says Seneca, constitute a sweatshop (*ergastulum*) of slaves, they have the capacity to "free" themselves from even their current "slavery." However, he insists that this liberation will not come

---

[6] Typical passages: *Suas.* 6.1 (Haterius): *sciant posteri potuisse Antonio servire rem publicam, non potuisse Ciceronem. . . . si intellegis, Cicero, non dicit "roga ut vivas" sed "roga ut servias"* (cf. Albucius at §9). §8 (Latro): *inutilis vita futura est et morte gravior detracta libertate. hic omnem acerbitatem servitutis futurae descripsit.* §10 (Cestius): *mors tibi utile est . . . ut numereris cum Catone qui servire ne Antonio quidem nondum domino potuit* (Winterbottom's text; reading is uncertain). §12 (Geminus): *quod ad servitutem pertinet, non recusabit; iam collum tritum habet. et Pompeius illum et Caesar subegerunt: veteranum mancipium videtis.* Cf. *Suas.* 7.3, 6, 8, 9, 10 (a closely related theme).

about through waiting for some outsider to depose the current "master," i.e., despotic ruler (*rex, dominus*) and so to claim these aristocrats as "free" through the process of *vindicatio* described above. Here again, these courtiers' relationship to their ruler is systematically structured as one of slave to master.[7]

These four examples, drawn from sources dating from the late 40s B.C. (example 2) to the 50s A.D. (example 4), instantiate a widespread metaphorical usage of the language and imagery of social status: certain words, images, and symbols that are closely associated with slavery and the slave experience are adduced to characterize the relationship between rulers, or the dynasts of the late republic and their (juridically) free subjects, especially aristocrats. Thus the master-slave relationship, made present through the vocabulary and symbols of social status, serves as a paradigm for aspects of the political experience of elites. The concrete, familiar social relationship of master to slave provides a structure, a set of categories, through which a different kind of relationship can be comprehended and experienced. The words, images, and symbols that mediate between these two relationships include the fundamental terms *liber, servus, dominus* ("free," "slave," "master"), and their cognates, as well as other, more specialized terms that represent slaves from a particular point of view: *verna, mancipium* ("homeborn slave," "possession"), etc. They also include certain images that are significant for aspects of slave experience, such as the *ergastulum* mentioned in example 4, the *pilleus* represented on the coin in example 2, the allusions in examples 1 and 4 to *manumissio vindicta*, and the yoke in example 3. Below we will see passages in which still other images and words particularly associated with slavery (e.g., "slavish" forms of execution, such as crucifixion) and certain legal terms (*sui iuris, alieni iuris, in potestate*) are used similarly. Finally, the Greek-language equivalents or near equivalents for these Latin terms are used in much the same way and will also figure in the discussions throughout this chapter.

The examples adduced above show that this language and imagery has at least two distinct domains of reference. One is the master-slave relationship itself, in the context of the social institution of slavery more generally. Following Cooper 1986, we may designate this as the "parent domain" of this language and imagery, the domain we regard as "proper" to it, with reference to which we regard this language as being used in a "literal," nonmetaphorical way. The other domain of reference, again following Cooper, may be called a "derived domain," in

---

[7] See section 6 below for further discussion of this passage. The *ergastulum* seems to have been a sort of building in which certain slaves were confined, often as a form of punishment; it was associated with particularly hard labor of various sorts (Fitzgibbon 1976).

which a social experience different from that of the parent domain — in this case, the experience of aristocrats in regard to their rulers or other especially powerful men — is expressed in terms of, and structured by, the categories of the parent domain.[8] Now, in their 1980 work entitled *Metaphors We Live By*, George Lakoff and Mark Johnson demonstrate that human conceptual systems are shot through with "conceptual metaphors," which they define as the systematic perception and experience of one kind of activity in terms of another. One conceptual metaphor, which they discuss in detail, is "argument is war." A variety of everyday expressions — "I took a position, she attacked it, and I defended it"; "we skirmished on that issue"; "I had to retreat and regroup"; "her criticisms were right on target"; "I won the argument and he lost it" — shows aspects of armed conflict (the parent domain) serving as a paradigm for aspects of verbal conflict (the derived domain). Any particular expression may be so familiar as to be virtually invisible as a metaphor (such as "I defended my position"), or may on its own admit of some other explanation. But such expressions cohere with other, more overtly militaristic expressions, which collectively reveal a deeper, systematic structuring of argument in terms of war, the underlying conceptual metaphor that generates all of these individual expressions. Moreover, conceptual metaphors tend to be productive, permitting the invention of novel expressions ("she nuked my argument") that, because they are manifestations of the familiar underlying mapping, are entirely comprehensible even if they have never before been uttered.[9] In a Roman context, I suggest that the use of the language and imagery of slavery to express and structure political relations among free members of society, and especially relations among the elites, is exactly such a conceptual metaphor: just as "argument is war," so "my relationship with my ruler (the derived domain) is, or significantly is not, a master-slave relationship (the parent domain)."

To identify such usages as verbal traces of a Lakoffian "conceptual metaphor" has several important corollaries. First, since the whole con-

---

[8] For the expressions "parent domain" and "derived domain," see Cooper 1986: 121–22, 130–31.

[9] For the "argument is war" metaphor, see Lakoff and Johnson 1980: 3–6 and ff. They further argue that it is usual for humans to comprehend relatively abstract domains of experience systematically in terms of relatively concrete domains (see pp. 106–114). By no means, however, are all metaphorical expressions manifestations of systematic conceptual metaphors. As a single example, consider the phrase *liber nubibus aether* (Lucan 3.522). The sky here is "free" of clouds, but is nowhere described as "slave" to the clouds; there is no systematic structuring of meteorological phenomena in terms of social status in Lucan's poem or anywhere else in Latin literature. In this and similar cases, no associations significant for the context are imported from the domain of social status. See further Cooper 1986: 144–52.

cept and structure of the master-slave relationship is projected *en bloc* into the derived political domain, then not only are a large number of individual terms and images made available for use in the political domain, but these terms and images also retain their connotations and the relations that obtain among them. Thus, if in the parent domain freedom is the condition of not having a master, so too in the derived domain; if crucifixion is a characteristically servile punishment in the parent domain, so "slaves" in the derived domain will be the ones "crucified." It further follows that an adequate semantic study of any of these words or images requires, first, that their usages in the derived domain be considered with reference to their usages in the parent domain, and second, that the whole complex of these terms and images be examined together, without any one term artificially being isolated from the others: for all are elements of the same underlying conceptual metaphor. These claims may appear so obvious as to go without saying. But over the past half-century or so, a number of scholars—Wirszubski, Hammond, Hellegouarc'h, and others—have studied in detail, or made general claims about, the meaning(s) of the word *libertas* and its cognates as they occur in political contexts. The focus in these studies on the derived, political domain results in little or no reference being made to the parent domain, which provides the political domain its conceptual structure; likewise, the focus on the word *libertas* and its congnates causes the other associated language and imagery of social status to be neglected.[10] Because of this inadequate contextualization, these studies contain systematic and characteristic distortions, which I will describe later. Other studies of *libertas* by Bleicken and especially Brunt are better, though even they are not entirely free of these difficulties.[11] In the

[10] In Wirszubski's (1950) study of *libertas*, the associated words *servitus, dominus*, etc., never receive sustained discussion (note too their absence from his index), and there are only a few references to the social institution of slavery (pp. 1–5); similarly in Hammond 1963. Hellegouarc'h's (1963) large-scale study of republican political vocabulary notes rightly (p. 543) that "*libertas* s'oppose continuellement à *servitus* ou *servitium*" in late republican sources (suggesting that these words might profitably be studied together), yet he devotes seventeen pages to a study of *libertas* in isolation (pp. 542–59) and just half a page to *servitium* (559). He then devotes an additional six pages total to *regnum, tyrannus, dominatus*, and *dominatio*. While the political associations of *libertas* discussed in these works are useful in themselves, they do not constitute an adequate semantic analysis of the word, let alone of the larger cluster of related terms and images. The methodology of these studies results from the implicit adoption of the "polysemy" or "homonymy" theory of metaphor; for this theory and its inadequacy in the face of conceptual metaphors, see Lakoff and Johnson 1980: 106–14 and Cooper 1986: 128–36; for the difficulties such issues pose the lexicographer, see Robins 1987.

[11] Bleicken's (1972) study, though also largely limited to the political usages of *libertas* (he mentions the parent domain only on pp. 19–20), makes many helpful observations, especially regarding the ad hoc nature of the usages of this word (pp. 52–56; cf. n. 27

next few pages, then, I will sketch the outlines of the kind of analysis I consider appropriate to this semantic cluster—an analysis that begins with the parent domain and establishes in that context the referents and interrelationships of these words and images. This analysis will provide the basis for my survey, in sections 3–4 below, of certain political uses of this language and imagery in late republican and Julio-Claudian Rome.

First for the words *servus* and *dominus*. In the context of the social institution of slavery, these words are almost always mutually entailing: the assertion of slavery invariably implies the existence of a master, while the mention of a "master" usually implies the existence of someone or something standing as a slave.[12] A different relationship holds between *servus* and *liber*. These words designate complementary social categories: any person not classifiable as a *servus* is necessarily *liber*, and vice versa; no other status is possible within this system of categorization. Likewise, any condition of which *servitus* can be predicated, literally or metaphorically, is ipso facto not a condition of *libertas*, and vice versa. This complementarity is implicit in almost any conjunction of these words, and is made explicit in certain in legal texts, which in this case seem to reflect the ordinary usage of these terms. Thus the jurist Gaius writes that "all men are either free or slaves" (*omnes homines aut liberi sunt aut servi*, *Inst.* 1.9) and Florentinus (*Dig.* 1.5.4. pr.

---

below). Brunt's chapter, entitled "*Libertas* in the Republic" (1988: 281–350) is by far the best study of the word: it begins by discussing legal definitions of chattel slavery, along with the sociology of this institution (pp. 283–91). The parent domain, and the significance of words and images in that domain, are kept in view throughout (esp. pp. 308–17). Yet his analysis remains too closely tied to questionable analytical structures set up by earlier scholars to allow him to exploit fully the new ground he breaks. Another study, notable for its ambitious cross-cultural analyses and comparisons, is Patterson 1991. He identifies three distinct subcategories of "freedom" in the Western tradition (pp. 3–5), categories that he applies (problematically, in my view) to all the cultures and periods his study covers (including Rome, pp. 203–90). On Patterson's contribution to our understanding of ancient slavery, see *Arethusa* 28 (1995) 87–112, a "Forum" containing three short essays by classicists.

[12] *Dominus*, however, has other meanings outside of the context of status relations: etymologically derived from *domus*, it refers to the "owner" of the household, everything inside it, and the associated land and buildings (Ernout-Meillet 1959: 183)—i.e., the *paterfamilias* (see further section 3 below). The common usage of *dominus* to refer to the master in relation to a slave is presumably a subset of this wider usage, since slaves are among the property that the *dominus* owns (see *TLL* s.v. *dominus* 1912–20). The word can also refer to a patron/gift creditor, a lover, the host of a convivium, any member of one's own family, and so on: these usages are discussed below (section 4). Meanwhile, the "master" of a slave is sometimes not an individual, but a corporate entity (as with slaves owned by the state); there is also a peculiar legal entity, the *servus sine domino*, on which see Buckland 1908: 274–79.

1) likewise defines *libertas* and *servitus* but no other statuses, implying that there is no other category of personal status in this scheme.[13]

Because of this complementarity, it follows that to define either of these categories is thereby to define the other. But it is usually the slave, not the free person, whom Roman writers attempt to define: it is the condition of slavery, not that of freedom, that is regarded as having specifiable and enumeratable characteristics. This is not to say that ancient writers found it easy to define slavery, or to determine someone's status as slave or free. For instance, Dio Chrysostom in two of his discourses (*Or.* 14 and 15) evaluates a number of possible criteria for slavery: whether money has been paid for one, whether one is owned like cattle or other goods, whether one is the offspring of slaves, and whether one is subject to arbitrary corporal punishment at another's hands, for example. Dio argues that none of these criteria is adequate by itself, since none embraces all persons who are generally agreed to be slaves, and each also includes certain persons whom all would agree are free (*Or.* 14.3–15, 15.1–28). But the fact that specific, positively-stated criteria for slavery are propounded and discussed at all suggests that this category has a conceptual core—that is, there exists conceptually a prototype of "slave" or "slavery" in which one or more of these criteria are met. Where the boundary lies between these complementary categories, however, may not be universally agreed upon: for how one classifies another in this scheme depends on what criterion or combination of criteria for slavery one considers to be decisive. I will argue below, for instance, that to be subjected to arbitrary corporal punishment, especially whipping and beating, was for Julio-Claudian aristocrats a particularly strong indicator of slave status. The categories of "free" and "slave," then, while complementary, are constructed differently. "Slavery" has a conceptual core that can be expressed through one or more positively stated criteria, though the necessity and/or sufficiency of any particular criterion is open to debate. "Freedom," on the other hand, is negatively defined, a default category with no conceptual core: it is merely "the condition of being not-a-slave," the absence of the decisive criterion or criteria, whatever it/they are accepted to be, that express the conceptual core of the category of slavery.[14]

Indeed, all of the explicit definitions of "freedom" that I have en-

---

[13] Cf. Wirszubski 1950: 1, who calls slavery (perhaps loosely) the "direct opposite" of liberty.

[14] The structure of the category "slave," as I describe it, accords with recent work on conceptual categories done by cognitive scientists, for which I follow Lakoff 1987. See e.g., his discussions of the categories "bachelor" and "mother" (70–71, 74–76), social categories that work similarly to "slave." For how a predicate like "subject to whippings" can indicate membership in a category like "slave," see Lakoff 52–54 on "cue validity."

countered in Roman texts are negative in this sense, making the absence of the restrictions associated with slavery primary and essential, and relegating to secondary importance any idea that freedom entails specific rights or powers in itself. Consider, for example, the discussion of monarchy in Cicero's *De Re Publica* 2.43, where the language of the master-slave relationship is applied to the derived domain of politics: "A people that is subjected to a king lacks many things, most importantly *libertas*, which resides not in experiencing our master as just, but in [experiencing] no master" (*desunt omnino ei populo multa qui sub rege est, in primisque libertas, quae non in eo est ut iusto utamur domino, sed ut nul<lo>. . .*). A substantial lacuna at the end of this passage makes the sense and direction of the argument uncertain, but the basic assertion that *libertas* requires the absence of a *dominus* reveals the fundamentally negative conception of freedom.[15] Similarly, freedom is sometimes defined as "subjection to no one" or "the power to do as you please": the first is clearly a negative definition, while the second, though positive in its articulation, is nevertheless conceptually negative, since it simply defers the questions of what constitutes constraint that may prevent one from doing as one pleases, and where such constraints may lie.[16] At least one other text — the first book of the *Institutiones* of

---

[15] For the supplement *nul<lo>*, cf. Cic. *Att.* 7.7.5: *pauci libertatem, magna pars iustos dominos volunt* (i.e., having a master, even a just one, is incompatible with *libertas*). Elsewhere too in Cic. *Rep.* the language of the master-slave relationship is applied in various ways to the relationship of a state's citizens to its government: e.g., *in optimatium dominatu vix particeps libertatis potest esse multitudo* (1.43.1); *ecce autem maxima voce clamat populus neque se uni neque paucis velle parere; libertate ne feris quidem quicquam esse dulcius; hac omnes carere, sive regi sive optimatibus serviant* (1.55.2); also 1.47.1–3, 1.50.1–3.

[16] A few instances of such articulations of "freedom" — some referring to chattel slavery, others to politics, still others philosophical: Cic. *Planc.* 16 (of the secret ballot): *datque eam libertatem ut quod velint faciant*. Cic. *Paradoxa* 33: *quid enim est libertas? potestas vivendi ut velis*. Persius 5.83–84: *an quisquam est alius liber nisi ducere vitam / cui licet ut libuit?* Dio Chr. *Or.* 14.3: . . . τὸ ἐλεύθερον εἶναι . . . τὸ μηδενὸς ὑπήκοον, ἀλλὰ πράττειν ἁπλῶς τὰ δοκοῦντα ἑαυτῷ. Epict. *Diss.* 4.1.1: ἐλεύθερός ἐστιν ὁ ζῶν ὡς βούλεται, ὃν οὔτ' ἀναγκάσαι ἔστιν οὔτε κωλῦσαι οὔτε βιάσασθαι, οὗ αἱ ὁρμαὶ ἀνεμπόδιστοι, αἱ ὀρέξεις ἐπιτευκτικαί, αἱ ἐκκλίσεις ἀνερίπτωτοι. Record of a manumission at Delphi: . . . ἐλευθέραν εἶμεν καὶ ἀνέφαπτον ἀπὸ πάντων τὸν πάντα χρόνον ποιοῦσαν ὅ κα θέλη καὶ ἀποτρέχουσαν οἷς κα θέλη (Collitz-Bechtel 1884 no. 1687; cf. 1685–86). Dig. 1.5.4 pr. (Florentinus): *libertas est naturalis facultas eius quod cuique facere libet, nisi si quid vi aut iure prohibetur*. Conversely, slavery entails constraints that keep one from doing as one pleases: Sen. *Suas.* 5.4: *confessio servitutis est iussa facere*; Sen. *Ep.* 61.3. Several of these passages are discussed in detail below. Most modern scholars also present the negative sense of *libertas* as fundamental: see Wirszubski 1950: 1; Bleicken 1972: 19–20, 54–55; Brunt 1988: 283–84, 313; Patterson 1991: 9. Likewise for Kuhlmann's *TLL* article on *liber*, which begins as follows: "[**I.**] **A**. negatur servitus singulorum hominum: 1. strictius respicitur is, qui dominio eri subiectus non est . . ." (*TLL* s.v. *liber* 1280.54–57; his discussion of *libertas* is organized similarly).

Gaius, a jurist of the second century A.D.—employs the same organizational scheme in classifying persons according to degrees of legal constraint: degrees of greater constraint are specified and articulated in positive terms, while degrees of lesser constraint are defined negatively, as that which is left over.[17] This text therefore provides a parallel for the conceptual ordering of the categories *libertas* and *servitus* that I propose here.

If the conceptual categories associated with slavery could be deployed metaphorically to structure the power relations found in the derived domain of politics, these categories also provided an ethical and affective commentary on those structures. The opening sentence of Augustus's *Res Gestae*, for example, implicitly presents the subjection of the state to the mastery of a faction as a bad and undesirable condition, and his own "liberation" of the state from that oppression as a good and desirable thing. This ethical/affective dimension of the language and imagery of social status derives immediately from its parent domain of usage, inasmuch as the condition of slavery in Roman society was strongly stigmatized, and freedom correspondingly valorized: for the grim social reality of slavery was before the eyes of aristocratic (and all other) Romans at all times, who would hardly have enjoyed envisioning themselves enslaved literally or metaphorically. Roman social practice in general, and legal practice in particular, produced a degradation of slaves that was both cruelly real and also powerfully symbolic.

The basic conditions of slave existence in Roman society are reasonably well attested; evidence for it has been collected and set out recently in a pair of books by Keith Bradley. He shows (1994: 81–106) that slaves in general experienced a low level of material existence, including few and poor clothes, poor and often scanty food, and frequently inadequate shelter; they also had always to fear being sold, thereby being abruptly and irremediably separated from parents, children, sexual partners, and friends.[18] The exceptions are certain domestics in wealthy

---

[17] Gaius *Inst.* 1.48–200. Throughout this classification, which he calls *alia divisio de iure personarum* (1.48), Gaius articulates degrees of empowerment negatively, as the absence of particular constraints. At 1.48–49 persons are classified as either *sui iuris* or *alieno iure subiectae*; the latter class is further subdivided into the categories *in potestate*, *in manu*, and *in mancipio*. In regard to these categories, Gaius says, *videamus nunc de iis, quae alieno iure subiectae sint: nam si cognoverimus, quae istae personae sint, simul intellegemus, quae sui iuris sint* (§50). Thus the lesser degree of constraint (*sui iuris*) is defined negatively, as the complement of the greater (*alieni iuris*). There follows a detailed discussion of the three subdivisions of the category *alieni iuris* (§§51–141), and the category *sui iuris* is duly ignored until §142. The whole procedure then recurs, starting at §142, to articulate decreasing degrees of constraint within the category *sui iuris*.

[18] Indeed, Patterson (1991: 9–10) argues that, in all slave societies, a slave is someone who should have died (e.g., in battle or from poverty), but whose physical death has been commuted in exchange for "social death," which entails the negation of all birthrights,

households, who were at least well fed and clothed—not necessarily for humanitarian reasons, but as elements in the competitive display of the household: one's cupbearers and litter-bearers must look good, though other slaves with less public exposure might well receive worse clothing and food. Elsewhere (1987: 113–137) Bradley examines the threat and reality of physical abuse—corporal punishment of various sorts, as well as sexual exploitation—that hung over slaves at all times. Anecdotes describing masters' cruelty toward slaves abound in Roman literature (Vedius Pollio's behavior, discussed in chapter 3.4 above, being but one striking instance). Although many of these anecdotes describe extreme and exceptional behavior on the part of masters, such behavior must have been at any rate credible if the anecdotes were to have any point for their audience.[19] While laws prohibiting excessive cruelty to slaves existed (e.g., Gaius *Inst.* 1.52–53), there were few if any mechanisms for enforcing such laws. No doubt the awareness that a law exists imposes a normative pressure on social actors, and hence a law may have some effect even in the absence of systematic enforcement mechanisms. Nevertheless, we know (for example) that Domitian, Nerva, and Hadrian each legally forbade the castration of slave boys; thus this practice must have persisted, despite each injunction, at a level that spurred further attempts to suppress it. Likewise, the legal remedies theoretically available for mistreated slaves (Bradley 1987: 123–28) are no more likely to have offered significant relief in the vast majority of cases. For an abused slave seeking legal recourse had to identify and locate the appropriate magistrate and approach him personally. None of these tasks would necessarily have been easy, since most slaves' knowledge of legal procedure, and perhaps their own movements as well, were limited; besides, in the end the magistrate might not be sympathetic.

---

kinship ties, and social connections, which are basic to a person's social existence. This view receives support in a Roman setting by texts such as *Dig.* 1.5.4.2, which derives the noun *servus* from the verb *servare*: *servi ex eo appellati sunt, quod imperatores captivos vendere ac per hoc servare nec occidere solent* (though note that in Roman society slave status was inherited through the maternal line, with the result that children of "socially dead" women were likewise socially dead); also Sen. *Ep.* 77.18. Consistent with this view is the slave's legal incapacity to form marriages and have legitimate children.

[19] Anecdotes describing masters' cruelty to slaves: Bradley 1987: 121–23; on fear as a device for controlling slaves, see 113–14, 134, 135–36; on castration see 128. Saller 1994: 142–53 further demonstrates that whippings and beatings by the *paterfamilias* were regarded as suitable and proper chastisement for slaves, but not for freeborn children (more on this in section 3 below). Finley 1980: 95–98 argues that slaves in general were made "answerable with their body" (i.e., subjected to torture, beatings, sexual abuse) as a way of degrading them and thus distinguishing them from human beings who are not property; he suggests that the use of *puer*/παῖς as form of address was another technique for degrading.

In fact, far from providing slaves with useful recourse, the law contributed significantly to their degradation. As is well known, slaves were in many respects property, as well as or rather than persons (to the extent that these categories conflicted). Under Roman law they could be owned, bought, and sold as chattel; the social disruptions this entailed have just been noted. Indeed, the semantics of the word *dominus* shows that there is a close conceptual connection between the *servus* and *res*: *dominus* is the usual word for "master" (of a slave) and is the *vox propria* for "owner" of property.[20] Slaves were excluded from most legal procedures, including their own defense in court if accused of a crime (Buckland 1908: 82–97). Moreover, in the late republic and into the first century A.D., the law sanctioned for slaves (and perhaps also for other noncitizens) particularly harsh and degrading forms of punishment: a slave who committed a captial crime, for example, could expect — and received — penalties such as *crematio* (burning alive), crucifixion, or *damnatio ad bestias* (being thrown to the animals in the arena). Persons of higher status were typically subject to lesser penalties for similar crimes, or at least less gruesome forms of execution. For a high-status person to be subjected to one of these typically "servile" punishments was regarded as singularly damaging to his status.[21]

---

[20] See Buckland 1908 chapters 2–3 for slaves as *res* and for the property laws that apply to them; also chapters 4–9 for slaves as persons, and for the respects in which they do or do not share the legal responsibilities and liabilities of other persons. Finley 1980: 72–73 implies that the Romans conceived of slaves fundamentally as property, albeit of a peculiar kind — though at 98–100 he notes the "ambiguity" inherent in the institution of slavery regarding a slave's status as person or property, especially regarding his actions. For example, a master was strictly liable for a slave's criminal deeds, yet in some cases a slave was liable for his own criminal actions (Buckland 1908: 91–92). Indeed, the property aspect of the slave could be emphasized at one time (e.g., Petr. *Sat.* 39) and the person aspect at another (e.g., Sen. *Ep.* 47.1) to advance different agendas.

A passage from Varro's *De Re Rustica*, classifying slaves within the *instrumenti genus vocale* (1.17.1), is frequently cited as evidence that slaves were regarded as property rather than persons (e.g., Hopkins 1978: 123, Garnsey-Saller 1987: 116, Griffin 1976: 263–64). This is a misreading: for as Varro later clarifies, slaves are adduced only as a representative instance of this class, which contains free laborers as well as slaves, both of whom moreover are *homines* (1.17.2: *omnes agri coluntur hominibus servis aut liberis aut utrisque*). Thus the classification of the slave as an *instrumentum vocale* is illustrative and does not distinguish him from the freeman as *res* from *homo*. See Perl 1977 for further discussion.

[21] The full dual-penalty system, in which these "slavish" penalties came to be applied to all *humiliores*, appears to have evolved only in the course of the second century A.D. On slave penalties, and on the character and origins of the dual-penalty system, see Garnsey 1970: 123–31, 158–72. Not just the laws themselves but also the very process of litigation was biased strongly in favor of those of high social rank or status: see at length Kelly 1966 (esp. chs. 1–3). Garnsey-Saller 1987: 109–11 and Garnsey 1970: 152, 260–65 discuss other aspects of the discrimination based on social rank or status in the Roman judicial system.

226 CHAPTER 4

Physical and legal degradation corresponded in Roman society to moral degradation. Literary texts produced by aristocratic authors — which is to say men who were themselves large slaveholders, or who identified themselves as belonging to this social stratum — reveal a stereotype of slaves as criminal, lazy, deceitful, intransigent, and implacably hostile to the needs and interests of their masters. These stereotypical representations presumably reveal at least some of the basic assumptions and biases of the aristocracy as a whole. Even Seneca's anecdotes demonstrating that slaves can confer *beneficia* upon their masters (*Ben.* 3.23–27) are notable, he says, because loyalty and willing self-sacrifice are anomalous in slaves (*Ben.* 3.19.4; cf. Finley 1980: 103–104). Most of Seneca's exhortations to his fellow aristocrats and slave owners to treat their slaves well engage, explicitly or implicitly, the aristocratic conventional wisdom that the master-slave relationship was by nature adversarial (e.g., *Ep.* 47.1–5, *Clem.* 1.18.1) — indeed, the phrase *quot servi, tot hostes* was a proverb.[22] This focus on stereotypes is not to deny that warm and loyal relationships could and did develop between some masters and slaves; the point is that aristocrats did not regard such relationships as the norm and did not assume that they would develop.[23]

---

[22] For the proverb, see Sen. *Ep.* 47.5: *deinde eiusdem adrogantiae proverbium iactatur, totidem hostes esse quot servos* (Macr. *Sat.* 1.11.13 paraphrases this passage). See also Curt. 7.8.28, comparing the relationship of masters and slaves to that between conquerors and conquered: *quos viceris amicos tibi esse cave credas. inter dominum et servum nulla amicitia est, etiam in pace belli tamen iura servantur*. Fest. 261.29 directly connects this proverb with the putative prisoner-of-war origin of the stereotypical slave. Bradley 1987: 26–31 and Brunt 1988: 287–89 further discuss the negative stereotypes and moral opprobrium associated with slaves by aristocratic writers. This degradation is particularly associated with sexual abuse: Sen. *Cont.* 4 pr. 10; Petr. *Sat.* 75.11.

[23] My interest here is in aristocrats' perceptions of the master-slave relationship, and in their imagination of the character of the slave experience. Scholars have however attempted to recover slave views of their own experience. Bradley 1987: 31–33 adduces slave revolts, running away, and reports of poor work performance (attested in Varro and Columella) as evidence for slave resistance to their condition; he also uses the works of Epictetus, a slave in his youth, as the basis for a discussion of slave psychology (1994: 174–82). Novels such as *Daphnis and Chloe* and the anonymous *Life of Aesop* (Bradley 1994: 102–105 and Hopkins 1993, respectively) also provide representations of slaves' viewpoints regarding their position and relationships (Hopkins 1993: 22, for example, notes that "the hostility between master and slave runs like a sore through the story"). Martin 1990, on the other hand, argues from primarily epigraphic evidence that slaves and even the poor freeborn could articulate fairly positive views of slavery, presenting it as a quicker and surer route to improved status and social integration than poor freebirth provided (pp. 28–29, 34, 41–42) — though such claims are subject to the cautions articulated by Scott 1990: 85 n. 38, namely that for slaves to speak well of their condition does not mean that they do not understand that they are subject to an unjust, brutal form of domination, even while they may perceive certain advantages in their condition. Scheidel

For Roman aristocrats, then, the word *servitus* and its cognates carried powerful negative connotations. These derived from the slave's stereotyped liability to moral and physical degradation, coercion by the threat and application of force, and circumscription of personal volition. Meanwhile *libertas* and its cognates, marking the absence of the undesirable conditions associated with slavery, could carry strongly positive connotations.[24] When these words are projected *en bloc* into a derived domain, they bring along these connotations, thus providing not just a formal structuring, but also an affective structuring, of that domain.[25] This affective structuring is visible in each of the four examples with which this section opened and is important in many further passages discussed below.

I conclude this section by showing how my socially grounded semantic analysis of this cluster of words and images relates to other semantic analyses, particularly of the much-studied word *libertas* and its cognates; I thereby also adumbrate the method I apply in the subsequent sections of this chapter. Scholars have long recognized that *libertas* carries positive connotations when used in political contexts. Consider Syme's brief but influential description of its semantics from the *Roman Revolution*, in a chapter entitled "Political Catchwords":

> *Libertas* is a vague and negative notion — freedom from the rule of a tyrant or faction. It follows that *libertas*, like *regnum* or *dominatio*, is a convenient term of political fraud. *Libertas* was most commonly invoked in defence of the existing order by individuals or classes in enjoyment of power and wealth. (Syme 1939: 155)

1993 further discusses the pitfalls of interpreting the exiguous evidence for slave mentality and viewpoints.

[24] Seneca acknowledges the importance of these connotations at *Ep.* 47.14: *ne illud quidem videtis, quam omnem invidiam maiores nostri dominis, omnem contumeliam servis detraxerint? dominum patrem familiae appellaverunt, servos, quod etiam in mimis adhuc durat, familiares; instituerunt diem festum, non quo solo cum servis domini vescerentur, sed quo utique; honores illis in domo gerere, ius dicere permiserunt et domum pusillam rem publicam esse iudicaverunt.* So the removal of *contumelia* from slaves is achieved in part by calling them *familiares* rather than *servi*, while *invidia* is removed from the master by calling him *paterfamilias* rather than *dominus* (cf. *Ira* 3.35.2). For the positive connotations of the son's relationship to his father, as opposed to the negative ones of the slave's relationship to his master, see sections 3–4 below.

[25] Brunt 1988: 287, 288 also observes that the positive connotations of *libertas*, in its political usages, arise through this word's complementarity to *servitus*, with its negative connotations: because the degradation of slaves "made it natural to connect freedom with morality [and] dignity" (p. 287), we find a mapping of moral value onto social status. Bleicken 1972: 54–55 makes essentially the same observation, but since he discusses only the political usage of *libertas*, he contrasts this word, and its positive connotations, with *regnum* and *tyrannis* rather than with *servitus*.

Although he makes no reference to the parent domain, Syme's analysis here is largely correct: he articulates the negative conception of *libertas*, he notes the importance of its affective, "catchword" quality (cf. ibid. 59, 516), and he sees at least two other words as semantically related. Ste. Croix, in turn, offers a critique of Syme's formulation:

> we need not discount *libertas* itself, with Syme, as *merely* 'a vague and negative notion.' . . . 'Vague' is not at all the right word for the majority of the most interesting uses of the term 'libertas.' In most cases the meaning of 'libertas' is *specific* enough: the point is that it is capable of expressing very *different* and even *contradictory* notions.[26] (Ste. Croix 1981: 368; all emphases in the original)

I will discuss aspects of this assertion in a moment, but in conjuction with a recent formulation by Duncan Kennedy:

> [T]he term *libertas* had for a long time been a central and "stable" one in the ideology of Republican Rome and was perhaps more potent and valued than any other. . . . However, this stability had been disrupted because of its appropriation by various interests in the turbulent and sectarian aftermath of the assassination of Julius Caesar. Each wanted the positive and valued connotations of this word to be associated with it. . . . Horace's insertion of [*libertas*] into his own integrational, quietistic discourse . . . constituted a reassertion of the positive connotations of a valued but disrupted and hence partially discredited term. . . . A term previously mobilised to support a non-monarchical system . . . changed direction to support an autocratic one. . . . The word *libertas* may have *looked* the same, but its *meaning* had changed. (Kennedy 1992: 31; all emphases in the original)

Pace Ste. Croix, *libertas* does not mean many different things, including opposite things; nor, *pace* Kennedy, is its meaning unstable and mutable. On the contrary, *libertas* means the same thing in all cases: it means "the (desirable) condition of not being a slave." It retains the fundamentally negative force it carries in its parent domain of reference, the social institution of slavery. What is occurring in apparently contradictory usages of the term is that people with differing political interests provide different, and even opposed, metaphorical structurings of political situations in terms of status, and thereby attempt to impose different understandings of those political situations.[27] In the first example cited

---

[26] Cf. Brunt 1988: 282–83 for a slightly different critique of Syme.

[27] Cf. Wirszubski 1950: 103–104, Hellegouarc'h 1963: 551–58, Brunt 1988: 297, 308–10 for the conflicting usages of the word *libertas* by different groups and persons. Bleicken's description of the semantics of this word (1972: 52–54) is congenial to my argument: he refers regularly to a political "*libertas*-Begriff," but denies that *libertas* is a unitary, abstract political "Idee" in and of itself: although there are certain patterns to its

at the beginning of this section, from the *Res Gestae*, Augustus labels the period immediately following Caesar's assassination as a *dominatio factionis*, with Antony, implicitly, being the *dominus* (whom Augustus in due course drove away). In the second example, however, Marcus Brutus portrays the very same period as one of *libertas*, as the *pilleus* on his coin shows, with Caesar, implicitly, being the (ex-) *dominus*. Ste. Croix and Kennedy are right to see contestation and a clash of political agendas in contradictory usages such as these, but the meaning of *libertas* is not being contested, nor does it differ in these two cases. What is being contested is the application of the social metaphor *as a whole* to the political situation at hand. Augustus and Brutus are each trying to persuade an audience of the same thing: that it had been "enslaved" to one or another "master," and that they (Brutus and Augustus) delivered it from that highly undesirable condition. They disagree, however, on the identity of the master, and therefore on the timing of both the period of enslavement and the moment of liberation.

Furthermore, it is commonly asserted that freedom has both a negative and a positive aspect: freedom *from* vs. freedom *to*. I have argued here for the primacy of the negative aspect in antiquity. Many classical scholars have however asserted that *libertas* has specific, positive associations. Thus Wirszubski 1950, in his first chapter, associates *libertas* with such positive concepts as the enjoyment of the privileges of citizenship, the proper functioning of laws and legitimate institutions, a distribution of governmental power over several power bases (rather than just one), and so on. He notes for example that, in texts discussing the conflict of the orders, the tribunes are commonly said to protect the plebeians' *libertas*, which he takes to mean equal treatment for both plebeians and patricians under the law (pp. 10–11). But his focus on a single element (*libertas*) in a systematic mapping of terms and images causes him to miss the bigger picture: for in the rhetoric of this struggle, the consuls and patriciate as a whole are often styled as "masters," actual or potential, who may succeed in "(re)enslaving" the plebeians if the latter lose their tribunician protections. Specifically, the plebeians fear being imprisoned, bound, beaten, and whipped by the patricians — forms of corporal punishment that are typically associated with slave status.[28] Thus, while the plebeians do associate *libertas* closely with the

---

positive associations, he says, its usage is generally ad hoc and context specific. I would add that the same is true of the other words in the semantic cluster; moreover, my argument here provides an explanation for this pattern of usage.

[28] For this language see e.g., Sal. *Or. Macri* 26: *abunde libertatem rati quia tergis abstinetur et huc ire licet atque illuc, munera ditium dominorum*. Also Cic. *Leg.* 3.9, 15–25; Dion. Hal. *Rom. Quaest.* 6.87.3; Livy 2.23.2, 28.7, 33.1; 3.9.2–4, 10.13–14, and passim in the decemviral narrative beginning at 3.37, where the suspension of tribunate leads to

functioning of the tribunate, they do so because the spectre of slavish treatment lies immediately behind the figure of the tribune: they imagine him precisely as a bulwark constraining the threat of slavish treatment and thereby creating the complementary domain of not-slavery, i.e., freedom, that they inhabit thanks to him; he is imagined, quite literally, as a physical boundary between freedom and slavery. Yet, while the plebeians thus map the language and imagery of social status onto political relationships in ways that serve their own interests, their usages do not preclude other, competing mappings that are inconsistent or even contradictory to this one. The decemvir Appius, for example, can argue that the very laws protecting the plebeians constitute a *dominatio* and impede *libertas* if the right of *provocatio* is not granted to everyone, including himself (Livy 3.56.13).

Similarly, in literary sources of the late republic and early empire, the word *lex* (law) is frequently linked with the word *libertas*. Most such usages refer to the political domain: *lex* and *libertas* are said to be threatened jointly by, and defended jointly against, those who threaten the state, and the laws themselves are sometimes said or implied to guarantee and sustain (political) freedom.[29] On the basis of such linkages, Wirszubski 1950 asserts that "libertas consists in rights which rest on positive institutions" (p. 5) and "libertas at Rome . . . is not an innate faculty or right of man, but the sum of civic rights granted by the laws of Rome; it consequently rests on those positive laws which determine its scope" (p. 7). But a closer look at the relevant passages again reveals a somewhat different picture. First, when *lex* and *libertas* are linked, other language and imagery of the master-slave relationship is also often present. The suppression of *lex* and *libertas* can be called a condition of *servitus* (e.g., Nepos *Timol.* 3; Livy 26.32.2); and Lucan's Brutus can declare that, when all of Rome's leading men have gone under Pompey's yoke — a symbol of enslavement, discussed below — there is then need to defend *leges* and *libertas* (2.277–84). Similarly Cicero, describing the character of Caesar's regime at *De Officiis* 2.24, condemns it as a rule of force that suppresses *leges* and *libertas*, compa-

---

beatings and executions of plebeians (3.37.5–8). The (metaphorical) usage of this vocabulary in this political context is finally literalized in the Verginia episode, where the decemvir Appius aims precisely to reduce this freeborn woman to slavery (*ut virginem in servitutem adsereret . . . manum iniecit, serva sua natam servamque appellans se sequi iubebat*, 3.44.5–6). On the thematization of *libertas* and *servitus* in the Verginia episode see Ogilvie 1965: 478, 481–83. I heavily document the association of corporal punishment with slavery in sections 3–4 below.

[29] *Lex* and *libertas* threatened and defended together: Cic. *Off.* 3.83; Phd. 1.2; Val. Max. 3.2.18; Sen. *Ep.* 86.2–3; Lucan 2.281–2, 3.137–40. Laws sustain political freedom: Sal. *Or. Lepidi* 4; Cic. *Clu.* 146, 155.

rable to the force by which masters control their slaves;[30] and a specific manifestation of such force is imagined by Seneca in his *Consolatio ad Marciam*, describing the character of a tyrant: "Dionysius the tyrant will be there [sc. in Syracuse], the destroyer of *libertas*, justice, and *leges*; greedy to be a master even after meeting Plato, and for life even after being exiled: some he will burn, others he will beat, still others he will order decapitated for a small offense" (*erit Dionysius illic tyrannus, libertatis iustitiae legum exitium, dominationis cupidus etiam post Platonem, vitae etiam post exilium: alios uret, alios verberabit, alios ob levem offensam detruncari iubebit*, §17.5). Thus, the *leges* in these passages are not only linked to *libertas*, but like it are also opposed to *servitus*, the condition of the slave, and in the latter example, to stereotypically slavish treatment such as arbitrary corporal punishment. What laws might these be? Cicero, in his *Pro Rabirio Perduellionis Reo*, accuses the tribune Labienus of imprisoning, crucifying, and whipping Roman citizens, sarcastically calling him a "truly popular tribune, guardian and defender of *ius* and *libertas*"; he then invokes a *lex Porcia* that forbids the beating of Roman citizens, and a *lex Sempronia* forbidding that a capital charge against a citizen be judged without an appeal to the people (§§12–13).[31] To the extent that the *lex* associated with *libertas* is specified, then, it is the body of law protecting citizens from whippings, beatings, imprisonment, and execution at the hands of magistrates without the possibility of appeal—that is, from suffering stereotypically slavish treatment. In these passages law is presented, like the tribunes discussed above, as a bulwark separating the domain of slavery (identified with subjection to arbitrary corporal punishment) from that of freedom.[32] It is perhaps not impossible that *libertas* could be associated with *leges* very generally in the civic community—the "sum of civic rights granted by law," as Wirszubski puts it—since free persons

---

[30] Cic. *Off.* 2.24: *sed iis qui vi oppressos imperio coercent sit sane adhibenda saevitia, ut eris in famulos, si aliter teneri non possunt: qui vero in libera civitate ita se instruunt ut metuantur, iis nihil potest esse dementius. quamvis enim sint demersae leges alicuius opibus, quamvis timefacta libertas, emergunt tamen haec aliquando aut iudiciis tacitis aut occultis de honore suffragiis: acriores autem morsus sunt intermissae libertatis quam retentae.*

[31] See also Cic. *Ver.* 2.5.160–63, invoking the same two laws under similar circumstances; also [Sal.] *In Cic.* 5–6. The *leges Porciae* of the early second century B.C. and a *lex Sempronia* of C. Gracchus seem to have established and secured the right of *provocatio ad populum* for citizens sentenced to death or scourging. On these laws see Lintott 1972: 249–53, 259–62; Rotondi 1962: 268–69, 309–10.

[32] Nicolet 1980 [1976]: 317–24 analyzes the linkage of *lex* and *libertas* in a similar way, holding the "rule of law" to be precisely the existence and effectuality of legal protections and remedies for citizens against the coercive power of magistrates.

were usually (if not always) embedded in that community as citizens.[33] Yet our sources, when at their fullest, indicate that the *leges* most closely associated with *libertas* are specifically those that protect the citizen from slavish handling, namely corporal punishment, by magistrates.

To conclude, I believe that it is incorrect to speak of *libertas* as being a "political idea" or as having a "political meaning" in Roman culture. Such formulations suggest that this term designates a coherent category of Roman political thought, independent of its function as a category of social status and its embeddedness in the institution of chattel slavery. Yet I see little evidence for such a function. The persistent assumption among modern scholars that this word does have an independent existence as a political term perhaps results from retrojecting modern conceptions of freedom into antiquity. In the Western liberal humanist tradition, "liberty" does unquestionably have political meanings, designating for example an individual's self-determination in the face of the power of a state apparatus (e.g., Berlin 1970 [1958]: 162–66, citing Benjamin Constant). But those Europeans who have theorized freedom over the past century and a half (at least) have mostly lived in and thought about societies in which slavery did not exist as an institution, much less the large-scale, vibrant institution that it was in classical Rome. Absent the social institution in which this language was originally grounded, the conceptual metaphor collapsed: meaning came to reside in the political domain—that is, a usage that was metaphorical in Roman antiquity came to be nonmetaphorical in the later Western tradition; the derived domain became the parent domain when the original parent domain ceased to exist as a social reality. Moreover, once the terms "liberty," "slave," "master," etc., were no longer bound together

---

[33] Wirszubski contends most broadly that the Romans identified *libertas* with *civitas*, since slaves manumitted "regularly" (i.e., by census, will, or *vindicta*), acquired citizenship along with freedom (pp. 2–4; similarly Hammond 1963: 93). If correct, this suggestion provides a conceptual basis for the metaphorical transfer of the language of social status into the domain of political relations, and also provides a mechanism whereby the negative conception of "freedom *from*" (the strictures of slavery) corresponds closely to a set of positive conceptions "freedom *to*" (partake of the privileges of citizenship). But I am not persuaded that this linkage is as immediate as Wirszubski suggests: for he himself notes (3 n. 4) that "informally" manumitted slaves were regarded as free in practice, though they did not receive citizenship; their status was even formalized in the early empire under the designation "Junian Latins." Perhaps such persons constituted an anomalous category: but their very existence proves that Romans could conceive of freedom without citizenship. Likewise Livy 2.5.8–10, describing the first *manumissio vindicta*, presents the fact that citizenship was conferred at the same time as freedom as striking and precedent setting. But if *libertas*, to his mind, immediately implied and necessarily entailed *civitas*, he would have no cause to remark on their conjunction here. On these matters see also Brunt 1988: 296–98.

by their shared reference to the (now nonexistent) institution of slavery, it became possible for each term to have its own history. Consequently, just one term, namely "liberty," has become central to modern political discourse, while the terms "slave," "master," etc., occur rarely in this context. This historical development in usage may account for the focus of contemporary classical scholars on the political usages of *libertas* in antiquity: they are wrongly projecting modern conceptions and categories onto the ancient sources.[34]

I turn next, then, to a closer examination of the language and imagery of chattel slavery as used metaphorically in the political domain—i.e., to describe social relations among free citizens, and particularly between the emperor and his aristocratic subjects in Julio-Claudian Rome. Central to this analysis is the use of this language and imagery by aristocrats to portray themselves as slaves of the emperor, an invidious comparison that implies the desirability of some sort of liberation from this master. But this straightforward portrayal of the relationship is open to challenge in several ways: by a different or opposing application of the language of slavery; by alternative interpretations of the crucial term *dominus*; and by the invocation of positive, ameliorative paradigms for imperial authority. These competing presentations of the character of imperial authority, the struggle to conceptualize and articulate it in terms of pre-existing social relations of authority, are important components of the multifaceted process of constructing autocracy in the Julio-Claudian period.

3. Father or Master? Two Models for the Emperor in Julio-Claudian Literature

I begin with an account of a conspiracy against the life of Alexander the Great, as related by the historiographer Quintus Curtius Rufus. The relevance of this account for the experience of this work's intended readership—Julio-Claudian aristocrats, provided we accept the usual identification and dating of Curtius[35]—is in no way diminished by the

---

[34] Thus, for example, I see no difficulty with Berlin 1970 [1958]: 165 speaking of liberty as entailing "rights" of individuals in the view of Constant, Mill, etc., but I think that Wirszubski is incorrect to take this same view regarding Rome (e.g., p. 7). The "rights" comprising Roman *libertas*, if any, are those granted by the specific laws that protect citizens from slavish treatment at the hands of magistrates. In Berlin's essay, incidentally, the words "slave" and "master" occur fairly frequently, sometimes in quotation marks: he is clearly aware that the term "liberty" is historically associated with a larger vocabulary cluster. But he does not discuss this association, or its grounding in the ancient social institution of slavery.

[35] See ch. 3 n. 47 above.

author's artifice of locating his narrative in a foreign culture and in a distant time and place. For the dynamics of the fraught relationship between the ruler and his aristocratic subjects, as well as the alternative social paradigms through which the character of the ruler's authority is articulated and contested, are essentially identical in Alexander's camp (as portrayed by Curtius) and in Julio-Claudian Rome.

The conspiracy in question, according to Curtius, originated among a group of noble adolescent youths, whose families had entrusted them to the king to provide a retinue in accordance with Macedonian custom (8.6.2–6). On the one hand, these youths kept watch by night outside the door of the king's sleeping chamber, managed his horses and his courtesans, and generally provided "services not much different from those provided by slaves" (*munia haud multum servilibus ministeriis abhorrentia*, §2). They were even subject to castigation by whipping, albeit only at the king's own hands (§§4–5).[36] On the other hand, they accompanied the king on hunts and into battle, were trained in the liberal arts, and dined at his table—activities plainly in accordance with their high birth, and presumably marks of honor. This group, says Curtius, constituted a sort of "nursery" of future military officers and prefects (*haec cohors velut seminarium ducum praefectorumque apud Macedonas fuit*, §6; cf. 5.1.42). Now, on a certain hunting expedition one of these youths, named Hermolaus, preempted Alexander in striking down a wild boar. Enraged at being deprived of his quarry, the king had the boy beaten (*verberibus*, §7). To avenge this disgrace (*ignominia*), Hermolaus and some of his peers formed a conspiracy to assassinate the king. The plot was exposed, and the conspirators were summoned before the king and a large council (*frequens consilium*), which included the fathers of the accused, to give an account of themselves (§§8–30).

In this situation, Curtius places in Hermolaus's mouth a dramatic speech rhetorically centered on a presentation of the king as a "master" who has "enslaved" his fellow Macedonians, particularly the nobility. Hermolaus begins, "we entered into a conspiracy to kill you because you have begun to command us not as people of free birth, but you lord it as if a master over his slaves" (*nos vero . . . occidendi te consilium iniimus quia non ut ingenuis imperare coepisti, sed quasi in mancipia dominaris*, 8.7.1). He does not speak overtly of the whipping he suffered on the king's orders (though Curtius makes this the original stimulus for the conspiracy), nor of the employment of his cohort in slave-like capacities, but rather of Alexander's cruelty in killing so many

---

[36] Whipping in Roman society was regarded as a characteristically slavish form of chastisement, not appropriate for freeborn (much less noble) persons: see the discussion of Saller 1994 below.

noble Macedonians (8.7.4–6). In particular, he jeers that the king imprisoned Callisthenes, his outspoken friend and adviser, because he could not bear to see his face or hear his "free voice" (*libera vox*, §9). Subsequently Hermolaus criticizes Alexander's adoption of Persian dress and manners: he has rejected the practices of his own victorious Macedonians in favor of those of their defeated enemies. This is indeed an innovative practice, sending the victors "under the yoke"—a symbol of enslavement after defeat in battle—and into the power of the vanquished (§§11–12).[37] He concludes by recapitulating this persistent figuration of the king's authority: free men cannot bear his arrogance; they are forced to choose between death or living in slavery (§14). Throughout this speech, Hermolaus draws upon the stereotyped characteristics of masters, slaves, and the relationship between them to characterize Alexander's exercise of power over his Macedonian nobles: Alexander makes them answerable with their bodies for offense they give, subjecting them to imprisonment, execution, or whipping (such as Hermolaus himself suffered); and the relationship is now implacably hostile, as this conspiracy demonstrates. In short, Hermolaus seeks to create in the aristocratic onlookers a perception of "status dissonance," a discord between what they consider themselves to be by birth, acculturation, and prior treatment (i.e., aristocrats), and what they are now being treated as (i.e., slaves).[38] This perception, he hopes, will rouse these audience members to oppose and resist Alexander: for no honorable noble would tolerate being treated as an honorless, degraded slave, *if* (and this is crucial) *he were persuaded that such treatment was occurring*.

Unsurprisingly, Alexander seeks to persuade this audience that no such treatment is occurring. On the one hand, he seeks to pick holes in Hermolaus's smooth presentation of him as a master lording it over his slaves. He states that his use of the whip to chastise the boy is sanctioned by custom: not only have Macedonian kings long disciplined

---

[37] *Quae tamen omnia tolerare potuimus, antequam nos barbaris dederes et novo more victores sub iugum mitteres. Persarum te vestis et disciplina delectat, patrios mores exosus es.* The "yoke," as Livy describes it (3.28.11), is an arrangement of two vertical spears with one horizontal spear as a crossbar, under which defeated, captured soldiers passed, marking their transition into slave status in the society of their victorious foes. The yoke thus becomes a synecdoche for slave status (e.g., Cic. *Phil.* 1.6; Sen. *Ira* 2.14.4). On Hermolaus' account, Alexander's imposition of Persian customs on the Macedonians creates an inversion of this procedure: in this case the victors pass under the yoke into the power of the vanquished. The idea that it is "slavery" or "captivity" for the Macedonians to adopt Persian customs is developed elsewhere in Curtius's text as well: see 8.5.13–20 (here too, Callisthenes's resistance to such initiatives marks him as "free" and as a protector of others' "freedom"), also 6.6.3–11.

[38] I borrow the expression "status dissonance" from Weaver 1967: 4–5, who uses it in a different context (see section 5 and n. 87 below).

members of their cohort in this way, but teachers so discipline their pupils, husbands their wives, and even slaves have been known to whip (presumably noble) boys of Hermolaus's age (8.8.3). By arguing that Macedonian social practice sanctions the use of the whip for reasons other than disciplining slaves, Alexander contests the implication that his chastisement of Hermolaus has effectively reduced this noble young man (and by extension the nobility in general) to slavery. On the other hand, Alexander actively proposes an alternative paradigm by which this audience may conceptualize his authority: he asserts that Hermolaus has sought to kill one he should regard as his "father" (*rabie . . . qua compulsus est me quem parentis loco colere deberet vellet occidere*, 8.8.2), and at the end of his speech (§17) calls the boy a "parricide." He also evaluates Hermolaus's actions within the ethical category of *pietas* (*impia caede*, §4), the central ethical category under which familial relations were organized at Rome. This move coheres with his self-presentation as "father," but is hardly applicable to the master-slave relationship (see below). Thus he adduces the model of the father's authority over a son, implicitly an ameliorative paradigm, to counter Hermolaus's invidious invocation of the model of the master's authority over a slave. Much, then, is at stake in the rhetoric of this debate, particularly in the competing paradigms for the king's mode of exercising power over his aristocratic subjects. His legitimacy in the eyes of the aristocratic audience, hence their acquiescence and assistance to him in furthering his aims, turns upon their acceptance of him as something other than a master figure — for example, as a father figure.

As we will see, the father-son relationship appears frequently in Julio-Claudian texts as an ameliorative paradigm for the emperor's relationship to his free subjects, particularly the aristocracy. As in Curtius's text, it is often invoked in opposition to the invidious paradigm of the master-slave relationship.[39] A brief discussion of the stereotypical characteristics and consequent affective overtones of the father-son relation-

---

[39] The use of the father-son and master-slave relationships as paradigms for positive and negative modes of monarchic rule has a long history in Graeco-Roman political theory. See for example Ar. *Nic. Eth.* 1160a36–b30 (with omissions): παρέκβασις δὲ βασιλείας μὲν τυραννίς· ἄμφω γὰρ μοναρχίαι, διαφέρουσι δὲ πλεῖστον· ὁ μὲν γὰρ τύραννος τὸ αὑτῷ συμφέρον σκοπεῖ, ὁ δὲ βασιλεὺς τὸ τῶν ἀρχομένων. . . . ἡ μὲν γὰρ πατρὸς πρὸς υἱεῖς κοινωνία βασιλείας ἔχει σχῆμα· τῶν τέκνων γὰρ τῷ πατρὶ μέλει . . . τυραννικὴ δὲ καὶ ἡ δεσπότου πρὸς δούλους· τὸ γὰρ τοῦ δεσπότου συμφέρον ἐν αὐτῇ πράττεται. Similarly Cic. *Rep.* 2.47: *videtisne igitur ut de rege dominus extiterit, uniusque vitio genus rei publicae ex bono in deterrimum conversum sit? hic est enim dominus populi quem Graeci tyrannum vocant; nam regem illum volunt esse, qui consulit ut parens populo, conservatque eos quibus est praepositus quam optima in condicione vivendi, sane bonum ut dixi rei publicae genus*. For still other paradigms for the positive and negative modes of rule, see *Rep.* 1.64.

ship is warranted here. For as with the master-slave relationship, so too the categories and images of the father-son relationship are projected *en bloc* into the political domain, structuring power relations there in terms of this familiar authority relationship within the family. And again, conventional expectations about the character of this relationship give the associated terminology an affective and ethical force, which makes implications about the desirability or undesirability of acquiescing in a political regime so modeled.

It is well known that the Roman *paterfamilias* held in law the same power over his children as over his slaves: for both slaves and children were usually *in potestate* ("under his power": e.g., Gaius *Inst.* 1.52, 55), a legal category encompassing broad powers of personal tutelage and property management. Under the category of personal tutelage, fathers held *vitae necisque potestas* (the "power of life and death," including the choice to rear or expose infants), the right to impose corporal punishment upon slaves or children; the right to hand them over to another as damages for crimes they commit (noxal surrender), the right to sell slaves, and some degree of control over their childrens' marriage arrangements. Regarding property, the *paterfamilias* legally owned everything the family had, meaning that he could alienate any and all of it, or dispose of it by testament, as he saw fit with little restriction.[40] But legal texts often provide poor and misleading evidence for actual social practices and attitudes. In this case, it is invalid to infer from the similar legal position of children and slaves that the father-son relationship in Rome was stereotypically hostile and abusive, like the master-slave relationship; there is a great deal of evidence to the contrary. The famous exemplary accounts of severe fathers who kill their adult sons for some transgression—accounts that may be thought to show the stark legal power differential actualized in practice—represent not typical attitudes and behaviors, but extreme ones that occur under extraordinary circumstances; these exempla are striking precisely because they presuppose and engage a widespread social expectation that fathers will favor and nurture their sons.[41]

---

[40] See Crook 1967: 113, whom I follow for this analysis of *patria potestas*. See also Harris 1986: 93–95, who argues that a father's *vitae necisque potestas* over a child is socially significant primarily in the matter of infant exposure—consigning a child to life or death at the very outset of life—rather than in the killing of adult sons for bad behavior.

[41] That legal strictures and archaic exempla of paternal authoritarianism do not adequately represent actual social practice, see Crook 1967: 118, Harris 1986, Dixon 1992: 117–18, 147, Saller 1994: 102–105, 114–30. Bucking this trend is Bettini 1991 [1986]: 5–13, who combines the archaic exempla with evidence for father-son avoidance in certain spheres, (e.g., a prohibition on bathing together) to support the position that the stereotypical Roman father-son relationship was distant, detached, and lacked intimacy.

Recently, Richard Saller (1994) has assembled convincing positive evidence that the father-son relationship in Roman elite society was conceptualized as normatively warm and affectionate. He surveys uses of the word *pietas* and its cognates—*pietas*, again, being the central ethical category under which familial relations were organized at Rome (see chapter 1.2 above)—from Plautus to late antiquity, demonstrating that throughout this period *pietas* marks affection and not merely emotionless "duty," and furthermore is reciprocal: not only do sons owe it to fathers, but fathers to sons; mothers and children to one another; and spouses to one another (pp. 105–114). He further shows that, despite their identical legal status in law, sons and slaves were sharply differentiated in their actual treatment by the *paterfamilias*. For as in the public sphere, where corporal punishment in the form of beatings was thought appropriate only for the honorless (i.e., slaves) and not for free men who had honor,[42] so in the domestic sphere the *paterfamilias* typically chastised his slaves, but not his sons, in this way. Indeed, while slaves are commonly presented as liable to be whipped if they transgress, sons were thought to be chastised appropriately by words or other noncorporal punishments precisely so as not to deprive them of honor and thereby conflate them with slaves (133–50).[43]

While Saller's evidence cannot reveal the actual incidence of corporal punishment applied (or not applied) to slaves and sons, it does reveal the stereotyped attitudes and conventional expectations that marked Roman thinking about the *paterfamilias's* relationships with his children and with his slaves, and it is these stereotypes that are important for my discussion here.[44] For example, we can now see why, for Ro-

---

But I do not think his argument can hold up against the objections just discussed, or the positive evidence for normatively warm father-son relations discussed below. At least one reviewer, Slagter 1992, shares these reservations about Bettini's analysis.

[42] Garnsey 1970 shows that most forms of legally imposed corporal punishment were thought to be typically servile, and therefore degrading if imposed on high-status individuals: see 131–146 for discussions of condemnation to the mines or public works; capital punishment by way of *crematio*, the *crux*, or *damnatio ad bestias;* beatings by rods or whips; and torture (e.g., p. 145: "When treason was the charge, no man was safe from torture . . . the theory was that whoever threatened the life of the Emperor had forfeited his rights and privileges: he could be treated as a slave").

[43] There are certain exceptions: beatings could be applied to free men (and citizens) in the military (Saller 1994: 139–40), and the teacher who whips under-performing pupils was a literary topos (148–49). Aristocratic pupils were inevitably of higher status than their teachers, who were typically slaves or freedmen.

[44] Indeed, Saller 1994: 151 and n. 62 adumbrates aspects of my discussion in this section, pointing out that emperors who presented themselves as a *pater* were marking themselves as "non-exploitative figures of benign authority looking after the best interests of their subjects," thus rejecting the pejorative master-slave model. Alföldi 1971: 40–46 offers strong corroboration of this positive stereotype: he shows that, in the literature of the late republic (though he also adduces some evidence from the early empire), for someone

mans, the master-slave and father-son relationships might seem to be paired naturally as opposed types of power relationship. For these two relationships occur together in the *familia*, and furthermore, the empowered roles in these relationships, the roles of *pater* and *dominus*, are engrossed in the very same person, the *paterfamilias*. These relationships are, in a sense, opposite sides of the same coin; thus there is no surprise that Alexander adduces the image of the father to counter Hermolaus's invocation of the spectre of the master. Curtius's description of this episode may or may not transmit significant information about Macedonian customs and social practices. But it unquestionably engages a Roman elite audience's stereotyped expectations about the character of these different yet closely linked social relationships. Indeed, the contestation that Curtius represents in this passage regarding whether and to what extent the master-slave relationship is an appropriate model for the ruler's relationship to his aristocratic subjects, and whether an alternative paradigm, specifically the father-son relationship, might be applicable instead, would have been thoroughly familiar to Curtius's contemporary readership: for there is copious evidence that exactly this debate, in these very terms, raged unabated in Roman aristocratic society from the late republic through the Julio-Claudian period.

In no text is the high-stakes competition among alternative paradigms for a ruler's authority more vividly on display than in Seneca's *De Clementia*. Written near the beginning of Nero's reign and addressed to the young emperor,[45] this text explicitly sets out to construct an idealized image of the ruler—that is, an image that serves the interests of Seneca's elite readership—for Nero to emulate. In constructing this ideal, Seneca sets forth a variety of paradigms for the emperor's relationship with his subjects, including negative ones (those he should reject, such as the master-slave relationship) as well as positive ones (those he should embrace, such as the father-son relationship). While Seneca urges Nero to emulate the nonoppressive models for exercising power, all of Seneca's paradigms implicitly or explicitly concede the aristocracy's disempowerment in relation to the emperor. Indeed, the essay

---

to use the term *parens* or *pater* of another who is not in fact his father is invariably to imply the latter's superior standing/power combined with benevolent oversight of the former, in the context of a mutually warm, affectionate relationship. I will discuss many such passages in this section and the next.

[45] The dramatic date of the treatise is approximately A.D. 56: *Clem.* 1.1.6–7 suggests that Nero's reign has begun only recently, and at 1.9.1 he is said to have recently turned eighteen (*hoc aetatis . . . quod tu nunc es, duodevicensimum egressus annum*). There is no reason to doubt that the treatise was also composed at this time. On the date of the work, and the punctuation of the crucial passage, see Griffin 1976: 407–11. I assume that this work, like all of Seneca's ethical prose works, is implicitly addressed to a wide audience of Roman elites, not merely to its stated addressee.

opens with a disquisition on the immensity of Nero's power. In Seneca's representation, this power altogether transcends the human scale: Nero is made to describe himself as the agent of *deus* on earth and as the mouthpiece of *fortuna* (*Clem.* 1.1.2). He goes on to say that he controls the status and wealth of persons, kings, cities, and nations (1.2–3)—precisely the power, in fact, that Seneca elsewhere ascribes to *deus* and *fortuna*.[46] Specifically, he can decide which ones to destroy, to move, to liberate, or to enslave; he even calls himself the "judge of life and death over whole peoples" (*vitae necisque gentibus arbiter*), hinting at *paterfamilias*-like power over huge collectivities (§1.2; cf. 14.2, 21.2). Prominent among the instruments by which he can bring about these transformations are military force and the threat of violence generally, whose capacity to destroy and terrorize is specifically noted—even if, as Nero is made to declare reassuringly, he is not currently using them for that purpose.[47] To give a slightly reductive summary of Seneca's presentation of Nero's power here, then, it is the power to deploy violent force at will, and thereby to change radically the status of the collectivities or persons who are the objects of this violence. The qualification "at will" is crucial, however. For Seneca points out that the emperor is not bound by human laws (though he warrants praise if he chooses to observe them: *sic me custodio tamquam legibus, quas ex situ ac tenebris in lucem evocavi, rationem redditurus sim*, §1.4);[48] rather, his decision to deploy or not deploy the instruments of force depends entirely upon whether he is moved by things such as anger, impulse, or pity (*ira, impetus, misericordia*, 1.1.3–4). In the absence of any countervailing force or constraint of law, then, it is only these internal states of mind that determine when and how he applies violent, status-altering force to those under his sway.[49]

[46] That *deus* and *fortuna* designate the same universal governing principle, but seen from different perspectives, see n. 101 below. For emperors portrayed as operating (in Stoic terms) like *deus* or *fortuna*, see section 6 and nn. 108–9 below.

[47] *Clem.* 1.1.3: *non . . . me ad iniqua supplicia compulit . . . ipsa ostentandae per terrores potentiae dira sed frequens magnis imperiis gloria: conditum immo constrictum apud me ferrum est*. Similarly 1.1.2: *haec tot milia gladiorum quae pax mea comprimit ad nutum meum stringentur*.

[48] Griffin 1976: 150–51, 158–65 notes that, while questions of jurisdiction and procedure (especially *cognitio*) under the principate are prominent concerns of Seneca in this treatise, they are not his only ones, for many instances of clemency that are adduced here have no particular legal context. Thus, for Seneca, clemency is a virtue to be exercised outside as well as inside the strictly legal sphere, and correspondingly, the sorts of punishment (especially corporal punishment) remitted by clemency can be understood to be threatened in extralegal as well as strictly legal contexts.

[49] Likewise at *Clem.* 2.3.1–5.5, actions taken by the emperor, such as remitting deserved punishment or punishing excessively, are said to be rooted in his mental states: for such actions are attributed to *clementia, crudelitas,* and *misericordia*, which are all defined here as one or another type of *temperantia animi* or *inclinatio animi* or *vitium animi*.

Having thus articulated Nero's power in the opening sections of the essay, Seneca concerns himself thereafter with setting forth schematically two contrasting modes in which such power can be deployed, one "good" and one "bad." Though elements of this dichotomy can be found throughout the essay, it is developed most systematically in 1.11–13. At §11.4 Seneca prescriptively uses the word "king" (*rex*) to designate the all-powerful ruler who uses his power in the "good" mode, and "tyrant" (*tyrannus*) to designate the ruler who uses this power in the "bad" mode.[50] First, however, he enumerates outward similarities in their status and power (*species enim ipsa fortunae ac licentia par est*, §11.4): both "are wont to kill" (*occidere solent*, §12.1), and both are "equally fenced around with weapons" (*uterque licet non minus armis valletur*, §12.4). But their modes of employing these instruments of force are sharply distinguished. Kings kill only from necessity and for the public good, and *clementia* is their characteristic virtue, while tyrants kill for pleasure and display *saevitia* (§§11.4, 12.1; cf. 25.1–2). Therefore the tyrant is hated and feared, and has a bad reputation (*fama*, §12.3–4; cf. 17.3, 18.3, 19.5). He cannot trust his guards, his relatives, or anyone else (§§12.3, 13.1–3)—indeed, he dehumanizes his guards and soldiers by using them as instruments of torture, just as he uses the rack, the axe, or wild beasts (§13.2)—and people are driven in desperation to plot and rise against him (§12.4–5; cf. 8.7, 25.3–26.1). Under these circumstances, countervailing force is in fact applied to the ruler: his subjects violently impose from without the control upon the ruler's actions that he failed to impose from within. A king, on the other hand, does control his great power from within, governing it with his judgment: for his soul is characterized by its temperance, moderation, and inclination toward gentleness, among other things.[51] He has a good reputation (*fama*): people speak well of him both in public and in private (§13.4–5; cf. 1.5, 9.6, 10.2–3). People love him, defending his

---

[50] Throughout, Seneca designates the "good" ruler by *princeps* as well as *rex* (e.g., 1.1.5–6; these terms are linked at 1.3.3, 1.4.3, 2.5.2). In §12.1 he implicitly concedes that his prescriptive usages of *rex* and *tyrannus* do not align perfectly with their conventional usages: he notes that, on his definitions, Dionysius of Syracuse is a *rex* rather than a *tyrannus*, and that Sulla must be counted as a *tyrannus*. Also, Seneca adheres to these prescriptive definitions only fitfully outside this essay. He maintains these usages (e.g.) at *Ep.* 114.24, yet at *Ira* 3.16.2–17.1 it is *reges* who are savage and are attacked by their subjects. A good ruler/bad ruler dichotomy similar to but longer than the one in *Clem.* is found in *Ira* 3.16–24; some of the exempla from this passage I have discussed in chs. 2 and 3 above.

[51] E.g., 1.11.2: [*clementia*] *est in maxima potestate verissima animi temperantia . . . non cupiditate aliqua, non temeritate ingenii, non priorum principum exemplis corruptum quantum sibi in cives suos liceat experiendo temptare, sed hebetare aciem imperii sui.* Cf. 19.4, 20.2, 2.3.1–2 for the condition of the *animus* that characterizes the king/clement ruler.

safety and rule with life and limb. He can trust his guards, since he uses them to secure collective safety, and he is subject to no plots (§13.1, 5; cf. 3.3–4, 19.6–8). His arms, which he carries at his side, are for adornment only (13.5). Throughout this passage (and indeed the entire work), Seneca maligns the model of the tyrant, his lurid descriptions of its shortcomings and ill consequences for all parties serving as a barely veiled warning. At the same time he urges the model of the *rex* upon Nero, even as he avers that Nero's reign already functions in this mode.[52]

A striking feature of this scheme is the role played by corporal punishment. We have seen that Seneca attributes to the ruler the power to kill, torture, or imprison at will, and that the criteria for distinguishing him as king or tyrant include whether he uses his weapons and soldiers to do away with those who offend him, or to chastise only those who really require severe correction, while being clement otherwise; whether he uses these instruments to beset subjects, or to protect them; whether he must fear the same from his soldiers and subjects in turn. But corporal punishment is also prominently thematized in many passages other than those already cited. Several times Seneca compares the tyrant to a wild beast on account of their shared appetite for blood and slaughter (1.3.3, 5.5, 25.1). Conversely, he insists several times that the greatest achievement of the king is to save lives, in view of his power to diminish or end them (5.6–7, 26.5); the ruler should note the example of the "king" bee, whom nature left unarmed so that it could not be savage or exact costly punishment (19.2–3; compare the human king's ornamental arms at 13.5). Indeed, the king's aim is to "blunt the edge of his ruling power" (*hebetare aciem imperii sui*, 11.2) — where the sword metaphor vividly concretizes the ruler's control over instruments of violence and marks this control as the central and crucial aspect of the power he wields. This weapon again stands by synecdoche for the emperor's power at 1.11.3, where Nero is said to have boasted that he has never shed any human blood throughout the whole world, a boast the more remarkable because "the sword has never been entrusted to anyone at a younger age" (*nulli umquam citius gladius commissus est*).[53]

---

[52] The stereotypical characteristics of the Graeco-Roman tyrant underpin the oppositions Seneca draws in this passage between the cruel leader who must hedge himself with bodyguards and weapons because he is hated, and the clement leader "fortified" only (but more successfully) by the good will and love of his subjects. Here the stereotypical tyrant provides a benchmark, a negative canon against which Nero or any emperor can be measured in regard to how he manifests, wields, and sustains his power. For a detailed discussion of the tyrant figure see Tabacco 1985: 89–116.

[53] Similarly Augustus, though a "mild *princeps*," is said to have "plied the sword" as a youthful triumvir (*mitis princeps . . . in communi quidem rei publicae <clade> gladium movit*, 1.9.1). In these passages where the sword stands by synecdoche for the emperor's power to inflict corporal punishment, there is probably an allusion to this weapon's em-

Augustus provides an exemplary illustration of these precepts in his handling of the conspirator Cinna (*Clem.* 1.9; see ch. 3.5 above), for Seneca presents this emperor's commutation of the expected death penalty as a notable instance of *clementia*. Seneca, then, like Hermolaus in the passage from Curtius Rufus discussed above, articulates the legitimacy of the ruler—the rightness or wrongness of the way in which he exercises his power—substantially in terms of the physical violence that he does or does not inflict upon his elite subjects.

Now, the figures of the king and tyrant in this essay, being rather schematic and abstract, are themselves compounded from a variety of other, more familiar paradigms for authority. Among these paradigms are earlier rulers, notably Augustus (1.9–11, 1.15.1–16.1), Tiberius (1.1.6), and Alexander (1.25.1); various animals such as bees and lions (e.g., 1.5.5, 19.2–4, 25.1); and a number of authority figures found in human society, such as physicians (§§17.1–2, 24.1, equating antisocial behavior to disease), teachers, and military officers (16.2–4). Horse breakers and other animal handlers also make an appearance (16.4–17.1). In each case, Seneca considers whether the empowered figure gains better results by using violence against those under his sway, or by using other means. Most prominent among these many paradigms, however, are the relationships of master to slave and father to son.[54] This is unsurprising, since we have seen that the selective application of corporal punishment is an important technique by which the *paterfamilias* distinguishes his sons from his slaves, and since anxieties about the emperor's ability and willingness to impose corporal punishment loom large in this treatise. That is, the *paterfamilias*, in his dual roles of *pater* and *dominus*, is the obvious social paradigm for the authority of the emperor as it is portrayed in this work. Indeed, Seneca twice attributes to the emperor the "power of life and death" (1.1.2, 21.2), which we have seen is one of the powers legally comprising *patria potestas* and which the *paterfamilias* normally holds over both his legitimate children and his slaves.

---

ployment for carrying out judicial beheadings, which apparently became standard early in the Julio-Claudian period. This mode of punishment may have originated in the military (cf. Sen. *Ira* 1.18.3–6), and continued to be delegated to military commanders (see *ILS* 9200, from the reign of Vespasian or Domitian, where a procurator in Rhaetia claims to hold the *ius gladii*), but this power also naturally resided with the emperor himself. For further discussion and references, see Mommsen 1899: 923–25.

[54] Note that Seneca is entirely aware of, and draws attention to, his participation in a process of setting and evaluating paradigms for the principate, of generating metaphors by which this locus of authority can be comprehended: at §16.2 he writes, *in magna imperia ex minoribus petamus exemplum. non unum est imperandi genus: imperat princeps civibus suis, pater liberis, praeceptor discentibus, tribunus vel centurio militibus.*

The father-son relationship is particularly privileged as a positive model for the ruler's relationship with his subjects, receiving a lengthy development in 1.14.1–16.1. The specific point of connection that Seneca establishes between these relationships is the chastisement and correction of misbehavior. For like a good father, we are told, a king (i.e., the "good" ruler) makes every effort to set his wayward charge straight by gentle means, and only when these have failed does he resort to stiffer forms of punishment; whipping is explicitly said to be an extreme, undesirable disciplinary recourse of the last resort (14.1, 16.3). Obviously, it is the stereotypical father's well-disposed attitude and warm feelings toward his child that Seneca wishes to make paradigmatic for Nero's attitude toward his subjects. Indeed, Seneca points out that the father-son relationship has been institutionalized as a model for the emperor through the title *pater patriae*: at §14.2–3 he writes, "that which must be done by a parent must also be done by the *princeps*, whom we have called 'father of the fatherland' with no empty flattery in view.... we have called him this that he might know that *patria potestas* has been granted him, which is as moderate as can be, taking consideration for the children and subordinating his needs to theirs. Only after much delay would a father cut off his own limbs; even when he had cut them off, he would wish to replace them, and in the cutting he would groan, hesitating a great deal" (*hoc quod parenti etiam principi faciendum est, quem appellavimus patrem patriae non adulatione vana adducti. . . . patrem patriae appellavimus ut sciret datam sibi potestatem patriam, quae est temperantissima liberis consulens suaque post illos reponens. tarde sibi pater membra sua abscidat; etiam cum absciderit, reponere cupiat, et in abscidendo gemat cunctatus multum diuque*). The paradigmatic qualities of the father explicitly enumerated here are his nurturing, loving concern for the child, and (conversely) his hesitation in resorting to violent punishment. Similarly at §10.3, Seneca declares that Augustus well deserved the "name of father" (*parentis nomen*) because no bloodthirstiness (*crudelitas*) was directed against those who insulted him, because he "appeared to suffer punishment when he was exacting it," and because he did not kill, but merely exiled, those who committed adultery with his daughter Julia. Here again, Seneca presents the reluctance to impose corporal punishment as the hallmark of the father.

Conversely, the master-slave relationship is presented at length as a negative paradigm for the ruler's relationship with his subjects. Consider the following passage:

(1.18.1) servis imperare moderate laus est. et in mancipio cogitandum est, non quantum illud impune possit pati, sed quantum tibi permittat aequi boni-que natura, quae parcere etiam captivis et pretio paratis iubet. quanto iustius iubet hominibus liberis, ingenuis, honestis non ut mancipiis abuti sed ut his, quos gradu antecedas quorumque tibi non servitus tradita sit, sed tutela. (§2) servis ad statuam licet confugere; cum in servum omnia liceant, est aliquid quod in hominem licere commune ius animantium vetet. quis non Vedium Pollionem peius oderat quam servi sui, quod muraenas sanguine humano saginabat? . . . (§3) quemadmodum domini crudeles tota civitate commonstrantur invisique et detestabiles sunt, ita regum et iniuria latius patet et infamia atque odium saeculis traditur; quanto autem non nasci melius fuit, quam numerari inter publico malo natos!

It is praiseworthy to command your slaves with moderation. Even regarding a chattel-slave one must consider not how much the slave can endure without striking back, but how much the nature of fairness and goodness permits you, which bids you to spare even prisoners of war and those obtained for a price. How much more justly does it bid that you not abuse the free, the freeborn, and the well born like chattel, but treat them as people you have surpassed in rank and whose protection, not bondage, has been placed in your hands. Slaves may take refuge at a statue: although one can do anything to a slave, there is something that the common right of all living creatures forbids one to do to a person. Who did not hate Vedius Pollio even worse than his own slaves, because he fed his lampreys with human blood? . . . just as cruel masters are pointed out throughout the whole city and are hated and detested, so too the injuries inflicted by kings are more widely exposed, and their bad reputation and the hatred they incur is handed down to the ages. But how much better it would have been not to be born, than to be counted among those born to public woe!

In this passage Seneca alludes again and again to the antagonism and violence that was a stereotyped feature of the master-slave relationship, particularly the antagonism of master toward slave. The repeated references to the master's unlimited power over the slave, to his potential cruelty, and to the slave's endurance in the face of abuse (at least until he strikes back) make it clear that Seneca is here invoking violent corporal punishment at the master's hands as the hallmark of the slave's condition.[55] Yet Seneca's contention is that the ruler's power over his subjects—most important, his aristocratic subjects, as the crescendo *liberis, ingenuis, honestis* suggests (§18.1), where each term marks a progressively more exclusive social status—is precisely the same as that of master over slave, insofar as the ruler, like the master, can impose arbitrary

---

[55] For a collection of other Senecan passages in which mutual hostility of masters and slaves is presupposed, see Viansino 1979: 187–89.

corporal punishment on these subordinates.⁵⁶ Seneca is urgently arguing that this is an inappropriate paradigm for the ruler's relationship to his free (especially aristocratic) subjects, and hence for Nero: he should regard these rather as "people he has outstripped in rank" or as "wards" (*tutelae*). At the same time, Seneca's criticism of Vedius Pollio's cruelty to his slaves (§18.2), his statement at §18.3 that cruel rulers, like cruel masters, are hated and have bad *fama*, and finally his assertion at §26.1 that nations avenge the cruelty of tyrants just as slaves do that of masters, all stand as warnings of the negative consequences for the emperor should he embrace the master-slave relationship as a paradigm for his relationship with his subjects.⁵⁷

To summarize: In Seneca's *De Clementia*, and also in Quintus Curtius's account of Hermolaus's plot against Alexander, the expressed or implied evaluations of the ruler's behavior toward his aristocratic subjects depend largely upon the presentation of his authority as that of a master over slaves, or as a father over children: if the former paradigm applies, the ruler is "bad," while if the latter applies he is "good." In both of these texts, moreover, the choice between these paradigms turns largely upon an evaluation of the ruler's deployment of corporal punishment, which is regarded as appropriately applied by the *paterfamilias* to his slaves but not to his legitimate children. An aristocrat who suffers such punishment at the hands of his ruler therefore perceives a dissonance between his status as marked and enacted at the moment (that of a slave) and his status as a matter of birth, acculturation, self-perception, and usual treatment (that of an aristocrat); he consequently adjudges the ruler a "tyrant" to be resisted and overthrown violently, if need be, to avenge the injury and eliminate the dissonance. In Curtius's

---

⁵⁶ Cf. *Ira* 3.18.3–19.2, where Seneca is indignant at Caligula's imposition of typically servile punishments on aristocrats. For the figuration of Caligula as *dominus*, see n. 81 below.

⁵⁷ Seneca even suggests that the mapping of roles of master and slave upon emperor and aristocrats is reversed in the case of a good ruler. He notes that the ruler must take care what he says (1.7.4–8.1), to which Nero responds, *ista . . . servitus est, non imperium*. Seneca then dilates on the ruler's "slavery," the things others do that he cannot do (§8.1–7): not only has he no *arbitrium loquendi* (§8.1) but he cannot go around the city unarmed and without attendants (§8.2). This is the "slavery of supreme greatness" (*summae magnitudinis servitus*); like the gods, Nero cannot become less great; he is "nailed to his pinnacle" (*fastigio tuo adfixus es*, §8.3) — an image, perhaps, from crucifixion (cf. *Tranq.* 10.6, where people who are "slaves" to their good *fortuna* are "nailed up" on their peak [*in fastigio suo . . . suffixos*] and can hope only to "hang more at ease" [*securius pendeant*]; cf. *Polyb.* 6.4–5, *Vit.* 19.3, *Tro.* 339). The understanding of "slavery" in play here is the very general one of "not being able to do as one pleases"; for this articulation see sec. 2 and n. 16 above. On kingship as *nobilis servitus* in Seneca, and on this idea's Hellenistic precedents (ἔνδοξος δουλεῖα), see Adam 1970: 27–31, 119–24; for Tiberius's exploitation of this idea, see sec. 4 and n. 80 below.

text, these contrasting paradigms are applied to Alexander after he has whipped a young aristocrat, in order to legitimate or delegitimate the young man's plot to kill his ruler. In Seneca's text, these paradigms are being held up as alternatives for Nero to choose for himself, as divergent paths he can take; indeed, the *De Clementia* may be regarded as an urgent effort to set a model for the young emperor that will direct him to act in ways advantageous to aristocrats, lest they suffer further humiliations and injuries of the sort that occurred in portions of previous reigns. The deployment of the competing paradigms of master and father in these Julio-Claudian texts is therefore politically and ideologically significant.

4. COMPETING PARADIGMS FOR THE EARLY PRINCIPATE

The competing paradigms for ruling power set forth in the texts of Curtius and Seneca are by no means unique creations of these authors, though I chose to discuss these two texts at length because they lay out with particularly rich detail and texture the grounds for adducing one or another paradigm, and the ideological implications of so doing. But such contestations were omnipresent in Roman society from the late republic down at least to the succession of Trajan at the end of the first century A.D. In this section I will chart this contestation of paradigms from the civil wars through the Julio-Claudian period, with references to later manifestations of the debate when they seem to illuminate earlier manifestations. My aim, on the one hand, is to provide context for the disputes in the texts of Seneca and Curtius that were traced above, and conversely to show that by presenting these disputes as they do these writers locate themselves centrally in a pressing public debate about the character of the new social and political order. On the other hand, I hope to suggest that it is through precisely these contestations that the new order is being invented; that the alternative paradigms for imperial authority that are constantly being promulgated and debated in these texts are central to the construction of the autocratic regime, providing the channels through which its power can be seen as flowing legitimately or illegitimately.

Both the master-slave and father-son relationships had long been available as models for political relationships between powerful elites and other Romans, or among elites. I noted above (section 2) that in the conflict of the orders, according to Cicero, Livy, and others, plebeians claimed to be reduced to slavery when they suffered or were threatened with physical coercion and corporal punishment at the hands of the consuls and other patricians; they regarded their liberty as secure only when the plebeian tribunate functioned effectively. I see no reason to doubt that plebeians of the fifth century B.C. could have presented their situation in these terms, though of course there is no way to be sure that our sources are not retrojecting onto this archaic social struggle the language of later social struggles. We are on solider ground in the early second century B.C. with Ennius's *Annales*. In a fragment (105–109 Sk.) describing the public reaction to the death of king Romulus, the bereaved Romans invoke him with the words *o pater, o genitor* — that is, modeling him as a father. Cicero, who preserves the Ennian fragment in question in his *De Re Publica*, declares it proof of Romulus's benevolent rule that these early Romans invoked him as a father rather than as a master: thus Cicero shows that these alternative models for monarchic authority, one pejorative and the other ameliorative, were available in the late 50s B.C., when he composed this work.[58] Indeed, contemporary evidence from the civil wars and triumvirates of the 50s–30s B.C. shows that these paradigms were invoked constantly by the various rivals, each trying to make himself out as a benevolent authority figure seeking to liberate, or preserve the liberty of, the Roman people from the despotic aspirations of the others, who have reduced their fellow-citizens to slavery or threaten to do so. While my focus here is on the Julio-Claudian period, it is worthwhile to examine these late-republican rhetorical contestations, for there is continuity between the competitive paradigm setting of the civil war era and that of the early empire. That is, the deployment of alternative paradigms to give interested, ideologically invested representations of the Julio-Claudian emperors is an outgrowth of a similar set of deployments during the convulsive struggles of the late republic.

Caesar and Pompey both appear to have been tarred as "masters" who had enslaved or threatened to enslave the Roman people and/or senate, while each conversely claimed to be defending collective "freedom" against the threat of despotism posed by the other.[59] Caesar anchored his self-presentation partly in the claim that he was defending

---

[58] Cic. *Rep.* 1.64: "*o Romule Romule die, / qualem te patriae custodem di genuerunt! / o pater o genitor o sanguen dis oriundum!*" *non eros nec dominos appellabant eos quibus iuste paruerunt, denique ne reges quidem, sed patriae custodes, sed patres et deos*. For the contrast see also *Rep.* 3.37: the soul commands the body as a king commands his citizens or a parent his children, but it commands the *libido* as a master does his slaves, "because it constrains and breaks it" (*libidini autem ut servis dominus, quod eam coercet et frangit*).

[59] If our later sources are correct, Pompey was sometimes figured as a "master" well before the outbreak of civil war: e.g., Dio 37.49.5, 40.55.3; Plut. *Pomp.* 30.3, 5; cf. 54.4; such a presentation coheres with Caesar's claims to be a "liberator," as at *B.C.* 1.22.5: *se non maleficii causa ex provincia egressum, sed . . . ut se et populum Romanum factione paucorum oppressum in libertatem vindicaret* (cf. Dio 41.34.3).

the sacrosanctity of the tribunes; thus he tapped the common contemporary mode of articulating the ancient tribunate's function, namely that it defended plebeian liberty against the threat of slavish treatment — physical coercion and corporal punishment — posed by magistrates and patricians.[60] According to Dio, the leaders each maintained this self-presentation right up to Pharsalus: for in his account, Pompey and Caesar address their troops before the battle in similar terms, each claiming to be a liberator opposing the tyranny of the other, and holding up the spectre of war captivity and subsequent (chattel) slavery if his side is defeated.[61]

After his victory, Caesar sought to institutionalize his self-presentation as "liberator": he was proclaimed as such by senatorial decree, and a temple of Freedom was constructed. A different paradigm also emerges in the mid-40s B.C., as he began to be called *pater* or *parens patriae*, like Cicero, Marius, and a few others before him. This designation, as Alföldi (1971: 80–89) has shown, was closely linked in the late republic and early empire with the idea of the "preserver" of life (*servator*): saving a life was but a short conceptual jump from giving it in the first place as procreator. The appellation *parens* may therefore be understood in conjunction with Caesar's clemency, the lifesaving consequences of which are symbolized by the crowning of his statues with the *corona civica*, the oak wreath indicating that the wearer had saved the life of a fellow citizen (ch. 3 n. 94 above). But the appellation *parens/pater* also, inevitably, conveyed the idea that Caesar was a benevolent tutor of his "children" in the stereotypically paternal fashion, bound to them by obligations of *pietas*.[62] His opponents, however, could figure

---

[60] For Caesar's claims to be preserving tribunician sacrosanctity, see *B.C.* 1.7.3–4, 8; 1.22.5, 1.32.6, 1.33.3–4; also Raaflaub 1974: 152–55, 174–80. Lucan, characteristically rewriting Caesar, makes him a conspicuous violator of tribunician sacrosanctity when he first verbally abuses and then threatens violence against the tribune Metellus, who attempts through a (literal) *intercessio*, a stepping-in-between, to keep Caesar from plundering the treasury (3.112–168). Here Metellus is said to be the embodiment of *libertas* (3.114), and he withdraws only when Cotta makes a remarkable speech (145–152) explaining that *libertas* is gone but for its shadow. Since all are now slaves of Caesar, and since slaves cannot own property, it follows (suggests Cotta) that there is no more collective property — *res publica*, represented here by the contents of the treasury — to defend. Thus Metellus is persuaded to step aside, withdrawing his tribunician veto; with this account Lucan shreds the historical Caesar's self-presentation as defender of tribunician power. On Caesar and Metellus see Raaflaub 177–79.

[61] Speeches before battle: Dio 41.57.2–3. The suggestion that all Romans would be "slaves" to the victor of this battle is already made by Cic. *Att.* 8.11.2; it becomes a trope of this battle in the Julio-Claudian period and after (Lucan 2.38–42, 314–23; Sen. *Ben.* 2.20.2, Dio 41.56.1, 41.59.4).

[62] Caesar as "liberator," temple of liberty: Dio 43.44.1. For Caesar being lauded as *servator*, and his statues crowned with the oak wreath, see e.g., Cic. *Lig.* 6, 19; App. *B.C.*

him as a "master" all the same. Cato is said to have declared that, having been reared in "freedom," he could not now learn "slavery"; indeed, in the early empire "Cato" and "freedom" become metonymies for each other, a figuration that is significant precisely in the context of a Rome putatively "enslaved" to Caesar, who therefore stands as master.[63] Moreover Caesar's assassins aggressively represented themselves as "liberators," as indicated not least by the coin of Marcus Brutus discussed at the beginning of this chapter, where the daggers flanking a *pilleus* figure Caesar's murder as an act of manumission. The assassination itself, as described by later sources, is a confrontation of the "master" model with the "father" model. For while the self-styled "liberators" presented Caesar as a master, Caesar's own enigmatic dying words to Brutus, "you too, child" (καὶ σύ, τέκνον: Suet. *Iul.* 82.2; cf. Dio 44.19.5) — whether regarded as a poignant reproach or as a curse — cast in Brutus's teeth the paternal model which Brutus, above all others, should have embraced. For Caesar had spared Brutus's life after Pharsalus, preserved his property, and advanced his career (appointing him governor of Cisalpine Gaul in 46, and *praetor urbanus* starting 1 January 44). The lifesaving in particular, as we have seen, could be regarded as placing Caesar in the position of *pater* relative to Brutus,[64] and the fact that Seneca, writing a century later, denies that Brutus had to regard Caesar as his parent constitutes further evidence for a widespread expectation in the early empire that one who had been saved would or should regard his savior in this way.[65]

2.106; discussion at Alföldi 1971: 66. For the connection between the *servator* imagery and the *pater/parens* appellation, ibid. 84–89. In general, Alföldi 80–101 offers a thorough and illuminating discussion of the phrases *parens patriae/pater patriae* in the late republic and early empire. Yet his overall contention that, in Caesar's case, these designations were a prerequisite to or perhaps dissimulated monarchic rule, has been questioned: for a critique see Yavetz 1983: 38–43.

[63] Dio 43.10.5: ἐγὼ μὲν ἔν τε ἐλευθερίᾳ καὶ ἐν παρρησίᾳ τραφεὶς οὐ δύναμαι τὴν δουλείαν ἐκ μεταβολῆς ἐπὶ γήρως μεταμαθεῖν (cf. Plut. *Cato Minor* 54.6, 59.8; on Cato and *libertas* see sec. 6 and n. 106 below). The victorious Caesar is also figured as a master at Suet. *Iul.* 80.1: *populo ... clam palamque detrectante dominationem atque assertores flagitante.*

[64] Thus the word τέκνον is not simply a generic endearment (though it is an endearment; see Dubuisson 1980: 882–84): it retains a particular point, even if the improbable story that Caesar was in fact Brutus's father (Plut. *Brut.* 5.1–2) is rejected. On the history of Brutus's relationship with Caesar see Dubuisson 1980 and Russell 1980. The latter shows that καὶ σύ is a colloquial apotropaic utterance to ward off the evil eye; hence the suggestion that Caesar's last words were a curse.

[65] Sen. *Ben.* 2.20.3: [sc. Brutus] *vitam accipere debuit, ob hoc tamen non habere illum parentis loco.* Conversely, Valerius Maximus regularly condemns Brutus and his fellow conspirators as "parricides" (*parricidae*: 1.5.7, 1.6.13, 1.7.2, 1.8.8), implying that they did incur the obligation to regard Caesar as *pater*, and Suetonius reports (*Iul.* 88) that the Ides of March were subsequently designated "parricidium" — a particularly pointed and public assertion of the "father" model.

By calling themselves liberators, however, the conspirators effectively imposed constraints upon their own actions, or at any rate this is the later tradition: for Dio reports that they refrained from killing Antony, Lepidus, and perhaps others at the same time as Caesar, because they wanted this self-presentation to remain credible; many corpses (says Dio) would have opened them to charges of seeking ruling power for themselves. A similar account given by Velleius Paterculus (2.58.2) shows that the tradition that the conspirators felt themselves constrained by their own paradigm setting was current at least by the reign of Tiberius; this tradition may well reflect their actual concerns.[66]

When Octavian emerged as Caesar's heir, Brutus redeployed his metaphor, now presenting Octavian as a "master" (actual or potential) in opposition to whom his own self-presentation as "liberator" remained meaningful. In a letter to Atticus, Brutus complains about Cicero's relationship with Octavian: "So long as he has people from whom he can get what he wants, and by whom he is cultivated and praised, he does not disdain slavery provided it confers honor." Later in the same letter he declares, "For *my* part, at any rate, no condition of slavery will be so good as to deter me from waging war against the real problem—i.e., against autocracy and unprecedented military posts and domination and power that aspires to be above the law—even if he [Octavian] is a good man, as you write, which I have never regarded him. But our ancestors did not wish even a parent to be a master."[67] By suggesting that Cicero stands as a (willing) "slave" to Octavian, and by asserting that the overall political arrangements made on Octavian's behalf im-

---

[66] For the assassins as "liberators," see e.g., Dio 44.1.2, 44.21.1, 44.35.1; for the constraints imposed by their claims to be restoring "freedom," see Dio 44.19.2: φοβηθέντες δὲ μὴ καὶ ἐκ τοῦ πλήθους τῶν ἀπολομένων διαβληθῶσιν ὡς καὶ ἐπὶ δυναστείᾳ ἀλλ᾽ οὐκ ἐπ᾽ ἐλευθερώσει τῆς πόλεως, <ἣν> προεβάλλοντο, τὸν Καίσαρα πεφονευκότες. Vell. Pat. 2.58.2: *quem* [sc. *Antonium*] *cum simul interimendum censuisset Cassius testamentumque Caesaris abolendum, Brutus repugnaverat dictitans nihil amplius civibus praeter tyranni (ita enim appellari Caesarem facto eius expediebat) petendum esse sanguinem* (cf. Plut. *Ant.* 13). Tac. *Ann.* 1.8.6 seems to adopt the assassins' rhetoric of "liberation," while noting the competing interpretations of the Ides of March: *diem illum crudi adhuc servitii et libertatis improspere repetita<e> cum occisus dictator Caesar aliis pessimum aliis pulcherrimum facinus videretur.*

[67] Brut. *apud* Cic. *ad Brut.* 1.17.4: *dum habeat a quibus impetret quae velit et a quibus colatur ac laudetur, servitutem honorificam modo non aspernatur.* §6: *ego certe, quin cum ipsa re bellum geram, hoc est cum regno et imperiis extraordinariis et dominatione et potentia quae supra leges se esse velit, nulla erit tam bona condicio serviendi qua deterrear, quamvis sit vir bonus ut scribis [Antonius], quod ego numquam existimavi. sed dominum ne parentem quidem maiores nostri voluerunt esse.* (Here Antony's name is apparently an intrusive gloss, and incorrect; Watt suggests that it displaced *iste*, i.e., Octavian). Cicero himself, at the very same time, was busily tarring Antony as a "master," to be resisted to the death by all freedom-loving Romans under the leadership of Brutus and Octavian (*Phil.* 3.34–36).

pose a general condition of "slavery" (which must be resisted), Brutus implies that Octavian is a "master." It would make no difference, he suggests, if Octavian were a good man (hence a benevolent authority figure), for even a "good condition of slavery" is no less slavery, and not even a parent (the most benevolent authority figure of all) should assume the role of a master. Thus, having initially constructed himself as "liberator" in opposition to Caesar, Brutus here maintains this self-presentation by positioning Octavian as a new or would-be "master." Indeed, he maintained this self-presentation to the very end, using *libertas* (or perhaps ἐλευθερία) as a watchword before the battle of Philippi (Dio 47.43.1; also 47.42.3–4).

Octavian himself, meanwhile, also sought to cast his opponents in the role of "master," and so arrogate to himself the role of "liberator." One attestation is discussed above (section 2): namely, the opening of the *Res Gestae*, where he declares "I claimed the republic as free, when it had been oppressed by the despotism of a faction" (*rem publicam a dominatione factionis oppressam in libertatem vindicavi*), apparently with reference to driving Antony from Rome in late 44 B.C. Later he levied an enormous fine upon the people of Nursia, who sided with the Antonians and suffered casualties resisting Octavian's forces: for they erected a commemorative inscription declaring that their men had fallen fighting for their liberty, thus casting Octavian as the would-be "master." His heavy retaliation suggests that he attached great importance to maintaining his self-representation in the valorized role of "liberator" and to evading the stigmatized role of "master."[68] Again in 28 B.C., a tetradrachm was minted in Asia minor bearing on the obverse Octavian's head and the legend "LIBERTATIS P R VINDEX."[69] Despite this aggressive self-presentation, however, his own actions continued to provide grounds for figuring him as a master. Suetonius (*Aug.* 27.4) reports an incident from 43 B.C. in which Octavian, wrongly suspecting the praetor Quintus Gallius of concealing a sword in his garment as he approached, had him seized, "tortured in a slavish manner" (*servilem in modum torsit*) and executed. Once again, then, a triumvir's application of arbitrary corporal punishment to an aristocrat triggers the invocation of the master-slave paradigm for his authority.[70]

For my purposes, the application of these paradigms in these civil-

---

[68] In Dio's version (48.13.2–6), the events in question occurred in 41 during Octavian's war with L. Antonius; in Suetonius's version (*Aug.* 12) they occurred in 43, the Nursians having sent a contingent to fight for the Antonians at Mutina.

[69] *RIC* I² p. 79, *BMC* I 112; for a discussion of the coin see Hammond 1963: 94–95.

[70] Again Marc Antony, in his speech just before the battle of Actium (as imagined by Dio), claims for himself the role of liberator, while presenting Octavian as a master who has enslaved all his supporters (50.22.3–4).

war contexts has three noteworthy aspects. First, a single social paradigm could be applied to a given political situation in different ways, to serve different interests: Caesar and Pompey could each claim to be a "liberator" and that the other was a "master." Second, alternative paradigms could be applied to a single situation, each giving that situation a specific complexion that served a particular interest: were Caesar and Octavian benevolent "father" figures, as they themselves maintained, who constituted a community of interest with their "children," or malevolent "master" figures lording it over their "slaves" in a relationship of implacable mutual hostility, as their opponents implied? Third, social paradigms were not simply picked out of the blue: anyone who sought to present himself as "liberator" had first to make a credible case that current circumstances constituted "slavery," and moreover had to conduct himself appropriately. Thus Caesar, seeking the support of certain groups (presumably subelites in particular), made an issue of tribunician sacrosanctity, tapping the ancient fear of corporal punishment associated with the absence of effective tribunician power. Similarly, Caesar's assassins feared losing credibility as "liberators" if the body count went higher than one. Each of these aspects remained important in the early empire, when these paradigms were used to model the relationship of the emperor to his subjects.

And so it is in the case of Augustus. Our sources declare that the people, the equestrians, and the senate vigorously urged him to accept "officially" the honorific appellation *pater patriae*; after initial resistance, he assented and regarded himself as highly honored (Suet. *Aug.* 58, Aug. *Res Gestae* 35, Ovid *Fasti* 2.127–28).[71] Conversely, Suetonius reports that Augustus considered it a reproach and an insult to be called *dominus* and, after observing the public acclamation for an actor who spoke the words *o dominum aequum et bonum* in his presence, he forbade that anyone ever refer to him by that term (*Aug.* 53.1, further discussed below; cf. Dio 55.12.2)—a stance consistent with his triumviral self-presentation as a liberator but not a master. A prominent element in both of these anecdotes is the implied dialogue between Augustus and his subjects: in both cases the latter put forward a paradigm for their relationship with him, labeling him *pater* and *dominus*; Augustus in turn publicly accepts the one and vetoes the other. He thereby participates in the construction of a benign, ameliorative public image of his authority: other Romans stand in relation to him as children to their father, and expressly not as slaves to a master. Not that parenthood is easy, however. Macrobius reports a wry witticism by Augustus

---

[71] Alföldi 1971: 92–93 notes that Augustus was already being addressed as *pater* well before the "official" senatorial act of 2 B.C. (e.g., Dio 55.10.10).

regarding his difficulties in handling children of both the biological and metaphorical varieties: "he said that he had two frivolous daughters with whom he had to put up, namely the state and Julia" (*dixit duas habere se filias delicatas quas necesse haberet ferre, rem publicam et Iuliam*, Sat. 2.5.4).

The Augustan poets also participate in this dialogical construction of imperial authority, propounding and evaluating alternative models. Ovid, as just noted, addresses Augustus as "blessed father of his country" (*sancte pater patriae*, Fasti 2.127–28), and a few lines later contrasts him favorably with Romulus as follows: *vis tibi* [i.e., to Romulus] *grata fuit, florent sub Caesare leges, / tu domini nomen, principis ille tenet* (2.141–42). That is, the model of the master is appropriate for Romulus, who embraced *vis*, unlawful violence (in the preceding couplet Ovid alludes to the rape of the Sabine women), but is not an appropriate model for Augustus, under whom the laws flourish: for him, *princeps* is the appropriate designation. Horace, on the other hand, offers up no such alternatives, but simple unanimity: in an apostrophe to Augustus he writes "here may you enjoy being called *pater* and *princeps*" (*hic ames dici pater atque princeps*, Carm. 1.2.50), which suggests not only that Augustus sanctions these particular paradigms, but also that the people who so address him agree with him that these are the proper terms. The designation *princeps*, as is well known, was applied to leading senators in the late republic to indicate high standing and great *auctoritas* (perhaps manifested in such perquisites as speaking first in senatorial deliberation), but did not mark any specific, definable "official" powers.[72]

There is a further complexity with the term *dominus*, however. I mentioned above a passage of Suetonius (*Aug.* 53.1) in which Augustus is said to have grown angry when a crowd hailed him by this appellation. Here is the passage in full:

> domini appellationem ut maledictum et opprobrium semper exhorruit. cum spectante eo ludos pronuntiatum esset in mimo "O dominum aequum et bonum!" et universi quasi de ipso dictum exultantes comprobassent, et statim

---

[72] Cicero frequently uses the word *princeps* in this sense (sometimes with a defining genitive such as *senatus* or *civitatis*, but usually without): referring to Pompey, see e.g., Pis. 25, Red. Quir. 16, Phil. 11.18; referring to Q. Catulus, Pis. 6; indicating no specific person, Dom. 42, Phil. 2.52. See also Sal. Or. Macri 23, where the role of a *princeps* (in this late-republican sense of the word) is opposed to and contrasted with *dominatio*. For the lack of "official" powers, cf. Aug. Res Gestae 34: *post id tempus* [27 B.C.] *praestiti omnibus dignitate, potestatis autem nihilo amplius habui quam qui fuerunt mihi quoque in magistratu conlegae*. For discussions of the designation *princeps* applied to the emperor, cf. Mommsen 1887: II 774–76; Wickert RE 22.2057ff. ("*princeps* als Bezeichnung des Kaisers").

manu vultuque indecoras adulationes repressit et insequenti die gravissimo corripuit edicto; dominumque se posthac appellari ne a liberis quidem aut nepotibus suis vel serio vel ioco passus est, atque eiusmodi blanditias etiam inter ipsos prohibuit.

> He always shuddered at the appellation *dominus*, considering it an insult and reproach. When he was watching a theatrical show and the words "O fair and good *dominus!*" were delivered during the performance of a mime, and the whole audience expressed its delighted approval as if these words were spoken about him, he immediately squelched this shameful flattery with his gesture and expression, and the following day he rebuked them with a stern edict. After this he did not permit himself to be called *dominus* even by his children and grandchildren, whether in earnest or in jest, and he even prohibited them from using blandishments of this sort among themselves.

If Augustus takes offense because he regards *dominus* as an invidious designation (*maledictum et opprobrium*), marking his relationship with this public as one of master to slave and involving all the mutual hostility and antagonism that we have seen was a stereotyped feature of that relationship—and I believe this is the correct interpretation, since he so diligently defended his self-presentation as "liberator" during the civil wars—then his interpretation is evidently at odds with the intentions of the spectators. For they label him a "good and fair" master, and Suetonius calls their behavior *adulatio*, suggesting that (in Suetonius's view) they suppose that this designation will please Augustus and make him well disposed toward them, far from implying that their relationship with him is mutually antagonistic and his power oppressive. Furthermore, if his children and grandchildren called him *dominus*, and even called one another *dominus* (*inter ipsos:* or does this mean that they were calling Augustus *dominus* out of his hearing?), these usages are hard to reconcile with this term's invidious, pejorative connotations as described above.

In fact, a variety of nonpejorative usages of *dominus* are attested in everyday parlance in the early empire. These usages are collected and discussed by Bang 1921, who shows that this word (and its Greek equivalent κύριος) was commonly used to address or refer to someone whom the speaker wished to present as his social superior. It constituted an attempt to gratify the addressee, and marked the speaker's deference to him. But it is also attested as a courteous form of address between persons not involved in any sort of social relationship, who were perhaps even unknown to one another. Furthermore, it was commonly used within the family: not only did wives and children address the *paterfamilias* in this way (as one might expect), but husbands also thus addressed their wives, parents their children, and siblings each other.

Bang also notes, without discussion, the common use of *dominus* and *domina* as terms of endearment addressed to one's lover, which is probably contiguous with the use of these terms to designate one's husband or wife. While the vast majority of Bang's evidence postdates the Julio-Claudian period (he surveys the first three centuries A.D.), there exist at least a few Julio-Claudian instances or attestations of almost all his categories of usage; thus his analysis seems applicable at least in its broad outlines to my investigation here.[73] The consequence of his demonstration is that the word *dominus* does not, on its own, automatically project into its context the invidious associations of the master-slave relationship; nor is this surprising, since, as noted above (n. 12), the word's basic meaning is "owner" of the household, of which slaves are but one part. Only in context can its tone be assessed as deferential but friendly, or intimate, or fawning, or on the other hand invidious, marking the oppressive, mutually hostile relationship of master to slave.

This very ambiguity, however, is an ideologically salient feature of the word, and crucial for my discussion here: for it is possible to contextualize and recontextualize a given occurrence of *dominus* so as to present it as polite/deferential or hostile, or even to retain the ambiguity artfully. Such strategic recontextualization is exploited by at least two authors at the end of the first century A.D. The emperor Domitian, we are told, demanded to be addressed as "master and god" (*dominus et deus*), which Suetonius says was characteristic of his arrogance (*adrogantia, Dom.* 13.1–2).[74] Martial, who did refer to Domitian as *dom-*

---

[73] The deferential usage directed at social superiors is best known from Martial, who commonly designates the men he cultivates as *dominus* or *rex* or both (1.112, 2.32, 2.68, 4.83, 5.57, 6.88, 9.92.5–6, 10.10). I have found no certain instances in Julio-Claudian texts, but this may be the sense at Petr. *Sat.* 57.2. For this usage see Bang 85. Calling one's father or grandfather *dominus*: aside from the passage of Suetonius just quoted (*Aug.* 53.1), see Bang 83. Other members of the family calling one another *dominus/domina*: again Suet. *Aug.* 53.1 (the children call one another *dominus* [?]); also Seneca casually refers to his brother Gallio as *dominus meus* (*Ep.* 104.1); for husband and wife calling one another *dominus/domina*, see Petr. *Sat.* 66.3, 67.9; on these interfamilial usages see Bang 87–88. Polite address directed at strangers: Sen. *Ep.* 3.1 (*quomodo obvios si nomen non succurrit "dominos" salutamus*); Suet. *Cl.* 21.5 (at games Claudius tried to be affable, counting out money on his fingers, making jokes, and calling everyone *dominus*); Dio 61.20.1 (Nero, when performing on the cithara, addresses his audience κύριοι ἐμοί, in the usual fashion of citharoidoi); Bang 86. See also Neumann *RE* 5.1305ff. ("*dominus als Kaisertitel*").

[74] On this appellation, see also Aur. Vict. *Lib. de Caes.* 11.2, *Epit. de Caes.* 11.6, and Dio 67.5.7, 13.4. Thompson 1986, however, recovers a more nuanced history: for he demonstrates that a wide variety of appellations were directed at Domitian, even in the last years of his reign, the vast majority of which were not *dominus et deus*. He therefore suggests that this particular appellation, which is manifestly fawning, should not be seen as dictated from above (for it was demonstrably not always used), but strategically de-

inus et deus (among other things) while Domitian lived (5.8.1, 9.66.3; cf. 7.34.8), declares in a poem written after the emperor's death (10.72) that his use of this designation was mere flattery, and he will use it no more: "In vain, Flattery, do you come to me, wretched with your worn lips: I am not going to say *dominus et deus*" (*frustra, Blanditiae, venitis ad me / adtritis miserabiles labellis: / dicturus dominum deumque non sum*, vv. 1–3). He then banishes Flattery to the land of the Parthians, declaring that in its shameful and abject suppliancy it should kiss the feet of their kings (5–7)—in other words, that such an address is appropriate to a tyrannical eastern despot. At this point, then, we perceive that the term *dominus* has been recontextualized: having at first been declared a flattering, and therefore false, designation for Domitian, it then is held a true designation for a despotic ruler—true in the pejorative sense of a master tyrannizing his slaves. This shift is further articulated in the next lines, where Martial contrasts *dominus* with other, ameliorative names by which the new Roman emperor will be designated: "This man is no *dominus*, but rather *imperator*, and the justest senator of all" (*non est hic dominus sed imperator, / sed iustissimus omnium senator*, 8–9); also "under this princeps" (*hoc sub principe*, 12); *dominus* is now marked not (or not merely) as a flattering address, but as an invidious one that can*not* be applied truthfully to the new emperor.[75] The younger Pliny also exploits this ambiguity. On the one hand, he condemns Domitian by saying that the emperor acted on a certain occasion "with the monstrousness of a tyrant, and the licence of a master" (*immanitate tyranni, licentia domini*, *Ep.* 4.11.6)—the accompanying words force *dominus* here to be understood pejoratively, as a master in relation to slaves—and he praises Trajan by negating these same labels and presenting alternative paradigms: "for I speak not of a

---

ployed by inferiors who sought to ingratiate themselves; it was then re-presented after Domitian's death as being his preferred/required form of address, and so offered as evidence of his tyrannical nature. This reconstruction facilitated the rhetorical use of Domitian as the negative pole in a bipolar contrast with the benevolent nature of Trajan. Thompson's thesis is persuasive, and congenial for my own argument: for he shows, as I seek to show, that these imperial appellations were deployed at different times to different ends by people with different interests.

[75] A similar recontextualization and reinterpretation occurs in Martial 2.68. He asserts at the beginning of the poem that he no longer addresses Olus as *dominus et rex* (v. 2) because he has decided to "buy his cap of freedom," despite the material cost involved (*totis pillea sarcinis redemi*, v. 4). In v. 2, where it is conjoined with *rex*, *dominus* implicitly carries polite, deferential connotations, suggesting that Martial has been cultivating Olus (see n. 73 above) in hopes of initiating an exchange relationship, and is positioning himself as the subordinate party. But these connotations are overturned by the manumission imagery in v. 4, which forces *dominus* to be (re)conceptualized, pejoratively, as "master" in relation to slaves.

tyrant, but of a fellow citizen; not of a master, but of a parent" (*non enim de tyranno, sed de cive, non de domino, sed de parente loquimur*, *Paneg.* 2; cf. 55.7). Yet in the letters of book 10, Pliny addresses Trajan as *domine* no less than eighty-two times; this usage is polite and deferential, apparently synonymous with his other, less common but manifestly polite, forms of address such as *imperator optime* ("most excellent commander," three times in book 10).[76]

The possibility for such recontextualization and reinterpretation suggests a way of understanding Augustus's reaction to his acclamation as "good and fair master" in the passage quoted above. In this phrase the adjectives seem to constrain the noun to be interpreted in an ameliorative way: Suetonius, at any rate, says that the address constituted "flattery" (*adulatio*) of Augustus, implying that the crowd meant to please Augustus through its display of deference. Augustus, however, either himself took the designation *dominus* in bad part, regarding it as an insult and reproach despite the presence of the ameliorative adjectives, or feared that others might take it in this way, as implying that he was a stereotypically exploitative, cruel master in a mutually hostile relationship with his slaves. Therefore he not only forbade others to address him so, but sought also to terminate the interfamilial usages of the term in his own household,[77] lest these usages too provide a handle for hostile presentations of his authority. Since the word was fraught with ambiguity, every occurrence potentially admitting of recontextualization and construction in the opposite sense, Augustus seems to have regarded the safest route to be to assume the worst (i.e., that the pejorative construction would always be available) and therefore sought to suppress the term altogether.

The contestation among paradigms for the new authority structure continued in following reigns as well. Like Augustus, Tiberius is said to have rebuked those who called him *dominus*, regarding it as an insult (Suet. *Tib.* 27, Tac. *Ann.* 2.87)—though again, I infer that those who used this address must have believed that he would find it a pleasing mark of their deference. He also never "officially" accepted the title *pater patriae* (as Augustus did in 2 B.C.), though it was offered repeat-

---

[76] *Domine* also appears as a form of address in a number of approximately contemporary (i.e., first to early second century) letters preserved on papyrus or wood tablets: see Cugusi 1992 no. 105 lines 4–6 (a letter from Vindolanda, datable to ca. A.D. 95–105), also no. 147 lines 8, 11.

[77] Suetonius presents this prohibition as surprising—*ne a liberis quidem; etiam inter ipsos*—as if such usages were completely unexceptional: for him, and presumably for his audience, it is the ban on these usages in this situation that is remarkable, not their occurrence.

edly.[78] But rather than merely reacting to and choosing among the models for his authority that were placed in circulation by others, Tiberius intervened actively in this collective process of paradigm setting. According to Dio, he often declared that "he was a *dominus* to his slaves, an *imperator* to his soldiers, and the *princeps* to everyone else," which I take to be an effort to dissuade people in general (i.e., those who were neither chattel slaves nor soldiers) from calling him *dominus* and *imperator*, and to promote the use of *princeps* instead.[79] Statements are also recorded in which he reverses the application of the master-slave paradigm. According to Suetonius (*Tib*. 24.2), he put on a show of hesitating to accept power after the death of Augustus, eventually taking it up after complaining that a "wretched and burdensome slavery" was being imposed upon him (*quasi coactus et querens miseram et onerosam iniungi sibi servitutem*). At another time he declared (*Tib*. 29) that a good *princeps* ought to be a slave to the senate (*senatui servire*), since he held power on their sufferance, and that he regarded the senators as "good, fair, and favorable masters" (*bonos et aequos et faventes vos habui dominos*); he further declared that his tasks should not be called "sacred" (as some had called them) but "laborious" (*Tib*. 27).[80] His advocacy of this inverted model failed to carry the day, however. For Tacitus (*Ann*. 3.65) says that the senate was always so excessively obsequious in its decrees that Tiberius, though no advocate of public freedom (*publica libertas*), grew weary of its overt servility, and whenever he left the curia would exclaim "men fit to be slaves!" We see, then,

---

[78] For his refusals see Tac. *Ann*. 1.72, 2.87; Dio 57.8.1, 58.12.8. Also, at Suet. *Tib*. 26.2 his rejection of the title *pater* is linked with his refusal to have the *corona civica* in his vestibule (for the connection between the symbolism of the civic crown and the designation *pater*, see on Julius Caesar above). But just as Augustus was called *pater* or *parens patriae* even before this title was "officially" conferred, so too Tiberius was in fact called this: e.g., Manilius *Astron*. 1.7, 1.925.

[79] Dio 57.8.2: πολλάκις γε ἔλεγεν ὅτι "δεσπότης μὲν τῶν δούλων, αὐτοκράτωρ δὲ τῶν στρατιωτῶν, τῶν δὲ δὴ λοιπῶν πρόκριτός εἰμι." Dio adds here that Tiberius was customarily addressed as Caesar, Germanicus, or πρόκριτος τῆς γερουσίας (= *princeps senatus*, 57.8.1). For Dio's own ruminations on the meanings and connotations of various imperial titles, see 53.18.2–3: regarding "father," he says that this was originally an honorific term of praise, marking warm, pious relations between ruler and ruled: ἵν' αὐτοί τε τοὺς ἀρχομένους ὡς καὶ παῖδας ἀγαπῶεν καὶ ἐκεῖνοι σφας ὡς καὶ πατέρας αἰδῶνται.

[80] I assume that the word *servire*, in conjunction with *dominus*, assures that the master-slave relationship is being adduced as the model for the Senate's authority, while the word *dominus* alone would provide no such assurance, given its alternative uses. Yet Tiberius suggests that this master-slave relationship is not a stereotypically hostile, exploitative one, since he insists that his masters are *boni et aequi et faventes* (though recall that Augustus took the address *dominum aequum et bonum* in bad part). A similarly tendentious attempt to present the state as master and the ruler as slave, rather than the other way around, is found at Sen. *Clem*. 1.7.4–8.3, discussed in sec. 3 and n. 57 above.

that Tiberius was not only the object of a public debate regarding how to model his relationship with with various groups in Roman society, but he actively participated in this debate. By approving or disapproving of paradigms that were in circulation or being proposed, and by proposing others himself, he attempted to exert control over public perceptions of his authority, or at least over what was expressed in public discourse about that authority.

Many more such examples of competitive paradigm setting could be adduced from the reigns of the later Julio-Claudian emperors. Such a multiplication of examples would add little new to my argument, beyond showing simply that these kinds of contestations continued throughout the Julio-Claudian period. A few broad points about these later emperors seem worth making, however. Caligula is said to have insisted on being called *dominus* (as Domitian later would do), in sharp contrast to his predecessors who strongly resisted being cast in this role. It is impossible to ascertain whether he imagined that all who so addressed him were being amicably deferential, or he actually wished to be seen as an oppressive master tyrannizing his slaves. The latter is perhaps not impossible, since Caligula's mutual hostility with the senate is well attested: both contemporary and later authors remark upon his penchant for exacting slavish services from aristocrats, and especially for imposing corporal punishment upon them, for which he is duly tarred as an oppressive and cruel master in relation to his slaves.[81] Claudius, though he too is said to have tortured free men despite having vowed not to do so (Dio 60.15.6), is usually implicated in a somewhat different set of social inversions: rather than conflating aristocrats with slaves through the imposition of servile duties or corporal punishments,

---

[81] For Caligula's insistence on being called *dominus*, see Aur. Vict. *Lib. de Caes.* 3.13: *his elatus dominum dici atque insigne regni nectere capiti tentaverat.* Also cf. *Epit. de Caes.* 3.8. For aristocrats discharging the duties of personal slaves to Caligula, such as running alongside his chariot and standing in attendance by his dining couch, see Suet. *Cal.* 26.2 (with Hurley 1993 ad loc.); *Galba* 6.3; also Sen. *Ben.* 2.12 for Caligula offering his foot to a senator to kiss, thereby "changing the customs of a free state into Persian slavery" and forcing an aristocrat to behave like a conquered enemy (hinting at the slave status of prisoners of war). For the slavish penalties, especially torture and whipping, that Caligula imposed on aristocrats, see Sen. *Ira* 3.18.3–19.5, esp. 19.1–2: *ceciderat flagellis senatores: . . . et hoc loco respondebitur: "magnam rem! si tres senatores quasi nequam mancipia inter verbera et flammas divisit homo qui de toto senatu trucidando cogitabat . . . ;"* also Suet. *Cal.* 27.3–4. On his hostility to the senate as a whole cf. Suet. *Cal.* 30.2, 49.1–2, and Dio 59.23.2–3 (discussed in ch. 3.6 and n. 105 above). Cf. Sen. *Apoc.* 15.2, where Claudius, newly arrived in heaven, is adjudged to Caligula as his slave, after Caligula adduces witnesses who had seen him beating his uncle. Note here both the representation of Caligula as physically abusive of aristocrats, and also the conceptual linkage between slavery and corporal punishment (to suffer beatings proves that one is a slave, or reduces one to that status).

Claudius is said to be a "slave" of his own slaves, freedmen, and wives, who are correspondingly elevated to positions of "mastery" over both him and others. Nero too is sometimes presented this way. Aristocratic ire at the elevation of imperial slaves and freedmen to aristocratic status, and at their undoubted power as confidants and deputies of the emperor, may be regarded as another manifestation of elite status anxiety in the Julio-Claudian period: not only are aristocrats subject to slavish treatment themselves, but certain slaves and freedmen are functioning socially and politically as senators and equestrians. I discuss these inversions at greater length in section 5 below. Furthermore Nero was regularly referred to after his death as a "master"—e.g., *extremum dominorum* (Tac. *Hist.* 4.42), *dominus nocens* (Stat. *Silv.* 2.7.61), and *dominus furens* (Martial 7.45.7), where the adjectives invite the pejorative interpretation of "master" in relation to slaves. Four of his challengers and successors, namely Civilis, Galba, Vitellius, and Vespasian, minted coins bearing the legends "LIBERTAS RESTITVTA" or "ADSERTOR LIBERTATIS PVBLICAE," suggesting that the moneyers thought at least some groups within the state, presumably including many of the elites, believed or could be persuaded that they had been "enslaved" to Nero and were now free.[82] Nero even had the political and ideological misfortune to face a rebellion led by one of his legates in Gaul, one Iulius Vindex (*PIR*^{2} I 628). This name served him well: Pliny the Elder, writing just a few years after the revolt and the subsequent civil wars, refers to *Iulium Vindicem, adsertorem illum a Nerone libertatis* (*Nat.* 20.160)—glossing the name Vindex as *adsertor* (*libertatis*), the man who claimed the state as free when it was wrongfully held in a slavish condition by Nero. Similarly, Dio calls Vindex a "lover of freedom" who sought to "free" the Romans, and the world, from Nero (63.22.1, 6; 24.4a). Suetonius adds (*Nero* 45.2) that people in Rome, by way of insulting Nero, would feign quarrels with their slaves in order to call out a demand for an avenger (*vindex*): here again, Vindex figures as a locus of resistance to Nero in part because his cognomen has meaning in the context of the social relations between masters and slaves.[83] Thus

---

[82] *Libertas restituta:* Galba (*RIC* I² pp. 205, 233, 254; the first of these concretizes the idea of "liberty restored" in a reverse type showing a *pilleus* flanked by two daggers, echoing the famous coin of Brutus), Vitellius (*RIC* I² pp. 268, 270–72), Vespasian (*RIC* II pp. 49, 68). *Adsertor libertatis publicae:* Civilis (*RIC* I² p. 214), Vespasian (*RIC* II pp. 65, 70). Manumission imagery is also found in Aur. Vict. *Epit. de Caes.* 5.9, who describes the public reaction to Nero's death as follows: *adeo cunctae provinciae omnisque Roma interitu eius exultavit, ut plebs induta pilleis manumissorum tamquam saevo exempta domino triumpharet.*

[83] Verginius Rufus's epitaph, given by Pliny *Ep.* 6.10.4, 9.19.1, includes the same gloss/pun on the words Vindex and *adsertor*, but in a way that distinguishes Verginius's aims from those of Vindex: *hic situs est Rufus pulso qui Vindice quondam / imperium adseruit*

at the end of the Julio-Claudian period as at the beginning and throughout, the emperor's power was reinforced and undermined, and the character and legitimacy of his authority was contested, through competing applications of familiar social relationships, principally those of master to slave and father to child.

In conclusion, I would suggest that this competition among alternative paradigms for the new social and political order was central to the development and evolution of that order. We have seen that not only the (potentially) oppressed aristocracy, but also the emperors themselves, participated in this debate, setting and rejecting different paradigms as appropriate or inappropriate, desirable or undesirable, and so were collectively involved in a continuing negotiation about the nature and limits of the emperor's authority. We have further seen that the affective connotations of the various term associated with these paradigmatic relationships (e.g., *servus, pater*) could motivate aristocrats and emperor to act (or not act) to change the character of their relationship; and that there was pressure on all parties to behave in accordance with the paradigmatic roles that they accepted as appropriate for themselves. To participate in this collective process of paradigm setting was to help invent the principate. In such a world, Seneca's attempt in *De Clementia* to persuade Nero to behave like a father was far from being a philosophical fantasy: it was an intervention in a vibrant, tense, high-stakes contemporary political debate, in which Seneca, as Nero's tutor, was well placed to speak influentially. To persuade Nero would indeed be to change the world.

My argument here, if persuasive, may have a further consequence, relating to the semantic questions raised in section 2 above. There I argued that the word *libertas* was fundamentally a negative term, meaning "the condition of not being a slave." This negative meaning was also sometimes reformulated in a positive way, as "the ability to do as one pleases." In the subsequent discussion, we have seen that when a power holder's relationship to other aristocrats is figured as that of a master in relation to slaves, he is most often said or implied to be im-

---

non sibi sed patriae. The implication may be that Vindex the *assertor* was not (in the elder Pliny's phrase) an *assertor libertatis*, but rather an *assertor imperii*—i.e., claiming it for himself (*sibi*)—yet was bested by Verginius who, though also an *assertor imperii*, claimed it rather for the state as a whole (*patriae*). It would be a neat convergence if Vindex himself had minted coins bearing the legend *assertor* (or *vindex*) *libertatis*, but no examples are known; he did however mint a type bearing the legend *Hercules adsertor* (*RIC* I² pp. 199, 207). The punning on the name Vindex and the word *adsertor* in political discourse during the years A.D. 67–71 has often been noted: for discussions of the literary and numismatic evidence, see Hammond 1963: 101–102, Baldwin 1975, Sutherland 1984, and especially Zehnacker 1987: 334–48 on the coinage of A.D. 68–69.

posing corporal punishments of various (stereotypically slavish) sorts upon them. That is, the salient feature of "slavery" in this respect is liability to beatings, torture, and execution in particular ways (*crematio, crux*, etc.).[84] If the frequency with which a theme appears in a society's documents is an indicator of the preoccupations and anxieties of members of that society, then anxiety about suffering these sorts of corporal punishments, and thereby potentially experiencing not only pain and death but also degradation to slave status, loomed large for Julio-Claudian aristocrats. The fear and/or reality of such penalties often stood as a barrier to "doing as they pleased." In many cases, then, what lurks behind deployments of the term *libertas* in the literature and political discourse of this period is a simple, gnawing fear of suffering corporal punishment—a powerful indicator of slavish condition, because closely associated with the slave experience—not a collection of abstract legal "rights" as Wirszubski and others have argued. This is true even in cases where the emperor's authority is not at issue. We saw, for example, that in late republican and early imperial articulations of the conflict of the orders, the plebeians' *libertas* is said to be secured by a properly functioning tribunate; when this office fails to function, plebeians suffer beatings, imprisonment, and executions at the hands of patricians, whereupon they claim to be treated as slaves. Similarly, the law that is sometimes appealed to in conjuction with *libertas* can be specified as that body of law granting citizens an appeal against physical coercion by magistrates. Even the power to speak one's mind is commonly formulated as *libertas* (see chapter 2.7 above), but only in explicit or implied counterpoint to some power that might punish such speech. These punishments, when specified, often include (but are not limited to) corporal punishment.[85] It would be false to claim that corpo-

---

[84] In addition to many passages cited above, a further striking instance of this conceptualization of slavery in the Julio-Claudian period is the declamation recorded by the Elder Seneca (*Cont.* 10.5) in which the Athenian painter Parrhasius is accused of harming the state because he purchased a war captive from Olynthus and tortured him to death, using him as a model for a painting of Prometheus. This case has many complications, but a particular question addressed by a number of the declaimers is whether this is an appropriate use of a slave, even though the law allows it (see e.g., the arguments "I bought him," "he is my slave," "it is permitted" at 10.5.1, 4, 15, 19). So while this declamation posits an extreme situation—the accused has purchased a slave for the purpose of inflicting corporal punishment on him; this is what the slave is *for*—it nevertheless supports my contention that vulnerability to corporal punishment is the major, perhaps defining, characteristic of slavery in the eyes of the aristocracy. Morales 1996 sensitively discusses the "limits of art" in this declamation.

[85] See, e.g., Sen. *Ira* 3.35.1–2: *respondisse tibi servum indignaris libertumque et uxorem et clientem, deinde idem de re publica libertatem sublatam quereris quam domi sustulisti. . . . quid clamas? quid vociferaris? quid flagella media cena petis quod servi loquuntur . . . ?* This passage neatly combines the idea that the emperor stands in relation to

ral punishment is *always* the implied fear or threat opposed to explicit assertions of *libertas*, for under particular circumstances other stereotypically slavish experiences — milder forms of castigation such as tongue lashings, or perhaps sexual (ab)use — may be more salient. But the prominent thematization of corporal punishment in those passages where aristocrats figure themselves as "slaves" to the emperor both implies and is in turn accounted for by the centrality of corporal punishment in aristocratic conceptions of slave experience.

5. Social Inversion and Status Anxiety

We have seen that emperors who imposed corporal punishment upon their aristocratic subjects, or treated aristocrats in other ways they regarded as stereotypically "slavish," stood to be portrayed pejoratively as "masters." In this section, shifting my focus somewhat away from the figure of the emperor himself, I further examine the anxieties about status that the imperial regime fostered among its elite subjects. For established aristocrats regarded their privileges and prerogatives as potentially threatened not only from above, by the degradation that emperors could impose, but also from below by upwardly mobile slaves and freedmen, primarily those in the imperial service. These anxieties are often articulated through a rhetoric of social inversion, where aristocrats are portrayed as slaves while slaves and freedmen are portrayed as these aristocrats' masters, or at the very least as aristocrats themselves. As with those ethical dilemmas discussed above in chapter 2, however, so in this situation Seneca offers his peers a Stoic solution, a way of stabilizing and reestablishing a social hierarchy with established aristocrats on top. For as I will argue below in section 6, aristocrats who embrace Seneca's philosophical ethics are promised status security both against challenges posed from above by the emperor, as were described in the last two sections, and from below by slaves and freedmen, as will be described in this section.

First, then, for aristocratic status anxieties associated with powerful imperial slaves and freedmen. While very few slaves and freedmen in the early empire actually accumulated sufficient economic, social, and cultural capital that they could plausibly be regarded and represented as

---

the aristocrat as the aristocrat does to his slaves, and that the subaltern in neither case has "free speech" in the sense of speaking out against the superior without having to consider that verbal or physical abuse may follow. Crook 1955: 142–47 collects instances in which emperors are said to tolerate the "free speech" of their aristocratic *amici* without retaliating physically. But the fact that they did not always retaliate physically does not eclipse the stereotypical expectation that they might and could.

claimants to aristocratic status, those who did created the perception among established aristocrats that radical social mobility was possible, and hence that crucial status distinctions could be (and indeed were being) effaced. The social phenomenon of powerful, wealthy, educated slaves and freedmen in the early empire has been well documented and thoroughly discussed; my interest here is in aristocratic expressions of unease or outrage at this phenomenon, and particularly in the rhetoric of social inversion that pervades contemporary discussions of this phenomenon.[86]

Politically engaged aristocrats had long employed skilled slaves and freedmen from their own households in various administrative and secretarial roles. When such slaves and freedmen, especially the latter, were in the immediate service of their master or former master, they could come to wield power as advisers, confidants, and deputies entrusted with making decisions on his behalf. Such men were acculturated as aristocrats, spent much time in an aristocratic social milieu, and in some cases disposed of large amounts of money; their lived experience in these respects strongly disaccorded with their degraded legal status.[87] An uneasy letter from Cicero to his brother Quintus, in 59 B.C. (*Q. fr.* 1.2), reveals that such a freedman provoked anxiety among established aristocrats even then, a full century before the heyday of the imperial freedmen. The freedman, named Statius, had arrvied in Rome to conduct business on Quintus's behalf; Marcus wrote his brother to describe both Statius's own conduct and that of others in relation to him:

> quod autem me maxime movere solebat, cum audiebam illum plus apud te posse quam gravitas istius aetatis, imperi, prudentiae postularet — quam multos enim mecum egisse putas ut se Statio commendarem, quam multa

---

[86] On the social mobility and power of Julio-Claudian freedmen and slaves, and on aristocratic reactions to them, see e.g., Weaver 1967, Millar 1977: 69–78, Saller 1982: 65–67. Wallace-Hadrill 1996 discusses how power devolves upon freedmen, slaves, and women by virtue of their proximity to a powerful man: he speaks specifically of the emperor and his "court," but the argument holds for other high-ranking aristocrats and their households, in both the republic and empire. On specific causes of elite resentment, see ibid. 299, and below.

[87] Millar 1977: 59–60, 70 argues that the existence of influential freedmen is an unsurprising result of the Roman tradition of exercising power in a domestic setting; he also notes the tensions that such power produced in aristocratic society. Ibid. 76–77 and n. 51 provides several examples showing that at least some of these powerful freedmen had, to one degree or another, internalized aristocratic ethics, engaged in aristocratic pursuits, and generally adopted an aristocratic lifestyle (Petronius's character Trimalchio is a fictionalized representation of such a freedman: he is represented as striving, with uneven success, to live and act as an *eques*). Weaver 1967: 4–5 uses the term "status dissonance" to describe the condition of these slaves and freedmen: they rank low according to certain criteria for assigning status (e.g., birth), but high according to others (e.g., wealth, education).

autem ipsum ἀφελῶς mecum in sermone ita posuisse, "id mihi non placuit," "monui," "suasi," "deterrui"? quibus in rebus etiam si fidelitas summa est (quod prorsus credo, quoniam tu ita iudicas), tamen species ipsa tam gratiosi liberti aut servi dignitatem habere nullam potest. (*Q. fr.* 1.2.3)

But what used to disturb me the most, when I heard that he had more influence with you than the weight of your years, your command, and your wisdom required—for how many people do you think requested of me that I commend them to Statius, and how often do you think he himself baldly declared, in conversation with me, "that didn't please me," "I advised him," "I urged him," "I discouraged him"? In these affairs even if he is utterly loyal (which I absolutely believe, since you consider him so), nevertheless the very appearance of a freedman or slave being in such favor cannot but be completely dishonorable.

The inordinate amount of influence that Statius is thought to have with Quintus is presented here as distorting, or even inverting, proper status relations. People who ask Cicero to commend them not to Quintus but rather to Statius cast the freedman in the role of the master. Also, Cicero's objection to Statius's use of expressions such as "that did not please me," "I advised him," and so on appears to be that Statius thereby adopts an imperious tone inappropriate for a freedman (the impropriety being conveyed by ἀφελῶς—"baldly," "artlessly") and so presents himself as being the authority who takes decisions rather than the mere agent of that authority. The very appearance of a slave or freedman enjoying such favor with his master, Cicero concludes, is lacking in *dignitas*—that is, Quintus's own social standing is damaged by his freedman's behavior, even as that behavior enhances Statius's standing.[88]

Julio-Claudian aristocrats too were bedeviled by perceived distortions in status relations, distortions associated with the prominence of certain imperial freedmen and slaves especially in the reigns of Claudius and Nero. For with the emergence of the emperor as the most powerful single individual in the Roman state, the power wielded by other members of his household, including women, freedmen, and slaves, inevitably increased proportionally. But great accumulations of power by such associates required the sanction, implict or explict, of the emperor. For example, Suetonius reports (*Aug.* 74) that Augustus always kept a strict account of status distinctions when inviting guests to dine with him; in particular, he never invited freedmen to to his table, with the single exception of Menas, who had warranted this honor by betraying Sextus Pompeius in 38 B.C, and besides had juridically ceased to be a freedman

---

[88] On Statius see Treggiari 1969: 158, 181.

since he was granted freeborn status, a gold ring, and made an equestrian.[89] By keeping his freedmen in the background in at least this respect, then, Augustus enacted in his own social practice the established aristocracy's sense of social propriety, its resistance to seeing freedmen socialize as aristocrats. Even Claudius, whose reign was notorious in the eyes of later aristocratic authors for the degree to which women and freedmen wielded power (e.g., Suet. *Cl.* 25.5, 29.1; Dio 60.2.4), was noted for conspicuously putting other peoples' slaves and freedmen in their places, and even some of his own—for example, confiscating the property of freedmen who took the initiative in socializing as equestrians (*libertinos qui se pro equitibus Romanis agerent publicavit,* Suet. *Cl.* 25.1; cf. Dio 60.12.2, 28.1; Pliny *Nat.* 33.33).

The power and prestige of Claudius's freedmen, however, is so frequently noted and lamented that it appears to have been regarded subsequently, and perhaps even contemporaneously, as one of the hallmarks of his reign. Consider first the status symbols that Suetonius says Claudius conferred upon various freedmen:

> Libertorum praecipue suspexit Posiden spadonem, quem etiam Britannico triumpho inter militares viros hasta pura donavit; nec minus Felicem, quem cohortibus et alis provinciaeque Iudaeae praeposuit, trium reginarum maritum; et Harpocran, cui lectica per urbem vehendi spectaculaque publice edendi ius tribuit; ac super hos Polybium ab studiis, qui saepe inter duos consules ambulabat; sed ante omnis Narcissum ab epistulis, et Pallantem a rationibus, quos decreto quoque senatus non praemiis modo ingentibus, sed et quaestoriis praetoriisque ornamentis honorari libens passus est. (Suet. *Cl.* 28)

> Of his freedmen he particularly esteemed Posides the eunuch, to whom he actually granted the *hasta pura* in the British triumph, along with the military men; no less did he esteem Felix, the husband of three queens, whom he put in charge of infantry cohorts and cavalry squadrons and the province of Judea. He also esteemed Harpocras, to whom he granted the right to be carried in a litter through the city, and the right to give public spectacles; and above these Polybius his literary secretary, who often went about between the two consuls. But above all he esteemed Narcissus his secretary of correspondence

---

[89] On Menas see chapter 3.2 above; on the significance of his gold ring, see Dio 48.45.7–9; on gold and iron rings as indicators of status, see Pliny *Nat.* 33.7–34, and n. 98 below. Weaver 1972: 282 suggests that receiving a gold ring actually conferred *ingenuitas* (similarly Treggiari 1969: 66, Millar 1977: 280, 488; at length, Duff 1928: 85–86, 214–20). The gold ring is also connected closely, but in a poorly understood way, with equestrian status: see Reinhold 1971: 279–87 on freedmen (and others) passing themselves off as equestrians by usurping the gold ring or other symbols of that status. Weaver 282–83 lists the few attested instances of imperial freedmen being granted *anuli aurei* in the first three centures A.D., concluding that the scantiness of this list is evidence for the actual exceptionality of such social mobility.

and Pallas the treasurer, whom he gladly permitted to be honored, by a decree of the senate no less, not only with immense monetary rewards, but also with the insignia of quaestors and praetors.

Each of these grants and favors is normally associated with equestrian or senatorial status, or is the prerogative of the emperor himself. Under the empire, the *hasta pura* was normally awarded to nobody in the army of rank lower than military tribune or prefect (both equestrian offices);[90] the right to give gladiatorial shows was by Claudius's reign restricted to those with equestrian census;[91] and the *quaestoria et praetoria ornamenta* provided to their bearer certain privileges (though apparently none of the responsibilities) of these senatorial magistracies, particularly the right to present himself publicly and socialize as a senator.[92] Also, the right to be carried within the city in a *lectica* may have been subject to age and status restrictions;[93] and the position between the consuls, obviously an honorific one, was sometimes occupied by Claudius himself (Suet. *Cl.* 23.2, Dio 60.16.3; cf. 59.12.2). In each case, then, freedmen are partaking, in one or more respects, in the privileges and responsibilities of the elites, and this apparent collapse or effacing of status distinctions makes the elites manifestly uncomfortable. Suetonius himself adduces these honors that Claudius bestowed upon freedmen as evidence of the ultimate social inversion: for at the start of the very next section (§29) he disapprovingly says that Claudius conducted himself not as *princeps* but as slave to his freedmen and wives, acting uncritically in accordance with their greed, prejudice, and lust.[94]

---

[90] An exception is the common soldier, M. Helvius Rufus, to whom Tiberius presented it (Tac. *Ann.* 3.21); this story is presumably related at least in part because of its exceptionality. For the military ranks and social statuses of recipients of the *hasta pura* at various times, see Maxfield 1981: 84–86, etc.; on Rufus see ibid. 65.

[91] In A.D. 27, after the collapse of a theatre, a *senatusconsultum* specified that no one whose census was less than 400,000 sesterces (the minimum equestrian census) might put on a gladiatorial show (Tac. *Ann.* 4.63).

[92] For the privileges and responsibilities conferred (and not conferred) by such *ornamenta*, see Borszák, *RE* 18.1111–12; also Lécrivain in Daremberg-Saglio 1887: IV 238–39. Claudius also granted *ornamenta consularia* to *procuratores ducenarii*, a fact that Suetonius presents as surprising (*Cl.* 24.1): presumably, the ground for this surprise is that such men, lacking equestrian census, are not of sufficiently high status to be placed symbolically among high-ranking senators.

[93] Julius Caesar, for example, imposed such restrictions in 45 B.C. (Suet. *Iul.* 43.1). See also Lamer, *RE* 12.1076–79.

[94] Suet. *Cl.* 29.1: *his, ut dixi, uxoribusque addictus non princpem se sed ministrum egit, compendio cuiusque horum vel etiam studio aut libidine honores exercitus impunitates supplicia largitus est, et quidem insciens plerumque et ignarus* (cf. Suet. *Vit.* 2.5). *Addicere* is the standard legal term for adjudging the possession of property, and in particular for assigning or making over a slave to the custody of a master. A *minister* is also generally a slave, either one who attends his master at a *convivium*, or a low-level functionary in-

The younger Seneca, a contemporary observer, also recognizes and describes such inversions. Arguing against the view that one cannot receive *beneficia* from a slave (*Ben.* 3.28), he ironically suggests that his aristocratic addressee (putatively Liberalis), to whom he ascribes this view, is not only a "slave" of lust, gluttony, and mistresses himself (§4; more on "slavery to the emotions" below), but also is carried around ostentatiously by an elaborately dressed band of slaves precisely so that he can pay his respects to someone else's slave, in hopes of receiving some favor, some *beneficium*, from him. In *Ep.* 47.8 Seneca similarly argues that one should not disdain one's slaves as unworthy dinner companions, lest one be disdained by them in turn. For he goes on to say (§9) that he saw a former master of Callistus (one of Claudius's freedmen: PIR^2 I 229), who had put him up for sale as being worthless, being denied entrance to Callistus's house, the latter now being far richer and more powerful than he: thus he is himself rejected as worthless in turn. Seneca does not express outrage in these passages at the social inversions he describes, but he presupposes that his audience will find them distasteful, and he seeks to mobilize this distaste so as to cause his audience to question its worldviews and behavior.[95] Other sources for this period describe contemporary outrage more directly. Dio reports (60.19.3) that in A.D. 43 soldiers under Aulus Plautius's command refused to cross from Gaul to Britain; Claudius sent his freedman Narcissus from Rome to address them. When Narcissus mounted the commander's tribunal to speak, however, the soldiers refused to let him utter a word: with one voice they cried *Io Saturnalia* (Saturnalia being the festival, as Dio helpfully explains, in which slaves don their masters' garb) and straightaway followed Plautius. Here the anger at a former slave impersonating an aristocrat (i.e., Narcissus mounting Plautius's platform), and so enacting the kind of social inversion appropriate only to the Saturnalia, comes not from an aristocrat, but from common soldiers who regard him as unworthy of the deference they would normally accord a senatorial commander. Similarly, Tacitus says (*Ann.*

---

volved in the service of some deity. The strong contrast between *princeps* and *minister* in this passage (*non principem se sed ministrum egit*) emphasizes the social inversion that Suetonius sees Claudius's behavior as enacting. For Claudius as a "slave" or "unfree," despite his ruling power, cf. Dio 60.2.5, 28.2, 31.8. The allegation that such status inversions occurred in the imperial household became a standard aristocratic reproach against "bad" emperors: e.g., Pliny *Paneg.* 88.1.

[95] Seneca himself solicited the clemency of Claudius, in hopes of returning from exile in Corsica, through the offices of the freedman Polybius (Sen. *Polyb.* 13; cf. Dio 61.10.2). Seneca alludes to the power and autonomy of Claudius's freedmen, as well as Claudius's ineffectuality in controlling them, at *Apoc.* 6.2. Here Claudius orders the head of the minor divinity Febris to be cut off, but he is ignored by everyone: *putares omnes illius esse libertos, adeo illum nemo curabat.*

14.39) that Nero dispatched his freedman Polyclitus to Britain in A.D. 61, to patch up a rift between the legate and the procurator as they sought to stamp out the last vestiges of Boudicca's revolt. But Polyclitus became "an object of mockery to the enemy" who, being free, "did not know the power of freedmen" and could not believe that the Roman commander and his troops obeyed slaves.[96]

In addition to ascribing resentment and derisive words to the contemporaries of these powerful freedmen, Tacitus also speaks resentfully of them in his own voice. The freedman Antonius Felix, whom Suetonius says governed Judea and commanded troops there (*Cl.* 28, quoted above), is the object of bitter invective at *Historiae* 5.9: "Claudius entrusted the province of Judea to Roman knights or to freedmen. One of these, Antonius Felix, exercised the power of kings with the spirit of a slave, employing every kind of savagery and lust" (*Claudius . . . Iudaeam provinciam equitibus Romanis aut libertis permisit, e quibus Antonius Felix per omnem saevitiam ac libidinem ius regium servili ingenio exercuit*). It is virtually certain that Felix had been granted equestrian status before being made a provincial procurator. Yet Tacitus nevertheless asserts that Felix had a "slave's nature" and governed accordingly.[97] Similar is the reaction of the younger Pliny upon reading an inscription on the tomb of Pallas, Claudius's freedman, describing honors bestowed upon him by a decree of the senate. This decree granted Pallas not only the *praetoria ornamenta*, but fifteen million sesterces (Tac. *Ann.* 12.54, Pliny *Ep.* 7.29.2; cf. Suet. *Cl.* 28), which he turned down; Pliny sees in these events an outrageous status inversion. As he writes to Montanus (*Ep.* 7.29.3), "Principally, however, this inscription reminded me how ludicrous and ill suited are the things that are sometimes thrown away upon this filth, this dirt—things that that *furcifer* was so brazen as to accept and refuse, and even to present himself to posterity as an exemplum of moderation" (*maxime tamen hic me titulus admonuit, quam essent mimica et inepta quae interdum in hoc caenum, in has sordes abicerentur, quae denique ille furcifer et recipere ausus est et recusare atque etiam ut moderationis exemplum posteris prodere*). Pallas, then, is "filth"; the term *furcifer* alludes specifically to his servile origins (the *furca* being a standard implement for punishing slaves). These comments on his status ground the claim that he was "brazen" in accepting and rejecting honors bestowed by the senate (this, at any rate, is the kind of thing the emperor does); and Pliny is

---

[96] Tac. *Ann.* 14.39: *sed hostibus inrisui fuit apud quos flagrante etiam tum libertate nondum cognita libertinorum potentia erat; mirabanturque quod dux* [i.e., the legate, Suetonius Paulinus] *et exercitus tanti belli confector servitiis oboedirent*.

[97] For the probable equestrian status of Felix, see Weaver 1972: 279 and n. 3; another attack on Felix occurs at *Ann.* 12.54.

further annoyed that Pallas presents himself as exemplum of moderation (presumably by inscribing on his tomb, for posterity to read, the fact that he rejected these honors): for thus Pallas seeks to install himself as one of the *maiores*, an aristocratic ancestor notable for the honors conferred upon him, and hence a model for future generations to emulate. This "filth," then, behaved as an aristocrat and was treated as such by the senate—a social inversion Pliny finds objectionable. These same tropes appear in more variety and at greater length in *Ep.* 8.6, a letter on the same subject again addressed to Montanus. Pliny has now hunted up and read the *senatusconsultum* itself. Its text is so fulsome, says Pliny, that Pallas's praises outstrip those of all the great heroes of the past put together (§2); he wonders why anyone would seek advancement in a state where the greatest reward of high office is to praise Pallas (§3); he is not surprised that praetorian insignia were granted to a slave, since it was "slaves" (i.e., senators) who granted them (§4); nor is there any surprise in the stipulation that Pallas wear a gold ring, since it would be degrading to the senatorial order for someone of praetorian rank to wear the iron rings that are actually appropriate to slaves;[98] and so on. Near the end of the letter Pliny again expresses horror at the Senate's stated reason for conferring honors on Pallas, namely that these honors might inspire others to follow Pallas's example: this rationale entails that freeborn people should strive to obtain what was given to a freedman or slave (*inveniebantur tamen honesto loco nati, qui peterent cuperentque quod dari liberto, promitti servis videbant*, §16)—rather than the other way around, which would be the proper social order. Pliny's objections, then, are framed almost without exception as social inversions: what is wrong with Pallas and his honors is that he conducts himself and is treated as a high-ranking aristocrat, while the senate, in conferring these honors, reduces itself to slavish status.[99]

Pliny's two letters to Montanus provide the fullest and most rhetorically sustained expression of elite resentment at powerful imperial

---

[98] That iron rings could symbolize captivity and slave status since they share the shape and material of a shackle, see Pliny *Nat.* 33.23, also §8; but cf. §§9, 11; also Pliny *Ep.* 8.6.4. The rings that Trimalchio wears (Petr. *Sat.* 32.3), which are of gilt iron and of iron-studded gold, therefore symbolize both his servile origins and his equestrian aspirations. On his tomb Trimalchio wishes to be represented wearing gold rings (§71.9), thus presenting himself to posterity as an equestrian. Martial draws attention to Zoilus's status in a like manner (11.37): he taunts him with the claim that the (presumably gold) ring on his finger weighs as much as the "rings" that once shackled his legs (cf. 3.29).

[99] The direct quotations or paraphrases of the *senatusconsultum* in Pliny's letter do not seem to convey any animosity by the senators toward Pallas, though such animosity would hardly be exhibited in a text like this. Sherwin-White 1966: 439, however, believes he can detect satire in the honorific wording of the decree.

freedmen. And while Pliny wrote these letters a half century or more after the events they discuss, I see no reason to doubt that his articulation of Pallas's position in terms of social inversions, along with the resentment he expresses, were also fundamentally the responses of many elites, indeed of many free persons of every status, who were contemporaries of these freedmen.[100] The extreme dissonance between these freedmen's birth on the one hand and their wealth and power on the other was seen as threatening the exclusiveness of aristocratic privilege. Thus the perception that the distinctions between aristocrats and slaves/freedmen were becoming blurred, and that the latter groups were being assimilated to the former in crucial respects, constitutes one further dimension in which the emergence of the imperial regime can be represented as reducing the established aristocracy to "slavery" in Julio-Claudian Rome.

6. Status Anxiety and Stoic Remedies

I argued in chapter 2 above that the younger Seneca promotes Stoic ethics in part as a means of addressing certain dislocations experienced by the Julio-Claudian aristocracy upon the advent of the principate. I identified two dislocations in particular that Senecan Stoicism in some way rectifies or makes good: it enables aristocrats to retain a claim upon *virtus* in a world in which the most prestigious military honors are no longer available to them, and it provides a way to stabilize ethical discourse in a world in which the expression of value judgments is distorted by flattery. Here, I suggest a third dislocation that Seneca's Stoic ethics addresses: the assimilation of Julio-Claudian aristocrats to "slave" status either through the threat of corporal punishment (or other characteristically slavish treatment) at the hands of the emperor, or through the perceived social inversions associated with the increased visibility, power, and wealth of imperial freedmen and slaves. For I will argue that Seneca deploys the language and imagery of the master-slave relationship to refer to mental states (which I call the "philosophical"

[100] Cf. Sherwin-White 1966: 439, who suggests that senators of Pliny's era might have found these upwardly mobile freedmen more objectionable in retrospect than did senators who were these freedmen's contemporaries, since the later group of senators were of more humble ancestry than the earlier and so would have felt a stronger need to distinguish themselves sharply from such freedmen. But this psychologizing explanation is unpersuasive. For even if the claim about the relative statuses of the two groups of senators is true, one could conjecture with equal plausibility that a senate of loftier lineage would be all the more offended by freedmen's incursions into its more ethereal social milieu, while a senate of humbler lineage, itself composed of arrivistes, might empathize with the freedmen's plight.

domain of usage); that he uses this language and imagery in ways that permit slippage or ambiguity of reference among the philosophical, political, and parent (i.e., "literal," chattel slavery) domains of usage; and that through this slippage he reconstructs the traditional Roman aristocracy as an aristocracy of virtue that maintains its "freedom" against threats both from above and from below.

First for the "philosophical" domain: Seneca regularly uses the language and imagery of social status to refer in various ways to a person's mental states, or more precisely (if more oddly) to a person's relationship with his own mental states. This usage constitutes another "derived" domain of usage for this language and imagery, in addition to the political domain: again, the concepts and categories proper to the social institution of chattel slavery are projected *en bloc* onto an altogether different set of relationships. Now, we saw in chapter 2.3 above that Seneca, in his ethical prose, articulates two different systems through which a person can confront the world as a moral agent. One system is more or less the traditional ethical system of the Roman aristocracy, in which moral value is inherently community oriented, constructed under the gaze of others on the basis of observed actions, status symbols, and other visible tokens. Seneca usually dismisses these tokens and symbols as "externals," which are not under one's control, but rather are capriciously given and taken away by *fortuna*; moreover people are tossed and turned on surges of desire and emotion as they struggle, with now favorable and now unfavorable fortune, to accumulate these things. The other ethical system, which Seneca privileges, is Stoic: only "internal" states (in Seneca's terminology) carry moral value proper, while the "externals" to which traditional ethics attaches moral value do not carry moral value at all, but instead are in the realm of "preferred" and "dispreferred" value. Accepting that the overarching structure and plan of the universe, as prescribed by the governing principle *deus/natura/providentia*, is by definition morally good, the wise man makes his wishes and desires conform to what must and does happen; being thus insulated from *fortuna* he does not suffer the emotional turmoil that the others suffer, but maintains a consistently joyful, placid bearing.[101]

---

[101] The two Stoic universal governing principles, namely *deus/ratio/natura/providentia* (alternative names for the same principle: see ch. 2 n. 4 above) on the one hand, and *fortuna* on the other, represent contrasting points of view regarding causes. The former terms are associated with the "top-down" view of the universe held by the Stoic wise man, who lives fully in agreement with nature and grasps its principles, inter alia the causal nexus in accordance with which all things happen. The latter term, *fortuna*, is associated with a "bottom-up" view of the universe, necessarily held by most people (Stoic fools), since they do not grasp these principles and consequently see events as occurring capriciously and arbitrarily. So while *deus* (etc.) and *fortuna* both designate the same

Those who confront the world as traditional moral agents Seneca commonly represents as "slaves" in one way or another: slaves of fortune, or of the externals they (wrongly) value, or of the emotions that toss them, or because they cannot "do what they want"—i.e., they desire things they cannot attain. Conversely Stoic sages, along with nonsages who are thinking in a Stoic framework, are often represented as "free" from fortune or externals or their emotions, or are said to be "masters" over them; and they are even free in the sense of "doing what they want" because their desires are in agreement with nature, with what must happen. Thus Seneca exploits the affective quality of the language of social status to reinforce and emphasize the desirability of displacing, or at least nuancing, the traditional ethical outlook with the Stoic one.[102]

---

causal power, the latter presents it as capricious and unforeseen, while the former marks it as morally good, knowable, and necessary. Inwood 1985: 122 makes this same distinction.

[102] I cannot document these claims exhaustively here, but the following passages offer a sampling. For most people being "slaves" to *fortuna* or to externals generally, but the good or wise man being either "free" from *fortuna* (and externals) or at least trying to free himself, see e.g., *Tranq.* 8.7, 10.1–6; *Polyb.* 6.4–5; *Vit.* 3.3, 4.4–5, 15.3, 26.1, *Marc.* 10.6, *Epp.* 26.9–10, 47.1, 51.8–9, 65.20–24, 104.34; see further Viansino 1979: 179–83. Seneca expressly denies that one can ever be a "slave" to *deus* (*Prov.* 5.5–6, cf. *Ep.* 96.2); on the contrary, following *deus* is *libertas* (*Vit.* 15.7), and *deus* stands in relation to one as father to son (*Prov.* 2.5–6, 4.11–12) or as commander to soldier (*Prov.* 4.8, *Vit.* 15.5, *Ep.* 107.9).

Few classical scholars have discussed the philosophical usages of the language of social status. One is Erskine 1990: 43–63, who examines the three different kinds of slavery articulated in Diogenes Laertius 7.121. On his account, these include "moral slavery" (pp. 44–46, i.e., usages of the language of social status to refer to states of mind or soul), chattel slavery (pp. 46–48), and other relationships of subordination referred to as slavery (pp. 48–58). Erskine rightly seeks to establish connections among these usages, but concludes only that these several kinds of slavery manifest different aspects of a single underlying concept, "the inability to act independently." This conclusion implies that the Stoics used the word δουλεία simply as an obfuscating synonym for ὑπόταξις. It does not recognize "slavery" as a metaphor that presents conditions of mind or soul in terms of social status; nor, therefore, can it explain the metaphor's significance (i.e., why this metaphor rather than another). Viansino 1979 offers a more fruitful treatment. He connects Seneca's interest in philosophical slavery, as well as his "humanitarian" concern for the way chattel slaves are treated, with Seneca's own experience of suffering exile at the emperor's command, and with his eventual disillusion with Nero. Viansino is right to see these domains of usage as significantly interconnected by their shared use of status language and imagery. But by making Seneca's personal experiences central to all these usages, Viansino risks turning Seneca's ethical prose treatises into a series of solipsistic ruminations on the wrongs he has suffered. This hinders a full understanding of these texts' intense social engagement—their status-anxious, class-interested exhortations to other aristocrats to consider new ways of thinking and acting so as to maintain their social privileges and exclusivity.

Here I examine passages where Seneca deploys the language and imagery of social status in such a way that the philosophical domain of reference is juxtaposed or conflated with the political domain or the parent (chattel-slavery) domain, or with both. Through these conflations, the mental states that are associated with free or master status in the philosophical domain are made relevant to the status anxieties—the threats to elite exclusivity and privilege coming from both above and below—of Seneca's aristocratic audience. By attending to Seneca's exhortations, his audience can learn patterns of thought and behavior that are rhetorically constructed, through the language and imagery of social status, as appropriate to it—that is, appropriate to those who are free and masters themselves, not "slaves" in any sense. Meanwhile, those who do not display these patterns of thought and behavior, including not only persons of lower status but also certain emperors, are dismissed as slaves in the philosophical sense. Hence, in Seneca's rhetoric, they are denied aristocratic status.

An example of the conflation of different domains of reference for the language and imagery of social status can be found in *Ep.* 77, where Seneca discusses considerations pertinent to the decision whether to kill oneself. Among the exempla he adduces is the following:

(§14) Lacon ille memoriae traditur, inpubis adhuc, qui captus clamabat "non serviam" sua illa Dorica lingua, et verbis fidem inposuit: ut primum iussus est fungi servili et contumelioso ministerio (adferre enim vas obscenum iubebatur), inlisum parieti caput rupit. (§15) tam prope libertas est: et servit aliquis? ita non sic perire filium tuum malles quam per inertiam senem fieri? quid ergo est cur perturberis, si mori fortiter etiam puerile est? puta nolle te sequi: duceris. fac tui iuris quod alieni est. non sumes pueri spiritum, ut dicas "non servio"? infelix, servis hominibus, servis rebus, servis vitae; nam vita, si moriendi virtus abest, servitus est.

The story of the Spartan has been preserved, still a boy, who as a captive used to cry out "I will not be a slave" in that Doric dialect of his, and he gave these words credence: as soon as he was bid to discharge a slavish and humiliating service (for he was ordered to bring a chamber pot), he broke his head by slamming it into a wall. Freedom is so near, and anyone is a slave? Would you not have preferred your son to die this way than to become an old man through lack of spirit? What is the reason you are confounded, if dying bravely is something even a boy can do? Suppose you are unwilling to follow: you will be led. Put under your own control what is now under another's. Will you not take up the boy's spirit, that you may say "I am not a slave"? Unhappy man, you are a slave to men, to your affairs, to life: for life is slavery, if the courage to die is lacking.

In the first sentence of this passage, all the occurrences of the language of social status refer to the parent domain, that of chattel slavery. The Spartan boy, a prisoner of war, is literally being enslaved and is asked to provide the demeaning personal service that a chattel slave stereotypically provides his master. By his suicide, he does indeed escape chattel slavery; death brings freedom.[103] But in the next few sentences, the boy's words and deed are also given a philosophical gloss. For when Seneca writes, "you are a slave to men, a slave to your affairs, a slave to life," he segues from the idea of chattel slavery to that of "slavery" to externals, specifically to one's everyday business (*rebus*, §15; also *curia, fori*, §17) and even to life itself. Now, one commonly adduced ground for suicide (though not the only one) expressed in prior Stoic sources, and implied elsewhere by Seneca himself, is that of finding that one is now suffering, or will soon be suffering, under a preponderance of dispreferred external circumstances[104]—which include illness, poverty, disgrace, etc. It is from this point of view that the Spartan boy's suicide becomes paradigmatic for Roman aristocrats. For it could be thought that the boy decided that he had crossed this threshold upon being ordered to handle a chamber pot; and in the sections following this anecdote (§§16–17) Seneca suggests that his aristocratic addressees themselves may be living near this threshold, if only by virtue of being sated in their pleasures (presumably a "dispreferred" state). If at any point, therefore, the aristocrat finds himself "enslaved" to these externals (*servis rebus, servis vitae*—the philosophical domain of usage) then death offers liberation, just as it liberated the Spartan boy from his chattel slavery (the parent domain).[105]

Elsewhere, Seneca conflates philosophical freedom and slavery not with chattel slavery, as in the previous passage, but with political slavery of the sort imposed upon aristocrats by tyrannical rulers. We return

---

[103] Spartan prisoners always choose death over slavery, in the Roman stereotype: e.g., Sen. *Suas.* 2, esp. §8: *captus Laco "occide," inquit, "non servio."* Cf. Plut. *Mor.* 234B (virtually the same account as Seneca's); also 219B, 234C, 235B.

[104] E.g., LS 66G (= Cic. *Fin.* 3.60–61), with discussion at I 428–29; also Griffin 1986: 73–74. For Senecan instances of this argument, see *Ep.* 70.5–6, 15–16, 24–25 (but see the counterarguments in §§8–11); also *Epp.* 77.5–6 (discussed in ch. 2.7 above) and 58.34–36. For a survey of the Stoic tradition on suicide, see Griffin 1986 and Rist 1969: 233–55.

[105] In *Ep.* 70.14–16 and 24 suicide is similarly presented as a route to "freedom" for aristocrats oppressed by dispreferred external circumstances; §§20–27 provide further parallels with chattel slaves who escape their condition by suicide. Seneca commonly asserts that death, or having the courage to die, constitutes "freedom" in one or several of its domains of reference. In addition to the passages discussed both above and below, see *Epp.* 4.8, 12.10, 26.8–10; *Marc.* 20.1–3; *Ben.* 3.23.5. Viansino 1979: 184–87 collects and discusses further passages.

once more to the Persian courtier Harpagus who, as a guest at a royal banquet, is fed the flesh of his own children by the king (*Ira* 3.15). Asked how he likes the dish, Harpagus replies, "at the king's table, all meals are pleasant" (§15.1). Seneca then asserts that all people who attend upon kings must behave as Harpagus did; their situation requires them to dissemble. He continues as follows:

> (§15.3) an tanti sit vita videbimus: alia ista quaestio est. non consolabimur tam triste ergastulum, non adhortabimur ferre imperia carnificum: ostendemus in omni servitute apertam libertati viam. . . . (§15.4) dicam et illi qui in regem incidit sagittis pectora amicorum petentem et illi cuius dominus liberorum visceribus patres saturat: "quid gemis, demens? quid expectas ut te aut hostis aliquis per exitium gentis tuae vindicet aut rex a longinquo potens advolet? quocumque respexeris, ibi malorum finis est. vides illum praecipitem locum? illac ad libertatem descenditur. vides illud mare, illud flumen, illum puteum? libertas illic in imo sedet. vides illam arborem brevem retorridam infelicem? pendet inde libertas. vides iugulum tuum, guttur tuum, cor tuum? effugia servitutis sunt. nimis tibi operosos exitus monstro et multum animi ac roboris exigentes? quaeris quod sit ad libertatem iter? quaelibet in corpore tuo vena."

> Whether life is worth this much, we will see: this is another question. We will not console so grim a sweatshop of slaves; we will not urge them to endure the commands of executioners: we will show that in every slavery there is an open path to liberty. . . . I will say both to him who has come under a king who shoots arrows at the breasts of his friends, and to him whose master sates fathers with the entrails of their children, "why do you groan, madman? Why do you wait for some enemy to free you by the destruction of your whole people, or for a powerful king to rush in from far away? Wherever you look, there is an end of your ills. See that cliff? By that route one may descend to freedom. See that sea, that river, that well? Freedom sits there, at the bottom. See that short, shriveled, barren tree? Freedom hangs from there. See your throat, your gullet, your heart? They are ways of escaping slavery. Am I showing you overly difficult deaths, requiring much spirit and strength? You ask what is the path to freedom? Any vein in your body."

Here Seneca uses the language and imagery of the master-slave relationship to characterize the position of courtiers in relation to such a king. They are called an *ergastulum*, a sweatshop of slaves; their condition is described as *servitus*; and in the first sentence of §15.4, the king himself is called a *dominus*, confirming the construction of this ruler-courtier relationship as a master-slave relationship. The basis for this characterization, as often, appears to be that the aristocracy suffers arbitrary corporal punishment at the ruler's hands. But if living in such circumstances is "slavery" for an aristocrat, he nevertheless (says Seneca) has a way to *libertas* (§15.3), namely suicide. On the one hand, the tyrant's power over his subject is manifestly abolished when the subject kills himself, so this *libertas* has significance in the political domain. But the very idea that suicide may be a valid course of action seems again to embody the criterion discussed above, that of the "preponderance of dispreferred externals," so that "freedom" resonates in the philosophical domain as well. Indeed, in this passage and the previous one chattel and political slavery emerge as particular cases of the much broader philosophical usage, since subjection to an actual master or tyrant can be regarded as specific kinds of "dispreferred external."

Nor is this assimilation of the philosophical to the political limited to foreign examples: the younger Cato comes to stand by metonymy for *libertas* in the Julio-Claudian period through exactly this process. Seneca can say that Cato's sword "will give to Cato the freedom that it could not give to the fatherland" *(ferrum istud . . . libertatem quam patriae non potuit Catoni dabit, Prov.* 2.10) — where the point is that the sword could either kill the "master," i.e., Caesar, and so confer political freedom on the state (see section 4 above on such rhetoric in the civil war era), or it can kill Cato and impart that freedom to him alone.[106] Yet his freedom also has a philosophical dimension in that he, an accomplished Stoic, judged the moment at which his personal burden of dispreferred externals became intolerable; thus he freed himself from this most general form of "slavery" at the same moment he freed himself specifically from Caesar's autocracy. Still another Roman example is Iulius Canus, the victim of Caligula whose death Seneca narrates in detail at *De Tranquillitate Animi* 14.4–10 (discussed in ch. 2.7 above). Speculating upon what Canus might have meant when he thanked Caligula for his death sentence, Seneca suggests as one possibility that he was "gladly receiving his liberty" *(tamquam libertatem libenter accepit,* §14.5): he subsequently praises him for the equanimity he displayed, and for philosophizing all the way to the grave *(nemo diutius philosophatus est,* §14.10). Here the moral agent's contempt for the suddenly unfortunate external circumstances of his life is revealed and enacted not in the decision to kill himself—since his fate was decided by Caligula—but in his tranquillity of mind, his refusal to be confounded or agitated in these circumstances. Yet the view that his death will constitute "liberty" again admits of interpretation in both the philosophical and political domains. For his death liberates him from

---

[106] Similarly, *Marc.* 20.6: [Cato] *libertati non suae tantum sed publicae natus*; even more concise at *Ep.* 13.14, where Cato's sword is simply an *adsertor libertatis.* For the metonymy Cato/*libertas* in other Julio-Claudian texts, see, e.g., Val. Max. 6.2.5; Sen. *Suas.* 6.10; Sen. *Const.* 2.2, *Epp.* 95.72, 104.29; Lucan *B.C.* 9.28–30.

the now-oppressive external circumstances of his life, circumstances brought about because Caligula, in deciding arbitrarily to execute him, has treated him as a slave.[107]

Elsewhere in Seneca there is still clearer evidence for the conflation, even identification, of the philosophical with the political; though in many cases "freedom" resides not in death, but in the mental serenity that the Stoic seeks to attain. In the sentences immediately preceding the Canus episode (*Tranq.* 14.3), Seneca describes two men who displayed notable tranquility of mind in the face of losses: Zeno, who lost all his possessions in a shipwreck, declared "*fortuna* bids that I philosophize with less hindrance" (*iubet . . . me fortuna expeditius philosophari*); and a philosopher named Theodorus received calmly (like Canus) the threats of a tyrant who promised to execute him and leave his corpse unburied. For Seneca's purposes, then, *fortuna* and the tyrant have exactly the same capacity to deprive people of their externals (whether property or life itself), and thereby also offer the same opportunities for victims to exercise and display tranquility of mind. Elsewhere Seneca describes an unspecified emperor who distributes magistracies, priesthoods, money, and other status symbols (*Ira* 3.31.2); and he mentions tyrants who execute the family members of aristocrats, or condemn the aristocrats themselves to imprisonment, torture, or death, and so on (*Ira* 2.33, 3.14–20): these rulers are allocating the very externals—namely life, death, property, bodily conditions, social status and standing—that Seneca elsewhere puts at the disposal of *fortuna*.[108] The Stoic wise man is said to regard "powerful men" as the instruments of *fortuna* (*Const.* 8.3); and Nero himself is made to declare that he is the representative of the gods on earth, and is the instrument of *fortuna* (*Clem.* 1.1.2).[109] In view of such passages, it is no surprise that the ideal Stoic attitude of serene, joyful, fatalistic acceptance of whatever life brings, which constitutes "freeing" oneself from *fortuna*, is also the proper attitude with which to face the threats and blows of the tyrant. Thus not only does Canus garner praise for thanking Caligula, and for his serene disposition as he approached his execution, but also Pastor's apparent joy and calm upon the execution of his son is presented as appropriate and advantageous, albeit possibly feigned, because it saved

---

[107] Other Senecan passages in which the language and imagery of social status is used in ways that are significant in the political and philosophical domains simultaneously: *Brev.* 5.1–2, *Tranq.* 5.2, *Ep.* 28.8.

[108] E.g., *Tranq.* 10.3, 11.1–3, 13.1–2, 16.3; *Marc.* 19.5, *Ben.* 3.20.2, *Prov.* 6.6.

[109] *Const.* 8.3: *et si fortunae iniurias moderate fert, quanto magis hominum potentium, quos scit fortunae manus esse! Clem.* 1.1.2: *egone ex omnibus mortalibus placui electusque sum, qui in terris deorum vice fungerer? . . . quid cuique mortalium fortuna datum velit, meo ore pronuntiat.*

his other son (*Ira* 2.33.3–6); likewise, Harpagus's smooth flattery of his king after being fed his own children is approved on the ground that Harpagus was spared having to eat the leftovers (*Ira* 3.15.1–2).

These latter two examples, along with others in the third book of *De Ira* (e.g., the exemplum of Praexaspes, *Ira* 3.14), are adduced in this treatise not primarily to show aristocratic victims of tyrants displaying tranquility of mind but specifically to show their suppression and control of anger, *ira*[110] — a crucial precondition for maintaining the serene attitude that constitutes freedom from *fortuna*. Indeed, Seneca's discussions of the degree to which *ira* is or is not controlled are shot through with the rhetoric of social status. Habinek (1992: 192–93) has shown that anger, as it is represented at the beginning of *De Ira* (1.1.2–4), "violates the aristocratic norms of decorum and taste.... It is anger's potential to destroy order, dissolve boundaries, and trample on hierarchies that makes it peculiarly dangerous and singularly inappropriate for members of the aristocracy." This assessment of the threat that *ira* poses, and its inappropriateness for aristocrats, is confirmed elsewhere in *De Ira* by Seneca's systematic use of the imagery of social status: the man who indulges his anger is described in terms that suggest low status, while the imagery of high status characterizes the man who controls it. At *Ira* 3.25.3, Seneca urges his addressee not to grow angry at those who attempt to harm his interests, for by suppressing his anger he can "remove himself from the crowd and stand higher" (*se exemerit turbae et altius steterit*), "look down" on those who harrass him (*despexit lacessentis*), and so display "true greatness" (*magnitudo vera*). On the other hand, at *Ira* 2.15–16 Seneca denies that anger has anything "noble" (*generosus*) in it, and at *Ira* 3.6.2–3 he asserts that the angry man ceases to display certain crucial aristocratic patterns of thought and action: he abandons all sense of shame (*verecundia*), whatever in him commands respect (*quidquid in se venerandi habuit*), all accounting of his duties (*numerus et ordo officiorum*), and various aspects of self-control (*quis linguae temperavit? quis ullam partem corporis tenuit? quis se regere potuit immissum?*). In sum, the angry man jettisons his aristocratic status altogether: at *Ira* 3.4.4, Seneca says that he is a "captive" of this emotion and consequently, regardless of what he does to other people, is actually neither powerful nor even free.[111] The metaphor

---

[110] For *ira* in each case, see specifically *Ira* 2.33.5–6 (Pastor), *Ira* 3.14.4 (Praexaspes), *Ira* 3.15.2 (Harpagus).

[111] *Ira* 3.4.4: *non vis ergo admoneam eos qui iram <in> summa potentia exercent et argumentum virium existimant et in magnis magnae fortunae bonis ponunt paratam ultionem, quam non sit potens, immo ne liber quidem dici possit irae suae captivus?* Again at *Ira* 3.3.3, the person in the grip of anger is a slave: *non it sed agitur et furenti malo servit.*

of the prisoner of war reduced to slavery, then, models this aristocrat's relationship to this most destructive of emotions.[112]

In all of these passages that articulate the suppression of emotion in terms of freedom, mastery, and high social standing, Seneca claims that the tranquil attitude he urges is appropriate specifically to his audience of elites—those who regard themselves as free, as masters, and of high status, but who may also feel anxiety about their status, which (as we have seen) they regard as threatened from both above and below in the Julio-Claudian period. Thus, in the interplay between the content of his assertions (say, the desirability of controlling one's anger, or maintaining one's equanimity, or having the courage to die) and the rhetoric of those assertions (these things make one free, or a master, or not a slave), Seneca presumes to show his status-anxious aristocratic audience the patterns of thought and action that are appropriate to them, that confirm their position in the upper echelon of society and whose absence topples them from this position. This is not to say that Seneca's recommended patterns of thought and action are simply identical with established aristocratic patterns. On the contrary: as I showed in chapter 2 above, Seneca often places his Stoic ethics in an adversarial engagement with traditional elite values of his addressees; in regard to anger too Seneca argues strongly against what he represents as the commonly held view that indulging one's anger is an indication of one's power and status.[113] So Seneca is indeed advocating new patterns of thought, action, and valuation for his aristocratic audience, but these new patterns incorporate many elements of the established patterns—concern for decorum and duty, for example.

It appears, then, that aristocratic status is a matter of acculturation, of education. Is it therefore available to all? Certainly, Seneca repeatedly asserts that virtue can reside in a person of any status (*Ep.* 44 passim; *Ep.* 66.3, 22; *Ben.* 3.18.2): even if a person's body is enslaved, that

---

[112] The role of other emotions too is sometimes articulated in terms of social status. People who experience them may be described as slaves to the emotion in question, or to the emotions generally, since they do not display the serenity associated with freedom in the philosophical domain, the attitude by which one is free from *fortuna*. Conversely, those who do not have emotional responses are "free" or "masters." Cf. *Ep.* 37.3–4 (the emotions are "in command" until banished by wisdom, which brings *libertas*); *Ep.* 80.4–6 (the addressee is slave to the fear of death and poverty, and must strive to free himself); *Ep.* 66.16 (fear is slavery); *Vit.* 4.3 (the *liber animus* is unafraid, placed beyond the reach of fear and desire); *Const.* 9.4 (the wise man is free from various vices and emotions). Viansino 1979: 181 and n. 29 offers further examples.

[113] In addition to his argument that *ira* has nothing *generosa* about it (*Ira* 2.15–16, discussed above), see also *Ira* 3.41.2: people who are *audaces* and whose actions are *animosa* are widely, but wrongly, held in high regard; also *Ira* 2.21.7: the inclination to indulge anger is greater in higher-status persons.

slavery does not necessarily extend to his internal states (*interior pars*, *Ben.* 3.20.2), and hence a slave may be "free" in soul (*liber animo, Ep.* 47.17). This displacement of a social hierarchy based on birth and wealth with one based on conditions of mind or soul has been called "revolutionary" (Viansino 1979: 189 n. 53). But caution is required here. In *Ep.* 88, for example, Seneca discusses the kinds of knowledge that constitute wisdom (*sapientia*), or lead to its acquisition—wisdom being that which confers "freedom," hence aristocratic status, in the sense that one's mental states are in good order. In this letter, Seneca expressly excludes from the realm of "wisdom" the kinds of specialist knowledge ordinarily gained, and sometimes taught to aristocrats, by freedmen, slaves, and the low freeborn. The letter opens as follows:

> (§1) de liberalibus studiis quid sentiam scire desideras: nullum suspicio, nullum in bonis numero quod ad aes exit. meritoria artificia sunt, hactenus utilia si praeparant ingenium, non detinent. tamdiu enim istis inmorandum est quamdiu nihil animus agere maius potest; rudimenta sunt nostra, non opera. (§2) quare liberalia studia dicta sint vides: quia homine libero digna sunt. ceterum unum studium vere liberale est quod liberum facit, hoc est sapientiae, sublime forte magnanimum: cetera pusilla et puerilia sunt. an tu quicquam in istis esse credis boni quorum professores turpissimos omnium ac flagitiosissimos cernis?

> You want to know what I think about liberal studies. I respect no study, and count none among the good, that ends in money making. These are skills for hire, useful only so far as they prepare the mind without keeping it occupied. For one should tarry among these only so long as the spirit can do nothing greater; they are our training, not our work. You see why they are called liberal studies: because they are worthy of a free man. But one study is truly liberal because it makes one free, namely the study of wisdom—lofty, brave, great spirited: the rest are insignificant and childish. Or do you believe there can be anything good in these studies whose teachers you perceive to be the most shameful and disgraceful of all men?

After the abrupt opening declaration that he counts no *studium* among the "good" if it aims at making money—though he concedes that studies falling under this rubric may "prepare" the mind for acquiring virtue—he proceeds (§2), in typically Senecan fashion, to offer two etymologizing definitions of *liberalia studia*, the first purportedly being the definition embraced by most people ("they are called liberal studies because they are worthy of a free man") and the second being his own prescriptive redefinition, his correction, of the common understanding ("one study is *truly* liberal because it *makes* one free: the study of wisdom"). The final sentence of this quotation explains why the first kind of study, the "insignificant and childish" ones, contain nothing good in them (hence, presumably, cannot set one free): their teachers are too morally degraded. Seneca does not directly connect this final statement with the opening one—the teachers are morally degraded *because* they take money for their services—but the aristocratic view that money making is shameful, unless it occurs on a massive scale, is familiar from a variety of other sources.[114]

In the remainder of the letter Seneca elaborates his distinction between the so-called *liberalia studia* (which actually are not) and the true *studium liberale*, the acquisition of wisdom through the study of philosophy. First he turns to the teachers whom he has just condemned, the teachers of the so-called liberal studies. The *grammaticus* (i.e., philologist and literary critic, §§3–8), along with those who teach music, geometry, and astronomy (§§9–17), are all declared to be teaching the wrong skills and asking the wrong questions. In §§18–19 Seneca further debars from the *liberalia studia* the skills and knowledge of painters, sculptors, athletic trainers, perfumers, and cooks. He again concedes in §20 that the so-called liberal studies have a propaedeutic function, preparing the mind for receiving virtue (recalling the claim in §1 that such *meritoria artificia*, skills-for-sale, can do nothing more than prepare the mind for better things; cf. §§24–27). But he insists that they themselves impart not even the smallest bits of virtue. The same concern to eliminate characteristically nonelite activities from the compass of *sapientia* is visible in other texts as well. In *Ep.* 90.26–27 Seneca declares that dancing, music, and even the arts of war are "too insignificant" for *sapientia*, which is rather the "skilled artisan of life" (but not of these lesser occupations). Again in *Ep.* 90.31 he rejects Posidonius's assertion that the wise man Anacharsis invented the potter's wheel. But if he did invent it, says Seneca, he did not invent it by virtue of being a wise man (*sapiens quidem hoc invenit, sed non tamquam sapiens*—presumably because such an object is not among the proper aims and concerns of wisdom); no more should the glassblower's skill be subsumed under *sapientia* (also §31). In these passages, then, Seneca not only sweepingly eliminates all remunerative activities from the fold of "liberal studies" (*Ep.* 88.1), but specifically rejects a number of skilled occupations, including teaching and the production of various kinds of art objects or crafts, that were in fact generally conducted by freedmen,

---

[114] Notably Cic. *Off.* 1.150–51, especially 150 where money-making occupations are all dismissed with words and phrases such as *improbantur, illiberales et sordidi, nec vero est quisquam turpius, minimae eae artes probandae*. As often, moral degradation and slave status go hand in hand: for among the phrases just quoted we also find *est enim in illis ipsa merces auctoramentum servitutis*, and *nec enim quicquam ingenuum habere potest*. For parallels and further discussion see Dyck 1996 ad loc. and Brunt 1975: 14.

slaves, or the poor freeborn. Presumably, those who engage in such activities cannot thereby acquire wisdom themselves any more than they can impart it to others.

Meanwhile the "true" liberal study is philosophy, the conferrer of wisdom and virtue, by which one may acquire the knowledge of good and bad; it is moreover the only self-sufficent art, building upon its own first principles and therefore needing no assistance from the (so-called) liberal studies just discussed (*Ep.* 88.28–32). In *Ep.* 65.15–21, Seneca shows that philosophy lives up to its billing as a *liberale studium:* he says that it is the only enterprise capable of setting someone free, and it does so by teaching the soul to contemplate the divine and so liberating it from its corporeal prison (e.g., *Ep.* 65.16). Similar assertions can be found elsewhere: he says that *liberalia studia*, which impart *sapientia*, fortify one against *fortuna* (*Helv.* 17.3–5) — or, in an even stronger metaphor, that philosophy provides an "unbreachable wall" (*inexpugnabilis murus*) through which the assaults of *fortuna* cannot reach one (*Ep.* 82.2–6); that the way to acquire *sapientia* is to spend time reading philosophy or talking to philosophers (*Brev.* 14; *Epp.* 62, 104.21–22); that this kind of activity will "claim the soul as free from its most wretched slavery" (*inter studia versandum est et inter auctores sapientiae . . . sic eximendus animus ex miserrima servitute in libertatem adseritur, Ep.* 104.16).

In all of these passages, then, we see a strong interplay between the status-conscious rhetoric of Seneca's assertions about acquiring wisdom — that *liberalia studia* are "appropriate to free men," or that they "set one free" in one way or another — and the content of those assertions, especially the exclusionary clauses that debar from the *liberalia studia* many, probably the large majority, of activities commonly pursued by nonelites and the fields of knowledge that they typically command. In a world of aristocratic status anxiety, where the elites perceive that the exclusivity of their privileges are threatened in part by the upward mobility of at least some imperial slaves and freedmen, Seneca proposes a reconstructed aristocracy of virtue — articulated as those who are "free" — to which one can gain entry by acquiring a body of knowledge that expressly excludes the kinds of knowledge monopolized by such slaves and freedmen. Of course, these low-status persons can in theory "free" themselves by studying philosophy and thus acquiring wisdom, just as elites can fail to do so and therefore fall into "slavery." But such study is not among the typical occupations of nonelites, while it is already a typical occupation of the elites. Habinek (1992: 192), in a discussion of the status-conscious rhetoric by which Seneca lays claim to the role of teacher of virtue, draws the following conclusion: "The distinction between the stampeding crowd and the followers of Seneca

... [is] an assimilation of the philosophical life to the political prejudices of the rich and high-born. Virtue may create its own nobility; but it is a nobility that mimics the old nobility's strategies of exclusion and contempt." Indeed, the nobility that virtue creates hardly extends beyond the circle of the old nobility, since the process of acquiring that virtue would seem to be available, in practice, almost exclusively to them.[115]

If persons of lower status are generally unable join Seneca's (re)constructed aristocracy because the necessary education is unavailable to them, tyrannical rulers are also excluded on the ground that they fail to display the patterns of behavior that are appropriate to that aristocracy. As we saw above, *ira* and other emotions are presented as inappropriate and even dangerous to this aristocracy: a person who displays these emotions is said to be a slave to them, while a person who suppresses them is free from or master over them. But tyrants are programmatically angry and fearful: the one described in *De Clementia* is savage, cruel, and fears both men and gods (1.11.4, 12.1, 13.2). Specific tyrants, such as those described in *De Ira* 3.14–21, are similar; all of these are invoked specifically as exempla for the destructiveness of anger (*Ira* 3.13.7). To take representations of Caligula as a test case, we are told that bloodthirstiness (*crudelitas*) was a pleasure (*voluptas*) for him (*Ira* 3.18.4); shortly thereafter we learn (§19.1) that *crudelitas* is an aspect of *ira*. In other passages, Caligula is said to have grown angry at heaven and feared thunderbolts (*Ira* 1.20.8), and furthermore in his mourning for Drusilla he is said to have lacked shame and self-restraint (*Polyb*. 17.4–6). Tyrants, then, reveal through their behavior and appearance the mental states that are characterized as "slavery," while their victims (such as Pastor or Canus), if they maintain their equanimity, thereby evince the mental states characterized as "freedom." Thus, the power relationship between tyrant and aristocrat, which may be modeled as a master-slave relationship in the political domain, is turned upside-down in the philosophical domain: here it is the properly acculturated, philosophically trained aristocrat who is a master or free, and the unacculturated, philosophically ignorant tyrant who is a slave. Tyrants are therefore not part of Seneca's aristocracy of virtue, and neither, for the most part, are persons of lower status: the established aris-

---

[115] The status implications of the phrase *liberalia studia* are expressed in animal terms at *Brev*. 18.4. Here Seneca chides his addressee Paulinus for holding a post that is beneath him. Seneca claims that this post, while honorable, is "not well suited to the happy life": for Paulinus's long cultivation of liberal studies have fit him for "something greater and loftier" (*maius quiddam et altius*). He then compares Paulinus to a "noble horse" of "well-born speed" (*nobiles equi, generosa pernicitas*) doing the work of "plodding oxen" (*tarda iumenta*).

tocracy's authority is thus preserved, even reconstructed, against the threats it perceives from the lower classes and from those emperors who afflict them with corporal punishment or other slavish treatment.

7. Conclusion

From my analysis of master-slave and father-son language and imagery, as it is used to model and characterize the position of the *princeps* relative to his aristocratic subjects — whether through the direct portrayal of the *princeps* as father or master, or the more intricate Stoic application of such imagery, as just discussed — it will be evident that the view of the principate articulated here is not a "constitutionalist" view. The "constitutionalist" view, familiar to all students of Roman history, is that the emperor engrossed a variety of specific powers that had been distributed among a number of magistrates and other officials during the republic. Specifically, the emperor usurped the power of supreme military command (*imperium*) historically held by the consuls — though his power in this regard was deemed higher than theirs (hence *maius imperium*) and his commands were not subject to veto, since the "position" of emperor was not collegial. He also appropriated the *potestas* of the tribunes of the plebs and the censors; and from late in Augustus's reign onward, he was *pontifex maximus*. He has even been regarded as a provincial governor on a statewide scale, not only because the so-called "imperial" provinces were under his direct oversight and control, but also because the de facto power he wielded was similar to that traditionally wielded within provinces by their governors. Thus the constitutionalist view presents the emperor as an amalgamation of familiar republican magistrates, and therefore suggests that his actions qua emperor are justifiable and explicable in the context of familiar republican magisterial powers.

The problem with this view is not that the concrete claims it makes are wrong: on the contrary, the emperor did indeed hold *tribunicia potestas, maius imperium*, and so on, and at least some of his initiatives were explicitly framed in terms of such powers. The problem, rather, is that it is inadequate, for these concrete powers do not adequately account for the emperor's actions and behavior. The emperor could and did do many things without reference to his "official" powers, and that these powers did not authorize him to do. Octavian was not hindered in the 30s B.C. by not "officially" holding the powers he was later granted by the senate, nor, I suspect, would it have mattered much to the subsequent conduct of his reign had he not been granted these powers in the 20s. This difficulty with the strict constitutionalist view is articulated at least as early as Premerstein (1937: 13), who traces it back still further. But it is perhaps worth reiterating since Veyne has recently reasserted the view of emperor as magistrate (1990: 345 = 1976: 620). More important for my purposes, however, is that I have found no indication that this constitutionalist view was widespread among Julio-Claudian aristocrats: that is, the aristocratic contemporaries of the early emperors did not, at least in the first instance, see the principate in these terms.

Focusing instead on widespread contemporary modes of comprehending and articulating the emperor and his regime, I have argued in this chapter and the last that his authority was figured largely through vigorous debates regarding which of several stereotyped, ethically loaded social authority figures could or should serve as models for him. On the one hand, I have surveyed the conditions under which the emperor might be presented as a "father" or "master" in relation to aristocrats, and the consequences of so modeling him. On the other hand, I have examined contemporary discussions and evaluations of his behavior as a transactor of objects and services, in the convivium and elsewhere, in the context of a society which uses such transactions to establish and challenge social hierarchies and hence to present social authority as legitimate or illegitimate. Furthermore, in chapters 1 and 2, I argued that the emergence of the principate was associated with various crises of ethical valuation and hence with the production of new systems of moral value that competed with the old; I showed that the ways in which Seneca and Lucan make such systems compete constitute an exploration of the new sociopolitical order, as well as an attempt to shape it, and to shape contemporary perceptions of it, in light of particular aristocratic interests. The ways in which Julio-Claudian aristocrats comprehended and constructed the autocracy in which they lived, then, was to focus upon various situations in which ethics and power intersected, and to debate vigorously the ethical ramifications of the configurations of power and authority they found at these intersections. There was no other conception of the new order that was external to, or prior to, these competitions among ethical systems, value judgments, and paradigms for authority that permeated Roman literature and thought from the civil wars onward. My aim in this book has been to trace some of these contestations, with the hope of elucidating contemporary ways of articulating the emerging social and political order of the principate.

BIBLIOGRAPHY

Adam, Traute. 1970. *Clementia Principis: der Einfluß hellenistischer Fürstenspiegel auf den Versuch einer rechtlichen Fundierung des Principats durch Seneca.* Stuttgart: Ernst Klett (= Kieler Historische Studien, Bd. 11).

Adkins, Arthur W. 1970. *From the Many to the One.* Ithaca: Cornell University Press.

Ahl, Frederick. 1976. *Lucan: An Introduction.* Ithaca: Cornell University Press.

Alewell, Karl. 1913. *Über das rhetorische Paradeigma.* Leipzig: August Hoffmann.

Alföldi, Andreas. 1971. *Der Vater des Vaterlandes im römischen Denken.* Darmstadt: Wissenschaftliche Buchgesellschaft.

Althusser, Louis. 1969. "Ideology and Ideological State Apparatuses (Notes toward an Investigation)." In *Lenin and Philosophy and Other Essays,* tr. Ben Brewster (London: New Left Books), 123–73.

———. 1971. "Marxism and Humanism." In *For Marx,* tr. Ben Brewster (New York: Pantheon Books), 219–47.

Amat, Jacqueline, ed. 1991. *Calpurnius Siculus Bucoliques, Pseudo-Calpurnius Eloge de Pison.* Paris: Les Belles Lettres.

Appadurai, Arjun. 1986. "Introduction: commodities and the politics of value." In *The Social Life of Things: Commodities in Cultural Perspective,* ed. A. Appadurai (Cambridge: Cambridge University Press), 3–63.

Atkinson, J. E. 1980. *A Commentary on Q. Curtius Rufus' Historiae Alexandri Magni, Books 3 and 4.* Amsterdam: Gieben.

Baldwin, Barry. 1975. "Vespasian and Freedom." *Rivista di filologia e di istruzione classica* 103: 306–308.

Ball, Terence. 1988. *Transforming Political Discourse.* Oxford: Blackwell.

Bang, M. 1921. "Über den Gebrauch der Anrede domine im gemeinen Leben." In Friedlaender, Ludwig, *Darstellungen aus der Sittengeschichte Roms* (9–10th ed.), IV.82–88.

Barton, Carlin. 1993. *The Sorrows of the Ancient Romans.* Princeton: Princeton University Press.

Bartsch, Shadi. 1994. *Actors in the Audience: Theatricality and Doublespeak from Nero to Hadrian.* Cambridge [Mass.]: Harvard University Press.

Basore, John W. 1928. *Seneca: Moral Essays.* 3 vols. London: Heinemann (= Loeb).

Bellincioni, Maria. 1979. *Lettere a Lucilio Libro XV: le lettere 94 e 95.* Brescia: Paideia Editrice.

Berlin, Isaiah. 1970 [1958]. "Two Concepts of Liberty." In *Four Essays on Liberty* (New York: Oxford University Press), 118–172.

Bettini, Maurizio. 1991 [1986]. *Anthropology and Roman culture: kinship, time, images of the soul.* Tr. John Van Sickle. Baltimore: Johns Hopkins University Press. (Originally published as *Antropologia e cultura romana: parentela, tempo, immagini dell'anima,* Roma, 1986.)

Bleicken, Jochen. 1972. *Staatliche Ordnung und Freiheit in der römischen Republik.* Kallmünz: Lassleben (= Frankfurter Althistorische Studien, Heft 6).
Bonhöfer, Adolf. 1894. *Die Ethik des stoikers Epiktet.* Stuttgart: Ferdinand Enke.
Bourdieu, Pierre. 1977 [1972]. *Outline of a Theory of Practice.* Tr. Richard Nice. Cambridge: Cambridge University Press. (Originally published as *Esquisse d'une théorie de la pratique, précédé de trois études d'ethnologie kybale,* Librairie Droz, 1972.)
———. 1991. *Language and Symbolic Power.* Ed. J. B. Thompson. Cambridge [Mass.]: Polity Press.
———. 1993 [1983]. *The Field of Cultural Production.* Cambridge [Mass.]: Polity Press.
Bradley, Keith R. 1987. *Slaves and Masters in the Roman Empire.* Oxford: Oxford Universtiy Press (= Editions Latomus, 1984).
———. 1994. *Slavery and Society at Rome.* Cambridge: Cambridge University Press.
———. 1998. "The Roman Family at Dinner." In *Meals in a Social Context,* eds. Inge Nielsen and Hanne Sigismund Nielsen (Aarhus: Aarhus University Press), 36–55.
Braund, S. H. 1992. *Lucan: Civil War.* Oxford: Clarendon Press.
Brunt, P. A. 1966. "The 'Fiscus' and Its Development." *JRS* 56: 75–91.
———. 1975. "Stoicism and the Principate." *Papers of the British School at Rome* 43 (n.s. 30): 7–35.
———. 1984. "Remarks on the Imperial Fiscus." *Liverpool Classical Monthly* 9: 2–4
———. 1988. *The Fall of the Roman Republic.* Oxford: Clarendon Press.
———. 1990. *Roman Imperial Themes.* Oxford: Clarendon Press.
Brunt, P. A. and J. M. Moore, eds. 1967. *Res Gestae Divi Augusti, The Achievements of the Divine Augustus.* Oxford: Oxford University Press.
Bryant, Joseph M. 1996. *Moral Codes and Social Structure in Ancient Greece.* Albany: State University of New York Press.
Buckland, W. W. 1908. *The Roman Law of Slavery.* Cambridge: Cambridge University Press.
Busch, Gerda. 1961. "Fortunae resistere in der Moral des Philosophen Seneca." *Antike und Abendland* 10: 131–54.
Cagnat, René, ed. 1906. *Inscriptiones Graecae ad Res Romanas Pertinentes.* 4 vols. Paris: E. Leroux.
Cairns, Douglas L. 1993. *Aidos.* Oxford: Clarendon Press.
Campbell, J. B. 1984. *The Emperor and the Roman Army 31 BC–AD 235.* Oxford: Clarendon Press.
Caston, Ruth Rothaus. 1997. "The Fall of the Curtain (Horace S. 2.8)." *TAPA* 127: 233–56.
Champlin, Edward. 1991. *Final judgments: duty and emotion in Roman wills, 200 B.C.–A.D. 250.* Berkeley: University of California Press.
Cloud, Duncan. 1989. "The client-patron relationship: emblem and reality in Juvenal's first book." In *Patronage in Ancient Society,* ed. A. Wallace-Hadrill (London: Routledge), 205–218.

Codere, Helen. 1950. *Fighting with Property: A Study of Kwakiutl Potlatching and Warfare, 1792–1930*. New York: J. J. Augustin (= Monographs of the American Ethnological Society, vol. 18).

Collitz, H., F. Bechtel et al., eds. 1884. *Sammlung der griechischen Dialekt-Inschriften*. Göttingen: Vandenhoeck & Ruprecht.

Conte, Gian Biagio. 1986. *The Rhetoric of Imitation*. Ithaca: Cornell University Press.

Cooper, David E. 1986. *Metaphor*. New York: Blackwell.

Cotton, Hannah. 1981. *Documentary Letters of Recommendation in Latin from the Roman Empire*. Königstein: Anton Hain (= Beiträge zur klassischen Philologie, Heft 132).

Crawford, Michael. 1974. *Roman Republican Coinage*. 2 vols. Cambridge: Cambridge University Press.

Crook, John A. 1955. *Consilium Principis: Imperial Councils and Counsellors from Augustus to Diocletian*. Cambridge: Cambridge University Press.

———. 1967. "Patria Potestas." *CQ* 17: 113–22.

Cugusi, Paolo. 1992. *Corpus epistularum Latinarum papyris tabulis ostracis servatarum*. 2 vols. Firenze: Gonnelli.

Damon, Cynthia. 1997. *The Mask of the Parasite: A Pathology of Roman Patronage*. Ann Arbor: University of Michigan Press.

Daremberg, Charles, and Edmond Saglio. 1875. *Dictionnaire des Antiquités Grecques et Romaines*. 5 vols. Paris: Hachette.

D'Arms, John. 1990. "The Roman *Convivium* and the Idea of Equality." In *Sympotica*, ed. O. Murray (Oxford: Clarendon Press), 308–19.

———. 1991. "Slaves at Roman Convivia." In *Dining in a Classical Context*, ed. W. Slater (Ann Arbor: University of Michigan Press), 171–83.

David, Jean-Michel. 1992. *Le patronat judiciaire au dernier siècle de la république Romaine*. Rome: École Française de Rome (= Bibliothèque des Écoles Françaises d'Athènes et de Rome, fasc. 277).

Davies, J. K. 1984. "Cultural, Social, and Economic Features of the Hellenistic World." In *Cambridge Ancient History* 7.1^2, 257–320.

Dixon, Suzanne. 1992. *The Roman Family*. Baltimore: Johns Hopkins University Press.

———. 1993a. "'A Lousy Ingrate': Honour and Patronage in the American Mafia and Ancient Rome." *International Journal of Moral and Social Studies* 8: 61–72.

———. 1993b. "The Meaning of Gift and Debt in the Roman Elite." *Echos du Monde Classique/Classical Views* 37: 451–64.

Dubuisson, Michel. 1980. "Toi aussi, mon fils!" *Latomus* 39: 881–90.

Due, Otto Steen. 1962. "An Essay on Lucan." *Classica & Mediaevalia* 23: 68–132.

Duff, A. M. 1928. *Freedmen in the Early Roman Empire*. Oxford: Clarendon Press.

Dunbabin, Katherine M. D. 1986. "'Sic Erimus Cuncti . . .': The Skeleton in Graeco-Roman Art." *Jahrbuch des Deutschen Archäologischen Instituts* 101: 185–255.

Duncan-Jones, Richard. 1982. *The Economy of the Roman Empire: Quantitative Studies*^{2}. Cambridge: Cambridge University Press.

Dyck, Andrew. 1996. *A Commentary on Cicero, De Officiis*. Ann Arbor: University of Michigan Press.

Earl, D. C. 1961. *The Political Thought of Sallust*. Cambridge: Cambridge University Press.

———. 1967. *The Moral and Political Tradition of Rome*. Ithaca: Cornell University Press.

Eck, Werner, Antonio Caballos, and Fernando Fernández. 1996. *Das senatus consultum de Cn. Pisone patre*. München: C. H. Beck'sche Verlagsbuchhandlung (= *Vestigia*, Bd. 48).

Edwards, Catharine. 1997. "Self-Scrutiny and Self-Transformation in Seneca's Letters." *Greece & Rome* 44: 23–38.

Ehrenberg, Victor, and A. H. M. Jones. 1955. *Documents illustrating the reigns of Augustus & Tiberius*[2]. Oxford: Clarendon Press.

Eisenhut, Werner. 1973. *Virtus Romana*. München: Wilhelm Fink Verlag (= *Studia et Testimonia Antiqua*, vol. 13).

Engberg-Pedersen, Troels. 1990. *The Stoic Theory of Oikeiosis*. Aarhus: Aarhus University Press (= Studies in Hellenistic Civilization, vol. 2).

Ernout, Alfred, and Antoine Meillet. 1959. *Dictionnaire etymologique de la langue latine*[4]. Paris: Klinksieck.

Erskine, Andrew. 1990. *The Hellenistic Stoa: political thought and action*. London: Duckworth.

Faider, P., C. Favez, and P. van de Woestijne. 1950. *Sénèque: De la clémence*. 2 vols. Gand: Van Rysselberghe & Rombaut.

Fantham, Elaine. 1992. *Lucan De Bello Civili Book II*. Cambridge: Cambridge University Press.

Farr, James. 1989. "Understanding Conceptual Change Politically." In *Political Innovation and Conceptual Change*, eds. T. Ball, J. Farr, R. Hanson (Cambridge: Cambridge University Press), 24–49.

Ferguson, John. 1958. *Moral Values in the Ancient World*. London: Methuen.

Finley, Moses I. 1980. *Ancient Slavery and Modern Ideology*. New York: Viking Press.

Fitzgibbon, J. C. 1976. "Ergastula." *Echos du Monde Classique/Classical Views* 20: 55–59.

Flower, Harriet I. 1996. *Ancestor Masks and Aristocratic Power in Roman Culture*. Oxford: Clarendon Press.

Foucault, Michel. 1986 [1984]. *The Care of the Self*. Tr. R. Hurley. New York: Vintage Books (= *The History of Sexuality*, vol. 3).

Fowler, Don. 1990. "Deviant focalization in Vergil's *Aeneid*." *Proceedings of the Cambridge Philological Society* 36: 42–63.

Fustel de Coulanges, Numa Denis. 1980 [1864]. *The Ancient City*. Tr. Willard Small. Baltimore: Johns Hopkins University Press.

Garnsey, Peter. 1970. *Social Status and Legal Privilege in the Roman Empire*. Oxford: Clarendon Press.

Garnsey, Peter, and R. Saller. 1987. *The Roman Empire: Economy, Society, and Culture*. Berkeley: University of California Press.

Gaudemet, Jean. 1953. "Testamenta ingrata et pietas Augusti." In *Studi in onore di Vincenzo Arangio-Ruiz* (Napoli: Jovene), III.115–37.

Geertz, Clifford. 1973 [1964]. "Ideology as a Cultural System." In *The Interpretation of Cultures: Selected Essays by Clifford Geertz* (New York: Basic Books), 193–233.
Gelzer, Matthias. 1968. *Caesar Politican and Statesman.* Tr. Peter Needham. Cambridge [Mass.]: Harvard University Press.
Gowers, Emily. 1993. *The Loaded Table: Representations of Food in Roman Literature.* Oxford: Clarendon Press.
Graver, Margaret. 1998. "The Manhandling of Maecenas." *AJP* 119: 607–32.
Gregory, Chris. 1982. *Gifts and Commodities.* London: Academic Press.
Griffin, Miriam. 1976. *Seneca: A Philosopher in Politics.* Oxford: Clarendon Press.
———. 1986. "Philosophy, Cato, and Roman Suicide I–II." *Greece & Rome* 33: 64–75, 192–202.
Grimal, Pierre. 1992. "Le vocabulaire de l'intériorité dans l'oeuvre philosophique de Sénèque." In *La langue latine, langue de la philosophie.* Rome: École française de Rome, 141–59.
Gruen, Erich. 1974. *The Last Generation of the Roman Republic.* Berkeley: University of California Press.
Gummere, Richard M. 1920. *Seneca: Ad Lucilium Epistulae Morales.* 3 vols. London: Heinemann (= Loeb).
Habinek, Thomas N. 1989. "Science and Tradition in *Aeneid* 6." *HSCP* 92: 223–55.
———. 1990. "The Politics of Candor in Cicero's De Amicitia" *Apeiron* 23: 165–85.
———. 1992. "An aristocracy of virtue: Seneca on the beginnings of wisdom." *Yale Classical Studies* 29: 187–203.
———. 1998. *The Politics of Latin Literature.* Princeton: Princeton University Press.
Habinek, Thomas N., and A. Schiesaro, eds. 1997. *The Roman Cultural Revolution.* Cambridge: Cambridge University Press.
Håkanson, Lennart. 1979. "Problems of Textual Criticism and Interpretation in Lucan's *De Bello Civili.*" *Proceedings of the Cambridge Philological Society* 25: 26–51.
Halkin, Léon. 1953. *La supplication d'action de grâces chez les Romains.* Paris: Société d'Édition (= Bibliothèque de la Faculté de Philosophie et Lettres de l'Université de Liège, fasc. 128).
Hall, Jon. 1998. "The Deference-Greeting in Roman Society." *Maia* 50: 413–26.
Hammond, Mason. 1963. "Res Olim Dissociabiles: Principatus ac Libertas. Liberty under the Early Roman Empire." *HSCP* 67: 93–113.
Harris, William V. 1979. *War and Imperialism in Republican Rome, 327–70 B.C.* Oxford: Clarendon Press.
———. 1986. "The Roman Father's Power of Life and Death." In *Studies in Roman Law in memory of A. Arthur Schiller,* eds. R. S. Bagnall and W. V. Harris (Leiden: Brill), 81–95.
Heinze, Richard. 1915. *Virgils epische Technik*[3]. Leipzig: B. G. Teubner.
Hellegouarc'h, Joseph. 1963. *Le vocabulaire latin des relations et des partis politiques sous la république.* Paris: Les Belles Lettres.

Henderson, John. 1987. "Lucan / the Word at War." *Ramus* 16: 122–64.
Herrmann, Peter. 1968. *Der römische Kaisereid*. Göttingen: Vandenhoeck & Ruprecht (= *Hypomnemata*, Heft 20).
Heyke, Waltraut. 1970. *Zur Rolle der Pietas bei Lucan*. Mannheim.
Higginbotham, James. 1997. *Piscinae: artificial fishponds in Roman Italy*. Chapel Hill: University of North Carolina Press.
Homans, George C. 1958. "Social Behavior as Exchange." *American Journal of Sociology* 63: 597–606.
Hopkins, Keith. 1978. *Conquerors and Slaves*. Cambridge: Cambridge University Press.
———. 1983. *Death and Renewal*. Cambridge: Cambridge University Press.
———. 1993. "Novel Evidence for Roman Slavery." *Past & Present* 138: 3–27.
Housman, A. E. 1926. *M. Annaei Lucani Belli Civilis Libri Decem*. Oxford: Blackwell.
Howell, Peter. 1980. *A commentary on book one of the Epigrams of Martial*. London: Athlone.
Humphrey, Caroline, and Stephen Hugh-Jones, eds. 1992. *Barter, exchange, and value: an anthropological approach*. Cambridge: Cambridge University Press.
Hurley, Donna W. 1993. *An Historical and Historiographical Commentary on Suetonius' Life of C. Caligula*. Atlanta: Scholars Press.
Inwood, Brad. 1985. *Ethics and Human Action in Early Stoicism*. Oxford: Oxford University Press.
———. 1995. "Politics and Paradox in Seneca's De Beneficiis." In *Justice and Generosity*, eds. André Laks and Malcolm Schofield (Cambridge: Cambridge University Press), 241–65.
Jal, Paul. 1962. "Bellum civile - bellum externum dans la Rome de la fin de la république." *Les études classiques* 30: 257–67, 384–90.
———. 1963. "Hostis (publicus) dans la littérature Latine de la fin de la république." *Revue des études anciennes* 65: 53–79.
Johnson, Terry, and Christopher Dandeker. 1989. "Patronage: relation and system." In *Patronage in Ancient Society*, ed. A. Wallace-Hadrill (London: Routledge), 219–41.
Kaster, Robert A. 1995. *C. Suetonius Tranquillus De Grammaticis et Rhetoribus*. Oxford: Clarendon Press.
———. 1997. "The Shame of the Romans." *TAPA* 127: 1–19.
Kautsky, John. 1982. *The Politics of Aristocratic Empires*. Chapel Hill: University of North Carolina Press.
Kelly, J. M. 1966. *Roman Litigation*. Oxford: Clarendon Press.
Kennedy, Duncan. 1992. "'Augustan' and 'Anti-Augustan': Reflections on Terms of Reference." In *Roman Poetry and Propaganda in the Age of Augustus*, ed. Anton Powell (London: Bristol Classical Press), 26–58.
Kerferd, G. B. 1978. "What Does the Wise Man Know?" In *The Stoics*, ed. J. Rist (Berkeley: University of California Press), 125–36.
Kidd, I. G. 1978. "Moral Actions and Rules in Stoic Ethics." In *The Stoics*, ed. J. Rist (Berkeley: University of California Press), 247–58.
Klauser, Theodor. 1944. "Aurum Coronarium." *Mitteilungen des Deutschen Archäologischen Instituts, Römische Abteilung* 59: 129–53.

Kloft, Hans. 1970. *Liberalitas Principis*. Köln: Böhlau Verlag (= Kölner historische Abhandlungen, Bd. 18).
Koestermann, Erich. 1963. *Cornelius Tacitus: Annalen. Erläutert und mit einer Einleitung versehen*. Heidelberg: C. Winter.
Konstan, David. 1995. "Patrons and Friends." *Classical Philology* 90: 328–42.
———. 1997. *Friendship in the Classical World*. Cambridge: Cambridge University Press.
Kuntze, Claudia. 1985. *Zur Darstellung des Kaisers Tiberius und seiner Zeit bei Velleius Paterculus*. Frankfurt am Main: Peter Lang.
Lacourse, Josée. 1987. "Réciprocité positive et réciprocité negative: de Marcel Mauss a René Girard." *Cahiers internationaux de sociologie* 83: 291–305.
Lakoff, George. 1987. *Women, Fire, and Dangerous Things: What Categories Reveal about the Mind*. Chicago: University of Chicago Press.
Lakoff, George, and M. Johnson. 1980. *Metaphors We Live By*. Chicago: University of Chicago Press.
Lebek, Wolfgang Dieter. 1976. *Lucans Pharsalia: Dichtungsstruktur und Zeitbezug*. Göttingen: Vandenhoeck & Ruprecht (= *Hypomnemata*, Heft 44).
Leigh, Matthew. 1997. *Lucan: Spectacle and Engagement*. Oxford: Clarendon Press.
Lendon, J. E. 1997. *Empire of Honour: The Art of Government in the Roman World*. Oxford: Clarendon Press.
Lintott, Andrew. 1972. "Provocatio." *Aufstieg und Niedergang der römischen Welt* 1.2: 226–67.
Litchfield, H. W. 1914. "National Exempla Virtutis in Roman Literature." *HSCP* 25: 1–71.
Long, Anthony A. 1986. *Hellenistic Philosophy: Stoics, Epicureans, Sceptics*^{2}. Berkeley: University of California Press.
———. 1991. "Representation and the self in Stoicism." In *Psychology*, ed. Stephen Emerson (Cambridge: Cambridge University Press), 102–120.
———. 1996 [1971]. "The logical basis of Stoic ethics." In *Stoic Studies* (Cambridge: Cambridge University Press), 134–55.
———. 1996 [1983]. "Greek ethics after MacIntyre and the Stoic community of reason." In *Stoic Studies* (Cambridge: Cambridge University Press), 156–78.
Long, Anthony A., and David Sedley. 1987. *The Hellenistic Philosophers*. 2 vols. Cambridge: Cambridge University Press.
Lounsbury, Richard C. 1975. "The Death of Domitius in the Pharsalia." *TAPA* 105: 209–212.
Lyne, R. O. A. M. 1987. *Further Voices in Vergil's Aeneid*. Oxford: Clarendon Press.
MacMullen, Ramsay. 1986. "Personal Power in the Roman Empire." *AJP* 107: 512–24.
Marti, Berthe. 1966. "Cassius Scaeva and Lucan's Inventio." In *The Classical Tradition: Literary and Historical Studies in Honor of Harry Caplan*, ed. Luitpold Wallach (Ithaca: Cornell University Press), 239–57.
Martin, Dale B. 1990. *Slavery as salvation: the metaphor of slavery in Pauline Christianity*. New Haven: Yale University Press.
Martindale, Charles. 1976. "Paradox, Hyperbole, and Literary Novelty in Lucan's De Bello Civili." *Bulletin of the Institute of Classical Studies* 23: 45–54.

Masters, Jamie. 1992. *Poetry and Civil War in Lucan's Bellum Civile.* Cambridge: Cambridge University Press.

Mauss, Marcel. 1990 [1924]. *The Gift.* Tr. W. D. Halls. London: Routledge. (Originally published as *Essai sur le Don,* Presses Universitaires de France, 1950.)

Maxfield, Valerie. 1981. *The Military Decorations of the Roman Army.* Berkeley: University of California Press.

Mayer, Roland G. 1991. "Roman Historical Exempla in Seneca." In *Sénèque et la prose latine,* ed. Pierre Grimal (Genève: Vandoeuvres), 141–69 (= Fondation Hardt, Entretiens sur l'Antiquité classique, tome 36).

McGinn, T. 1989. "The Taxation of Roman Prostitutes." *Helios* 16: 79–110.

Millar, Fergus. 1977. *The Emperor in the Roman World.* Ithaca: Cornell University Press.

———. 1984. "The Political Character of the Classical Roman Republic." *JRS* 74: 1–19.

Miller, William Ian. 1993. *Humiliation.* Ithaca: Cornell University Press.

Minyard, John D. 1985. *Lucretius and the Late Republic.* Leiden: E. J. Brill (= *Mnemosyne* suppl. 90).

Mommsen, Theodor. 1887. *Römisches Staatsrecht*^{3}. Leipzig. (Reprint by Akademische Druck- u. Verlagsanstalt, Graz 1969.)

———. 1899. *Römisches Strafrecht.* Leipzig: Duncker & Humblot.

Moore, Timothy. 1989. *Artistry and Ideology: Livy's Vocabulary of Virtue.* Frankfurt am Main: Athenäum (= Beiträge zur klassischen Philologie, Bd. 192).

Morales, Helen. 1996. "The torturer's apprentice: Parrhasius and the limits of art." In *Art and Text in Roman Culture,* ed. J. Elsner (Cambridge: Cambridge University Press), 182–209.

Morford, M. P. O. 1967. "The Purpose of Lucan's Ninth Book." *Latomus* 26: 123–29.

Nicolet, Claude. 1980 [1976]. *The World of the Citizen in Republican Rome.* Tr. P. S. Falla. Berkeley: University of California Press. (Originally published as *Le métier de citoyen dans la Rome républicaine,* Paris, 1976.)

Ogilvie, R. M. 1965. *A Commentary on Livy, Books 1–5.* Oxford: Clarendon Press.

Patterson, O. 1991 *Freedom.* Vol. 1, *Freedom in the Making of Western Culture.* New York: Basic Books.

Pelling, C. B. R. 1988. *Plutarch: Life of Antony.* Cambridge: Cambridge University Press.

Perl, G. 1977. "Zu Varros Instrumentum Vocale." *Klio* 59: 423–29.

Powell, Anton. 1992. "The *Aeneid* and the Embarrassments of Augustus." In *Roman Poetry and Propaganda in the Age of Augustus,* ed. Anton Powell (Worcester: Bristol Classical Press), 141–74.

Premerstein, Anton von. 1937. *Vom Werden und Wesen des Prinzipats.* München: Verlag der Bayerischen Akademie der Wissenschaften.

Raaflaub, Kurt. 1974. *Dignitatis Contentio.* München: C. H. Beck'sche Verlagsbuchhandlung.

Rawson, Elizabeth. 1991. "Cassius and Brutus: The Memory of the Liberators."

In *Roman Culture and Society: Collected Papers* (Oxford: Clarendon Press), 488–507.
Reinhold, Meyer. 1971. "Usurpation of Status and Status Symbols." *Historia* 20: 275–302.
Richardson, Scott. 1990. *The Homeric Narrator.* Nashville: Vanderbilt University Press.
Rist, John. 1969. *Stoic Philosophy.* Cambridge: Cambridge University Press.
Robins, R. H. 1987. "Polysemy and the Lexicographer." In *Studies in Lexicography*, ed. R. Burchfield (Oxford: Clarendon Press), 52–75.
Rogers, R. S. 1947. "Roman emperors as heirs and legatees." *TAPA* 78: 140–58.
Roisman, Joseph. 1997. Review of Bryant 1996. *American Journal of Sociology* 102: 1789.
Roller, Matthew. 1998. "Pliny's Catullus: The Politics of Literary Appropriation." *TAPA* 128: 265–304.
Rosenstein, Nathan. 1990. *Imperatores victi: military defeat and aristocratic competition in the middle and late Republic.* Berkeley: University of California Press.
Rotondi, Giovanni. 1922. *Leges Publicae Populi Romani.* Milan (reprint by G. Olms, Hildesheim 1962).
Rudich, Vassily. 1993. *Political Dissidence under Nero: the Price of Dissimulation.* London: Routledge.
Russell, James. 1980. "Julius Caesar's Last Words: A Reinterpretation." In *Vindex Humanitatis: Essays in Honour of John Huntly Bishop*, ed. B. Marshall (Armidale), 123–28.
Rusten, Jeffrey. 1989. *The Peloponnesian War Book II.* Cambridge: Cambridge University Press.
Säflund, Gösta. 1972. *The Polyphemus and Scylla Groups at Sperlonga.* Stockholm: Almqvist & Wiskell (= Stockholm Studies in Classical Archaeology, v. 9).
Saggese, Paolo. 1994. "Lo Scurra in Marziale." *Maia* 46: 53–59.
Sahlins, Marshal. 1972. *Stone Age Economics.* Chicago: Aldine-Atherton.
Saller, Richard. 1982. *Personal Patronage under the Early Empire.* Cambridge: Cambridge University Press.
———. 1983. "Martial on Patronage and Literature." *CQ* 33: 246–57.
———. 1989. "Patronage and friendship in early Imperial Rome: drawing the distinction." In *Patronage in Ancient Society*, ed. A. Wallace-Hadrill (London: Routledge), 49–62.
———. 1994. *Patriarchy, property and death in the Roman family.* Cambridge: Cambridge University Press.
Saylor, Charles. 1986. "Wine, Blood, and Water: The Imagery of Lucan Pharsalia IV." *Eranos* 84: 149–56.
Scheidel, Walter. 1993. "Slavery and the Shackled Mind: On Fortune-telling and Slave Mentality in the Graeco-Roman World." *Ancient History Bulletin* 7.3/4: 107–114.
Scott, James C. 1990. *Domination and the Arts of Resistance.* New Haven: Yale University Press.

Seitz, Konrad. 1965. "Der pathetische Erzählstil Lucans." *Hermes* 93: 204–32.
Shackleton Bailey, D. R. 1982. *Anthologia Latina*. Vol. 1. Stuttgart: B. G. Teubner.
———. 1988. *Lucanus De Bello Civili*. Stuttgart: B. G. Teubner.
Shaw, Brent. 1984. "Bandits in the Roman Empire." *Past & Present* 105: 3–52.
———. 1985. "The Divine Economy: Stoicism as Ideology." *Latomus* 44: 16–54.
Sherwin-White, A. N. 1966. *The Letters of Pliny: A Historical and Social Commentary*. Oxford: Clarendon Press.
Skinner, Quentin. 1989. "Language and Political Change." In *Political Innovation and Conceptual Change*, eds. T. Ball, J. Farr, R. Hanson (Cambridge: Cambridge University Press), 6–23.
Slagter, M. 1992. Review of Bettini 1991 [1986]. *Bryn Mawr Classical Review* 3.2.2.
Smith, Martin S. 1982. *Petronii Arbitri Cena Trimalchionis*. Oxford: Clarendon Press.
Smith, R. E. 1976 [1947]. "The Aristocratic Epoch in Latin Literature." In *Essays on Roman Culture*, ed. A. J. Dunston (Toronto: A. M. Hakkert), 187–223.
Ste. Croix, G. E. M. de 1981. *The Class Struggle in the Ancient Greek World*. Ithaca: Cornell University Press.
Stückelberger, Alfred. 1980. "Seneca: Der Brief als Mittel der persönlichen Auseinandersetzung mit der Philosophie." *Didactica Classica Gandensia* 20: 133–48.
Sullivan, J. P. 1985. *Literature and Politics in the Age of Nero*. Ithaca: Cornell University Press.
Sumner, G. V. 1970. "The Truth about Velleius Paterculus." *HSCP* 74: 257–97.
Sutherland, C. H. V. 1984. "The Concepts of Adsertor and Salus As Used by Vindex and Galba." *Numismatic Chronicle* 144: 29–32.
Syme, Ronald. 1939. *The Roman Revolution*. Oxford: Clarendon Press.
———. 1961. "Who was Vedius Pollio?" *JRS* 51: 23–30.
Syndikus, Hans Peter. 1958. *Lucans Gedicht vom Bürgerkrieg*. München: "Uni"-Druck.
Tabacco, Raffaella. 1985. "Il tiranno nelle declamazioni de scuola in lingua latina." *Memorie dell'Accademia delle Scienze di Torino, Classe di Scienze morali, storiche e filologiche* 9: 1–141.
Talbert, Richard J. A. 1984. *The Senate of Imperial Rome*. Princeton: Princeton University Press.
Thévenaz, P. 1944. "L'interiorité chez Sénèque" In *Mélanges offerts à M. Max Niedermann* (Receuil de travaux 22, Université de Neuchâtel), 189–94.
Thompson, Leonard. 1984. "Domitianus Dominus: A Gloss on Statius *Silvae* 1.6.84." *AJP* 105: 469–75.
Treggiari, Susan. 1969. *Roman Freedmen during the Late Republic*. Oxford: Clarendon Press.
Treu, Max. 1948. "Zur Clementia Caesaris." *Museum Helveticum* 5: 197–217.
Tsekourakis, Damianos. 1974. *Studies in the Terminology of Early Stoic Ethics*. Wiesbaden: Franz Steiner Verlag (= *Hermes* Einzelschriften, Heft 32).

Van Sickle, John. 1987. "The Elogia of the Cornelii Scipiones and the Origin of Epigram at Rome." *AJP* 108: 41–55.
Veyne, Paul. 1976. *Le pain et le cirque: sociologie historique d'un pluralisme politique*. Paris: Éditions du Seuil.
———. 1990. *Bread and Circuses: Historical Sociology and Political Pluralism*. Tr. Brian Pearce. London: Penguin (abridged translation of Veyne 1976).
Viansino, Giovanni. 1979. "Studia Annaeana II." *Vichiana* 8: 168–96.
Wagenvoort, H. Hendrik. 1980 [1924]. "Pietas." In *Pietas: Selected Studies in Roman Religion* (Leiden: E. J. Brill), 1–20.
Wallace-Hadrill, Andrew. 1989a. "Introduction." In *Patronage in Ancient Society*, ed. A. Wallace-Hadrill (London: Routledge), 1–13.
———. 1989b. "Patronage in Roman society: from republic to empire." In *Patronage in Ancient Society*, ed. A. Wallace-Hadrill (London: Routledge), 63–87.
———. 1996. "The Imperial Court." *Cambridge Ancient History* 10^2 (Cambridge: Cambridge University Press), 283–308.
———. 1997. "Mutatio morum: the idea of a cultural revolution." In *The Roman Cultural Revolution*, eds. T. Habinek and A. Schiesaro (Cambridge: Cambridge University Press), 3–22.
Wardle, D. 1994. *Suetonius' Life of Caligula: A Commentary*. Brussels: Universa (= Collection Latomus, v. 225).
Warren, Brian. 1996. *Authority, Gift-Exchange, and Senecan Clementia*. Unpublished MS, Baltimore.
Watson, Alan. 1967. *The Law of Persons in the Later Roman Republic*. Oxford: Clarendon Press.
Watt, W. S. 1988. *Vellei Paterculi Historiarum ad M. Vinicium Consulem Libri Duo*. Leipzig: B. G. Teubner.
Weaver, P. R. C. 1967. "Social Mobility in the Early Roman Empire: The Evidence of the Imperial Freedmen and Slaves." *Past & Present* 37: 3–20.
———. 1972. *Familia Caesaris: a Social Study of the Emperor's Freedmen and Slaves*. Cambridge: Cambridge University Press.
Weinstock, Stefan. 1971. *Divus Julius*. Oxford: Clarendon Press.
Wheeler, Everett L. 1988. "*Sapiens* and Strategems: The Neglected Meaning of a Cognomen." *Historia* 37: 166–95.
White, Peter. 1993. *Promised Verse: Poets in the Society of Augustan Rome*. Cambridge [Mass.]: Harvard University Press.
Williams, Bernard. 1981. *Moral Luck*. Cambridge: Cambridge University Press.
———. 1993. *Shame and Necessity*. Berkeley: University of California Press.
Wirszubski, Ch. 1950. *Libertas as a Political Idea at Rome during the Late Republic and Early Principate*. Cambridge: Cambridge University Press.
Wistrand, Erik. 1979. *Caesar and Contemporary Roman Society*. Göteborg: Kungl. Vetenskaps- och Vitterhets-Samhället.
Woodcock, Eric C. 1959. *A New Latin Syntax*. London: Methuen.
Woodman, A. J. 1975. "Questions of date, genre and style in Velleius: Some literary answers." *CQ* 25: 272–306.
———. 1977. *Velleius Paterculus: The Tiberian Narrative (2.94–131)*. Cambridge: Cambridge University Press.

---. 1983. *Velleius Paterculus: The Caesarian and Augustan Narrative (2.41–93)*. Cambridge: Cambridge University Press.
Yavetz, Zwi. 1983. *Julius Caesar and his Public Image.* Ithaca: Cornell University Press.
Zehnacker, Hubert. 1987. "Tensions et contradictions dans l'Empire au Ier siècle: les témoignages numismatiques." In *Opposition et résistances à l'Empire d'Auguste à Trajan.* Genève: Vandoeuvres (= Entretiens sur l'Antiquité classique, tome 33).

GENERAL INDEX

Acilius Buta, butt of convival jokes, 148
adulatio. See flattery
Aemilius Lepidus, M.: military achievements of, 101
Afranius, L. (character in Lucan), 51n
Agathocles, in convivium as host, 160n
Ahl, Frederick, 19
Alexander the great: in convivium as host, 159–60; exemplum of vice in Seneca, 88–90, 102; figuration in Curtius Rufus (father, master), 234–36, 239; as munificent gift-giver, 201n
Alföldi, Andreas, 238, 249–50
Althusser, Louis, 23n
amicus minor, 113, 115–19. *See also* friendship
Antistius Sosianus, 168n
Antonius, M. (Marc Antony): in convivium, 141, 152; figuration as liberator, 252n; figuration as master, 214, 215–16, 251n; vulnerability to flattery, 152
Antyllus, in convivium as host, 150
apophoreta, 151n
Appius Claudius (the decemvir), 229n, 230
Apronius Caesianus, military achievements of, 100n
Aristides, exemplum virtutis in Seneca, 96–97
aristocracy of virtue, 142n, 273, 284–85
aristocrats: competition among, in early empire, 99–100, 107n; defined, 6–7; and flattery (*see* flattery); and gift-debt, dislike of, 194–98 (*see also* gift-debt); socioeconomic domination by, in republic, 4–6, 10
— confronting rulers: in convivia, 144–46, 150–52, 154–73; as gift-debtors, 176–93, 211–12 (*see also* gift-debt); with alternative paradigms for authority, 233–72. *See also* emperor; king; tyrant; father-son relationship; master-slave relationship
See also under individual names
Asinius Pollio, 164n; exchange relations with Augustus and Antony, 180

assentatio. See flattery
assertor (or *vindex*) *libertatis*, 214–17, 250n, 252, 261
Athenodorus, 142
auctions: as commodity-exchange framework, 146, 204; with gift-exchange components, 205. *See also* Caligula
Augustus, and advisers, 115
— in convivium: as guest, 168–71; as host, 144–45; as participant, 141; power extended by *delatores*, 157–58
— exchange and legitimation: 144–45, 157–58, 178–79, 185–88, 200–202, 207–208; *clementia* of, 157, 185–88; and false charges, 205; incurs/reciprocates gift-debt, 144–45, 207–208; resists incurring gift-debt, 202; patronage of veterans, 207–208
— figuration: as father, 253–54; as liberator, 214, 252; as master, 251–55, 258
See also emperor
Aulus Plautius: 269

bad. *See* good/bad
Ball, Terence, 9n
Bang, M., 255–56
Barton, Carlin, 62n, 139n, 150n, 156n
Bartsch, Shadi, 111n
Bellincioni, Maria, 89n
blanditiae. See flattery
Bleicken, Jochen, 219n, 227n, 228n
bona damnatorum, 199–200, 205–206
bonum/malum. See good/bad
Bourdieu, Pierre, 21n
Bradley, Keith, 223–24, 226n
Brunt, P. A., 77n, 197n, 219n, 227n
Brutus, M. Iunius: exchange relations with Caesar, 177, 188–89; figuration as liberator, 215, 230, 250; figuration as (un-grateful) son, 250

Caelius Rufus, M., 184; in convivium as host, 152
Caesar, C. Iulius
— character in Lucan: "alienating" viewpoint of, 38, 41–43, 59–61; vs. histori-

Caesar, C. Iulius (*cont.*)
  cal Caesar, 54–63; figuration as *dominus*, 54n; polyvalence of name, 37–38; speech before battle of Pharsalus, 42–43, 44
— exchange and legitimation: *clementia* of (see *clementia*); incurs/reciprocates gift-debt, 207; rises by giving, 175–78; reckons gift-debts scrupulously, 184n; patronage of veterans, 190n, 207
— figuration: as father, 249–50; as liberator, 248–49; as master, 248–50
— triumphs of, ideological significance, 56–58
  See also Index Locorum
Caesarians, historical vs. Lucan's, 55–56
Cairns, Douglas L., 22n, 24n
Calidius, Q., exchange relations with Metelli, 196–97
Caligula: in convivium as host, 144, 145–46, 161–64; exactions of, 209; figuration as master, 260, 278–79; figuration as tyrant, 285–86; and Iulius Canus, 120–21, 278–79
— exchange and legitimation: auctions of, 145–46, 203–205 (*see also* auctions); and false charges, 205; and prostitution, 205n; resists incurring gift-debt, 198–99, 203–205; and ungrateful wills, 179–180
  See also emperor
Callistus (imperial freedman), 269
Cambyses, 3–4, 116, 121; in convivium as host, 162
Campbell, J. B., 57n
Canus, see Iulius
carnifex, metaphor for ruler, 160, 164
Caston, Ruth, 153n
Cato, M. Porcius (the younger)
— character in Lucan: and Caesar, 54n; and participation in civil war, 52n; and Stoic ethics, 53–54
— exemplum virtutis in Seneca: electoral defeat, 96; military defeat, 104, 107
— and *libertas*, metonymy for in early empire: 250, 278
— Stoic mouthpiece: in Cicero, 74n; in Lucan, 53–54
Chrysippus, 77n, 98

Cicero, M. Tullius: in convivium as invitee, 143; exemplum in Dio Cassius, 97n; figuration as *pater patriae*, 249; figuration as slave (or not) to Antony, 215–16; figuration as slave to Octavian: 251. *See also* Index Locorum
Cinna. *See* Cornelius
civil war: confounds *cives* and *hostes*, 28–29; divides community, 28–29; vs. external war, 36–37; in Lucan's narrative voice, 51–53
civis: and "assimilating" viewpoint, 29–30; defined, 28n; vs. *hostis*, 38
civitas, and *libertas*, 232n
Claudius (the emperor): in convivium as host, 171–72; figured as slave (to Caligula, to slaves and freedmen, etc.), 260–61, 267–70. *See also* emperor
Claudius, Appius (the decemvir), 229n, 230
Claudius Marcellus, M.: exemplum virtutis in Seneca, 97
clementia: of Augustus, 157, 185–88; of Caesar, 43n, 51n, 176–77, 183–85; characteristic of good ruler, 241–42; as gift requiring gratitude/reciprocity, 157, 176–78, 182–88; as symbolic violence, 183–85
— and reciprocity: inaugurates or fails to inaugurate amicable reciprocity, 182–92; terminates or reverts to hostile reciprocity: 182–89
Clitus, in convivium as guest, 159–60
commoda/incommoda. *See* preferred/dispreferred
commodity exchange: in auctions, 145–46, 203–205; in dinner invitations, 139–41; defined, 133; in prostitution, 205n. *See also* gift-debt; gift exchange; patronage; reciprocity
common conceptions, 65. *See also* ethics/traditional Roman
conscientia: as external judge, 84–88; as internal judge, 82–84; vs. reputation and witnesses, 82–84, 86–88
"constitutionalist" view of principate, 286–87
Conte, Gian Biagio, 53n
convivium
— equipment of: drinking-cups (breakage and theft), 169–72; napkins (theft),

GENERAL INDEX 303

172; wine, as trigger for abusive speech, 149, 153, 157–61, 165–66, 173
— as hierarchical social event: guest of higher status than host, 141–44, 168–71; host of higher status than guests, 135–41; emperor as host (*see* emperor); participants of equal status, 141; status coding of seating, food, etc., 138–39
— incompatible with mourning, 163–64
— as locus of exchange, 146–54; amicable and hostile exchange, 146–72; and *apophoreta*, 151n; and *propinatio*, 151; speech as object of exchange, 146–54, 157–68
— as object of exchange: functioning as gift, 135–46; in exchange for diverse offerings, 138; in exchange for *salutatio*, 136–38, 140; reciprocated by diverse offerings, 139; functioning as commodity, 140–41
— speech in: topics of conversation, 147; abusive speech as apotropaic device, 150n; abusive speech giving pleasure or displeasure, 148–54; flattering speech giving pleasure or displeasure, 148, 152–53
Cooper, David, 217–18, 219n
Cornelius Cinna, exchange relations with Augustus, 185–87
Cornelius Cn. f. Scipio, virtues of, 24–25
Cornelius Scipio Africanus, exchange relations with Terentius Culleo, 197–98
Cornelius Scipio Barbatus, virtues of, 22–24
Cornelius Sulla. *See* Sulla
corona civica, 39, 188n, 249
corporal punishment. *See* master-slave relationship
Cotta, Aurelius, gratitude of, 79
Cotta Messalinus, exchange relations with Tiberius, 167–68
Crook, J. A., 263n
crown gold, 210
Curio, Scribonius, 184n; character in Lucan, 38n, 44n
Curtius Rufus, Q., 159n. *See also* Index Locorum

Damon, Cynthia, 138n, 148n
D'Arms, John, 139n

David, Jean-Michel, 78n, 134n, 143n
death. *See* good death; suicide
Decii, exempla virtutis in Seneca, 103–4, 107
Decimus Brutus, exchange relations with Caesar, 177–78
delatores, in convivial settings, 155–58, 167–68
dining. *See* convivium
Diogenes the Cynic, 142n
Dionysius of Syracuse: in convivium, 166n; as good ruler, 241n
dispreferred. *See* preferred/dispreferred
dominus: as address to various emperors, 254–58, 260; as model for relationship to rulers, *fortuna*, etc. (*see* master-slave relationship); semantics of, 220, 255–58. See also *libertas*; master-slave relationship; *servus/servitus*
Domitian: in convivium as host, 151n; figuration, 256–57. *See also* emperor
Domitius Ahenobarbus, L. (character in Lucan): "assimilating" viewpoint of, 191–92; and Caesar's *clementia*, 189–92
Domitius Corbulo, military achievements of, 100n, 101
Dyrrachium, battle of (in Lucan), 32–33, 34, 41–42

Eisenhut, Werner, 25n
emperor: as "Caesar," 37–38, 62; controls instruments of violence, 239–43; in convivium as guest, 168–71; in convivium as host, 144–46, 150–52, 154–55, 161–64, 171–72; and *delatores*, 155–58, 167–68; and flattery (*see* flattery); and oaths of loyalty, 59–62; socio-economic domination by, in early empire, 8–9
— exchange and legitimation: 173–212; apparent non-reciprocation of gifts received, 209–10; avoidance of gift-debt, 199–206, 208–10; *clementia* of (see *clementia*); as gift-debtor, 198–99, 206–8; as dominant gift-giver, 173–76, 178–82, 185–88, 200–203, 211–12; patronage of soldiers and veterans, 203, 207–8; reciprocation of gifts received, 200–201, 203; sources of revenue, 199–200, 203–6, 209–10

—figuration: as master, 244–46, 253–64 (*see also* tyrant); as father, 244, 249–50, 254, 262 (*see also* king); as slave, 246n, 259
See also *under individual names*
ergastulum, 216–17, 277
Erskine, Andrew, 274n
Ethics, in society broadly, 10–11, 17, 97–99, 124–26
—Stoic: and Cato, 53–54, 74n, 104, 278; described, 65, 66–70; divinity in, 66–67, 273; in early imperial Roman society, 98–99, 125–26; exempla in (*see* exempla); and flattery, 117–22; and frankness, 119–22; and freedom, 274–86; and friendship, 117–19; in Hellenistic monarchies, 98–99; and nature (*see* nature); paradox, 74, 77n, 82n; proper functions (*kathekonta*)/right actions in, 91–94; and traditional Roman ethics (*see* ethics/traditional Roman); voiced by Seneca, 70–74, 79–81, and ch. 2 passim
—traditional Roman: described, 21–28, 64–65; exempla in (*see* exempla); in early imperial Roman society, 21–23, 124–26; presupposed by Seneca's interlocutors ("common conceptions"), 70–73; and Stoic ethics, dialogue in Seneca between, 65, 73, 76–77, 70–126 passim
See also *virtus*; *pietas*; *gratia*; moral; good/bad; indifferents; preferred/dispreferred; internal/external
euergetism, in contrast to norm of reciprocity, 174, 193, 212
exchange. See commodity exchange; gift exchange; gift debt; reciprocity
exempla: canon of, in early empire, 107; redeployment by Seneca, 88–108; traditional Roman mode of ethical argumentation, 73
external. See internal/external

Fabricius, C., exemplum virtutis in Seneca, 92–93
Farr, James, 9n
father-son relationship: as paradigm for ruler-aristocrat relationship, 235–37, 244, 246–47, 249–50, 254, 262; sociology of, 236–39; stereotypical warmth of, 237–38

—father-figure: and lifesaving, 188–89, 249–50 (see also *corona civica*); and *pater patriae*, 244, 249; and *patria potestas*, 237, 243; and *vitae necisque potestas*, 237, 240, 243
—and master-slave relationship: contrasted with, 239, 243; similarity to, under law, 237
Felix (imperial freedman), 267–68, 270
Finley, M. I., 224n, 225n
fiscus, 199–200
fishponds, 169–71
flattery: of aristocrats by subordinates, 108–10; and falseness, 111–15; vs. friendship and frankness, 112–13; of kings and emperors by aristocrats, 110, 115–16, 256–58; of kings and emperors by others, 254–55; and status, 108–11; and Stoicism (or philosophy broadly), 117–22
Flower, Harriet, 21n
focalization, 48, 75, 191
fortuna (Stoic cause), 72; assimilation to ruler, 279–80; endurance of, as *virtus*, 104–106; and "externals," 240, 279–80; figuration of one's relationship to as master-slave relationship, 216–17, 246n, 273–80, 284; vs. knowability of Stoic divinity, 273; mutability of, 118; unknowability of, 81–82
Foucault, Michel, 98–99, 124
frankness: danger of, when speaking to power, 116, 119–22; and friendship, 112–13, 116; and Stoicism, 119–22
freedmen: as advisers of powerful aristocrats, 265–66; in imperial service, 264–72; figured as masters, 267–70; figured as slaves, 270. See also *under individual names*
freedom. See *libertas*; master-slave relationship
friendship: and *amicus minor*, 113, 115–19; and frankness, 112–13, 116; Stoic, 117–19
Furnius, C., exchange relations with Augustus, 187–88

Gaius (emperor). See Caligula
Galba: exchange and legitimation, 201n; figuration as liberator, 261. See also emperor

GENERAL INDEX   305

Gallius, Q., tortured by Octavian, 252
Garnsey, Peter, 238n
Geertz, Clifford, 9
gift-debt: incurred/avoided by aristocrats, 194–98; incurred/avoided by emperor (*see* emperor); and social subordination, 132–33, 144, 165–66, 173–88. *See also* commodity exchange; patronage; reciprocity
gift exchange: and aristocrats (*see* aristocrats); defined, 132–33; and emperors (*see* emperor); two modes of, "hostile" and "amicable" (*see* reciprocity)
good/bad: in *De Providentia*, 70–73; inconsistency of Seneca's usage, 75–77; predicated of "internal" states in Seneca, 72–73; predicated of "moral" value in Stoicism, 67–68
good death: of Decii, 103; exemplary force of, 105n; of Iulius Canus, 120–22
gratia, 115, 118; "enacted" vs. "dispositional," 78–82; and exchange, in traditional Roman ethics, 78–79. *See also* gratitude
gratitude: owed to emperors on account of *clementia* in particular, 176–78, 182–88; owed to emperors on account of their giving generally, 177–93; and expressions of thanks, 196; and subordination, 195–98. *See also* gift-debt; gift-exchange; reciprocity
Graver, Margaret, 95n
Griffin, Miriam, 18–19, 240n
Gruen, Erich, 8n

Habinek, Thomas, 20, 76n, 87, 280, 284–85
Harpagus, 116, 121; in convivium as guest, 162–63; figuration as slave, 216–17, 276–78
Harris, William, 21n, 25n, 27n, 101n
Hellegouarc'h, Joseph, 219n
Helvius Rufus, M., 268n
Hermolaus (character in Curtius Rufus) figured as slave, 234–35, 239; figured as son, 235–36, 239
Herrmann, Peter, 59–62nn
honor-community, 21n
Hopkins, Keith, 7n, 226n
Horatius Cocles, exemplum virtutis in Seneca, 92–93

hostis, and "alienating" viewpoint, 37; vs. *civis*, 38; defined, 28n
Hurley, Donna, 146n

Ilerda, battle at, 46n, 51, 189n, 190n
indifferents, in Stoicism, 67–69; not a "moral" form of value, 67–68; preferred and dispreferred, 68–69
internal/external: as alternative modes of evaluation, 22n, 82–88, 123; as alternative modes of speech, 123; central ethical distinction in Seneca, 71–73, 273–74; figuration of one's relationship to externals as master-slave relationship, 274–79. *See also* good/bad; preferred/dispreferred
Inwood, Brad, 80n
ira: figuration of one's relationship to *ira* as master-slave relationship, 280–81, 285; inappropriate for aristocrats, 280–81, 285
Iulius Agricola, military achievements of, 100n
Iulius Caesar. *See* Caesar
Iulius Canus, exemplum virtutis in Seneca, 120–24, 278–79
Iulius Civilis, figuration as liberator, 261
Iulius Vindex, C.: ideological value of cognomen, 261; figuration as liberator, 261
Iullus Antonius, exchange relations with Augustus, 179
Iunius. *See* Brutus
ius gladii, 37n, 242n

Johnson and Dandeker, 130n
Julius. *See* Iulius, Caesar
Junius. *See* Brutus
Junian Latins, 232n

Kaster, Robert, 24n
kathekonta. *See* ethics: Stoic: proper functions
Kautsky, John, 7n
Kennedy, Duncan, 19–20, 228–29
king: in convivium as host, 159–60, 162–63, 165–66; and flattery (*see* flattery); as munificent gift-giver, 201n; *nobilis servitus* of, 246n
— as good ruler in Seneca's *De Clementia*: *clementia* of, 241; figuration as father,

king (*cont.*)
244; vs. "tyrant," the bad ruler, 241–46
See also *under individual names*
kolakeia. See flattery
Konstan, David, 134n, 137n
Kuhlmann, H.?, 222n
Kuntze, Claudia, 181n

Laelius (character in Lucan): "alienating" viewpoint of, 40–41, 43, 59–61; speech of, 39–41
Lakoff, George, 221n
Lakoff, George, and Mark Johnson, 217–18, 219n
latro, 28n, 55
Leigh, Matthew, 49n, 51n
Lendon, J. E., 21n, 131, 143n, 168n, 194, 197n, 210n
Lentulus Spinther, exchange relations with Caesar, 184n
lex Porcia, 231–32. See also *libertas*
lex Sempronia, 231–32. See also *libertas*
liberalia studia: appropriate to free men, or make one free, 282–86; lower classes and tyrants debarred from, 283–86
Liberalis, Aebutius (Seneca's addressee in *De Beneficiis*), 195–96, 269
libertas: and Cato the younger, 250, 278; and *civitas*, 232n; and "doing as you please," 74n, 222–23, 262–64, 274; and freedom of speech, 153–54; and *lex*, 230–32; and the tribunes of the plebs, 229–31, 247–49, 253, 263
—semantics of, in context of master-slave relationship: complementary to *servitus*, 220–21; conceptually derivative, 221–23, 227, 262–64; isolated wrongly from other language/imagery, 219–20; positive affective/ethical connotations 223, 227; other semantic studies of, 219–20, 227–33
See also *dominus*; master-slave relationship; *servus/servitus*
Libo Drusus, ingrate to Tiberius, 179
Livius Drusus, M.: exemplum in Velleius Paterculus, 85; recipient of oath of loyalty, 61n; rises by giving, 175n
Long and Sedley, 77n, 92n

Lucan (M. Annaeus Lucanus), and Caesarian ideology, 58–59. *See also* Index Locorum
Lucilius, C. (Seneca's addressee in various works), 106n, 119

MacMullen, Ramsay, 174n, 177n
Maecenas, C.: in convivium as guest (in Horace), 168n; exemplum of vice in Seneca, 94–95; frank adviser to Augustus, 115
manubiae, 200
manumission: *manumissio vindicta*, 214, 217, 232n; and *pilleus* (see *pilleus*)
Marcellus. *See* Claudius
Marius, C.: exemplum of vice in Seneca, 89; figuration as *pater patriae*, 249
Marius, Sex., victim of Tiberius, 205
Maro, Iulius? *delator* in convivium, 155–56
Masters, Jamie, 51, 59n, 62n
master-slave relationship: language and imagery of, 217; as paradigm for one's relationship to *fortuna*, or externals generally, 273–81, 284–86; as paradigm for ruler-aristocrat relationship, 54n, 234–35, 239, 244–47, 253–64, 276–80, 285–86; "parent" vs. "derived" domains, 217–18, 227, 233, 273; stereotypical hostility of, 223–27
—and father-son relationship: logically contrasted with, 239; legal similarity to, 237
—masters: corporal punishment at disposal of, 168–71, 237–38, 245–46; *vitae necisque potestas* of, 237, 240, 243
—slaves: and corporal punishment, 168–71, 224, 238, 245, 262–64; legal degradation of, 224–25; moral degradation of, 226; other physical degradation of, 223–24; manumission of (see manumission; *pilleus*); and war-captivity, 197, 223n, 226n, 235
See also *dominus*; *libertas*; *servus/servitus*
McGinn, T., 205n
Menas, exchange relations with Octavian, 144–45, 266–67
Messalla Corvinus, exchange relations with Octavian, 180–81

metaphor, 213, ch. 4 passim; conceptual, 217–18
Metellus Numidicus, 196–97
Metellus Pius, exchange relations with Q. Calidius, 196–97
Metellus Scipio, *exemplum virtutis* in Seneca, 104–5, 107
Milichus, exchange relations with Nero, 201
military commands, changing distribution of in early empire, 99–101, 106–7
military honors, limits on in early empire; 99–101, 106–7
Millar, Fergus: 131, 210n, 265n
moral point of view, 64–65
moral value, admits predicates "good" and "bad" in Stoicism, 67–68
mourning, incompatible with dining, 163–64

Narcissus (imperial freedman), 267–69
narrator, in epic poetry: in general, 47–48; in Lucan, 47–53; embodies civil war in Lucan, 51–53
nature, in Stoicism: acting in accordance with, 65, 68–69, 84; living in agreement with, as Stoic end, 66–69
Nero: figuration as master, 261–62; power of, as described in Seneca's *De Clementia*, 240
— exchange and legitimation: 168n, 201; *clementia* of, with Augustus as exemplum, 186–87; and false charges, 205; and ungrateful wills, 179–80
See also emperor
Nicolet, Claude, 231n

oaths of loyalty, in early empire, 59–62; manifest "alienating" view, 60–62; origins of, 60n, 61n. *See also* emperor
Octavian. *See* Augustus
Octavius, Cn., invites Cicero to dinner, 143
ornamenta quaestoria, praetoria, consularia, 268, 270
Otho, rises by giving, 175–76. *See also* emperor

Pallas (imperial freedman), 267–68, 270–71

Panaetius, 77n, 118
paradox. *See* ethics: Stoic
Parrhasius, 263n
Pastor, in convivium as guest, 163–64
pater patriae, 244, 249
patronage: emphasizes enduring elements of social relationship, 173, 211; as modern category of social analysis, 130–32; vs. *patronus* (ancient usage), 130, 132. *See also* commodity exchange; gift-debt; gift exchange; reciprocity
Patterson, Orlando, 219n, 223n
Paulus, in convivium as guest, 155–56
penates, 39n
Petreius, M. (character in Lucan), 36–37, 48
Pharsalus, battle of: figuration of leaders in, 248–49
— in Lucan: aftermath, 49; battle proper, 45–47; Caesar's speech, 42–43, 44; ethics in, 43–47; Pompey's speech, 35–36
Philotas, in convivium as guest, 150
pietas: in civil war context of Lucan, 30–54 passim; "enacted" vs. "dispositional," 27; and familial relations, 26–28, 55n, 236, 238; in traditional Roman ethics, 26–28
pilleus, 215, 217, 229, 250, 257n, 261n. *See also* manumission
piscinae, 169–71
Pisistratus, in convivium as host, 166n
Piso, L., in convivium as guest, 150–51
Pliny (the younger): angered at honors given to Pallas, 270–72; indebted to Trajan, 144n
politics: of literature, 17–20; narrow vs. broad sense of, 18–19
Polybius (imperial freedman), 267–68, 269n
Polyclitus (imperial freedman), 269–70
Pompeians, historical vs. Lucan's, 55
Pompeius, Cn. (Pompey the great): exemplum of vice in Seneca, 88–89; figuration as liberator or master, 248–49; ideological significance of triumphs, 56n
— character in Lucan: embraces "assimilating" viewpoint, 30–36 ("strong" version, 32–36; "weak" version, 30–32);

308 GENERAL INDEX

Pompeius, Cn. (Pompey the great) (*cont.*)
speech before battle of Pharsalus, 35–36
Pompeius, Sex., 145, 266–67; in convivium, 141; as *pius*, 55n. See also *pietas*
Pomponius Flaccus, in convivium as guest, 150–51
Praexaspes, 3–4, 116, 121; in convivium as guest, 162; as slave to king, 216–17
preferred/dispreferred: predicated of "externals" in Seneca, 72–73, 103–4; predicated of "indifferent" value in Stoicism, 68–69. See also ethics: Stoic
Premerstein, Anton von, 59–62nn, 131, 286–87
princeps, as designation for emperor, 254. See also emperor
principate, as a system of government, 6–9
proper functions/right actions. See ethics: Stoic
propinatio, 151. See also convivium
prostitution, 205n. See also Caligula
Pyrrhus, and diners, 165–66

Raaflaub, Kurt, 55–56
rational-legal administrative system, 146n, 174
reciprocity: amicable vs. hostile, 133, 210–11, ch. 3 passim; in convivium, 146–72; contingency of each transaction, 173, 211–12; norm of, in contrast to euergetism, 174, 192–93, 212; as symbolic violence, 211n. See also commodity exchange; gift-debt; gift exchange; patronage
Regulus, M. Atilius, exemplum virtutis in Seneca, 104, 107
republic, as a system of government, 6–9
rings, and status: gold, 145, 267, 271n; iron, 271n
Romulus: figuration as father, 248; figuration as master, 254
Rufus, aristocrat in convivium, 157–58
Russell, James, 250n
Rusten, Jeffrey, 24n
Rutilius Rufus, exemplum virtutis in Seneca, 106n

Sahlins, Marshall, 133n
Saller, Richard, 130–32, 224n, 238

salutatio, in exchange for convivium. See convivium
Satellius Quadratus, in convivium as guest, 149
Saturnalia, 269. See also status: inversions of
Scaeva, Cassius (character in Lucan), 41–42, 49
Scaevola, Mucius: exemplum virtutis in Seneca, 105–107
Scipio. See Cornelius; Metellus
Scott, James, 111n, 124
Scylla, in sculpture group at Sperlonga, 170n
Senatus Consultum de Pisone Patre, 202n
Seneca, L. Annaeus (the younger): as moral instructor to aristocrats in general, 65–66, 95–97; to Nero in *De Clementia*, 239, 246, 262; seeks recall from exile through offices of Polybius, 269n. See also Index Locorum
servus/servitus, *nobilis*, 246n, 259. See also status: inversions of
—semantics of, in context of master-slave relationship: 220–21, 227; conceptually primary, 221–23, 227; complementary to *libertas*, 220–21; mutually entails *dominus* (usually), 220; negative affective/ethical connotations, 223, 227
See also *dominus*; *libertas*; master-slave relationship
Shaw, Brent, 98–99, 124
Sherwin-White, A. N., 272n
Silius, C., exchange relations with Tiberius, 198
Skinner, Quentin, 9
slaves. See master-slave relationship; *servus/servitus*
Socrates, exemplum virtutis in Seneca, 96, 106n
speech: in convivia, 146–54, 157–68; flattering or frank (*see* flattery; frankness)
Statius (freedman of Q. Cicero), 265–66
status: dissonance in, 235, 246, 265n, 272; equestrian, assumed by freedmen, 266–68; senatorial, assumed by freedmen, 266–71
—inversions of: emperor as slave (see *servus/servitus: nobilis*); and Saturnalia,

269; slave or freedman as master, 266–72
Ste. Croix, G. E. M. de, 228–229
Stoicism. *See* ethics: Stoic; good/bad; preferred/dispreferred; indifferents
strena, 200–201, 209
suicide, 117–18, 275–79
Sulla, L. Cornelius: exemplum of cruelty in Lucan, 32–33; as tyrant in Seneca, 241n
Sullivan, J. P., 18–19
Syme, Ronald, 8n, 227–28

Terentius Culleo, Q.: exchange relations with Scipio Africanus, 197–98
testamenta. *See* wills
theft, in convivium: of drinking cups, 171–72; of napkins, 172
Theodorus, exemplum of constantia in Seneca, 120, 279
Thévenaz, P., 72n
Thompson, L., 256n
Thrasea Paetus, exchange relations with Nero, 168n
Thrasippus, in convivium as guest, 166n
Tiberius
— in convivium: as host, 150–52; power extended by *delatores*, 155–56, 167–68
— exchange and legitimation: 181–82, 200–201; avoids incurring gift-debt, 208–9; and false charges, 205; incurs gift-debt, 198; patronage of soldiers and veterans, 203
— figuration: as father, master, *princeps*, slave, 258–59
See also emperor
Trajan
— exchange and legitimation: addressee of Plutarch, 203n; recipient of Pliny's praise/gratitude, 144n
— figuration: addressed *domine*, 258; as parent, not master, 257–58
See also emperor
Trebonius, C., exchange relations with Caesar, 177–78
tribunes of the plebs, 229–31, 247–49, 253, 263, 286. See also *libertas*
triumphs: of Caesar, 56–58; of Pompey, 56n

Tullius Marcellinus, 117–18
tyrant: stereotypical, 236n; figured as bad ruler and master in Seneca's *De Clementia*, 244–46; opposed to good ruler ("king") in Seneca's *De Clementia*, 241–46

Valerius Asiaticus: in convivium as guest, 161–62; exchange relations with Caligula, 161–62
Varus, convivial joker, 148
Vedius Pollio: in convivium as host, 168–71; cruelty of, 168–69, 246; exchange relations with Augustus, 171
Velleii, exchange relations with emperors, 176–82. *See also* Index Locorum, *s.v.* Velleius Paterculus
Verginius Rufus, 261n
Vespasian: in convivium as guest, 144; figuration as liberator, 261. *See also* emperor
Veyne, Paul, 131, 174, 193, 202n, 212, 287
Viansino, Giovanni, 274n, 282
Vibius Serenus, exchange relations with Tiberius, 201–2
Vindex, C. Iulius. *See* Iulius
vindex (or *assertor*) *libertatis*, 214–17, 250n, 252, 261
Vinius, T.: in convivium as guest, 171–72; exchange relations with Claudius, 172
virtus: in civil war context of Lucan, 30–54; "enacted" vs. "dispositional," 24–25; in philosophical contexts broadly, 26; in Senecan Stoicism, 101–8; specifically in Stoicism as the endurance of ill-fortune, 104–6; in traditional Roman ethics, 22–26, 99–108
vitae necisque potestas, 237, 240, 243
Volusius Proculus, exchange relations with Nero, 201

Wallace-Hadrill, Andrew, 8n, 130n, 211–12, 265n
Warren, Brian, 186n
Weaver, P. R. C., 235n, 265n, 267n
White, Peter, 131n

wills: source of revenue for emperor, 199; ungrateful, 179–80
wine. *See* convivium
Wirszubski, Ch., 215n, 219n, 221n, 229–33, 263
Wistrand, Erik, 183n

yoke, symbol of enslavement, 216–17, 230, 235

Zeno: exemplum of constantia in Seneca, 120, 279; philosophical views, 77n, 123n

INDEX LOCORUM

This index contains only those passages discussed, quoted, and/or translated; mere citations are not listed.

Appian
  B.C.
    2.104: 55n
    2.146: 178n
    5.113: 181n
Aristotle
  Nic. Eth.
    1089b12: 73n
    1160a36–b30: 236n
Augustus
  R.G.
    1: 214–15, 223, 229
    15: 200
    17: 210n
    21.2: 200
    34: 254n
    35: 253
Aurelius Victor
  Epitome de Caesaribus
    5.9: 261n
  Liber de Caesaribus
    3.13: 260n

Boethius
  Cons.
    1.3: 107n

Caesar
  B.C.
    1.7.3–4, 8: 249n
    1.22–23: 184n
    1.22.5: 248n, 249n
    1.86–87: 189n
  B.G.
    1.18.3–5: 175n
Catullus
  Carm.
    12.1–5: 171–72
Cicero
  ad Brut.
    1.17.4, 6: 251n
  Att.
    7.7.5: 222n
    8.9a.2: 185n
    8.11.2: 249n
    8.16.2: 184n
    9.7C 1–2: 183–84, 189
    10.4.8: 184n
    13.36.1: 177n
  Cat.
    1.1.3: 25
  Fam.
    7.9.3: 143
    7.16.2: 143
    8.15.1: 184
  Fin.
    2.116: 23n
    3.33–34: 93n
    3.48: 74n
  Inv.
    2.66: 79
    2.159: 26n
    2.161: 79n
  Lael.
    89–99: 108–114 (passim in nn.)
    89, 98: 112
    89–92: 113n
    97–99: 111n
    99: 114
  Leg.
    1.44–45: 26
    3.9, 15–25: 229n
  Off.
    1.53–56, 107–25: 91
    1.90: 118n
    1.144: 92n, 147n
    1.150–51: 283n
    2.24: 230–31
    2.28: 57n
    2.66: 79n
    2.69: 143, 194–95
  Parad.
    33: 74n, 222n
  Phil.
    3.3–5: 214n
    3.34–36: 251n

Cicero (cont.)
    3.37–38: 214n
    14.21–25: 58n
  Planc.
    16: 222n
    72: 188n
    80: 27n
  Q. fr.
    1.2: 265–66
  Rab. Perd.
    12–13: 231
  Rep.
    1.2: 25n
    1.43.1: 222n
    1.55.2: 222n
    1.64: 236n, 248n
    2.43: 222
    2.47: 236n
    3.37: 248n
  Rosc.
    66: 27n
  Sul.
    86: 39n
  Top.
    83: 109n
    85: 109n, 113
  Tusc.
    2.43: 22n
  Ver.
    2.4.17: 39n
Curtius Rufus, Quintus
  Hist.
    6.2.1–3: 159n
    7.8.28: 226n
    8.1.22–8.2.12: 159–60
    8.2.2: 163, 165
    8.5.13–20: 235n
    8.6–8: 234–36, 239
    9.7.24–26: 172n

Digest
    1.5.4 pr. (Florentinus): 220–21, 222n
    1.5.4.2: 223n
Dio Cassius
    37.26.1–2: 97n
    41.52.1: 57n
    41.57.2–3: 249n
    42.18.1: 57
    43.10.5: : 250n
    43.44.1: 249n
    44.19.2: 251

    47.42.3–43.1: 252
    48.45.7–9: 267n
    50.22.3–4: 252n
    53.4.1–2: 179n
    53.18.2–3: 259n
    54.23.3–6: 171
    54.35.1: 200
    55.4.2: 208n
    55.12.4: 202, 210n
    55.14–22: 187n
    55.25.3: 202
    57.8.1–2: 259nn
    57.8.6: 200
    57.10.5: 205
    59.8.3: 205n
    59.11.4: 205n
    59.14.1–4: 204–205
    59.18.5: 205
    59.21.4: 209
    59.23.2–4: 198–99
    59.24.4–5: 209n
    59.27.1: 144n
    59.28.8–9: 205n
    60.15.6: 260
    60.19.3: 269
    61.10: 110n
    61.20.1: 256n
    62.18.5: 209n
    63.22.1, 24.4a: 261
    67.9: 151n
Dio Chrysostom
  Or.
    3.12–24: 109–114 (in nn.)
    14: 74n
    14.3: 222n
    14.3–15: 221
    15.1–28: 221
    34.7–8: 210n
Diodorus Siculus
  Bibl.
    20.63: 160nn.
    37.11: 61n
Diogenes Laertius
  Vit. Phil.
    6.29–30: 142n
    7.53: 93n
    7.85–89: 67n
    7.89: 96n
    7.92–93: 68n
    7.94: 67n
    7.101–103: 67

INDEX LOCORUM 313

7.104: 67n, 69n
7.109: 91n

Ennius
  Ann.
    fr. 105–109 Sk: 248
    fr. 278–86 Sk.: 113
Epictetus
  Diss.
    2.10: 92n
    3.24.99: 92n
    4.1: 74n
    4.1.1: 222n

Gaius
  Inst.
    1.9: 220
    1.48–200: 223n
    1.52–53: 224

Herodotus
    3.34–35: 4
Horace
  Carm.
    1.2.50: 254
    3.29.1–16: 143n
  Epist.
    1.7.46–95: 138n
    1.7.73–74: 141n
    1.18.15–20: 152
  Serm.
    1.4.86–90: 149–50
    2.6: 147n
    2.8: 153, 168n
    2.8.6–7, 42–53, 90–93: 139n
    2.8.77–83: 148

Juvenal
  Sat.
    3.212–22: 202
    5.12–23: 136, 139
    5.39–41: 172n
    5.125–27: 153–54

Laus Pisonis
    122–27: 140–41
Livy
    2.5.8–10: 232n
    2.10–13: 24nn
    2.10.12: 78n
    3.28.11: 235n

3.37: 229n
3.44.5–6: 229n
6.34.8: 27n
26.32.2: 230
Lucan
  B.C.
    1.1: 52n
    1.1–8: 29–30
    1.2: 44
    1.41: 37
    1.59: 37
    1.185–92: 38
    1.195–203: 38
    1.203: 44n
    1.278–79: 38n
    1.279: 44n
    1.299–356: 39
    1.357–88: 39–41
    1.373–74: 43
    1.373–86: 59–62
    1.475–84: 31n
    1.667–68: 44n
    2.277–84: 230
    2.319–20: 31n
    2.439–46: 41
    2.507–25: 189–92
    2.531–95: 30–32
    3.112–68: 249n
    4.24–265: 48n
    4.26–28: 46n
    4.157–205: 36
    4.169–72: 46n
    4.189–92: 37–38n
    4.212–35: 36
    4.337–401: 51
    4.363–64, 381–400: 190n
    4.823: 37
    5.385–86: 38n
    6.130–34: 34
    6.140–262: 41–42
    6.165–257: 48
    6.147–48: 44n
    6.257–62: 49
    6.299–305: 32–33
    7.51–53: 33
    7.95–96: 33–34
    7.103–104: 33
    7.164: 31n
    7.207–13: 37n
    7.259–63: 44
    7.269–76: 37n

Lucan (cont.)
  7.312–15: 43n
  7.318–22: 42–43, 59–62
  7.342–82: 35–36
  7.462–585: 45–47
  7.604: 192
  7.617–30: 46n
  7.638–46: 49–50
  7.706: 50
  7.749–86: 49
  7.764–80: 47n
  8.627–29: 192n
  9.1–949: 53–54
  9.248–83: 54n
  9.272–76: 43n
  9.593–96: 53–54n
  9.980–86: 37n
  9.1059–62: 192n

Macrobius
  Sat.
    2.4.26: 201
    2.4.27: 207–208, 209
    2.4.29–30: 201
    2.5.4: 253–54
Manilius
  Astron.
    1.7, 925: 259n
Marcus Aurelius
  Med.
    1.16.2: 164n
Martial
  Epigr.
    1.44: 137n
    2.27: 137
    2.68: 257
    3.52: 202
    3.82.16–17: 156n
    3.82.33: 153n
    5.78.22–25: 139n
    6.44: 154n
    6.44.3–4: 149n
    7.86: 138, 140n
    8.59: 172n
    9.9(10): 154n
    9.19: 137
    9.35: 147
    9.100: 138, 140
    10.19(18): 138
    10.72: 257
    11.37: 271
    12.27(28): 139n
    12.29(26): 137n
    12.48.1–4, 15–18: 141
    12.74.7–8: 170n
    12.82: 137

Nepos
  Timol.
    3: 230

Ovid
  Fasti
    2.127–28, 141–42: 254
  Tr.
    1.2.37: 27n

Persius
  Sat.
    5.83–84: 222n
Petronius
  Sat.
    32.3: 271n
    34: 139n
    47.7: 148
    48.7: 148
    51: 170n
    52.7: 148
    57.2: 256n
    61.1–2: 147
    64.2: 147
    64.10–13: 171n
    66.3, 67.9: 256n
    71.9: 271n
Philodemus
  Peri Parrhesias
    XXIIb–XXIVa: 109n
Plato
  Gorgias
    524E: 95n
  Rep.
    560D: 45n
Plautus
  Merc.
    105: 79n
Pliny the Elder
  Nat.
    9.76: 170n
    9.167: 168n
    14.140: 151n
    14.141: 160
    14.145: 151n

20.160: 261
33.7–34: 267
33.23: 271n
Pliny the Younger
  Ep.
    2.6: 139n
    4.11.6: 257
    6.10.4, 9.19.1: 261n
    7.29: 270–72
    8.6: 271–72
    8.12.2–3: 79n
    10.52: 27n
  Paneg.
    2: 258
    49.6: 166n
    88.1: 268n
    90–92: 144n
Plutarch
  Alex.
    51.1–5: 159n
  Ant.
    24.7–12: 152
    28.7–12: 150
  Brut.
    5.1–2: 250n
  Cato Minor
    6.1: 139n
    64.7–9: 192n
    66.2: 192n
  Caes.
    5.8–9: 175
    55: 57n
    56.7–9: 58
  fragmenta (Sandbach)
    211: 120n
  Galba
    12: 171–72
  Mor.
    48E-74E: 108–114 (passim in nn.)
    49E-51E: 113n
    51C-D: 114–15
    56B-C: 114
    60C-D: 110n
    66B: 113n
    124A: 164n
    172B-C: 203n
    176A-B: 166n
    615E-619F: 139n
    629E-634F: 149n, 154
    682A: 147
    1042E-F: 95n
    1058E-1086B: 74n
    1069E: 69n
  Otho
    4: 175
  Sert.
    26.10: 170n
Polybius
  6.39.6–7: 188n
  31.24.4–5: 113

Quintilian
  [Decl. Min.]
    301: 142
    301.14: 169
  Inst.
    5.11.41: 87–88
    6.3.10: 165
    6.3.14, 105: 148
    12.2.29–31: 88n

Rhetorica ad Herennium
  4.57: 78n

Sallust
  Cat.
    54.4: 25
  Hist.
    Or. Cottae 5: 79
    Or. Macri 23: 254n
    Or. Macri 26: 229n
  [ad Caes.]
    2.6.4–5: 175n
Seneca the Elder
  Cont.
    2.5.10–13: 208n
    4 pr. 5: 164n
    4.1: 164n
    9.1.9–11: 208n
    9.1.10: 96n
    9.2.4: 169n
  Suas.
    2.8: 276n
    5.4: 222n
    6: 215–16
Seneca the Younger
  Apoc.
    6.2: 269n
    15.2: 260n
  Ben.
    2.11.2–3: 144
    2.12: 260n

Seneca the Younger (*cont.*)
  2.12.1: 189n
  2.12.2: 159
  2.16: 201n
  2.17.5–7: 196n
  2.17.6: 203n
  2.20.1–3: 188–89, 250
  2.21.1–2: 141n
  2.22–25: 144
  2.23–24: 196
  2.25.1: 187–88
  2.31.1, 4: 82n
  2.34.3–5: 93n
  2.35.2: 76
  3.1.3–2.3: 207n
  3.9: 82n
  3.18–26: 158
  3.18–28: 92
  3.19.4: 226
  3.20.2: 282
  3.26.1–2: 155–56
  3.26–27: 167
  3.27.1–4: 157–58: 165
  3.27.4: 183n
  3.28: 269
  4.7.1–2: 66n
  4.21.1–5: 80–83
  4.26–27: 76
  4.40.4: 141n
  5.2.1–4.2: 195
  5.3.2: 104n
  5.6.2–7: 142n
  5.7.4: 111n
  5.22–23: 207n
  5.23: 207
  5.24: 207, 209
  5.25.1: 207
  5.25.2: 208–209
  5.25.3: 123n
  6.4: 189n
  6.13.3–14.2: 174n
  6.19–23: 174n
  6.29–34: 92, 115–16
  6.30.4–5: 112
  6.33.1: 162
  6.33.1–3: 118
  6.42.2: 83
  6.43.3: 84n
  7.1.7: 86n
Brev.
  14.5–15.2: 119n
  18.4: 285n
[*Carmina*], in Shackleton Bailey 1982
  396–400: 56n
  460.19, 28: 45n
  461: 51n
Clem.
  1.1.2: 279
  1.1.2–4: 240, 243
  1.1.6–7: 239n
  1.5.5–7: 242
  1.7.4–8.3: 246n, 259n
  1.9.1: 239n, 242n
  1.9.1–10.3: 185–87
  1.9.11: 188n
  1.10.3: 244
  1.11–13: 241–42, 285
  1.13.5–14.2: 111n
  1.14.1–16.1: 244
  1.16.2: 243n
  1.18.1–3: 244–46
  1.18.2: 170nn
  1.19.2–3: 242
  1.21.1: 186
  1.21.2: 190n, 243
  1.26.2: 161
  2.3.1–5.5: 240n
Const.
  8.3: 279
  9.4: 281n
  11.2–3: 150n
  18.1–3: 161–62
Ep.
  3.1: 256n
  13.14: 105n, 278n
  19.11–12: 136–37, 198n
  24.1–3: 106n
  24.5: 105–106
  24.6: 106n
  24.9–10: 105
  26.9–10: 274n
  27.5–8: 149
  37.3–4: 281n
  42.1: 67n
  43.5: 86
  44: 281
  45.7: 113n
  47.5: 226n
  47.8–9: 148, 269
  47.14: 227n
  47.17: 282
  59.1–4: 76

INDEX LOCORUM 317

59.11: 113–14
65.15–21: 284
65.20–24: 274n
66.5: 73n
66.14–23: 68n
66.16: 281n
66.36–39: 73n
66.38: 69n
66.39–40: 67n
67.4–5: 103n
67.9–13: 102–104
70: 276nn
71.10: 105n
71.16: 105n
77.5–7: 117–18, 276n
77.14–17: 275–76
79.13–15: 95n
80.4–6: 281n
81.3–8, 15–18: 189n
81.31–32: 196
82.2–6: 284
82.5: 72n
82.10 (and ff.): 73n
83.19: 159n
85.24–29: 75–77
85.38–40: 69n
85.38–41: 75–77
87.36–37: 70n
88: 282–84
89.8: 106n
90.26–31: 283–84
91.17: 88n
92.14–16: 70n
94.50, 55, 59–60 (etc): 95–96
94.60–68: 88–90, 92, 96
94.69–71: 84
94.69–74: 95–96
95.57–59: 123n
95.65–66: 95n
99.16–18: 84
102.11–17: 122–23
104.1: 256n
104.16, 21–22: 284
104: 29–30: 104
113.1–2: 26n
113.32: 83
114.4–8: 94–95
115.6–7: 72n
117.8–9: 73n
120.4–13: 92–94
122.12–13: 148

fragmenta (Haase)
14: 83
24: 84–85
Helv.
9.4–6: 97
10.9–10: 204n
13.4: 83n
13.4–8: 96–97
17.3–5: 284
19.6: 24n
Ira
1.18.3–6: 242n
1.20.8: 285
2.15–16: 280
2.21.7: 281n
2.24: 136
2.33: 279
2.33.2–6: 163–64, 279–80
2.35–36: 95
3.3.3: 280n
3.4.4: 280
3.6.2–3: 280
3.8.6: 152
3.13–21: 285
3.13.5: 161
3.14–20: 279
3.14.1–2: 3–4
3.14–15: 116, 121, 162–63
3.15: 3–5
3.15.1–2: 280
3.15.3–4: 216–17, 277–78
3.16.2–17.1: 241
3.17.1–4: 159
3.18.3–19.2: 246n, 260n
3.23.1: 159n
3.25.3: 280
3.31.2: 279
3.37.1: 154n
3.40: 168–171
3.41.1–2: 83
3.41.2: 95, 281n
Marc.
16.2: 24n
17.5: 231
20.6: 278n
Nat.
1 pr. 13: 66n
2.45.2–3: 66n
3 pr. 2, 5–9: 118n
3 pr. 5, 10: 102
3.18.3–5: 170n

318 INDEX LOCORUM

Seneca the Younger (cont.)
  4A pr.: 108–114 passim in nn., 119n
  4A pr. 13: 119
  4A pr. 18–19: 113n
Polyb.
  13: 269n
  17.4–6: 285
Prov.
  1.1: 70
  2–3: 69n
  2.5–6: 274n
  2.9–10: 104
  2.10: 278
  3.4–14: 73, 97
  3.14: 104
  4.8–12: 274n
  5.5–6: 274n
  6.1–6: 71–72
Tranq.
  1.16–17: 111n
  7.1–2: 142–43
  8.7, 10.1–6: 274n
  10.6: 246n
  14: 119–22, 278–79
  14.4: 107n
  17.9: 97n
Vit.
  3.3, 4.4–5: 274n
  4.3: 281n
  15.3–7: 274n
  20.4: 86, 87
  20.5: 85, 87
  22.4: 73n
  24.4–25.8: 68n
Stobaeus
  2.96–97 WH: 91n
Suetonius
  Aug.
    27.4: 252
    53.1–2: 110n, 253–256n, 258
    57.1: 200
    57.2: 202
    58: 253
    70.2: 205
    74: 144–45, 266–67
  Cal.
    18.2: 151n
    26.2: 260n
    32.2: 169n
    38–42: 203–205
    38.2: 179
    39.2: 145–46
    41.1: 205n
    42: 209n
  Cl.
    17: 56n
    21.5: 256n
    24.1: 268n
    25.1, 5: 267
    28: 267–68
    29: 268
    32: 171–72
  Dom.
    13.1–2: 256
  Galba
    6.3: 260n
    12.3: 201n
  Iul.
    43.1: 268n
    80.1: 250n
    82.2: 250
    88: 250n
  Nero
    32.2: 179–80
    38.3: 209n
    45.2: 261
  Tib.
    24.2: 259
    26.2: 259n
    27: 110n, 258, 259
    29.1: 259
    34.1: 139n
    34.2: 200
    42.1–2: 150–52
    54: 152
  Vesp.
    2.3: 144
Tacitus
  Ag.
    39–40: 100n, 101n
    42.2: 121n
  Ann.
    1.8.6: 251n
    1.14: 110n
    1.69: 203n
    2.12: 110n
    2.87: 258, 259n
    3.21: 268n
    3.65: 259

4.18–19: 198
4.29.3: 201–202
4.63: 268n
4.64: 202n
6.5: 167–68
6.6: 95n
6.7.2–3: 167–68
6.11.3: 151n
6.19.1: 205
6.45: 202n
11.20: 101
12.26: 110n
12.41: 110n
14.10: 110n
14.39: 269–70
14.48: 168n
14.56.3: 121n
15.43.2–44.2: 202n
15.51.2: 201
15.54.4: 201
15.59: 110n
15.71.1: 201
Hist.
1.48: 171–72
2.71.2: 121n
4.3: 78n
4.4: 57n
5.9: 270
Thucydides
2.45.2: 24n
3.82.4: 45n, 114n
3.82.6: 40n

Varro, Marcus Terentius
De Re Rustica
1.17: 225n
Valerius Maximus
1.5.7: 250n
2.8.4: 56
2.8.7: 56n
5.1 ext. 2: 166n
5.1 ext. 3: 165–66, 183n
5.2.5: 197
5.2.7: 196–97

6.1.1: 24n
7.5.6: 97n
Velleius Paterculus
2.13–14: 85
2.52–57: 188
2.52.5: 177
2.56–57: 176–77
2.58.2: 251
2.61: 179
2.62.5: 179
2.63.3–64.2: 178
2.69.1: 178
2.69.5: 181
2.71.1: 180–81
2.76.1: 181
2.86.3: 180
2.100.4: 179
2.102.3: 108n
2.104.3: 181
2.111.3: 181
2.115.1: 181
2.115.3: 101
2.121.3: 181
2.124.4: 181
2.127–28: 181n
2.129.2: 179
2.130.3: 179n
Vergil
Aen.
1.378: 27n

Epigraphic Texts
Collitz-Bechtel (= *GDI*) 1687: 222n
ILS
1: 23
2–3: 23 nn
7: 24–25
190: 59–60
939: 100n
8781: 60–61
9200: 242n
Senatus Consultum de Pisone Patre
lines 52–57: 203n
lines 66–68: 164n

Printed in Great Britain
by Amazon